The Things Things Say

Jonathan Lamb

PRINCETON UNIVERSITY PRESS

PRINCETON AND OXFORD

Published by Princeton University Press
41 William Street, Princeton, New Jersey 08540

In the United Kingdom: Princeton University Press,
6 Oxford Street, Woodstock, Oxfordshire OX20 1TW

Library of Congress Cataloging-in-Publication Data

Lamb, Jonathan, 1945–
The things things say / Jonathan Lamb.
    p.   cm.
Includes bibliographical references and index.
  ISBN 978-0-691-14806-9 (hardcover : alk. paper) 1. English literature—
18th century—History and criticism. 2. Personal belongings in literature.
3. Property in literature. I. Title.
PR448.P47L36 2012
820.9'36—dc22   2011001680

British Library Cataloging-in-Publication Data is available

This book has been composed in Sabon

Printed on acid-free paper. ∞
press.princeton.edu
Printed in the United States of America
10 9 8 7 6 5 4 3 2 1

For Charlie

Contents

Acknowledgments

To Bill Brown I owe the opportunity and the encouragement to think deeply about things in literature. His collection of essays, *Things*, appearing as a special issue of *Critical Inquiry* in 2001, together with the publication of his own study in 2003 whose title so happily invoked Campanella, *The Sense of Things*, fetched my ideas into focus, and what I offer here is really an expansion and wider application of the argument I formulated then, entitled "Modern Metamorphoses and Disgraceful Tales." The influence of him and his colleagues at Chicago, notably Sandra Macpherson, Heather Keenleyside, and Jim Chandler, is plainly evident throughout. The conversation of Chris Pinney, and his work on South Asian chromolithography and photography, has been an inspiration to me since the beginning of this enterprise.

I record my gratitude to Joe Meisel and the Andrew W. Mellon Foundation for funding two summers of graduate seminars at Vanderbilt from 2006–7. They were called "The Souls of Brute and Stupid Things" and attracted students whose enthusiasm was a great fillip to all of us who taught them: Lynn Enterline, Colin Dayan, and David Wood (all from Vanderbilt), Oliver Berghof (San Marcos and Irvine), Mark Blackwell (Hartford) Wolfram Schmidgen (Washington University), Helen Thompson (Northwestern), Sandra Macpherson (Ohio State), Tony Brown (Minnesota), Frank Palmeri (Florida), and Heather Keenleyside (Chicago). Their collaboration was invaluable. During 2005–6, I held the R. Stanton Avery Distinguished Fellowship at the Huntington Library which put me in the middle of an opulent archive where many a vagrant idea was brought to heel. To Roy Ritchie and the trustees I am grateful for that opportunity. A visiting fellowship in 2008–9 at Kings College, Cambridge caused me to gather in and consolidate all the information I had assembled over the previous eight years. I thank the Provost and the Fellows for their hospitality, and in particular Peter de Bolla and Alex Regier for the rigorous scrutiny they gave three of my chapters over as many days of intense discussion early in 2009. To my respondents at that event, Markman Ellis and Andrea Haslanger, and to Peter de Bolla, who chaired each of the sessions, I am much indebted. Concurrently in the Michaelmas Term of 2008 I held a fellowship at the Centre for Research in the Arts, Social Sciences and Humanities. To the staff at CRASSH, and to Professor Mary Jacobus, the director, I say a big thank you.

Julie Park read an early version of the chapter 2, and Michael McKeon and Nick Paige read chapter 7, offering observations and suggestions from which I have benefited. Two anonymous readers at Princeton University Press gave me splendid advice about the structure of the argument, which I hope I have followed. During my visits to Cambridge over the last five years Mark Phillips has been an invaluable interlocutor, and I thank him for his patience. Between 2009–10 the History Department at Vanderbilt ran a stimulating series of seminars on things under the direction of Gary Gerstle, and I am glad I was invited to contribute to it. In the Fall Term of 2009 Lynn Enterline and I jointly taught an undergraduate class on metamorphosis. I hope it was as exciting for the students as it was for me; certainly a good number of the ideas we discussed appear in the following pages. Last Spring, Nick Paige and I convened a colloquium at Vanderbilt under the rubric of "The History of Fiction," and this afforded me a view of the topic that influenced considerably the last revision of *The Things Things Say*. Nick Paige, Margaret Cohen, April Alliston, Michael McKeon, Francoise Lavocat, Lynn Festa, Andrea Haslanger, and Mark Phillips all deserve my thanks for the range and subtlety of what they brought to the table.

Without the extremely generous policy for leave and research funding of Vanderbilt University, I doubt if this book could have been written. Richard McCarty and Carolyn Dever, successive deans, deserve thanks for their active faith in the project, also my chair Jay Clayton for his goodwill, and Janis May, Susan Crisafulli, Dan Spoth, Amanda Hagood, Beau Baca, Amanda Johnson, Adam Miller, and Killian Quigley for all the work they have done on my behalf. My wife Bridget Orr has throughout the decade been a cheerful supporter, and Charlie, to whom I dedicate the book, has proved an exemplary enthusiast for things of all sorts—fleets of wooden boats, squadrons of paper aeroplanes and battalions of tin soldiers have defined his association with frogs, tadpoles, fish, water and most especially mud.

Prologue

This book explores the difference between objects that serve human purposes and things that don't. The properties of objects of most interest to us are their mobility in the world of exchange, expressed as commercial and symbolic value, and their interpretability as specimens and curiosities, expressed as knowledge. We are interested in their contribution to the circulation of information, goods, and money because of the importance it imparts to us, the owners of them. Things, on the other hand, are obstinately solitary, superficial, and self-evident, sometimes in flight but not in our direction; they communicate directly only with themselves, and have no value in the market that they reckon. It has been suggested recently that this difference between objects and things is only apparent, a paradox of portability or an illusion of commodity fetishism that allows objects to masquerade for a while as lonely literal things, until such time as they re-enter the system of communication as figures, characters, and signs (Plotz 2008: 26; Freedgood 2006: 9). To be sure, many a thing has been an object until it was changed, like the three hats, one cap, and two non-matching shoes Robinson Crusoe sees lying on the beach after the shipwreck; but these particular items are never to be valued again, either as objects to be exchanged or used, or as signs of a definite idea. What makes them so sinister or implacable (to use Adorno's word) is their irrelevance to any human system of value, even though humans once made, bought, and wore them. The transformation from object into thing tends to be final and irreversible, not dialectical. When they ride away on their speckled horses, Edward Lear's sugar-tongs and nutcrackers have gone for good: "They faded away, and they never came back" (Lear 2002: 273). Once having made the change, things do not return as anthropomorphized items in the systems of exchange and symbolic labor. They are positioned starkly in opposition to objects that represent other objects, or descriptive facts that serve as metaphors, or sheer surfaces that advertise hidden meanings.

Hobbes's definition of an idol does very well for a thing: it is a "Materiall Body" made of "Wood, Stone, Metall, or some other visible creature" which represents (on St. Paul's authority) *"nothing"*: nothing in the sense that all there is of it is present in the material of which it is composed; and nothing in the sense that there is no surplus over and above its substance which it is concerned to represent (Hobbes 1996: 448–9, 445). It is as full of itself as it is empty of every thing else. It subsists in a material universe where "there is no reall part thereof that is not also Body" (269). For a human who is, in Hobbes's use of the term, a person, that is to say, a civil subject defined by a political system of representation, the encounter with such a thing is unnerving because it stands in an unrecognizable space where nothing is represented and nothing stops a thing demonstrating this. An unmediated meeting between a thing and a human will result therefore in these alternatives: either its emptiness will be derided as un-meaning matter, or its fullness (its faculty of being exactly what it is) will be worshipped. In the latter case the passions of the spectator—bewilderment, fear, hope—are invested in the thing and instantly it is trans-formed into a personification or a god. At this point, a perfect alignment has taken place between Hobbes's bodily thing and Hume's "empire of the imagination" (Hume 1978: 662). The idol's incontrovertibly physical nature absorbs the impressions it has made on the human imagination, and there it stands the visible cause of its fantastic effects. The thing, the idol, and the personification are all exempt from what Hobbes and Locke identified as the limitation of empiricism, namely, that objects striking on our senses do not leave reliable prints of themselves: "the object is one thing, the image or fancy is another" (Hobbes 1996: 14). The thing (or the idol) is both things at once.

Of course, it is strange that Hobbes should offer such a contemptu-ous account of idols since his own Leviathan appears to be a very good example of one. The loose and flying elements of a crowd are impelled by fear to worship the shape of a mortal god who confers unity upon them on condition they agree to mortgage the sum of their authority in return for the preservation of their lives; thus the Commonwealth comes about. There is a critical difference, however, between Leviathan and other idols inasmuch as it emerges from the consent of the crowd to be represented as a person. One of the impulsive causes of fear allayed by Leviathan is the emptiness of non-representation (Esposito 2010: 141). Now ev-eryone is represented, and each citizen confronts the other as a person; even things may be represented as persons by other persons, who derive their power from the person of what was once a crowd or multitude. Bruno Latour has observed how representation silences the thing, equally in Hobbes's Commonwealth and in Boyle's laboratory, leaving a parlia-ment of mutes represented by a sovereign or a witness who, in speaking for all, says nothing for certain that a thing or a fearful human might say for themselves: "We shall never know whether representatives betray or translate" (Latour 1993: 143). Why does Hobbes's idol exhaust the energy of a thing? The answer must be that representation introduces a medium between the materiality of the thing and its effect—its image, fancy, or passion—that diverts power to the figure of the sovereign, the person of the personate multitude, who is (unlike the crowd from which he derives) distinct from the material of which he is composed. Hobbes distinguishes the truth of his mortal god from all other material fictions of things and idols on the basis of the real political and historical effects of representation. Latour calls Hobbes's achievement a reconstruction of the vertical relation between the three orders of gods, humans, and nonhumans, one that successfully obscures "the separation between humans and nonhumans on the one hand and between what happens 'above' and what happens 'below' on the other" (Latour 1993: 13). All gods except the mortal one are an illusion, and active matter, including things that speak themselves, are supplanted by the fictions of their representational form, for "there are few things, that are uncapable of being represented by Fiction" (Hobbes 1996: 113).

Oddly, it is in fiction that the disturbances are to be found that restore the vertical divisions that Hobbes had concealed. Before he describes the sea-wrack of headgear and footwear, Crusoe says, "I walk'd about on the Shore, lifting up my Hands, and my whole Being, as I may say, wrapt up in the Contemplation of my Deliverance, making a Thousand Gestures and Motions which I cannot describe, reflecting upon all my Comerades that were drown'd" (Defoe 1983: 46). Immediately afterward his mood changes; he thinks that wild beasts will kill him, "and this threw me into terrible Agonies of Mind, that for a while I run about like a Mad-man" (47). This is one of the very few occasions—the footprint is another—when Crusoe's passions are exalted and depressed by things so very much themselves they loosen and agitate his imagination, leaving him without a narrative or conjecture to explain what has happened. In an ecstasy of relief he raises his hands as it were in praise of a god, and in despair he places himself below the animals. "In this disordered scene, with eyes still more disordered and astonished [he] see[s] the first obscure traces of divinity" (Hume 1956: 28).

Alternatively, humans finding a certain voluptuous satisfaction in beholding things purely as they are, when, as Defoe's Roxana puts it, "the Sence of things . . . began to work upon my Sences" (Defoe 1981: 200), enjoy a reflection not of critical judgment but of pleasure so intense it evades representation, and culminates in idolatry. Basking in the "fullness of Humane Delight" with her lover, Roxana says, "As the Prince was the only Deity I worshipp'd, so I was really his Idol" (70). And when he carries her in front of the mirror, she stands in wonder at her own image, "all on fire with the Sight" (73). Excitements like these are risky, for it is not long afterward that Roxana calls the prince a beast for falling in love with a whited sepulcher such as herself. However, the point is made by Defoe that in states of heightened emotion, provoked by things striking us as things, the three levels that Latour says are sacrificed to a system of representation come back into play. There are two terms or poles to this experience: idol and author. Things are idolized when their fantastic energy remains their own, which requires either that they desert the system of representation underlying the ownership of property and the circulation of goods; or that, never having been in it, they remain outside it. The return of stolen goods organized by Jonathan Wild before his death at Tyburn in 1725 provides many examples of commodities that rediscover themselves as things, attracting in the process such a zealous desire on the part of their former owners to transcend the limits of mere possession that it is not too extravagant to name such zeal worship or infatuation. Paradoxically, the intemperate longing of a human to own a thing beyond the limits prescribed for property can lead to the independence even of things as immobile as estates. The law of entail allowed mortals to contend for a kind of immortality in relation to land that, legally speaking, they could own forever. In the following pages, I shall show how the exorbitant desire to own a thing absolutely liberates it; also I shall examine five parallel examples of the transformation of humans into idols, which I take to be not figurative but real—Bottom the weaver, Gay's Thomas Peascod, Pope's Belinda, Captain Cook, as well as Roxana herself. Here the thinghood of a human is proved in the unmediated manifestation of a former person as fully and unconditionally another thing altogether. Cook is not like a god, he is one. When Bottom gives up playing games of representation, saying things such as, "I Pyramus am not Pyramus," he becomes the very idol of idols, half horse and half human, a metamorphosis he is incapable of representing. That these changes should occur beyond the walls of the city, or at the limit of the known world, out of reach of justice and common sense, is consistent with the freedom of idols, whether animate or inanimate, to subsist in their material form immune to the pressure to mean or signify anything of value to civil society.

To the word "author" itself I attach the same primitive meaning Hobbes assigns it, namely, a solitaire endowed with undefended natural rights occupying a vulnerable condition outside or on the rim of civil society, without the advantages of covenants, mortal gods, personate selves, and representations. Authors are distinguished not only by their nakedness and isolation, but also by their delight in being looked at, especially in mirrors, by their hostility to being symbolized or interpreted, and by their impatience with language that does not say the thing which is, including the thing each author is. Like other things, they experience the peculiar reflexive exactness of entities, whether they are things, personifications or gods, who do what they are and embody nothing but what they do. Like those pieces of nature in Marvell's *Upon Appleton House* vitrified by the river which has licked its own back into a mirror ("Where all things gaze themselves, and doubt/ If they be in it or without" [Marvell 1971: 1.82]), human figures turned to things accomplish themselves, such as the mower who mows himself with his own scythe, or the poet who sits in the shade of a tree and thinks nothing but green. Reflexivity of this order, as Steven Knapp has pointed out, is the product of a degree of self-experience unmatched in empirical consciousness, and is therefore difficult to express in words that are not part of the reflection. Authors are to the civil subject what things are to objects; consequently, they are not often read or viewed in a manner faithful to their own active and immediate conceptions of themselves. The hostility growing up between them and their audience accounts for certain ruptures in their narratives and fissures in their self-portraits. This kind of authorship is evinced by Lord Shaftesbury, the Author of Swift's *A Tale of a Tub*, Lemuel Gulliver, John Dunton and Laurence Sterne, to name a few.

What then can a thing say, if it is isolated from all relative and conventional modes of significance? Without the vestige of a common language, it cannot find a seat even in that mute parliament of things proposed by Bruno Latour. Its circumstances resemble not so much those of a representative body as of Hobbes's state of nature, where community, law, letters, and time are not yet operating. In Ovid's metamorphoses, the change of an object, most often a human one, into a thing is accompanied by the attenuation of voice into a cry, gesture, or tears, spontaneous expressions of emotion that bid farewell to a specific language community. If metamorphosis is the material form taken by passions reacting to an unparalleled emergency—crystallizing into flowers, birds, or stones—then color, sound, or volume are their natural language, and they mean what they neglect explicitly to say. Like Humpty Dumpty's portmanteau, "impenetrability," or his impudent commentary on the word "brillig," the words used by things and idols cannot say what they mean; they may only mean what they say: the sound comes first and meaning afterward. The words and names they utter mean them: "*My* name means the shape I am," says Humpty Dumpty. Language of this order strikes the senses as a powerful aesthetic or synaesthetic event, heard by the eye and seen by the ear, as Bottom testifies, a dramatic and overwhelming encounter with matter, moisture, noise, pigment, and (in the case of authors) ink. The portal of this aesthetic language is constructed from decaying words, so that we understand what Hecuba is saying before she starts barking as a dog, and what Actaeon has tried to say before he weeps as a deer. Metamorphosis of kind and tongue go in lockstep. Passion transforms what was formerly sociably human—a person or a commodity with a social life and a repertoire of representational options—into a thing at the same moment as words turn into the things things say, the expressive material creature of what belongs solely to them.

❦

With Charles Gildon's strange story of talking gold coins, *The Golden Spy* (1709), a genre of fiction was inaugurated in Britain that shadowed its senior colleague, the novel, for well over a century. Autobiographies of inanimate things proliferated—of coins, ornaments, utensils, land, clothing, vehicles, and furniture—and of animate ones too, such as dogs, horses, insects, and body parts. Soon afterward, the same two-step was performed by fiction in France. The stories themselves are episodic, usually recording a series of unhappy encounters between things and humans, in which the things come off badly. Furniture and vehicles are involved in events they would rather have avoided. Coins and chattels get used up, and are forsaken or destroyed. Animals provide a little diversion and then are tortured or killed. The narrative usually begins when a thing comes out of circulation and looks back at its career, sometimes nostalgically, but mostly with incomprehension, disapproval, or resentment. Gulliver's memory, for instance, is organized by his identification with horse-kind, and as he reaches back through the era of his humanity, he is overcharged with disgust and horror.

In a landmark essay on the topic, Aileen Douglas called these stories "novels of circulation" (Douglas 1993 [2007]), a term that alternates with "it-narratives" and "object-narratives" in the important subsequent work of Christopher Flint, Deidre Lynch, Barbara Benedict, Lynn Festa, Markman Ellis, Cynthia Wall, and Mark Blackwell. With varying degrees of emphasis these scholars have understood the generic self-consciousness of the fiction of things in the eighteenth century to reside generally in notions of property and specifically in the market for print. Without a broad and consistent demand for ephemeral literature, it-narratives would have remained under the horizon, never more than a branch of didactic fables for children. In Flint's powerful argument, the development of Grub Street as a center of print capitalism was the *terminus a quo* for this novelty, as Swift's Author partly demonstrates in *A Tale of a Tub* when he reports that the tales of Dick Whittington's cat, Tom Thumb, and the Hind and the Panther have acquired new currency and importance in the market (Swift 1920: 68–9). This development had nothing to do with the intrinsic merit of the tales, rather with an industry that required a certain mass of printed material to be offered to the public week by week, branded as new even if it wasn't. The story of a cat or a tub is to be understood therefore not merely as a transitory event in a commercial process, but more particularly as a token or emblem of its *terminus ad quem*, the phenomenon of circulating popular print. The story is the occasion for the existence of a manufactured product—written, printed and bound, and offered for sale—whose brief life on the huckster's stall and in the hands of readers is as it were the story of the story. Its passage from hand to hand is re-enacted in the shifting of clothes from back to back (*Adventures of a Black Coat* [1760]), vehicles from place to place (*Adventures of a Hackney Coach* [1783]), or animals from owner to owner (*The Adventures of Pompey the Little* [1751]). Flint closes the circle with stories such as `Adventures of a Quire of Paper,' published in the *London Magazine* 1779, in which the materials of print become themselves directly the subject of the narrative (Flint 2007: 172–73).

This important insight into the invention and consumption of it-narratives lies at the heart of one of the most thorough-going of recent revisionist histories of the novel, Deidre Lynch's *The Economy of Character* (1998), in which she suggests that the reader's experience of a circulating object in print is continuous with the circulation of commodities and money at large. For example, the fictional memoirs of fiduciary paper such as *The Adventures of a Bank-Note* (1770) and an actual endorsed bill, with the history of its transfers written on its back, are reporting an identical set of events. An it-narrative uses print to make legible the series of exchanges that all marketable goods have as it were written on their backs, what Lynch calls their *characters*, fully exploiting the pun on character-as-sign and character-as-identity. Such a narrative gives literal and material point to the function of character as some sort of inscription, commodity, or specie that will pass in the market as a sign of value, "character ... ascribes discursive centrality to the marketable products of the press and to the voluble ... face of the page" (Lynch 1998: 97, 38). Coaches, coins, clothes, and other mobile appurtenances are objects whose histories as commodities are delivered in the "character" of type, impressed on sheets, and circulated in the vast web of contracts that constitutes civil society. Between one sign and another, whether it be manifest in print, metal, fabric, or flesh, there is an unbroken continuity. Characters take their places on the whirligig of the commercial and fashionable worlds, a situation, as Pope puts it, "Where Wigs with wigs, with sword-knots sword-knots strive,/ Beaux banish beaux, and coaches coaches drive" (*The Rape of the Lock* 1.101–2). These are worlds where there is little to choose between the human and the material character, for they all move, speak, and are valued in the same sociable way.

Ever since Arjun Appadurai published the important collection of essays, *The Social Life of Things* (1986), the idea governing the critique of it-narratives has been commodity fetishism of one sort or another. The volubility and activity of things was derived from an equality between manufactures and humans that was claimed when the former usurped the latter's modes of sociability. The exuberant celebration of exchange value that goods exhibit in Marx's *Capital I*, for example, where tables dance on their heads and convivial commodities congregate to preen themselves, proclaims the commonalty of things and people in this regard at least, that they come together for the purpose of exchange and the determination of value. But this assumption concerning commodity fetishism relies on two others that many it-narratives neglect to illustrate, namely, that active and talkative things want to be like human beings, and that they always function as property. For example, the bank-note mentioned above talks indignantly of the venality of bankers and their hideous method of putting paper-money to death (anon. 1770: 207, 167). That is to say, it assigns itself an importance outside the scope of its service to humans. In Gildon's *The Golden Spy*, the stories told by money of human depravity are so alarming that the guinea's tale has to be edited, "for fear the Sense of Things should destroy all Confidence betwixt Man and Man, and so put an End to human Society" (Gildon 1709: 116). The realism of these narratives—the "Sense of Things"—is not intended, as Johnson in his fourth *Rambler* paper supposed modern realist fiction did intend, to expand and ameliorate conversation with mankind. Often it identifies such a radical distinction between the interests of things and humans that there can be no question of the one wishing to be like the other, or of participating willingly in the transactions which make up the sum of its woe or disgust. Since the passions of things are a measure of resistance to the laws of the market and the actions of those who stand in it, might there be another means of tracing a connection between a Grub Street author and the story of a thing than through the meshing of the cycles of exchange?

In the comic romance of *Don Quixote*, the termini cited by Flint for the narratives of things are entirely reversed. The *terminus a quo* of the knight's adventures is the expanded market in print, calculated to have produced some 200 million volumes by 1600 (Anderson 1983: 41), whereas its *terminus ad quem* is a world of enchanted things, such as windmills, sheep, and barbers' basins, all harking back to the origins of fiction in romance and fable. Is it possible to suppose that this Quixote-effect—the return to the metamorphoses of ancient fiction via the extensive circulation of modern romances within the print-market—is in fact the restoration of a forgotten genre of fiction under the guise of modernity, much as Swift's Author suggests? Huet says the old romances were closely linked to fable, that their common theme was metamorphosis, and that their invention of "Imaginary Spaces and Impossibilities" corresponds to the "restless Emotions which continually actuate the Mind of Man" (Huet 1715: v, 13–99, 125). His favorite examples are the stories of humans turned to asses, told variously by Lucius of Patras, Lucius Apuleius, and Lucian. Here, the wilder improbabilities of fable are attuned to the extravagance of romance, and in Apuleius's inset story of Cupid and Psyche the adjustment of extreme passion to the activity of things such as rocks, water, and birds, culminating in the transformation of a mortal into a god, brings the art of fabular romance to its apogee.

The introduction of an older form of fictionality on the back of the modern distribution of print is of special interest to Cervantes, whose hero is animated by restless emotions that are at first aroused and finally quelled in his encounters with books. The story begins with the burning of Quixote's library by the barber, the curate, and the housekeeper in a futile effort to purge the knight's brain of fiction; and it ends shortly after he goes into a printing house in Barcelona, where he finds a workman printing off sheets of Avellaneda's counterfeit sequel. "I have heard of that Book before, said Don Quixote, and really thought it had been burnt, and reduc'd to Ashes for a foolish impertinent Libel" (Cervantes 1991: II.473). Between the first mention of incinerated books and the last, the hero's reinvention of himself as a knight-at-arms and his transformation of the localities of La Mancha into an imagined space of wonders combine to secure him an unparalleled and unique identity, and to cast over all the quotidian things in his circuit a luster that may only be lost by enchantment. A wineskin is a giant until it is reduced by magic to the common thing it only seems to be; by means of spells and charms, Mambrino's helmet is made to masquerade as a basin; Quixote himself is transformed by envious enchanters into Alonso Quixada, a non-armigerous yeoman. If Descartes supposed a malign genie had transformed the sensible world into an improbable fiction so that he could secure the single certainty of being a solitary individual thing that thinks, no less does Cervantes's hero exalt himself by regarding all empirical phenomena surplus to his mission as part of a fantasy wrought by his enemies. This proviso ensures that nothing in the real world is not continuous with his idea of himself, even the author of the story in which he appears, who begins Quixote's second sally by imagining how the knight imagines the author's beginning of this very adventure. Such blurring of authorship and action Hobbes set aside as pure fiction, "the internal gloriation of mind" of those braggarts for whom no lie is too enormous (Hobbes 1994: 50); but here in the very romance he cited as the model of such mendacity it achieves a subtlety outside the reach of simple distinctions between what is probable and what isn't—a subtlety that is not lost even when print turns enchanter, and transforms the truth of this fabulous history into a fake, and the fake into a commodity.

The authority of the improbable which impels the story of Don Quixote was appreciated by the inventors of it-narratives, whose tales—equally improbable but on a lower level—were responses not simply to a widening circulation of printed products, but also to a world that challenged their imaginations. The authors of the lives of things, sitting in garrets in Grub Street and racking their brains to invent the thoughts and deeds of a corkscrew, a dog, or a coat so that they could eat or pay the rent, doubtless dipped into their own circumstances for anecdotes, reminding themselves as they did so that market forces were not phenomena for which they felt much esteem. The result of finding some equivalence between their own situations and those of the things they were ventriloquizing was less likely an insight into the social lives they shared with artifacts and animals than a rueful sense of their common lot as unaccommodated singular things. But in that recognition lay an opportunity imaginatively to transform the world they didn't like into one they preferred. Swift's Author in *A Tale of a Tub* is lonely, poor, diseased, periodically insane, and well-apprised of the fickleness of the market for print in which he is trying to trade, as well as of the venality of the booksellers who are its brokers. He tries to exercise a social role, listing himself as the delegate of corporations of poets, modern authors, political groups, even the insane; but it is a feeble pretence. Rather than social relations, the terms that seem to define the production of print-ephemera in this writer's world are solitude, faction, and war—pretty much the state of nature described by Hobbes, a philosopher to whom he several times refers. When the Author considers his tub, it is not as a successful commodity bustling in a commercial world; it is a thing like him perched on the edge, awaiting annihilation. He and it are atoms of the same quantum of matter, little more. Even if the material circumstances of the Author were less dire, his bewilderment in the face of a market where the analogy between clothes and the qualities of the mind strikes him as exact, where the only reason for people to gather together seems to be to fight, and where by means of ink and paper words are made into missiles, is enough to tempt him into a thoroughgoing Lucretian materialism. If a surface declares all there is of the essence of a thing, and if a human soul can inhabit a shoulder knot, why may he not stop pretending that shapes are emblems of occult meanings and that skin is a disguise? He turns instead to enjoy the meaningless beauty of varnish and tinsel, and to let his pen leave its pointless trail of ink on the surface of the page. Print is made to serve his turn by restoring a sort of fabulous immediacy to nonsense.

I have said that things resume the clarity of their being when we who handle or view them are shocked or disturbed, like Crusoe on the beach. In Grub Street, the fragile and uncertain state of the market itself was the reason that the imaginations of writers responded so directly and vividly to the life and vocality of things. Far from enjoying the buoyancy of production, marketing, sale, and consumption, creators of the raw material of print capitalism were subject, as Charlotte Lennox put it, to "slavery to the Booksellers" (Gallagher 1994: 197), tormented in body as well as brain, as Fielding's Mr. Wilson attests. With a very slender assurance of the comforts of civil society, they were inclined to idealize their loneliness as virtuous privacy, and to consider their enforced participation in the routines of exchange as an injury that dispossessed themselves of themselves (Gallagher 1994: 145–202). That is to say, they began to treat themselves as things by considering their public emptiness as a private plenum, and finding in the lives of animals and artifacts an existential simplicity with which they could sympathize. Plagued by fears and anxieties they were unable to lodge in the body of Leviathan, authors invested them instead in lapdogs, slippers, and non-current cash.

No one understood better the effects of market uncertainties upon the imaginations of people than Mandeville, in whose *The Fable of the Bees* (1724) the unintelligibility of commercial society reaches shocking proportions, with virtue depending for its efficacy upon vice, prudence finding itself inseparable from heedlessness, and chastity colloguing with licentiousness. Anyone acknowledging even a fraction of truth in Mandeville's analysis had reasons for intense personal anxiety, because it left them unable intentionally to prepare for what was coming next. Mandeville was exploiting a common fear about civil society that was seldom expressed as anything but moral outrage aimed arbitrarily at examples of hypocrisy, lasciviousness, or greed, as if their shaming would insure the system against further shocks:

> One, that had got a Princely Store,
> By cheating Master, King and Poor,
> Dar'd cry aloud, *The Land must sink*
> *For all its Fraud*; And whom d'ye think
> The Sermonizing Rascal chid?
> A Glover that sold Lamb for Kid.
> (Mandeville 1988 [1924]), 1: 27)

But the problem, as Mandeville well understood, went much deeper. With the market, human beings had invented an engine that they could not control. It operated according to laws they could neither fathom nor influence. Credit, like public opinion, taste, and fashion, was a mystery that left their ability to order the chain of events at the mercy of Fortune; and this perplexed considerably their ideas of identity and human agency, not to mention reality (Pocock 1985: 111–13). Whether they wanted to or not, men and women living in these circumstances were forced to *imagine* who they were and how they related to things.

Mandeville's choice of genre, an expanded version of the Aesopian fable he had learned from translating La Fontaine fifteen years before, in which creatures allegedly dumb speak out loud of human infirmity, struck him as ideal for this modern confusion, in some respects so like primitive times.

> Before the Reign of buxom Dido,
> When Beasts could speak as well as I do,
> Lyons and we conversed together,
> And marry'd among one another.
>
> (Mandeville 1966: 41)

The story of the lion and the merchant told in Remark P of *The Fable of the Bees* brings ancient times up to the present, specifically the present of trade and exchange, in which it seems appropriate that beasts resume their voices in order to quell the pointless vanity of creatures whose worth derives from nothing more important than the circulation of goods. However, Mandeville does not wish to treat this encounter as a homily, any more than he means the "Moral" of his *Fable* to function as instruction. Unlike Ogilby, he is not using fable in order "to make Men lesser Beasts" (Ogilby 1651: 1. [i]); instead, like Aesop and La Fontaine, Mandeville is aware that fables are inconsistent, as likely to recommend opportunism and bad faith as equitable dealing, and that, taken as a whole, they add up to nothing very much. Fables such as "The Fox and the Mask" or "The Camel and the Driftwood" advertise their own emptiness; that is the extent of their boast, that there is nothing in them, and if they are to say anything at all, it will emerge from the angle at which they are approached (Henderson 2004: 58). As La Fontaine puts it: "Il dépend d'une conjoncture/ De lieux, de personnes, de temps" (La Fontaine 1865: 215; ['L'Horoscope,' VIII: xvi]). When such a conjuncture occurs then it becomes clear, but only for a moment, how power, nature, and chance are configured: "And sure the wolf is only wrong/ When he is weak and you are strong" ("Bergers, bergers! Le loup n'a tort/ Que quand il n'est pas le plus fort"—La Fontaine 1865: 274 ["Le Loup et les bergers," X: vi]). Having told the story of a cat who defends its friend the sparrow from another bird by killing and eating it, only to find a relish for the food and to finish his meal upon his friend, La Fontaine demands, "Quelle morale puis-je inférer de ce fait? / Sans cela toute fable est un oeuvre imparfait;/ J'en crois voir quelques traits, mais leur ombre m'abuse" (La Fontaine 1865: 313 ["Le Chat et les deux moineaux"; XII: ii]. In Remark P the lion, briefly in a strong position vis-à-vis humankind, explains to the merchant shipwrecked on his desert shore how the colossal and urgent hunger natural to lions might now be appeased, at which point the merchant faints. British novelists flirt with these possibilities, not simply by inserting fables into their stories, a technique of which Richardson was inordinately fond, but by their alignments of humans with animals and things. The hero of William Godwin's *Caleb Williams* (1794) describes in one of the alternative endings how he is turning into a thing: "I wonder which is the man, I or my chair" (Godwin 1988: 334). Robinson Crusoe, covered with the hair and skin of goats and echoed by a parrot, fears that his solitude amidst the stranded trophies of world trade might have left him with no other narrative than a fable called "The eminent History of a Dog and two Cats" (Defoe 1983: 64).

In his *Natural History of Religion* (1757), Hume reflected at length on the commotions of mind that confound, as Latour says, what happens above with what happens below. He suggested that in ancient times the surge and tumult of imagination excited by inexplicable events and broken sequences resulted in a visible union between the material and spiritual worlds that left a void in the human zone between.

> Convulsions in nature, disorders, prodigies, miracles, though the most opposite to the plan of a wise superintendent, impress mankind with the strongest sentiments of religion; the causes of events seeming then the most unknown and unaccountable. Madness, fury, rage, and an inflamed imagination, though they sink men nearest to the level of beasts, are, for a like reason, often supposed to be the only dispositions, in which we can have any immediate communication with the Deity. (Hume 1956: 42)

In this distracted state there was a strong propensity among humankind "to rest their attention on sensible, visible, objects," with the result that along with the personification of the moon, stars, waters, and forests, divinities were found even in "monkeys, dogs, cats, and other animals" (38). Swift's Author runs up and down this scale in the eighth section of *A Tale of a Tub*, where the fancy sports amidst ideas of what is highest and best until it "becomes over-short, and spent, and weary, and suddenly falls like a dead Bird of Paradise to the Ground," or alternatively it begins in the abyss of things—spermatic fluid or dunghill vapors—and rises by degrees into visions of empire and philosophy (Swift 1920: 158). The digression on "The Use and Improvement of Madness in a Commonwealth" synthesizes the materialism of modern religion. Devotees locate their gods in casks, clothes, and wind; followers of fashion adore the tailor-idol, whose associate divinities are a flat-iron and a louse, whose hell is a rag-bag, and whose product is fabric assembled in the human figure. The difference between Swift's examples and Hume's is that he is talking about the earliest phases of ancient polytheism, while Swift is dealing with the modern age. Hume is describing the kinds of transformations that occur in Apuleius's *The Golden Ass*, where the superstitious curiosity of the hero precipitates his transformation into an animal until, purged by pain and the humiliation of inhabiting the body of the lowliest of working creatures, he is fit to join the cult of the goddess Isis. Swift is exhibiting a kind of hopeless fetishism that cannot elide the fact that the empire of imagination terminates in an idol of which "there is no reall part thereof that is not also Body" (Hobbes 1996: 445). It is not that things act like humans but the reverse. "What do I see from the window," Descartes had demanded, "but hats and coats which may cover automatic machines?" (Descartes 1996: 69). Swift gingerly goes the next step in his Author's history of clothes: "These *Postulata* being admitted, it will follow in due Course of Reasoning, that those Beings which the World calls improperly Suits of Cloaths, are in Reality the most refined Species of Animals, or to proceed higher, that they are Rational Creatures, or Men" (Swift 1920: 78).

Like Mandeville, Adam Smith considers the fragility of identity to arise from commercial pressures which aggravate the imagination. The paradoxes heaped up by Mandeville to illustrate the amorality of market-providence are deployed by Smith to show how its exorbitances are controlled by an invisible hand that structures the contradictions of supply and demand, ease and industry, individual aspiration and social equity so that they operate for the benefit of everyone. Mandeville typically puts the case more cynically when he says of his bees, "They mended by Inconstancy/ Faults, which no Prudence could foresee" (Mandeville 1988 [1924]: 1.25). But Smith, though as deeply attached to the Stoic doctrine of self-control as to the self-regulating principles of commercial society, knew that no amount of self-inspection could guarantee moderation, and no system of providential oversight could preserve a just equilibrium. To keep human beings from fits of excess such as those Hume identified in ancient times and Swift in modern ones, it was necessary in extreme cases to adapt not reason or reflection but the imagination, the very faculty responsible for immoderate passions, for the cure for them.

He located the problem (as Hume had done) in an imagination alarmed by whatever interrupts the rhythm of daily life: natural convulsions, prodigies, miracles.

> Nature ... seems to abound with events which appear solitary and incoherent with all that go before them, which therefore disturb the easy movement of the imagination; which makes its ideas succeed each other. ... by irregular starts and sallies; and which thus tend, in some measure, to introduce those confusions and distractions ... this chaos of jarring and discordant appearances ... this tumult of imagination. (Smith 1980: 45–6)

The singularity of these disturbances may be mitigated however by a further effort of imagination. If an individual is able to communicate or receive the pain of an alarmed imagination by means of sympathy, that is, by "an imaginary change" of situation with another person (Smith 1982 [1976]: 317), then a social force counteracts the natural one. Imagination tames the anguish of imagination. However, a licensed imagination is much less biddable than self-critique. Smith conceded at the outset of *The Theory of Moral Sentiments* that sympathy might well exceed its brief, and out of the imaginary change of situation create a scene of horror. He says we often indulge an unavailing sympathy with the dead, stunning ourselves with the misery of their forlorn situation by as it were putting ourselves into it. "It is from this very illusion of the imagination, that the foresight of our dissolution is so terrible to us, and that the idea of those circumstances, which undoubtedly can give us no pain when we are dead, makes us miserable while we are alive" (Smith 1976: 13). Imagination that is to say brings us back to the tumult and confusion from which it was supposed to free us by exchanging a social fiction ("imaginary change") for a fantasy of perpetual isolation ("this very illusion"). Thus, each individual is found in that castaway or private situation in which the shrinkage of the ego is proportionate to the salience of things and the power of their speech.

That Smith is not, like Hobbes, simply distinguishing between useful fictions (the persons of churches, hospitals, or bridges, for instance [Hobbes 1996: 113)] and the outrageous lies of Quixotic braggarts, is evident from the fact that an alarmed imagination reflects, if not a real state of affairs, then a level of feeling appropriate to what he calls the irregularities of Fortune. These may occur at any time; the traces of them scar public and private histories alike: so it is not mischievous or ridiculous to imagine them. His prime historical example of this irregularity is the institution of chattel slavery in the Caribbean and American plantations, of which he says this: "Fortune never exerted more cruelly her empire over mankind, than when she subjected these nations of heroes [on the coast of West Africa] to the refuse of the jails of Europe" (Smith 1982: 206). The ravages of Fortune in private life he finds illustrated in tragedy. His prime exemplars are Sophocles' Oedipus, Otway's Monimia, and Southerne's Isabella, characters whose innocent actions produce appalling consequences, so far from what they intended and yet so freighted with the guilt of parricide, adultery, and incest that they lose any sense of coherence in their lives (107). In history and tragedy the problem is that a narrative framed from predictable elements—moderate passions, social conscience, and moral agency—is ruptured by another belonging to Fortune, altogether tumultuous and unaccountable. The sociability based on the imaginary change of sympathy is usurped by the singularity associated with the illusion of a living death. The switch is radical, transforming what one thought was doing for the best into what has happened for the worst. Deeds have turned into accidents. While Smith allows that the finest and most compelling scenes of tragedy involve the disclosure of these unintentional crimes, it is clear that in history there is no discernible form of providence capable of justifying the transformation of humans into saleable items and working beasts, a transformation effected not only by men and women rendered brutal by avarice but by the precedents of common law. This is something that has happened to us all, though very few of us intended it or did it. Can we mend that state of affairs by prudential inconstancy? Smith thinks not.

Around the issue of Fortune Smith weaves a discussion of what was known in Scottish law as piacular guilt, or faultless trespass. Not meaning to do what you did was not regarded in law as a mitigating factor; nor was the instrument by which the trespass committed, say a horse or a cow, any freer of guilt than its owner, although both were acknowledged innocent of evil intent. In the course of these meditations Smith considers how even in the passages of ordinary life the passions aroused by accidents, and the metamorphoses they provoke, are parallel to those identified in the law of the piaculum, and affectively justify it. We blame the stone that bruises our foot; we curse it for its malice and would like to destroy it (94). On the other hand, there are inanimate objects for which we feel an adventitious and irrational love, such as the plank of wood that saves us from shipwreck, or a favorite snuff-box. Just as we demonize the stone, we deify these. "The Dryads and the Lares of the ancients, a sort of genii of trees and houses, were probably first suggested by this sort of affection, which the authors of those superstitions felt for such objects, and which seemed unreasonable, if there was nothing animated about them" (94). Similarly, human beings anciently projected their passions as gods—at first the worst, such as lust and revenge, and then latterly feelings more friendly to humanity, such as indignation and admiration, "And thus religion, even in its rudest form, gave a sanction to the rules of morality" (164).

No matter how providential this advance from the vengeful tumults of imagination to the amenities of true religion is supposed to be, it is clear that early in the process humans endowed things with the force of their passions and what was left of their reason; animating them with an energy impossible to construe as human. Unintelligible accidents provoked furor among the passions and imagination, forcing humans to confront a wild animal or worship a god. It is the same sequence that Hume had traced, whose modern versions are repeated, *mutatis mutandis*, in the philosophies of Hobbes and Descartes, in the despair and joy of Crusoe the castaway, in the erotic delight experienced by Roxana, and, by way of mockery, in the materialism of Swift's *Tale*. What Smith manages to make clear with the example of slavery is that the ameliorative narrative leading from savagery to civility may be interrupted at any time with accidents belonging to another agent, one who controls a different story in which our actions are converted into passions, our deeds into events, and our expectations into horrors. Modernity is insured neither from this tumult, nor from the metamorphoses that go with it. Smith points out that the dominion of Fortune makes her a divinity for his contemporaries, and that the proof of it is seen in the transformation of humans into beasts. Hobbes's narrative of the origin of civil society is the naturalization of this shock, with a god set over affairs rendered less than authorial, and to that extent less than human. Civil society that is to say was the child of a rupture that shattered the narrative of feudal duty and obligation, replacing it with another that was just as liable to interruption. A disciple of Hobbes, Mandeville enjoyed pointing out how the offspring of the fiction of the original contract spawned the vast network of trespasses and contracts which constitutes the unpredictable cycles of the market, of all human inventions the one most fruitful in the kinds of irregularity Smith assigns to Fortune.

If we attempt to transpose Smith's idea of irregularity to the history of instrumental fictions such as the state of nature and the original contract, it seems that he has to suppose like Hobbes and Locke that there are two sorts, a fiction that obeys the laws of probability and serves our purposes, and another that is neither probable nor useful. In Smith's terms this would be the difference between the fiction of the imaginary change and the fiction of the isolating illusion. The first looks very like the emergent novel in recording those customary associations that allow us to entertain secure ideas of identity, trace the necessary connection between cause and effect, and judge of what we call the real. The other looks like romance or fable, or any other fiction that is told in contempt of our ideas of personal identity, moral consequence, and truth. As the learned doctor points out at the end of *The Female Quixote*, the best fiction (a category from which he explicitly excludes romance and fable) reflects the orderly stream of custom: "A long Life may be passed without a single Occurrence that can cause much Surprize, or produce any unexpected Consequence of great Importance; the Order of the World is so established, that all human Affairs proceed in a regular Method" (Lennox 1989: 379). The ideological function of the novel is not to reflect the real, however, as Johnson points out in *Rambler* 4. It is fiction because it reflects what may be imagined as real; that is to say, it is structurally aligned with the normalization of the shock out of which civil society emerges. It creates reality by acting *as if* what were imagined were real, that we really did come in from the forests as individuals and subscribe to a contract that made a mortal god whose dominion would be more powerful than Fortune's, as long and only as long as we kept on believing in the reality of the consequences of having imagined that primordial scene.

Romance is a reminder of the older kind of fiction this new fiction replaced, which explains why so many English novels (along with English philosophers) try to lay the ghost of quixotism, the internal gloriation of the mind that reverses the values of the real and shows the stream of custom to be a figment or an enchantment. Fable, the earliest example of the slave narrative genre, reminds its readers that the dominion of Fortune has never ceased, and that at any moment they could change places with things or animals and start worshipping idols. This is why Mandeville, peculiarly alert to the delusions necessary to the regular conduct of civil society, chose fable to show that it was based on nothing but a congeries of imagined scenes created by imagined persons, each straining "all his Faculties to appear what his shallow Noddle imagines he is believ'd to be" (Mandeville 1982: 1.54). In the world of the fable, all these illusions are dispelled: there is no justice, no steady meaning, no identity, just conjunctures of bodies in given spaces. Caxton's proleptic choice of Aesop as one of the first printed texts to be sold in England ties fable to the very engine that will multiply the possibilities of such conjunctures. Machiavelli, the most astute analyst of the politics of conjuncture, sets a short but devastating analysis of history within a framework of a romance he named, in honour of Apuleius, *L'Asino d'oro*.

The it-narrative is, among other things, a modern fable, the autobiography of something not human, formerly inanimate but now inspired with enough passion, reason, and speech to launch upon its own story. In what sense this narrative constitutes an "I" or first person is an important question to settle. There are some it-narratives (*Adventures of a Hackney Coach*, for example) which claim a sympathetic intimacy with humankind. In such a case, the relationship between the thing and the human is merely a variant of Smith's temperate sympathy, an imaginary change of situation with another person or character in which the thing is anthropomorphized, awarded social relations and a personal identity. If on the other hand the thing is located anomalously beyond the limits of the proper, like a corpse, then it has no person to exchange and can function entirely on its own account, just like Hobbes's "author" in a state of nature or like Swift's Author in his garret, with obligations to nothing but itself. Such a thing is the antithesis of property, free from all human control and proof of Fortune's dominion, although the language expressive of that freedom sometimes may be hard to distinguish from nonsense. Like slave narratives. the best it-narratives chronicle an emancipation that divides the portion of their earlier lives as property from their later lives as an unowned thing. So the first issue to determine is the difference between property and what is no longer owned or ownable, and how the unowned thing finds itself idolized as a subaltern deity of Fortune. And then the road will be clear to determine more fully the difference between the two sorts of fiction, that of imagined change and that of horrid illusion, giving special attention to the differences on which it depends, namely, the differences between persons and authors, humans and idols, and objects and things.

PART ONE

Property, Personification, and Idols

CHAPTER 1

Owning Things

Bags without people don't make sense.

—Notice on municipal river transport plying the
Brisbane River, Queensland, Australia

Spinoza thought that volatility of the human mind and the velocity of things were largely remedied by justice, "a fixed intentment to assign to each person what belongs to them" (Spinoza 2007: 203). This would slow the passage of property and calm the emotions. Hume was not so sure. Although distributive justice certainly hindered the rapid movement of things from hand to hand and caused a corresponding drop in turbulence of mind, there were plenty of events capable of disturbing "the stability of possession" (Hume 1978: 491) and precipitating "looseness and easy transition" among things (488). Invasions of property from outside, in the form of theft or war, could do it; or disturbance could come from the inside in the form of caprice, madness, and death. In such cases, three distinct factors would affect the tenure of property: first, the fixedness of possession would be disturbed; second, the continuity of the consciousness of possession would be interrupted; and third, a thing would be freed from the dominion of an owner, moving with varying degrees of impetus toward another, or toward independence. In the event of these contingencies, the fugitive qualities of minds and things characteristic of a state of great scarcity are restored: the food of humans flies at their approach (485), and they themselves recur to "that savage and solitary condition" that Hume always wanted to call a fiction, "a mere philosophical fiction," "an idle fiction" (496, 493, 494) but which here defines for him the uncertain tenure of property. In the wilderness outside the city limits of Athens, the effects of such uncertainty are exactly noted by Robin Goodfellow:

> Their sense thus weak, lost with their fears thus strong,
> Made senseless things begin to do them wrong.
> For briers and thorns at their apparel snatch;
> Some sleeves, some hats—from yielders all things catch.
> (*A Midsummer Night's Dream* 3.2.26–30; 1994: 190–1)

In this chapter I mean to chart the change from fixed possession to the looseness of things, and from calmness to passion, by way of introducing the manifold transformations that will be the theme of the rest of the book. But in anticipation of its eighth and tenth chapters, I want to suggest also that there is a kind of fixed tenure possible outside the government of civil society to which authors and intellectual property may jointly aspire. I have already outlined in the Prologue how sudden emergencies capsize the hierarchy of things and people, elevating the former to the condition of gods and depressing the latter to the condition of animals. These emergencies seem to arise from two antithetical motives. On the one hand, we find that the desire to fix property contractually beyond the faintest likelihood of truancy is a sure method to make it delinquent; and on the other, it is plain that to gain property without contracts is a state of war, in the course of which passions are stirred and all sorts of things take flight. The chief example I shall give of an overweening attachment to property is entail, a late innovation in the law of feudal tenure which appeared to allow an owner to own a thing forever, posthumously and without limit. I want to show how this attempt to glue things to the person was counterproductive. As for the state of war, it is useful to consider Nestor's characterization of the man addicted to battle as cursed and outcast, "void of law and right,/ Unworthy property" (Homer 1959: 166 [IX, 63]), together with Aristotle's comment on "the war-mad man" as one who is "like an isolated piece in a game of draughts . . . the figure of a man as an amputated hand is the figure of a hand, but neither enjoys the *condition* of man or hand, and is thus *another thing*" (Aristotle 1992: 60). I hope it will appear that as humans become more like things, things acquire the serene self-sufficiency typical of all personifications, in representing only what they are and nothing else. These personifications are the consummate agentive form of loose things, under whose dispensation human figures are so confused and passive that they can scarcely begin a history of their subjection unless they learn a thing or two from those very things, so secure in themselves.

Property

> Mankind labours always in vain, and to no purpose . . .
> because it does not know the limits of possession.
>
> —Lucretius, *De Rerum natura*

When Blackstone said that the owner of property enjoys "that sole and despotic dominion, which one man exercises over the external things of the world, in total exclusion of the rights of any other individual in the universe" (Blackstone 1773: 2.2), he summarized a tendency in the theory and practice of property-owning that had been growing stronger since the Reformation and became explicit by the seventeenth century. Basically this tendency involved a weakening of the feudal conception of property as a conditional right, held within a network of political and social obligations, and a corresponding strengthening of an impulse toward the unconditional and exclusive appropriation of what Blackstone calls "the very substance of the thing" (2.4). The desire of such absolute possession was destined to revise the feudal division between chattels real (land and the privileges belonging to its occupier) and chattels personal, such as clothes and ornaments. Under the system of feudal tenure, the latter were considered ephemeral and relatively unimportant because they fell outside the law of seisin, which by the end of the middle ages referred solely to property recoverable in real actions—real estate in short. You could be seized in a fee—tenure of an estate—but you could not be seized in portable property. The ancient law-books, says Blackstone, "entertained a very low and contemptuous opinion of all personal estate, which they regarded as only a transient commodity" (1773: 2.384). This explains why medieval law never mentioned ownership as such, concerning itself rather with the details of the fee, which embraced rights and restrictions deriving from an original act of homage to the king extending to embrace the future line of heirs to whom the real estate would descend (Simpson1986: 41, 116, 61). This distinction between real and personal property was buttressed by a paradox. The quality which rendered tenured land real was not just its immobility but also its incorporeality, for even though it subsisted in houses, fields, and streams, these were the clothing of a set of ideas about duties and rights which cohered under the general heading of tenure. Advowsons, views of frankpledge, fee-farms, escheats, reliefs, rents, and reversions—the litter of invisible entitlements and duties that constitute the estate of Shandy in the marriage contract of Tristram's father in *The Life and Opinions of Tristram Shandy*, for example—distribute fiefs as abstract entities throughout political space and genealogical time. Contrariwise it is the mere materiality of chattels personal that renders them inconsiderable and evanescent. They are no more than the weight in your hand at the moment of holding them: the substance of a thing lasts no longer than that.

The opposition between the high value of the incorporeal real and the low value of the ephemeral substance was destined to alter. Blackstone observed that the extension of commerce and trade brought mobile chattels, or personalty, almost to the level of realty. Merchants and stockjobbers took the private possession of the substances of things very seriously, having greatly augmented both the circulation and the value of articles such as "animals, household stuff, money, jewels, corn, garments, and everything else that can properly be put into motion" (2.387). What

Blackstone calls "possession absolute" (2.389) comprises both right and occupancy resulting in that sole, despotic, and exclusive dominion exercised by an owner over the substance of a moveable thing; and this is owing to the elevation of personalty from its precarious status under feudal law into its robust modern form of the exchangeable commodity. As that division of property strengthened, so realty weakened, never having been susceptible to absolute possession. Various adjustments were made to laws of tenure to deal with the problem. The terms *forinsec* and *intrinsec* were coined in order to distinguish inalienable feudal duty to the crown from subinfeudation, a bargain struck over subsidiary grants and fees that were carved from the original feud (Simpson 1986: 5). Blackstone calls this the difference between proper and improper (or derivative) feuds, the former being founded on military obligation and honor, the latter being "bartered and sold . . . for a price" (2.58).

The most improper feud of all was an entail, although it masqueraded as a return to the feudal ideal of real estate as immobile in space and indivisible in descent. By means of an entail, the holder of an estate nominated a line of inheritance, usually through the males (tail male), although it could be devised for females (tail female) or for either gender (tail general). James Boswell and his father quarreled over the entailing of the Auchinleck estate, whether it should be secured for the succession of heirs general or heirs male (Boswell 1980: 666). In three important respects entail departed from the concepts on which the abstraction of real estate was founded; and in another it seemed to sustain them. What it sustained was the physical integrity of the estate, which had to descend undamaged from heir to heir; and in this it seemed to provide a guarantee for the imperishability of realty. But in the case of entail there were no heirs in the feudal sense of the term, for each succeeding occupant was in fact a tenant for life, a steward of what was only held in trust for another tenant, and so on down the line. The fee simple was lodged forever with the original donor, long dead, and each succeeding tenant was obliged to trace title not from the previous occupant of the estate, but from that first donor, leading to tangled and improbable lines of descent which made less and less sense in human terms, as Mrs. Bennett remarks in *Pride and Prejudice* (Simpson 1986: 61; Macpherson 2003). Johnson believed that entails ignored the change of times and opinions, adding, "I know not whether it be not usurpation to prescribe rules to posterity, by presuming to judge of what we cannot know" (Boswell 1980: 668). With regard to the tenants, there were limits set on feudal penalties for failure of service because they were not vassals: for an act of treason the entailed estate could not be forfeit beyond the life of the traitor, and after that the entail resumed. It was clear at least to Blackstone that the originator of an entail was intending to defeat three principles of feudal law. The first was continuity of blood, for if it was impossible to attaint an heir in tail, there was no true genealogical line of descent. The second was the axiom of common law that all property must cease at death:

> For, naturally speaking, the instant a man ceases to be, he ceases to have any dominion: else, if he had a right to dispose of his acquisitions one moment beyond his life, he would also have a right to direct their disposal for a million of ages after him; which would be highly absurd and inconvenient. (2.10)

Yet this immodest aim impels an entailed estate through all the odd traverses and casualties of successive tenancies. In the motive for the immortality of a fee simple lies the third breach of feudal law, namely, the transformation of realty into personalty, the metamorphosis of a conditional into an absolute possession. Blackstone assigns responsibility for this innovation to noble families who wished to keep their estates intact within the family (2.112). Brian Simpson thinks it more likely to have been the ingenious plan of savvy parvenus, particularly lawyers, who, having purchased land, took steps to prevent its subsequent alienation by exercising a special form of despotic dominion over it (Simpson 1986: 209, 235). In any event, under entail immobile property began to function as if it were mobile, but not by means of the contracts and bargains which stimulate the rapid movement of commodities. Instead, the absurd ambition of a dead person endowed an estate with a kind of autonomy. It moved from hand to hand by virtue of its never being thoroughly owned at all, although the impulse that actually set it free was the human ambition to own its substance fully and without limit.

Blackstone says that, as a result, entails "were justly branded as the source of new contentions and mischiefs unknown to the common law" (2.116). Lord Hailes thought them an encroachment upon the dominion of providence (Boswell 1980: 673). Lord Kames called entail the idolization of property, a "swollen conception" that transgressed nature and reason (Kames 1788: 4.449). The breaking or barring of an entail could be accomplished only by means of fictions as absurd as the ambitions of those who, as Lord Nottingham said in his judgment upon the Duke of Norfolk's case, "fight against God, by effecting a stability which human providence can never attain to" (cited in Simpson 1986: 226). These were fictions of entry, recovery, and settlement, by whose means a tenant collaborated with his heir in the pretence of occupying and then alienating the estate from the defunct owner of the fee, who was now no longer in a position to object to the injury. Alternatively, there were ways of mortgaging the estate almost to its full value, and then buying another (Simpson 233; Blackstone 2.117). Effectually a fiction of immortal and absolute possession is confronted by a counter-fiction of sudden occupancy and usurpation, proving (if any proof were needed) that the thing in contention, the real estate, was more "real" than the methods of owning it.

FICTIONS OF THE CIVIL STATE

> How the wit of man should so puzzle this cause to make
> civil government and society appear a kind of invention and
> creature of art, I know not.
>
> —Lord Shaftesbury, *Sensus Communis, An Essay on the*
> *Freedom of Wit and Humour*

If this was happening at law, what was happening in the zone of political theory? In 1646, feudal tenures were abolished by Parliament, followed three years later by the execution of the king, an event that put a decisive end to the continuity of royal succession on which the concepts of feudal tenure necessarily depended. The incorporeality of realty and the rights of personalty required radical redefinition, and this was largely supplied by Thomas Hobbes and John Locke in their rival theories concerning the origin and structure of civil society and the nature of property. These were developed against a background of Continental thought concerning natural and civil law whose chief architects were Hugo Grotius and Samuel Pufendorf. The premise guiding the work of all these thinkers was that the state is constructed by human beings for their own advantage: that it has a distinct point of origin in an agreement to unite in a commonwealth, and that its history is an account of how the ends proposed by its foundation, chiefly self-preservation and the securing of property, are fulfilled in action. At the core of every discussion of civil society is the conjectural transition from the state of nature to the amenities of civil life, when some form of contract or covenant is supposed to have been ratified between the people as a whole and the representatives of the government to which they submit. In order to establish this point of origin in the history of rights, it was necessary to invent an account of the state of nature, a condition of life that was unrecorded and unremembered. Rather like the breakers of entails, then, theorists of civil society made their approach to the real by way of a fiction.

Not surprisingly, these fictions varied. Both Pufendorf and Hobbes believed the state of nature to be one of extreme privation, both savage and uncertain, although Pufendorf allays the horror of it by claiming a limited kinship among its inhabitants (Pufendorf 1991: 119). Hobbes makes no such concession, maintaining that there is no natural right, especially the right to property, that can be vindicated in such a condition, which he calls a state of war: every man against every man. Grotius, on the other hand, dates the human dominion over nature from this period. "From hence it was, that every Man converted what he would to his own Use, and consumed whatever was to be consumed; and such a Use of a Right common to all Men did at that Time supply the Place of Property, for no Man could justly take from another, what he had thus first taken to himself" (Grotius 2005: 2.420–421). Locke is not so hesitant, declaring that whatever thing is taken from nature and converted by labor into the means of self-preservation is a property, and so inalienably ours that it can be no one else's except by a singular breach of natural law (Locke 1963: 328; 314–15 [2.11.25; 2.26.1–18]). Moreover, the development of property from articles of present use into materials stored against future emergencies, and thence into commodities at first bartered and then exchanged for money, is a process consistent with a state of nature. Civil society, as far as Locke is concerned, comes about by an act of free will on the part of each individual, not as a compact forced upon creatures fearful for their lives, "For Truth and keeping Faith belongs to Men as Men, and not as Members of Society"' (Locke 1963: 318 [2.14.20]). Of the four versions of the state of nature, Locke's aims to be the least fictional because the transition from a natural to a civil state is a continuum involving a consistent self and an unrestricted right to the property necessary for its preservation. What is real now was real then; there is no fictional beginning—a proposition tested by Defoe in one of the earliest English novels, *Robinson Crusoe* (1719) and found (at least by a majority of its readers) to be true.

In their histories of the establishment of property Hobbes and Locke are therefore diametrically opposed. During the war that persists in a state of nature, there is, according to Hobbes, "no Knowledge of the face of Earth, no account of Time; no Arts; no Letters; no Society" (Hobbes 1996: 89). There is nothing one can call one's own, or even remember, until a property is made. So histories of the self and nations begin only when (as Hobbes says again) "every man [has] his own": for "where there is no *Own*, that is no Propriety, there is no Justice" (Hobbes 1971: 58). And to those like Locke who might say that property is acquired and justice maintained in the peaceful conversion of natural things to use, he puts this devastating rhetorical question: "How gottest thou this Propriety but from the magistrate.... We would have our Security against all the World, upon Right of Property, without paying for it.... We may as well Expect that Fish and Fowl should Boil, Rost and Dish themselves, and come to the Table; and that Grapes should squeeze themselves into our Mouths, and have all other Contentments and ease which some pleasant Men have Related of the Land of Coquany" (Hobbes 1971: 66). When Locke says that the venison that nourishes the American Indian "must be his, and so his, i.e. a part of him, that another can no longer have any right to it" (Locke 1963: 328 [2.26.14–18), in Hobbes's opinion he is dreaming of a utopia or a romance, where deer offer themselves to be eaten, just like the grapes, nectarines, and peaches in Marvell's *The Garden*. In Hobbes's narrative of the transition from a state of war into a state of civil peace, the problem of self-preservation without security becomes so urgent and terrifying that people agree with one another to come under the government of a commonwealth, a union he figures as Leviathan or the body of the people, which union is represented in its turn by a sovereign. Natural men, authors of their actions, are now obedient to an artificial man who acts on their behalf. The world is thus divided between those who formerly had rights they were incapable of enforcing, and a sovereign who enforces them with his sword. This is the difference between individuals who once were natural persons and acted by their own authority ("Authors") and artificial persons who represent them and operate vicariously by virtue of the authority transferred to them from the people ("Actors") (Hobbes 1996: 112). From that source of sovereign power duly delegated derives the capacity of the magistrate to exercise justice and apportion property. There is no other way to own a thing.

Despite their radically different approaches to property, Hobbes and Locke agree that justice is a matter of an individual's relation to things and not, as Aristotle maintains, a proportionate or fair relation between people (Aristotle 2003: 257 [V.i.8]). The issue is not one of fairness but of security of possession: being sure of owning a thing. Once property is guaranteed, then a sequence is formed that can be delivered as an account. Each sees an intimate connection between possessing and telling things. A self preserved by what is its very own can begin a narrative of its life: "For that which in speaking of goods and possessions is called an Owner . . . speaking of Actions is called an Author . . . he that owneth his words and actions, is the AUTHOR" (Hobbes 1996: 112). So says Hobbes, eliding the distinction between the "Actor" and the "Author"; but Locke would not disagree. Having demanded, "Can [a man] be concerned in his actions, attribute them to himself, or think them his own?" (Locke 1979: 2.27.14; 339), he affirms that a man can and must, and so produces his definition of a forensic personality as one which "extends itself beyond present existence to what is past . . . whereby it becomes concerned and accountable, owns and imputes to itself past actions" (2.27.26; 346). The word "own" extends itself to comprehend both the means of self-preservation, what one *owns*, and the account of the experience of preservation, what one also *owns*. The security of the one account warrants the truth of the other. The action of preserving the self, the history of its preservation, the ownership of property, and the authority of the civil state are all inextricably entwined in the one narrative enterprise.

Hobbes recognizes there is no longer any pure authorship in his commonwealth, so his narrative is filled with useful fictions, chiefly composed of the artificial figures of Leviathan and the sovereign who, together with their delegates, represent the authority that was consolidated with the establishment of civil society. Government is transacted not by authors but by a series of actors, artificial persons representing people whose real authority lies in an immemorial past. When Hobbes includes in this pattern of state authority representations of things that never could have been authors, such as fools, madmen, churches, hospitals, and bridges, then the level of fiction necessary to the conduct of the state rises. "There are few things, that are uncapable of being represented by a Fiction" (Hobbes 1996: 113). How can authors of such fictions draw limits around their inventions and determine their relation to truth when they are themselves creatures of similar fictions, owning actions that are not theirs? The answer as far as Hobbes is concerned is that there is a difference between good and bad fictions. Good ones serve the cause of the commonwealth, bad ones give individuals the illusion of a power they no longer possess, for example when they claim what is not theirs, or say they have done what they never did. When, for example, Locke declares that a man in a state of nature can lay claim to absolute dominion over whatever he picks up, or claims that a convention or contract requires no sacrifice of personal authority, he would be embarked in Hobbes's view upon a bad fiction. For his part, Locke would rejoin by pointing out that anyone who is obliged to own an action in the name of someone else has forsaken title to property and identity alike, and is no different from the man who thought he was simultaneously the mayor of Queenborough and Socrates.

In his discussion of justice, Hume inclines to Hobbes's judgment insofar as he distinguishes between the usefulness of those artifices and contrivances which secure property to an owner, despite the selfishness of individuals and the scarcity of goods, and the "idle fiction" of the state of nature, "a mere philosophical fiction, which never had . . . any reality" (Hume 1978: 494, 496). On the other hand, property is secured by a contrivance that looks very like Locke's idea of incorporated ownership, namely "by putting these goods, as far as possible, on the same footing with the fix'd and constant advantages of the mind and the body" (489), as if they were as naturally a part of the owner as a limb, or a talent for mathematics. However, this security is achieved by means of an artifice, not a right, and it is made necessary because of the fugitive and mobile state of material goods, their "looseness and easy transition" as well as their scarcity (489): When the primitive human goes hunting, "The food, which is requir'd for his sustenance, flies his search and approach" (485). So the good fictions stabilize the relation of the individual to "the situation of external objects" (494), and the bad ones bring about the fluxing state of affairs invented by philosophers, "that savage and solitary condition, which is infinitely worse than the worst situation that can possibly be suppos'd in society" (497).

What is it that molests this fictional stability imagined by Hobbes and Hume, or the evolving state of nature that Locke believes at last merged into the social contract? Well, any event that disturbs the relation of civil subjects to the things that they own, what they both hold and tell, will break up the narrative and alter the relation of human to thing. These events may occur on the outside, in the shape of accidental loss, fraud, theft, or war; or they may originate from within, when madness or death dissolves a person's right to hold property. The framers of entails try to remove a threat that can never be neutralized. Horace Walpole wrote "The Entail: A Fable" to make the point: the butterfly means to entail his manor, the rose; but a small boy trying to catch the insect destroys both insect and flower (Walpole 1758). The moral of uncertain tenure is advertised in the custom of Maori called *muru*, which required that any misfortune, not just insanity and death, be met with the pillage of every item belonging to the afflicted party: "A man's child fell in the fire, and was almost burnt to death. The father was immediately plundered to an extent that almost left him without the means of subsistence: fishing-nets, canoes, pigs, provisions—all went" (Maning 1863: 97). Samuel Butler incorporated this system of double jeopardy into his utopia Erewhon, where illness is regarded as an offense and crime as a malady. However odd such usage may seem to us, it indicates the close correspondence between the degree of a misfortune and the looseness of things that is generally acknowledged in the case of death, when the worst exigency of all prompts all belongings real and personal to shift to new quarters or new owners. Johnson wisely observed in his discussion of entails that an individual in society is never "fully master of what he calls his own" (Boswell 1980: 668).

Things on the Loose

> Recover, resist, repel, strive, arm.—War! War!

> —Lord Shaftesbury, *The Philosophical Regimen*

If we put Blackstone's definition of personal property (absolute dominion exercised by a human being over the very substance of a thing) alongside these difficulties of Hobbes and Locke and Hume, it is evident that there is a disparity between what the structure of society allows and what individuals desire. When people go about to obtain absolute dominion over things—for example by means of entails—it is evident that the two meanings of owning (possession and narrative) come under strain. Because we are unable to "judge of what we cannot know" (Johnson in Boswell 1980: 668), it is impossible for the donor of an entail, who has committed what Johnson calls usurpation and Hailes a breach of providential government, to give an account of what he or she has done. It is a story that might be told in a multitude of ways, none of them accessible to its originator. In such a narrative vacuum, the possibility of a thing's appearing to own and move itself becomes very strong, as when an entailed estate follows the vagaries of a line of descent that becomes less and less predictable, having much more to do with chance or fortune, or maybe with the inclinations of the fief itself, than with the will of the person who set it in train. No one wrote a novel called *The Life and Adventures of an Entailed Estate*, but in *Sense and Sensibility* and *Pride and Prejudice* it is possible to see the outlines of the plot, and how volition passes from people to the land itself. If civil society is conceived of as the occupation of limited tenures in which fictions serve as probable accounts consistent with justice, it is flanked on one side by the dream of natural dominion over things exhibited by Locke's Indian with his venison, so much his it can never be anyone else's, and on the other by the fantasy of absolute possession encouraged by legal definitions of personalty. In either case, should an individual entertain the fiction of embodying possession rather than merely representing it, things will start to evacuate the realm of property, challenging the authority of owners and returning to the looseness and scarcity of the savage state.

Grotius's definition of war describes a limited release of property from absolute dominion. He says, "Before the Right of War can entitle us to any Thing taken, it is requisite that our Enemy had first the true Propriety of it" (Grotius 2005: 3.1323). Grotius's just war is like trade, except that things move from hand to hand by force of arms instead of by exchange. For him war becomes a problem only when violence prevents the thing passing whole from one hand to another, rendering the principle of property and ownership vulnerable, and amplifying the meaning of the word "spoil." Fruit trees should be spared destruction because "Trees cannot, as Men may, rise up in Arms against us" (3.1459). He goes on to cite a number of authorities who conjecturally personify this kind of property, as if wittily to emphasize its immobility: First Philo, who has the figure of the Law demand of careless warriors, "Why are you angry with Things inanimate. . . . Do they like Men, discover any hostile . . . intentions against you?" Then Josephus, whose trees reproach men with injustice, being injured in a war that was none of their making. He is followed by Cicero, who calls that species of war horrid and abominable "which was made against Walls, Houses, Pillars and Gates" (3.1460–61). As far as Grotius is concerned, these prosopopeias are amusing but fallacious, since even in a state of nature it is impossible to conceive of things performing as agents other than by way of trope. It is impossible because things are always owned, and even as booty they ought to pass from hand to hand as property, whole and unbroken.

However, the closer war approaches the injustice of total conflict, where property is alienated not in an orderly passage between successive owners but so violently as to leave things of value broken and destroyed, the more likely it is that the fiction of personified things will start to solidify and have to be taken seriously. Grotius resists this proposition. Tackling the topic of unintentional injury, he remarks on the absurdity of supposing a man in a state of nature may have satisfaction of a beast that has wounded him, implying that the animal can bear the fault. This is a purely figurative and inexact way of speaking: "I should as soon say, that when a Tree falls on a Man in a Forest, and wounds him, that he might have taken Satisfaction for the Damage by cutting the Tree" (2.896 n. 1). By setting the scene in a state of nature, he means to say that even in circumstances the most remote from civil government these fictions of active things are inappropriate, and derogate from the dominion of humankind. Like Locke, he wishes to vindicate the continuum of ownership common to all stages of the evolution of social life, and to recommend the exact mode of speech that belongs to it. Things have never not been owned, he insists, and the story of our possession of them has always been a full and true account. But the circumstances of total war are anomalous and seem to contradict him; for then human beings act as if there were a perfect but uncanny equality between themselves and things, no matter what reasonable people might say in non-figurative language to the contrary. This is why Aristotle is interested in Homer's comparison between the stateless man and a warrior maddened by war, "having no family, no law, no home . . . like an isolated piece in a game of chess": such a creature will appear in the human figure but be another thing altogether (Aristotle 1992: 60).

When Blackstone says the legal fictions associated with entail were without precedent in common law, he was himself being not altogether exact. The law governing unintentional injury identified the deodand, the instrument by whose means the damage was inflicted, as "an accursed thing" and liable to forfeiture or destruction, just like Grotius's tree. Scottish law excluded inanimate objects from the category of deodand as incapable of committing felonies; but at the same time it allowed a place for felonious animals (Holmes 1991: 21; Tamen 2001: 80–86; Macpherson 2010: 157). That is to say, the deodand was not simply a figure for an accidental injury as Grotius understood it, but was in fact an agent capable of motion and will. After its trespass, if an animal should escape or be sold, the former owner was cleared of blame and the new owner acquired the liability (Holmes 1991: 9). Fault lay with the thing and traveled with the thing; the owner simply provided the route to retribution. Marvell's nymph reverses the sequence of trespass (here it is man against animal, not animal against man), but the indelible guilt of the deodand is still plain:

> And nothing may we use in vain.
> Ev'n Beasts must be with justice slain;
> Else Men are made their *Deodands*.
> Though they should wash their guilty hands
> In this warm life-blood, which doth part
> From thine, and wound me to the Heart,
> Yet could they not be clean; their Stain
> Is dy'd in such a Purple Grain.
>   (Marvell 1971: 23; ll. 15–22; see Macpherson 2010: 165–169)

At the heart of common law then lies an idea of the guilty thing, capable of causing harm and consequently deserving punishment. The idea is not treated as a fiction but as a true state of the case. Even today, when ships are prosecuted for the damage they do as persons, this is not a dramatic way of saying somebody's property is about to be sold but an actual "proceeding against the vessel" (Holmes 1991: 26). A corporation functioning as a person absorbs the responsibilities of those who run it. Responsibility for keeping a parish bull was not Tristram Shandy's father's, although he takes the beast's failures personally: it was an obligation falling on the land itself (Holmes 392).

This raises some interesting questions about the status of things like deodands: are they absurd fictions that serve a legal purpose; are they prosopopeias with an imaginative or emotional value; are they dead metaphors that once stood for a power beyond human government; or are they what they are taken to be in common law, things with a real and culpable autonomy? Might they be inclined to take autonomy a further step and challenge the narrative of their guilt by proclaiming as false or wrong what humans say is real and right, and telling a different story? Is it possible to suppose that a thing might supplant its human master, and initiate its own actions, possessed of its own substance, not a person at all but another kind of author or idol? When Ulysses falls silent in an agony of grief after Demodocus has sung the history of the fall of Troy, incapable of answering the questions put to him by Alcinous, the king thinks it might be more useful to ask his ship; and Chapman adds this note: "Those inanimate things having (it seemd) certain Genij, in whose powers they supposed their ships' faculties . . . others have affirmed Okes to have sence of hearing: and so the ship of Argos was said to have a Mast made of Dodone—an Oke that was vocall and could speake" (Homer 1956: 148 [8. 770–75]). Cowley's vocal oak tells the story of Charles I, until it gets to his execution and then like Ulysses is stifled by passion:

> Here stopt the Oak,
> When from the bottom of its Root there broke
> A thousand Sighs, which to the Sky she lifts,
> Bursting her solid Bark into a thousand Clefts.
>
> (Cowley1881: 2.252)

STONES

> Revenged?—Of what? Of a stone? . . . Who is so mad?—for a chance hurt, against thought or intention?
>
> —Lord Shaftesbury, *The Philosophical Regimen*

The point Oliver Wendell Holmes makes about the personification of things in common law is that the passion of resentment is conserved by a legal fiction, and deliberately so: "Without such a personification, anger towards lifeless things would have been transitory at most" (11). It does not need to be anger. Livy mentions the citizens of Alba Longa who kissed the stones of the city they were being forced to leave. But Aristotle says we do not desire either the good or ill of a thing: we do not enquire about the feelings of a bottle of wine (Aristotle 1934 (2003): 457). So what is the point of keeping warm our anger or our grief over a thing, and formalizing what amounts to superstition? The answer seems to be that it depends how severely we are harmed by the thing, and not (as Grotius chiefly argues) how badly we damage it.

At this stage, the argument has to take a wider sweep. Let us say the deodand was a stone, an inanimate thing upon which we chose to wreak vengeance, like the one mentioned by Adam Smith: "We are angry, for a moment, even at the stone that hurts us. A child beats it, a dog barks at it, a choleric man is apt to curse it" (Smith 1982: 94). Smith adds that the passion soon abates when we realize that an inanimate object is not a fit object of resentment: "What has no feeling is a very improper object of revenge" (94). But this is not always the case, as he points out in the next two sections of *The Theory of Moral Sentiments*, where he discusses the effects of Fortune, and its contribution to the irregularity of our senti-ments. He says that a castaway is bound to have affection for the plank of wood which saves his life, and that we would hate any object (say a stone) that killed a friend. Smith then goes on to discuss the deodand and

the "piacular" or fallacious guilt attaching to the perpetrators of accidental harm, whose trespasses are involuntary and yet are punished because
the feelings of those harmed demand that an injury have a real cause, and
perpetrator who is responsible for it. Even the impartial spectator must
"feel some indulgence for what may be regarded as the unjust resentment
of the [victim]" (104). A law that punishes the authors of unintended
harm can equally well find things guilty too, for no matter how improperly a judgment against the deodand is made, it sorts with the rugged passions that incline us to see it as necessary—the same passions which the
contrivances of civil society are designed to soothe and disable, according
to Hume (Hume 1978: 487).

So, of Smith's three conditions determining the propriety of gratitude
or resentment—that the object cause pain or pleasure, be sentient, and act
by design—only the first is applicable to the stone, or any other deodand.
As for the human agent who never meant to do what he or she actually
did, Smith says tragedies owe their finest and most interesting scenes to
the discovery of faultless trespass—Oedipus's incest and parricide, Monimia's adultery (Otway, *The Orphan*), and Isabella's bigamy (Southerne,
The Fatal Marriage) (107). The connection between rebellious property
and actions productive of the opposite of what was intended by them,
that is to say between deodands and tragedy, is strengthened; for both
generate narratives outside the scope of human intention and understanding. They describe a situation in which the element of passion is a
measure of the enforced passivity and degradation of the human agent
when faced with the actions of personified things, all operating under the
license of a divinity called Fortune.

In following an irregular line of thought that ends up justifying a passionate relation to inanimate things he began by explicitly rejecting, Smith
imitates Hume who, in the *Treatise of Human Nature*, lists the four passions (pride, humility, love, and hatred) which must be activated before
a thing can attract or repel us. "Suppose we regard together an ordinary
stone ... causing of itself no emotion ... 'tis evident such an object will
produce none of these four passions.... [Even] a stone that belongs to
me ... [a] trivial or vulgar object ... will [never], by its property or other
relations, either to ourselves or others, be able to produce the affections of
pride or humility, love or hatred" (Hume 1978: 333–4). However, Hume
makes two large concessions in respect of the psychology of faultless trespass and the nature of passion itself which combine to blunt his remarks
on the inertia of stones. He says, "Any harm ... has a natural tendency to
excite our hatred, and ... afterwards we seek for reasons upon which we
may justify and establish the passion. When we receive harm from any
person, we are apt to imagine him criminal.... Here the idea of injury
produces not the passion, but arises from it" (351). And he points out

that such a passion does not, as in his favorite examples of the double relation of impressions and ideas, involve a reflexive relationship to persons and imagination: "A passion is an original existence. . . . When I am angry, I am actually possest with the passion" (415). What is more, anger is put into possession of a person by means of a thing. In contrasting two cases, of a stone touching a hand and a stone lying against a stone, Hume points out that sensation distinguishes the first from the second, and that the nerves of the hand convey an impression, whole and unmodified, to the mind (230–31). Put Smith's case that his foot strikes a stone in the road, that it hurts him and that he is possessed by anger which forces him to suppose that an injury has been done him. The passion provoked by the impression of the stone drives this narrative of harm, and reason does its best to supply the evidence. When Swift's Houyhnhmns hit their hooves against a stone, even those models of rational stoicism call it a Yahoo stone "Ynlhmnawihlma Yahoo" [Swift 2005: 257]), personifying it in order to align it with the phenomenon of evil in their horse-world. Contrariwise, when facing what he thinks is the statue of his ill-used wife Hermione, Leontes asks, "Does not the stone rebuke me/ For being more stone than it?" (Shakespeare 1976: 155–6 [5.3.35–6]).

In these examples, passion prompts the human victim (who is very often figured as beyond the protection of the law, such as a castaway or someone unintentionally guilty of homicide or incest) to tell a story from a thing's point of view—not owning a thing, but the very opposite: imagining what a thing might own. In this state of superstition, Lucius begins the story of his transformation in an ass: "Every thing seemed unto me to be transformed and altered into other shapes . . . insomuch that I thought the stones which I found were indurate [were] turned from men in that figure . . . and further I thought the Statues, Images, and Walls could goe, and the Oxen and other brute beasts, could speake and tell strange newes" (Apuleius 1923: 39). The same ambiguity hangs over the strange news told by Gulliver in his fourth book, whose reader absorbs two stories simultaneously: one is a man's story of his life among horses; the other is a horse's story of its life among men. The first is what happened to Gulliver; the second is what he owns of his life. But the author of that second story is no longer human.

Of all philosophers of the passions, Spinoza most clearly distinguishes between action and passion, between doing something and having something done to oneself. "We act when something takes place within us or outside of us whose adequate cause we are" (Spinoza 1993: 83). On the other hand, passion arises in proportion as the power to act is diminished. "Insofar as the mind has adequate ideas, thus far it necessarily acts, and insofar as it has inadequate ideas, thus far it is necessarily passive" (84). A mind operating under the influence of passion is in vain pursuit of an adequate idea. The reason it will never find one is owing to the fact that the body has been changed by the power of something beyond it. It may try to invent an adequate idea, but such an explanation will always be a fiction. "The essence of passion cannot be explained merely through our essence ... the power of passion cannot be defined by the power with which we endeavour to persist in our being ... it must necessarily be defined by the power of some external cause compared with our own" (146). Passion is what happens to us when we are involved in an event not of our making, and not our own. As Hume says, passion is a real existence and it possesses us. Here is Spinoza's defiance of the verisimilitude of Hobbes's contract, designed to cure fear by turning authors into actors: "Weakness consists in this alone, that man allows himself to be led by things which are outside him, and is determined by them to do those things which the common constitution of external things demands" (164). Things make us do the things that make us creatures of things. Hobbes was incredulous at such propositions: "As if Stones ... had a desire, or could discern the place they would bee at, as Man does" (Hobbes 1996: 468).

A complex narrative of harm forms what there is of the story of *Tristram Shandy*. It begins in the trenches of Namur, when uncle Toby was wounded in the groin by a fragment of stone dislodged from a parapet by a cannonball. The basic fact of this disaster is that the stone fell on him. His surgeon tells him that it was its weight that did the damage, not the projectile force of it. Although this is construed as a fortunate circumstance by the surgeon. it does nothing to soothe the "passions and affections of the mind" (Sterne 1983: 68) which are excited not only by the agony of the wound, but more particularly by Toby's failure to explain exactly how it occurred. Once he has a map, his explanatory techniques get him only so far toward a cause. He studies cannonballs and the parabolas in which they move; and he is evidently fascinated by artillery and the impetus behind the ball which broke off the stone which fell on his groin. But he cannot identify a gunner who pulled the lanyard of the gun, or an artillery officer who gave the command to fire. There is no person at the breech fit to represent an adequate cause.

Undoubtedly one of the most rapturous and private moments of his mock sieges is when he plays a battery of six brass cannon against the walls of Lille by puffing tobacco smoke through their barrels, as if occupying himself the position of the cause he seeks. But he feels it necessary to disappear into the sentry box in order to do so, rendering this mimic cause less than visibly adequate by a maneuver Tristram entirely discommends.

On his best days, when the news from Flanders allows him to take a citadel, Toby does what his passions and affections would teach a man in his situation to do, he takes revenge upon the deodand, the stone that wounded him. The exclusive point of every one of his sieges in the War of Spanish Succession is to make himself master of the works by battering down bastions and ruining defenses, including parapets (Sterne 1983: 363). It is a curiously formal and repetitious pursuit of ruin, but it completes the shift from pain to pleasure. "What intense pleasure swimming in his eye as he stood over the corporal ... lest, peradventure, he should make the breach an inch too wide,—or leave it an inch too narrow" (357). Never in this book is accident so perfectly contrived or so effortlessly fetched into the scheme of intention; and it is a feat performed again and again. Towns and siege architecture are constructed with no other end in mind than putting them in "a condition to be destroyed" (372). Toby is the impresario of this ruin, not its victim. Even though what he fashions mimics the scene of his overthrow, now he appears to act and not to suffer, destroying stonework like that which once nearly ruined him—again and again until he meets more dangerous artillery in the shape of Mrs. Wadman's eye. The pleasure swimming in his own tells us however how far he is from an adequate idea of his personal history. Still possessed by passion, he constructs a scene that is supposed never to change, since it has no other purpose from his point of view than the regular rhythm of its being built and then demolished. The story of the bowling green is less like a narrative than a rite, with Toby the priest and the works the sacrifice. As for the ultimate agent, the external force with the adequate idea of what this is all about, Tristram locates it in the benign personification of Fate, who "recollected for what purposes, this little plot, by a decree fast bound down in iron, had been destined, —she gave a nod to NATURE—'twas enough—Nature threw half a spade full of her kindliest compost upon it" (Sterne 1983: 356).

But there is another female presence in the back garden, rather more aggressive, that might exert a stronger claim to tutelary divinity. Mrs. Wadman is heavily ornamented with metaphors of war (cavalry, artillery, phalanx) and resembles the personification of the very business Toby has been so intently following. Cesare Ripa says that the icon of siege architecture is "a woman of ripe Years, in a noble Garment of divers Colours ... in one Hand the Mariner's Compass, in the other the Description of an hexagon Fortification" (Ripa 1709: 6). That she should lead Toby at least figuratively back to his groin and the wound it sustained at Namur, restoring him to the mute confusion his assembly of siege miniatures had banished, is consistent with the paradox of all obsidional structures. Like other fractal forms, whether of fern-leaves or crystals, fortified positions extend by reinforcing with identical chevrons those angles imagined to be weak. They are elaborate patterns of their own ruin rebuilt, and in this respect much like Toby, who has mended his weakness in exactly the same way, by an accumulation of supplements. But their fate is always to return to ruin, for no matter how well they anticipate the improvements in artillery with the multiplication of their curtains, ravelins, and horn-works, cannon will always outstrip them. Likewise, Mrs. Wadman's artillery is too much for Toby, even though he retreats to what he foolishly believes to be the place of maximum security, his sentry box. So blown up once again, silence once more envelops the wounded soldier, this time dignified by his nephew with the name of modesty.

Lucretius is very cogent in his assault on the stupidity of doing what Toby and his nephew are doing. He says stones have nothing to do with vital sense, and that it is superstitious folly to believe that matter is sentient. Personification incarnates accident as intention; so when passion inclines us to invest an inanimate thing with sensation and intelligence and call it an adequate cause, a god, an idol, or a deodand, we delude and disturb ourselves: "It is no piety to show oneself often with covered head, turning towards a stone" (Lucretius 1924 (1997): 165, 169, 471). Hobbes makes the same point about the materials of which the thrones of kings are made, their "visible creature." We attribute to the stone and wood the spirit of royalty and divinity, and worship them as idols (Hobbes 1996: 449). He also says that personifying Fortune is a way of disguising ignorance (468). Hume explains the whole history of polytheism as figures of the passions, lodged in various materials, personified and then worshipped as if they really existed. He says these are instances of false piety magnified by our own confusion into a pantheon of causes of fresh vicissitudes (Hume 1956: 47).

In the early modern period, the idea of a sphere of spiritual power freely mingling with the material world gained considerable currency. Tommaso Campanella's *De Sensu rerum* (1620), a book that had a powerful influence on Charles Gildon and seems also to have affected Defoe's Roxana, treated the sense of things as a literal truth exhibiting the vitality of the "world animal." He wrote, "We affirm that the sense with which animals seem to be equipped and which seems to distinguish them from inanimate things, can be found in every thing" (cited in Heller-Roazen 2007: 171–2). Campanella pictured experience as perpetual metamorphosis and perception as extensive sympathy. To feel movement is to be moved, to see light is to be brightened; and this truth depends upon another, namely the sapience of all things: "We see that the existent is, because it knows that it is, and there is no existent that does not know itself" (172). Campanella adapts the curious self-awareness of Ovidian metamorphosis, of which Narcissus's self-absorption is exemplary, to an anti-Lucretian theory of motion. Where Lucretius was at great pains to deny any link between consciousness and constituent matter ("One can laugh although not grown from laughing things"), Campanella locates sensation everywhere, and finds all things capable of perception, for "there can be no sensation without the sensing being's acquiring a likeness of the sensed" (173). For his part, Francis Bacon pointed to the lodestone as an example, and drew a conclusion very like Campanella's: "No body when placed near another either changes it or is changed by it, unless a reciprocal perception precede the operation . . . in short there is Perception everywhere" (Bacon 1863: 9.56).

The issue has pursued thinkers to the present day. Heidegger asks what is proper to a stone, and he answers that it is the sum of those traits that are empirically stated of it, which renders a stone a mere object, the inert predicate of the human subject's empirical observation. When he poses a different question, "What in the thing is thingly?" the answer comes out differently, more like Campanella's or Bacon's account of the sense of things, or Spinoza's of the passions. Stones move us, he says, when we perceive what lies behind the manifold of given properties. Like the undistinguished drops in Leibniz's waterfall, we hear a door shut only when we "listen away from it" (Heidegger 2001: 22–3, 165, 25). And, like the odor of Pope's rose, so keen it can scent a man to death, this is an experience which reverses the order of agency, for the door does the shutting and the rose organizes the fatal smelling. In *Minima Moralia*, Theodor Adorno, referring to the alarming efficiency demanded in the shutting of modern doors, laments what humans are exposed to when they are plunged into events managed by things and submit to: "the implacable, as it were ahistorical demands of objects" (Adorno 1974: 40; see Pinney 2002: 125–61).

Things acquire powers of moving us when they emerge from a human system of representation into a zone of experience which is as it were self-organizing. Panpsychism, the modern version of Campanella's and Bacon's theories of immanent perception, is a philosophical position based on the impossibility of an intelligence that is not distributed through all matter. Panpsychists maintain that it is incoherent to think that thinking matter such as ourselves could emerge from matter merely inert: if we laugh we are made of potentially humorous stuff, despite Lucretius's derisive jokes about atomic hilarity (Lucretius 1997: 77; 1.915). Similarly, what humans call experience is derived from matter's own experience. To put it in Galen Strawson's words, "[You] cannot deny that when you put physical stuff together in the way in which it is put together in brains like ours, it constitutes—is—experience like ours; all by itself" (Strawson et al. 2006: 12). In his defense of the category of properties, or what he called *coniuncta*, Lucretius encountered this problem of anomalous experience, which he distinguished as accidents, or *eventa*, pointing out that these could not possibly have an existence of their own (Lucretius 1992 [1975]: 39 [i.449–82]. This is precisely what Strawson denies: "There cannot be a subject of experience, at any given time, unless some experience exists for it to be a subject of, at that time" (Strawson et al. 2006: 192). Talk of properties he says is a blind, designed to introduce the counterfactual possibility of a subject with none, accident-free and purely autonomous.

PERSONIFICATION

> To acknowledge the reality of affliction means saying to oneself: "I may lose at any moment, through the play of circumstances over which I have no control, anything whatsoever that I possess, including those things which are so intimately mine that I consider them as being myself."
>
> —Weil 2005: 90

The idea of a subject of experience thinned by affliction and war, more provisional, passionate, and uncertain than was ever thought possible, seems to me a useful way of getting closer to the questions of property and personification that have been raised earlier in the chapter. Locke and Hobbes between them were aware that a civil subject required a fictional supplement if it were to function in a predictable way. The creature in perpetual flight for fear in Hobbes's state of nature finds refuge within the artificial man, a figure made in his likeness who *acts* for the citizen and out of many individuals embodies a unity, namely the state or commonwealth. From the discontinuous and passionate fragments of the experience of the self, Locke fashioned an internal representative in the form of the person, who likewise renders coherent what otherwise would be inchoate. Each is aware that the price paid for unity is a fictive representational synthesis, what Hobbes calls "the unity of the representer" or Leviathan (Hobbes 1996: 114) and Locke "a precise multitude (Locke 1979: 289 [2.22.2]): the inchoate considered as a unity. Therefore, they are very deliberate about drawing the boundaries between what deserves to be represented by a person and what doesn't. Let us say that in the very moment of inventing a political subject capable of emerging from the state of nature by means of contracts, Hobbes and Locke are forced to deal in a sidelong way with that thinner sort of subjectivity that makes people vulnerable to things and the sense of things, liable to play parts in narratives that are far different from the veridical first-person records on which civil society depends for its own history. Locke smells this danger in the alienation of property by payment of money, expediting "the partage of things" that once were our very own, and so much so it was supposed impossible they could belong to anyone else (Locke 1963: 344). Hobbes knows that the necessary fictions of a civil state may slip into gloriation, and that the figure of an artificial man might become nothing but an idol. Such dangers can only be skirted by re-inflating the civil subject to dimensions as large and round as is consistent with the delegation of power (for Hobbes) or with the forensic duties of a public self (for Locke).

In this respect, personification is a critical index of where things have got to in the relations of humans to things. As Quintilian and, later, Hume point out, it is the great resource of poets. Quintilian specifies two fundamental forms of substitution in personifications: animate for inanimate and cause for effect. He praises the sublime feelings that erupt "when we attribute some sort of action and feeling to senseless objects" (Quintilian 2001: 3.431). Likewise, he draws attention to those locutions which emphasize the dual function of agent and patient in personification, such as "pale Death," "pale Disease," and "slothful Ease" (3.441). The passions embodied by these figures generate this ambiguity in acting both as the force behind what is felt and the feeling itself: "Fear, however, is to be understood in two ways: fear which we feel and fear which we cause in others. Likewise envy: one kind makes a person 'envious,' the other 'invidious,' though the first applies rather to persons and the second to things" (Quintilian 2001: 3.55).

Like Longinus, Quintilian is fascinated by the reciprocity between the symptoms of passion and their springs, which he refers to *enargeia*, "not so much talking about something as exhibiting it" (3.61). And, like Lucretius, neither he nor Longinus is interested in the representation of sensations in the form of idols or deities, only in the physical immediacy of them. Both critics call sublime that sort of oratory or poetry which succeeds in generating passion by moving rapidly from a quotation or an imperfect description of experience to the experience itself via a figure which, like personification, acts simultaneously as the trigger of the feeling and the feeling itself. This rhetorical maneuver Longinus called being sublime on the sublime and it is one which Quintilian associates directly with personification, clearly for him a far more potent figure than Grotius believed it to be. *Enargeia* is therefore a powerful inducement to sympathy, along the same lines as Campanella's brightening light or Bacon's lodestone. If we are to identify with the sufferings of those whose misfortunes we lament, then we have to act as if theirs were ours until the transfusion is complete: "We play the part of an orphan, a shipwrecked man, or someone in jeopardy" (Quintilian 2001: 3.63). One way or another, *enargeia* reaches a point where it is hard to distinguish between those who introduce and describe the experience and those who endure it. When the circumstances of fear are exhibited not as the properties of another person in peril but as Fear itself, then the conventional distinction between action and passion breaks down, and Fear is what it does to you and me. Personification abbreviates the reversal of sequence to be found in doors that shut to one side of us, or roses that smell us dead, or actions of our own that turn into the events which happen to us. Fear does not represent itself; it is what it does, the author of itself.

The problem with personification is that, of all literary ornaments, it is the one most threadbare and trite, especially in the eighteenth century when every abstraction seems to have had a machine-life of its own ("Can Honour's voice provoke the silent dust,/ Or Flattery soothe the dull cold ear of Death?"). It is profitable therefore to consider how Quintilian analyzes the language involved in making the change from the description of things and emotions to the action of things and passions. He chooses as his example the siege and capture of a city.

> No doubt, simply to say "the city was stormed" is to embrace everything implicit in such a disaster, but this brief communiqué as it were, does not touch the emotions. If you expand everything which was implicit in the one word, there will come into view flames racing through houses and temples, the crash of falling roofs ... then will come the pillage of property ... the frenzied activity of plunderers carrying off their booty. (3.379)

He is recommending such a multiplication of circumstances of war that the panoptic point of view implied by the passive voice ("the city was stormed") is replaced by personified destruction (racing flames and crashing roofs) and by scenes of what Hume calls the "looseness and easy transition" of property (Hume 1978: 489). Personification, like the deodand in common law, conserves the intensity of passion and the activity of things. The circumstances and properties of animated things familiar to Grotius as an empty trope are presented by Quintilian as not only rhetorically successful but true to the experience of destruction, or more accurately Destruction; that is, the experience of roofs that engineer their own fall, flames that delight in their own motion, and booty that rides off on the backs of frenzied pillagers. Their ideas of themselves are as adequate as ours are inadequate who passionately register or assist in what they do.

It is surprising how inevitably personification invades descriptions of extreme distress, such as shipwreck, plague and war, and sieges. Here are some examples, taken almost at random from fiction and historical accounts. This is James Cook reporting from the Endeavour Reef, where his ship was holed by coral and apparently sinking, owing to an error in the reading of the water level in the hold: "A Mistake soon after happened which for the first time caused fear to operate upon every man in the Ship" (Cook 1955: 345). Notice it is the mistake, or Mistake, which happens and Fear that then affects the whole crew, no human agent visible.

Here is Joseph Banks in the same predicament: "The Capstan and Wind-lace were mannd and they began to heave: fear of Death now stard us in the face" (Banks 1962: 2.79). Capstan and Windlass do the heaving; Death does the staring. And here is Don Juan in an open boat: "Twelve days had Fear/ Been their familiar, and now Death was here" (Byron 2000: 445; [II, 49, 391–2]). "Death now began not, *as we may say*, to hover over every ones Head only, but to look into their Houses, and Chambers, and stare in their Faces" (Defoe 1990: 34). 'The yellow fever stalked openly through the city of the Cape . . . now it had become like a giant person that could no longer be hid away' (F. Tennyson Jesse 1981: 90). "I had felt Death's hand once before . . . but this time his grip was more and more determined" (Jünger 2004: 281). Here is Victor Hugo: "The Saint-Antoine barricade used everything as a weapon, everything civil war can hurl at the head of society . . . a mad thing, flinging inex-pressible clamour into the sky. . . . It was a pile of garbage, and it was Sinai" (Hugo 1982: 889–90).

W. G. Sebald has talked of the hollowness of descriptions such as these. "The reality of total destruction, incomprehensible in its extremity, pales when described in such stereotypical phrases as 'a prey to the flames,' 'that fateful night,' 'all hell was let loose,' 'we were staring into the in-ferno,' and so on and so forth. Their function is to cover up and neutral-ize experiences beyond our ability to comprehend" (Sebald 2003: 25). Yet when he is faced with the job of describing the destruction of the city of Hamburg by a firestorm in 1943, in astonishment he resorts to the same language:

> The fire, now rising 2000 metres into the sky, snatched oxygen to itself so violently that the air currents reached hurricane force, resonating like mighty organs with all their stops pulled out at once. . . . At its height the storm lifted gables and roofs from buildings, flung rafters and entire advertising hoardings through the air, tore trees from the ground and drove human beings before it like living torches. (28)

He takes the necessary next step in the representation of ruin recom-mended by Quintilian in making the effects so vivid that they embrace the function of causes. Here is an example from a bombardment of Row-ton Heath during the English Civil War, where the same thing happens: "Our houses like so many splitting vessels crush their supporters and burst themselves in sunder through the very violence of these descend-ing firebrands . . . two houses in the Watergate skip joint from joint and create an earthquake, the main posts jostle each other, while the frighted casemates fly for fear' (Duffy 1979: 155). Houses do the work of their collapsing, rather like Toby's towns, each falling according to a pattern some power other than he, the contriver of ruin, has decreed. In Ernst Jünger's description of the bombardment of the village of Fresnoy, the antics of things take over the scene. "As if by some magical power, one house after another subsided into the earth; walls broke, gables fell, and bare sets of beams and joists went flying through the air, cutting down the roofs of other houses. Clouds of splinters danced over whitish wraiths of steam. Eyes and ears were utterly compelled by this maelstrom of devastation" (138). And Edmund Blunden, on the other side of the same conflict, noticed how "A small brick building between our trench and Festubert village behind began to jump away in explosions of dusty yellow smoke" (Blunden 2000: 11).

I want to look more closely at this process. When Plume is advancing an argument for fornication in *The Recruiting Officer*, Ballance objects, "War is your Mistress, and it is below a Soldier to think of any other" (Farquhar 2000: 700). To coin Holmes's phrase, is this just a dramatic way of saying that military duty lies in the field rather than the tent; and if it is more than that, what does the personification amount to? Guy Chapman offers a more hectic version of War as lover. "Once you have lain in her arms you can admit no other mistress ... [we] arise from her embraces pillaged, soiled, it may be ashamed, but [we] are still hers" (Chapman 1988: 226). He gives examples of lovers transmogrified by War. He mentions the inquisitive idler who catches himself being watched, "but if you turn to surprise the watcher, there is nothing except the fog filtering between the trees" (43). More dramatically, he pans across the vista of wreckage in no-man's land, listing the accidents of his mistress, "The shovels, water bottles and tin hats, maps stamped and ground into brown mud, the cotton bandoliers ... boxes of bombs, of Very-lights, odd rounds of Stokes shells, flares, entrenching tool handles, stretchers" (218). "That war was a jealous war," says Blunden of the deity who makes her votaries attend to the singular difference that prevails in all the things she owns as hers: "no single brick, no wheelbarrow, no sandbag should be omitted" (Blunden 2000, 1, 179). Like the three hats, one cap, and two non-matching shoes that take the measure of Crusoe's nakedness when he is cast away on his island, or like the multitude of familiar phenomena Gulliver lists as absent from the land of the horses, these things belong to the experience of total destitution Hobbes called the state of war. Such details make up their own account, they are that species of "facts [that] stare us straight in the face" (Sebald 2003: 53). To be War's paramour is to be possessed by the experience of such things.

Chapman begins his memoir of the First World War with an epigraph from Hobbes on the state of nature: no account of time, no traffic, no arts or letters, and very little of human life. There are many accounts of extreme suffering that talk of the weird sense of suspended time, of the fantastic importance acquired by things, of the perpetual fear, and above all of the impossibility of putting the experience into language. For instance, in *If This Is A Man* (published in the United States as *Survival in*

Auschwitz), Primo Levi attempts an illustration of the intense and unre-mitting hunger of the victims of Auschwitz, which he can render logically in no other form than as absorption into a personified experience ("the Lager *is* hunger: we are ourselves are hunger, living hunger" [1996: 74]). There is a picture of a steam-shovel moving earth that shows dramati-cally how thin Levi's subjectivity has become, and how full of activity is every thing beyond it: "At every bite of its mouth our mouths also open, our Adam's apples dance up and down. . . . We are unable to tear our-selves away from the sight of the steam-shovel's meal" (ibid.). Under such a revision of the relationship between human and thing, where nothing is owned, and nothing can simply be told from a secure position by a subject, personification ceases to be a rhetorical choice; it proclaims its ownership of the experience itself, and refuses to be depicted in a frame or reported in a sequence. Levi includes a persistent nightmare of survi-vors: "They had returned home and with passion and relief were describ-ing their past sufferings, addressing themselves to a loved person, and were not believed, indeed were not even listened to" (Levi 2005: 2). To be placed so precisely on the other side of authenticity and even of verisi-militude, where every enormity endured contributes to the improbability of a vile romance, is to endure a special kind of silence. It is not owing to the want of words, or an ability to articulate them, but to a re-orientation in the relationship of the individual to experience so severe it cannot be expressed as true or even likely. To make such an account plausible, everything remembered by the narrator would have to be sacrificed to a criterion that judges such memories to be false. "In reality, *wood* cannot feel, nor *iron think*," says a child's toy faithlessly of its own report (Anon n.d.: 34). But if the circumstances of misery and fear were to overtake the toy's audience, then wood and iron would feel, speak, think, and move about, as they do at Rowton Heath, Festubert, and Auschwitz.

Authors and Books

> Are these *propria*? are they thine? thy very own true
> and certain possessions properly belonging to thee and
> naturally thine?
>
> —Lord Shaftesbury, *A Philosophical Regimen*

An individual metamorphosed by war or the Lager loses the rank of per-son or character, and with it most of what represents a secure relation to social and literary affairs. Alice finds this out when she tries to recite fa-miliar verses in the worlds underground or behind the looking-glass, and they all come out as nonsense. Words printed in books, no matter how familiar, are changed, and mean something different or nothing at all. Caught in the artifices of those who have read his book and now want to read him as if he were print, Don Quixote wishes to destroy the false history of himself he finds in the press of the Barcelona printing house. Ernst Jünger explores a ruined house at Guillemont and discovers how strange it feels to come across a book there, even one he used to know very well:

> I took a walk through the ravaged gardens, and looted delicious peaches from their espaliered boughs. On my wanderings I happened into a house surrounded by tall hedges, which must have belonged to a lover of antiques. . . . Old china sat in piles in large cupboards, ornate leather-bound volumes were scattered about the floor, among them an exquisite old edition of *Don Quixote*. I would have loved to pick up a memento, but I felt like Robinson Crusoe and the lump of gold; none of these things were of any value here. (Jünger 2004: 103)

The very novel which, according to Hobbes, drives people into fits of romantic vainglory is set aside here as antithetic to the state of war, exemplified by reference to another novel, as if it were not fictional enough to do justice to the extremity of it. There is an example even more peculiar from the anonymous *A Woman in Berlin*, a story told by a woman who experienced the first months of the Russian occupation in 1945. She has to resort to special metaphors and locutions in order to show how acts of war, especially rape, reduced her to a category beyond the human. The measure of her own metamorphosis is given by the booty that comes her way, named with "its own specialized jargon . . . 'my major's sugar,' 'rape shoes,' 'plunder-wine,' and 'filching-coal'" (Anon. 2003: 190). Like the hats and shoes that stare Crusoe in the face on the beach, these things are not property and trace their genealogy not from their manufacture and sale but from the violence that liberated them from ownership. While in this condition of servitude to alien stuff, the woman opens a book and reads the following sentence, "'She cast a fleeting glance at her untouched meal, then rose and left the table.'" "Ten lines later," she confesses, "I found myself magnetically drawn back to that sentence. I must have read it a dozen times before I caught myself scratching my nails across the print, as if the untouched meal—which had just been described in detail—were really there and I could physically scrape it out of the book" (4). A page of print divides her from the world she once enjoyed. She is now on the other side of it, what is written rather than she who reads and eats and has choices to make. So she scratches at the paper in a hopeless effort to reclaim dominion over the substance of things, emphasizing by the futility of her gesture the fictionality of the world that was once her own, and the pointless and scarcely communicable materiality of the one she is in now, which isn't her own at all.

In respect of the eighteenth-century novel, several questions are raised by such a state of affairs. How was it owned, for example, and what was owned in it? What kind of property did it embody, or represent, and what kinds of persons, or characters, handled it? I shall tackle these questions later, but I want to finish this chapter with a brief account of the relation of authors to books, and the equivocal thingliness of this form of property.

By the Statute of Anne, 1710, known as the Copyright Act, it became possible to negotiate the limited sale of literary property. For a period of fourteen years a bookseller had the right to print copies and sell them; afterward, the right returned to the author. Discussions of copyright seemed to hew closely to the new definitions of portable property and the doctrine of absolute dominion. Defoe wrote in *The Review*, "A Book is the Author's Property . . . 'tis as much his own, as his Wife and Children are his own" (No. 2, 1710, cit. in Rose 1993: 37). John Dunton, author and bookseller, stood up for his "sole Right and Property for the Children of his Brain" (Dunton 1705: 255). So literary property made its way into the marketplace from the author's point of view as something totally possessed, so much the author's own it could be no one else's. This led to a host of metaphors of authorship involving gestation, birth, and tutelage, all strongly suggestive of an embodied good not easily alienable. Nevertheless, the point of owning literary property was to plan for its sale or "partage" to a bookseller. By means of the limited copyright, authors hoped to reconcile their embodied and peculiar ownership of the copy with the need to exchange it for money. But from the booksellers' point of view, the alienation of literary property ought to have been like the contract of sale of any other commodity—forever. It seemed to them an impossible novelty to sustain a contract of sale for only a certain number of years.

There were various attempts to define literary property—as the print-run of a single edition of a work, as the name on the title-page, as a common-law right in the fruits of literary labor, as the patent of an invention, or as a supplement to common-law right. In his *A Letter from an Author* (1747), William Warburton took up the cudgels for authors. "Surely if there be Degrees of Right, that of Authors seemeth to have the Advantage over most others; their Property being, in the truest Sense, their own, as acquired by a long and painful Excercize of that very Faculty which denominateth us Men" (Warburton 1747: 2). William Blackstone thought it was in the very idea of composition, and not in the labor of actual writing, that a property was formed; it was lodged therefore in the sentiment, not the script, and literally constituted sentimental value. The sentiment and style of a literary work, "These alone," he said, "constitute its identity" (cited in Rose 1993: 76, 89). Warburton called this

essence of literary property its "Doctrine" or "ideal Discourse," "the true
and peculiar Property in a Book" (Warburton 1747: 13, 8). John Dunton
named it "the very Life and Soul ... of the Copy" (Dunton 1705: 248).

Unlike any other bargain, the exchange of literary property confounded the meaning of property; for it was something belonging entirely to an individual, yet its value was determined by a quality inherent
in the thing itself. No matter how hard Defoe, Dunton, Warburton, and
Blackstone argued for the inalienable essence of literary property, only
in the material form of a printed book and via an act of exchange that
made its contents public could its sentiment or "doctrine" be known to
have a value. Booksellers paid a standard miserly rate for copy that was
almost always a gamble, with publication alone justifying the price paid.
This uncertainty no doubt influenced their view that the sale should be
final and unconditional, and their ownership of the copyright absolute.
On the other hand, no amount of emphasis laid by them on the price
and materiality of the print commodity could obliterate the truth that in
paper, board, thread, glue, calfskin, and printer's ink there lodged an immaterial quality that gave one book a value greater or less than another.
Is knowledge to be scratched out of a page with a penknife, as Walter
Shandy thinks, or is a meal to be scraped from the page with a finger-nail,
as the woman of Berlin believes? If not, is a book assumed to have an immaterial core or soul deriving from the mysterious quality of sentiment,
originality, doctrine, ideality, or genius like that which inhabits the mast
of Ulysses' ship?

Mark Rose names this genius the "ownness" of literary property, which
he understands to be both the result of its reification, treating thought
and invention as a thing, and of the recognition of its distinctive quality,
or what Warburton calls its "true and peculiar Property" (Rose 1993: 88,
118). The property of authors is, Warburton maintained, "in the truest
Sense, their own" (Warburton 1747: 2); but at the same time the author
"should be owned and protected in a Property ... which he hath not
merely acquired to himself, but which is generously objective to the Benefit of others" (11). These inner and outer aspects of literary property, that
which is publicly owned in respect of what an author personally owns,
are handled too by Edward Young, who said of the author and his works,
"His [is] the sole Property of them; which Property alone can confer the
noble title of an Author" (Young 1759: 53–4; Rose 1993: 115). It is not
quite a tautology. Consider what he is saying: the works must first confer
the title of an author, and only then may the author claim the work as
his own. The author sues for title from the "ownness" of the book itself;
and only after the transformation of manuscript into print, author into
vendor, and book into semi-commodity, does this proprietory ingredient
become evident.

In this first essay in the law of intellectual property it was clear that other commentators such as Defoe and Dunton, both of whom were professional writers living by their pens, wished to locate authorial property in the copy prior to publication, lasting as long as the interval between its creation, or birth, and its partage to a bookseller. When Defoe talks about it as an infant conceived and born, or Dunton as a thing with life and soul, it is clear that the copy is the embodiment in ink and paper of a virtue whose "ownness" is complete and unconditional as it stands: totally the author's own property. The "ownness" that survives after sale in the printed text, on the other hand, is the shrunken commodity form of absolute possession, amphibian in the sense that it straddles the interiority of originality and the public realm of trade and value, and likewise in the sense that it belongs both to the present moment of alienation and the future when it will come back home. Richardson was a rare exception to this difficulty in being both author and seller of his books. For many others, the totality of ownness must have seemed a pointless fantasy, any alternative to publication being bound to strike them as absurd: why write only to oneself and keep secret what was meant to be communicated? Nevertheless, it was evidently a dream of some Grub Street writers that they might be able to reserve to themselves what they regarded as peculiarly their own. In his *A Pocket Library; or, A Voyage Round the World* (1691), John Dunton (who like Richardson was both a producer and an agent in the book trade) uses the forum of print to chide readers who expect him to reveal all of himself, invoking as his warrant the quality of authorial glory: "So great a Glory do I esteem it to be the Author of these Works, that I cannot . . . endure that any should own 'em who have nothing to do with 'em" (Dunton 1691: 2.19). He goes on, "[No] other Person[s] yet named or suspected, are the real Authors of this Book, or the real Evander, but that I, and I only am he; and who I am, is yet, and ever shall be a Secret" (2.23). By means of digressions, lacunae and Swift adapts the ploy of an author writing solely to himself at the end of *A Tale of a Tub*; and a similar ambition of publishing only what cannot fully be told informs one of the strangest novels of the eighteenth century, Defoe's *Roxana*, where the suppression of the story is the story. The accident of Tristram Shandy's autobiography, whose narrative retreats in geometrical proportion as it advances, requires constant allusions to Tristram's life as a writer, with inkhorn, pen, and sheets of paper held up for inspection, the badges of his experience of serendipitous privacy. Shaftesbury and certain writers of slave narratives, as we shall see, have in common a preference for ink over type, and one of his most interesting works, *A Philosophical Regimen*, lay a long time in manuscript, just like Hannah Crafts's *A Bondwoman's Narrative*. When the abstractions of intellectual property began to proliferate in the nineteenth century, Samuel Warren and Louis

Brandeis articulated a legal defense of the right to privacy, identifying as objects of concern words which a person did not wish to communicate, which they called a "secret-writing," a term Dunton seems intuitively to have understood and embraced. "In every such case," they wrote, "the individual is entitled to decide whether that which is his shall be given to the public" (Warren and Brandeis 1890; 199; cited in Best 2004: 50).

The question is whether the desire among authors to own their literary productions absolutely is identical with other ways of seeking dominion over the very substance of things; and it seems as if it is not. According to Hobbes, property is acquired by means of the magistrate, a vicar of the sovereign who assigns us what is our own on the basis of a system of distributive justice originating in the sovereign. According to Grotius we enter nature like a theater, and occupy a vacant seat which we call our own and to which we then have a right. Locke comes closest perhaps to what authors understand as property when he says that by means of labor we somehow incorporate what we take from nature, making it so far our own it cannot possibly be anyone else's. But in all these theories of property, an object comes to the individual from the outside as a good which is then assimilated and owned. But children of the brain are on the inside to begin with, until such time as the parents choose to part with them; hence, for the duration of that magical interval they are "in the truest Sense, their own" (Warburton 1747: 2). That is to say, no force other than invention, imagination, judgment, or wit has made them property: not the magistrate, right of occupancy, or labor expended on nature. They are the closest it is possible to get in civil society to an action owned by an author, or natural person, as Hobbes would say, as opposed to an action performed or acted by authority lodged in some representative or institution of civil order. Thus, Tristram Shandy is at a loss to explain the operations of originality, and is forced to construe them as a form of ideal theft, as though composition were a war waged in a state of nature: "I wish you saw me half starting out of my chair, with what confidence, as I grasp the elbow of it, I look up—catching the idea, even sometimes before it half way reaches me—I believe in my conscience I intercept many a thought which heaven intended for another man" (Sterne 1983: 436).

Whatever quality of fugacity or independence belongs to things which have escaped human dominion belongs to authors, too. They are consubstantial with a kind of property whose thingness they share, and which more than one of them calls *glory*. Dunton described it in the third person: "What his industrious Toes do tread, his ready Fingers do write, his running Head dictating" (Dunton 1691: 1.9). Hobbes was quite right to associate this authorial superbia with Don Quixote, a man whose actions are exactly synchronized with the rhythm of his author's pen, and whose proximity to print therefore is measured by artifices whose unpleasantness—deceit, dispossession, and disappointment—declares their distance from ink. "Gloriation of mind" was understood by Hobbes to be an egregious self-delusion, but it is experienced in situations that are not easily gained or maintained in being in every sense extreme, on the edge of what is known, allowed, or intelligible, not civil and sometimes not even safe. The manuscripts of such authors are what Hobbes would call idols, being the material substance in which the products of the imagination are lodged; and authors are an unbloody species of human *figure*, to coin Aristotle's term, cut off from ordinary systems of tenure by a kind of idolatry. They arrive at a perfect equivalence with a thing, from which it is impossible to part or be parted, like the castaway with his plank.

As I write this, Internet search engine Google's attempt to settle issues of copyright flowing from its planned digitization of 30 million books is proceeding through a court in New York's Southern District. The company is attempting on a vast scale what booksellers in the eighteenth century wanted instead of the Copyright Act—namely, total control over the copy for an indefinite period. This includes seven million so-called orphan books which are still in print but whose rights holders are unknown. Google, it seems, wishes to annihilate the anomaly of a book's ownness at the same time that it puts authors into a petitionary relation to the terms on which their works will be read. Nation-states such as France and Germany are offering memoranda to the court pleading for value of the book, "a product unlike other products" (Darnton 2009: 83). If what I have written in this chapter has any truth, then the usurpation of dominion over the substance of book-things and their authors by a global corporate network cannot possibly succeed. I wonder how it will fail.

CHAPTER 2

The Crying of Lost Things

A man cannot possess that which he possesses.

—Plato, *Theaetetus*

Guy de Maupassant tells a story exemplary of the flight of portable property from an owner falsely secure in the possession of it. Called "Who Knows?" it concerns a man who has become very attached to his furniture and bibelots until one night he comes home to find everything in his house evacuating it. "What should I see waddling over the threshold of my own room but the big armchair in which I used to sit and read . . . followed in turn by low settees crawling crocodile-like along . . . my other chairs leapt out like goats, with footstools lolloping alongside. . . . I watched everything down to the smallest, the most modest of my former possessions, including some whose existence I was not even aware, all disappear" (Maupassant 2004: 280). The unfortunate gentleman goes to Italy to recover from the shock, and when he returns to his home town he passes an antique shop, where he sees his things stacked up. From the shopkeeper, an enormously fat and grotesque dwarf, whose small head shines like a moon amidst his wares, he buys back three of his chairs for an extortionate sum. By the time he reports this event to the authorities, the shopkeeper has disappeared, and his empty house has been reinhabited by all the things that left it; but he refuses ever to live there again, and instead commits himself to an insane asylum. It is a fable that not only establishes the tight link between things on the loose and the distraction of human beings; it also introduces the figure of an ill-favored and scarcely human broker who arranges for the purchase of goods already owned by the purchaser. The mystery of this double sale, and how it re-orients the relation of people to things, is the subject of this chapter.

Jonathan Wild's organization of crime in London during the first quarter of the eighteenth century was a phenomenon that many people found astonishing. How was it that a man who had been a notorious thief could insert himself between property-owners and the criminals who preyed upon them, maintaining a fat living by arranging for the return of stolen goods while plausibly proclaiming himself a public benefactor not only for delivering to every man his own but also for periodically betraying the thieves who worked for him? Like the mysteries of credit and the South Sea Bubble, he was one of the many anomalies thrown up by modern commercial society. If in this new dispensation chastity depended on prostitution, accumulation upon profligacy, public benefits upon private interest, and good upon evil, as Mandeville was currently arguing, then it was congruent with such a state of affairs that the law could be served by criminals, and property secured by thieves. From his office in the Old Bailey, Wild dominated the sector of felony known as redemption or payback. Although it was plain to everybody that he was multiplying the wages of crime by exploiting both the thieves who stole the goods and a diffident public who wished earnestly to purchase what was already theirs, he thrived for many years because there was no legal remedy against him. Not until the passage of 4 Geo I, c 11, a law which made it a capital crime to take a reward for returning stolen goods and chattels, did Wild become vulnerable, and even then the interpretation of the statute had to be wrenched in order to secure his conviction and execution (Radzinowicz 1948: 1.683).

Like all great innovators in the market, Wild used the latest techniques of communication. He reached his public through his Old Bailey quarters, a clearing house for information and a forerunner of Fielding's Universal Register Office, also by publishing advertisements in the *Daily Courant*, the *Postboy*, the *Gazette*, and the *Daily Post*. "If any Thing was Lost (whether by Negligence in the Owner, or Vigilance and Dexterity in the Thief) away we went to Jonathan Wild. Nay, Advertisements were Publish'd, directing the Finder of almost every Thing, to bring it to Jonathan Wild, who was eminently impower'd to take it, and give the Reward" (Defoe 1725: 20). Soon the owners of missing things would themselves be placing advertisements in the hope that a deal with the thief might be brokered. But they had to make sure that their messages ended with the promise of a substantial reward and the magic words, "no questions asked"; otherwise the process of redemption would never begin, and as for the missing articles, "seldom or never [would they be] heard of any more" (Defoe 1725: 7).

There are two common assumptions about Wild's enterprise I want to tackle and to modify. The first is that he was a kind of super-capitalist, extending the mechanisms of exchange and profit across the boundary dividing legal exchange from illicit dealing. Certainly this is how Fielding regarded him, and to some extent Gay: a sort of nefarious factory-owner of the underworld commanding the maximum number of hands to labor purely for his benefit. Wild's market, however, was much more focused and more anomalous than that. It involved its two or three participants in a very strange transaction where the price was not, as Marx put it, a wooing glance sent in the direction of money by the commodity; rather, it was the measure of a value outside the scope of exchange, a private calculus involving a person and a thing. The second assumption is that the advertisements of the kind Wild pioneered were precursors or outriders of the formal realism of the early novel, exhibiting in miniature the techniques of probability developed by authors concerned, in Ian Watt's phrase, to bring "an object home to us in all its concrete particularity" (Watt 1957: 29). The objects Wild succeeded in bringing home were in fact illicit; their owners had compounded a felony in order to get them back. As for the particulars of their description, they were oddly exorbitant to the case, for what was being described had already been at home. The owner needed no prompt to imagine what it was like, and neither did the thief who had the article in his hands. As for any narrative implicit in such a description, that seems to have favored the liberated item rather than the owner, reading as we shall see more like a satire than a tale of lost property.

Let us begin with Wild's relation to the market and the world of commodities. Although his system of information exchange seems to belong to the expansion of techniques of publicity characteristic of the emergent public sphere, and to be devoted to the enhanced circulation of goods and money, what he really secured was an extraordinarily intimate and conspiratorial connection between thieves and their victims in which the value of a thing had nothing at all to do with the relation of commodity to commodity, but was instead determined solely by the desire to resume the pleasure of absolute possession, what Blackstone called despotic dominion over moveables, and ownership of "the very substance of the thing" (Blackstone 1773: 2.4). As we saw in the previous chapter, the growing importance of personalty in relation to realty was responsible for the belief that ownership might be entire and even (by means of the law of entail) last for all time. Mandeville mentions the husband of a fine wife or the owner of a fine horse: "[He] take[s] Delight in [it] . . . not for the use he makes of it, but because it is His: The Pleasure lies in the consciousness of an uncontrolable Possession" (Mandeville 1924: 1.227). The pleasure of an uncontrollable possession breeds an appetite for a "vast Quantity of Trinkets as well as Apparel," all intended to flatter the vainglory of owners. When a thief stole something the owner could not bear to lose, and challenged him or her to pay more money again than it had originally cost in order to have it back, a metamorphosis overtook the very substance of portable property.

What had distinguished personalty from realty had been the materiality of things in motion on the one hand, and the incorporeality as well as immobility of real estate on the other. Now that substance had vanished from personal property, having been stolen and no longer in the hands of the owner, it became the target of desires and passions more intense and poignant than any that had accompanied what had been mistaken for its absolute possession (Benedict 2004: 227). To be reacquainted with the desiderated article, a sacrifice needed to be made of the sort Georg Simmel calls "the unique constitutive element of value, of which scarcity is only the external manifestation, its objectification in the form of quantity" (cited by Appadurai 1986: 3). Theft introduces scarcity in its most dramatic objective form, precipitating an idealization of property that renders it more intensely attractive to the imagination than it had ever been while possessed. The many details lavished on the description of missing articles in advertisements were superfluous in all empirical respects. As Defoe pointed out, "The Advertising or Publishing their Loss [was not] any real Service, or of any use to the Loser, for that the only Person who could assist in the Recovery of the Goods, was quite out of the question, having no need of the Information, but coming by his Intelligence another way, viz. from the Thief himself" (Defoe 1725, 11). Advertisements were the wooing glances sent in the direction of the re-membered possession, and the price was the sacrifice required for its re-materialization. Particularity was a conjuration or spell designed for an idol, the visible creature of a fantasy, not an attempt at realism.

Often these stolen things had no market value, such as pocketbooks and shopbooks. Even if they still bore a face value, such as a banknote, a lottery ticket, or scrip, their value had altered, for these were usually "stopped" and no longer current. But if they were intrinsically valuable, such as a watch, an ornamented cane, or a snuffbox, the bullion weight was already discounted in determining what they were worth to their owners. So what was being measured arose solely from the opinion or sentiment of the owners who wanted back what had been theirs for little better reason than that it had been theirs, and that they very much liked it being theirs. They wanted their own, their very own, back—proving, if any proof were still needed, that Johnson's maxim was good: "A man is, therefore, in society, not fully master of what he calls his own" (Boswell 1980: 668). Personal property in a state of illicit partage involved a valu-ation of purely private matters incommensurable with any other, or with any public criterion. In the case of watches and snuffboxes, what was being negotiated was known as "the fashion of the thing," or what Pufen-dorf called the "fancy price" (Pufendorf 1994: 193). Fielding is mordant about this *je ne sais quoi* because he thinks it is pure caprice:

> Wild had ... established an office, where all men who were robbed, paying the value only (or a little more) of their goods, might have them again. This was of notable use to several persons who had lost pieces of plate they had received from their grandmothers; to others who had a particular value for certain rings, watches, heads of canes, snuff-boxes, etc., for which they would not have taken twenty times as much as they

were worth, either because they had them a little while or a long time, or that somebody else had had them before, or from some other such excellent reason, which often stamps a greater value on a toy than the great Bubble-boy himself would have the impudence to set upon it. (Fielding 1982: 139)

Mandeville's opinion of sentimental value is pretty much Fielding's: "If what we want is a Trinket, either enamel'd, or otherwise curiously wrought; if there is Painting about it, if it be a particular Ring, the Gift of a Friend; or any Thing which we esteem above the real Value, and offer more for it than Mr. Thief can make of it, we are look'd upon as good Chaps, and welcome to redeem it." The payment is for the value above or to one side of the real value, irrelevant to "any Thing but the Fashion" (Mandeville 1725: 3–4). Roxana makes the same complaint as Fielding and Mandeville in respect of her own body, "this Carcase of mine," which can never sufficiently be possessed by her lover, the prince; a perpetual longing she generalizes like this: "In a Word, they raise the Value of the Object which they pretend to pitch upon, by their Fancy; I say, raise the Value of it, at their own Expence; give vast Presents for a ruinous Favour, which is so far from being equal to the Price, that nothing will, at last, prove more absurd, than the Cost Men are at to purchase their own Destruction" (Defoe 1981: 74)—that is, in the case of her own lover, to purchase by extravagant gifts what he has already bought.

The fancy price of the fashion of an alienated thing arises from the fantastic exaggeration of what was originally a judgment of taste. The pleasure of having owned it, whether it arose from its beauty, from its associated ideas, or simply from the habit of possessing it, was set at a new rate, beyond the intrinsic, exchange, or fiduciary value of the commodity. More specifically, it was the residue of "propriety" in the thing, that quality each owner believed had made it peculiarly the owner's own, which was being negotiated. Locke had defined primitive non-alienable property as an object stained with "something that is his own [that] thereby makes it his own." Thus, the venison that nourishes the wild Indian "must be his, and so his, i.e. a part of him, that another can no longer have any right to it" (Locke 1963: 328). Hume's most forcible illustration of the doctrine of the double relation of impressions and ideas involves this intimate and loving relationship with what is yours. "Every thing belonging to a vain man is the best that is any where to be found. His houses, equipage, furniture, cloaths, horses, hounds, excel all others in his conceit; and 'tis easy to observe, that from the least advantage in any of these, he draws a new subject of pride and vanity" (Hume 1978: 310). It is this remainder of personal identity or pride, confounded with the element of taste, that Wild and his cohort had to sell, and which the former owner was bidding for. The thieves did nothing to alienate that remainder, nor did they consider it alienable: they put it into abeyance until its worth could be assessed; and if it could not, then its vehicle or medium (snuff-box, cane, or watch) was melted down or sent to Holland.

The analogies between payback and reprieve from execution are strangely exact. In payback, the niceties of the law are overlooked and criminal injuries are forgiven in the project of reversing "the partage of things" (Locke 1963: 344), a sort of wild justice whereby every man might resume what is his own and the rider have his mare again. Similarly, a reprieve restores a delinquent to society by an extra-legal and non-procedural act of mercy which many people believed served the cause of justice poorly. "Examples of Justice are more merciful than the unbounded exercise of Pity," thought Fielding (1988: 167). The failure of a payback deal and the execution of criminals likewise run parallel. In the destruction of stolen property, no one annihilates the owner's right to what is lost, that "something that . . . makes it his own," any more than the law threatens the extinction of the immortal soul of a felon when it puts an end to his or her life. And as the souls of felons such as Moll Flanders are never so brilliantly displayed as when they hover between these two possibilities of reprieve and execution ("let any one judge what kind of motion I found in my soul," she declares at that juncture [Defoe 1971: 290]), so the unique quality of a thing is apprehended most vividly not when it enters the market as a commodity, but when it absents itself from the realm of possession. It-narratives are attentive to this pause in the life of thing, for often it is during that equivocal caesura in the sequence of ownership that they begin to speak. Whipping Top begins his story when he is cast away on a riverbank (Anon. n.d.: 72); the One Pound Note starts speaking when he is put in a strongbox (Anon. 1819: 7); the Parrot reports in articulate words that it cannot, like Sterne's starling, get out of its cage (Oulton 1826: 89); Pegtop's narrative begins in a drawer (anon. n.d.: 18); the Rupee's in a pawnbroker's shop (Scott 1783: 119); and the gold in Charles Gildon's *The Golden Spy* (1709) acquires the attributes of soul and speech once it is locked up and no longer circulating. Gildon calls this quality in gold that has ceased to circulate a "peculiar Mark of Excellence invisible to human Eyes" (Gildon 1709: 30). Let us call it for the time being the soul of the thing.

The law recognized no such value, nor any right in the thief to treat with the owner about it, which is why the determination of value in bargains of payback or redemption was such a singular and exclusive procedure. The law was plain on two points: a lost or stolen thing still belonged to its owner; and any attempt to re-purchase title to it was illegal. In his *Dialogue of the Common Laws*, Hobbes had demanded, "How can that be given me which is my own already?" (1971: 58). Pufendorf wrote, "It is evident that if we lose possession of some other thing against our will ... its dominion does not pass from us ... unless it is later on determined that we have given the thing up for lost" (Pufendorf 1994: 188). On the topic of theft, Blackstone has this to say: "If my goods are stolen from me, and sold, out of market overt, my property is not altered, and I may take them wherever I find them" (Blackstone 1773: 2.449). A clandestine sale, even if the purchaser is the owner, is a void contract. In his pamphlet on the subject of theft and punishment, *An Enquiry into the Causes of the Frequent Executions at Tyburn* (1725), Bernard Mandeville cites the "Act for the further Preventing Robbery, Burglary, and other Felonies" of 1719 (4 Geo I, c. 11 that was aimed specifically at Wild by making receipt of stolen goods a felony equivalent to theft). He shows that owners buying their property over again are by no means guiltless in the terms of the statute, for they are engaged in compounding a felony: "He who by publick Advertisements, with Promises of Secrecy, and that no Questions shall be asked, invites others to commit Felony, is guilty of a great Misdemeanour" (Mandeville 1725: ix–x). Mandeville insists that owners should never cease to regard thieves as enemies, and that they ought to keep faith with the property right, even if it means (as it most probably does according to Defoe) never hearing of their goods again. In his view, that is the sacrifice that property demands.

This is a paradox close to the others that Mandeville cites as typical of a market-driven economy. The virtue of possession lies in the sacrifice of the thing; but the vice of possession is to sacrifice money and true title in order to have it again, as it were uncontrollably. In either case, he suggests, possession will be imperfect, either by owning something that is no longer to be had, or by taking possession of it by criminal means. It is worth studying the language of the act in question to see how the degeneration of the owner takes place. It states, "Any Person tak[ing] Money or Reward, directly or indirectly, under Pretence or upon Account of helping any Person or Persons to any stolen Goods or Chattels, every such Person ... (unless such Person doth apprehend, or cause to be apprehended, such Felon who stole the same) ... shall be guilty of Felony, and suffer the Pains and Penalties of Felony ... in such and the same Manner as if such Offender had himself stolen such Goods and Chattels" (Radzinowicz 1948: 1.683). Brokers like Wild are turned into the persons or delegates of thieves, having already represented themselves as the persons of owners. And those owners themselves are implicated in this personate conspiracy, being the "Person or Persons" encouraged to break the law by gaining access to their chattels via other nefarious persons. Here the forensic function of the person, the sole groundwork of civic responsibility according to Locke and Hobbes, contaminates everyone involved in the transaction. Mandeville suggests that in circumstances such as these it is better to have no person at all, and to retreat to the exiguous status of an unrepresented and unpropertied self.

As owners decay into guilty persons, the thing comes into its own. The illicit attempt at recovery actually releases the thing (at least temporarily) from its character of property, and via the advertisement that opens the criminal channel between the person of the owner and the person of the thief, the thing gets access to the public. Its "fashion" is then revealed as autonomous glamour, and the thing itself resonates with potential vocality. It is necessary to distinguish sharply therefore between the soul of the thing as the residue of "propriety" or owner-identity and the soul of the thing from its own point of view. The one is the abstract form of ownership, the shadow of the self in the imagined ideal of a missing thing, the object of the owner's fantastic desire for uncontrollable possession. The other is a power lodged within the thing itself. So from the side of the owner, the soul of a thing is expressed as an aesthetic judgment about a silent and invisible object; but the soul of the thing in its own opinion is more like the *hau* of the gift in Polynesian systems of prestation—a power that transcends ownership and makes an artifact move perpetually from hand to hand, not as a commodity but as an object endowed with a capacity for will and action, rather like an entailed estate.

The conflict between these rival views of the souls of missing things is perhaps best rendered in Arjun Appadurai's idea of tournaments of value. Whether in that great circuit of gifts in the Trobriand islands known as the kula ring, or in an auction at Sotheby's, a tournament of value occurs when personal prestige or *mana* is invested in arresting or diverting the passage of highly valued items such as arm-rings and old masters. Such tournaments are distinguished by the exclusive and privileged company of people who take part in order to calculate the price of a thing "by some negotiated process other than the impersonal forces of supply and demand" (Appadurai 1986: 19). Within this enclave, the price may affect but it cannot restrict the movement of the thing; and it is the path taken by the thing that will finally determine the prestige of those trying to calculate its price. So the contest takes place both at the level of taste and the level of autonomous movement. The success of advertising, Appadurai concludes, arises from its ability to mimic this enclave of value (55) and to reproduce the contest between human desire for possession and the independence or *hau* of the thing. The analogy is close therefore between the intimacy of Appadurai's enclave and the clandestine familiarity of thieves and owners who operated under Jonathan Wild's supervision. For the latter were making judgments of taste which they hoped would influence the route taken by things, and their advertisements were the means of accomplishing this. But when things are liberated from the condition of property, they can assert their own interests and importance, likewise through the medium of an advertisement.

The person who has lost a thing either has it "cried" or listens for its cry. Moll Flanders says a single unadvised woman is like a lost piece of gold or a jewel, and "if a man of virtue and upright principles happens to find it, he will have it cried, and the owner may come to hear of it again" (Defoe 1971:128). In Wild's system of redemption, it depends on the owner asking questions or refraining from asking them whether the thing will or will not be "heard of." The reason it needs to be heard at all arises from its having been "spoken with" (in the cant) by the thief. "Advertisements were daily cram'd into the Publick News-Papers, calling loudly out for all sorts of stray'd Valuables, to be brought in to Mr Jonathan Wild's, in the Old-Baily, upon Promise of great Rewards, and no Questions" (Smith 1726: 13). Consider where the volubility lies in this orgy of advertising. In calling loudly for the goods in an advertisement, the owner promises to be silent (asking no questions)—these are public advertisements promising secrecy, as Mandeville points out. This leaves the calling or crying peculiarly focused on the things themselves, which can cry as well as be cried. The simplest way to contrast the cry of the owner with the cry of the thing is to notice in the advertisement the difference between description and narration. Insofar as an advertisement expresses the desire of owners to be reacquainted with a material portion of their selves, the language is exhaustively descriptive and lover-like in its attention to detail. But insofar as it commences what could become the testimony of the thing, it functions as the outline of a story, and one not at all flattering to the former owner. This intriguing difference between the cries of owners and things marks the point at which the failure of the project of uncontrollable possession includes a loss of narrative control. As usual the two senses of "own" go together, and what is lost cannot be owned either in the sense of being possessed or in the sense of being told—it can only be described.

Even the least distinguished objects are closely observed, and the circumstances of their loss minutely given. "Lost on Friday 23rd Instant, a black shagreen Pocket-book, without the pencil" (*Daily Courant*, 31 July 1725); "Lost a paper Pocket-book ... in riding from London to Little Ilford in Essex, on Wednesday last, either in the great Road, or the Black Lamb, through Westham, or in the Grass or Stubble-fields adjoining to the said Roads" (*Daily Courant*, 9 August 1725). The more the object inclines to fashion, however, the more lavish the description: "Lost Monday 27th in White Conduit Field, a small Spaniel Dog, all white on the Right side, two Liver coloured Spots on the Left side, white streak down the Face, with a Bell about his Neck, ty'd with a Yellow String" (*Heathcote's Intelligencer*, 31 July 1724). Undoubtedly the most particular accounts are given not of things, but of humans who have become things—prisoners, slaves, or indentured servants. Perhaps because they are more valuable, or perhaps because they are situated more critically between the status of thing and the status of human, they are described with extraordinary attention, as if they were entirely singular. "Whereas a Young Man, 25 Years of Age, or thereabouts, fair Complexion, pretty large Nose, wide Mouth, stooping very much in the Shoulders, with a Mark on each Hand in the Shape of a Spur, done with Gun-Powder, has an uncommon Gait in his Walk, and speaks a little thickish, of a middle Stature, thin vis-aged, wearing a light Cloth-colour'd Druggit Suit, or a dark Cloth Suit, did on Sunday last absent himself from his Master's Service" (*Post-Boy*, 7 July 1722).

Remember that in the realist account of the language of advertise-ments, description is supposed to bring an "object home to us in all its concrete particularity" (Watt 1957: 29). In commenting on that phrase in the context of early advertisements for missing things and persons, Jill Campbell suggests that descriptive density brings what is lost home in two senses: to the imagination of the finder, and to the hands of the owner, in order that the incomplete advertising self—the self minus the missing thing—might be restored to unity (Campbell 2002: 251–2). And this circumstantial account of the thing, she argues, runs parallel with techniques of verisimilitude in the novel. We have already seen that at-tempts to repossess possessions unsettles and compromises the status of owners, placing them on the wrong side of the law, and that the detailed descriptions of advertisements are superfluous since they are addressed not to a finder but to a thief who knows very well what the missing thing looks like. This is especially true of missing servants, who are sometimes directly entreated by their masters in the midst of their descriptions to re-turn themselves and their clothes and to collect the reward. The descrip-tion that is to say is not directed necessarily at a public readership, nor does it characterize or personalize its object. It is focused on a singular phenomenon subsisting in the imagination between the zones of visibility and invisibility. The absence of any narrative background reinforces that singularity. The effect is exactly the same as the description of Gulliver's watch and hat in Lilliput, or the ownerless articles of headwear and foot-wear washed up on the shore of Robinson Crusoe's island. As for the neglect of narrative, whether owners believed that lengthy concatena-tions of cause and effect might breach the code of secrecy and silence that payback demands, and lose them forever the chance of repairing their loss; or whether they lacked the confidence in ownership that a narrative of possession requires; or whether in the case of human objects there was a history best suppressed, owners never give the history of how they came by a thing and how they lost it; they stick to description, the "trembling search for a clear sense of belonging" (Schmidgen 2002: 40). Wolfram Schmidgen, whose phrase that is, reads *Robinson Crusoe* as a dramatic oscillation between the certain possession claimed by a narrative, and the uncertain tenure of description. If we transpose his insight to these advertisements, the more a thing is described, the less discretion and the more passion about ownership the advertiser betrays.

Certainly, the more a thing is described, the less it is supposed to speak. It is surprising how commonly advertisements mention that missing persons, whose features are so exactly delineated, are reported as imperfect in speech. The twenty-five-year-old cried so exactly in the *Postboy* "speaks a little thickish." James Watlington, a decamped servant, is reported to speak in "a very hoarse and slow Voice" (*Daily Courant*, 3 August 1724). After his breaking out of the condemned hold at Newgate, Jack Shepherd's physical characteristics are listed, including "an Impediment in his Speech" (*Daily Courant*, 8 September 1724). Daniel Mendoza goes missing on 13 February 1720, described as wearing a dove-colored camblet coat and speaking broken English; the next month, "A Negro Boy called Ebo, about 15 Years old, well favour'd, having a Scar on the right Side of his Head, like a half Moon, [and] an Impediment in his Speech," disappears in a fustian waistcoat and leather breeches (*Daily Courant*, 17 March 1720). In Fanny Burney's *Cecilia* (1782) the heroine is cried in the *Daily Advertiser* as "a crazy young lady" incapable of uttering coherent language (Burney 1988: 901). Here is the description of the companion of Charles Price, an impostor who himself spoke "in general very deliberately, with a foreign accent": "She is rather tall and genteel, thin face and person, about thirty years of age, light hair, rather a yellow cast in her face, and pitted with the small pox, a downcast look, speaks very slow" (Anon. 1786, 203). One of the first *Spectator* papers to mention newspaper advertising tells the story of a man so sparing of his words that when he leaves his lodgings for others, his former landlord is unaware that he has decamped and cries him as a missing person (No. 12, 14 March 1711).

The more volubly an advertisement attempts to portray the missing thing as personal property, whose mark of excellence is the trace of the owner's self, the less the object is presumed to talk on its own account. It might be possible to speculate upon the connection between Ebo's scar and the difficulties he has in talking, but there is no remnant of that story in the advertisement. Ebo is cried, and the owner does the crying. But in notices of missing things, the beginnings of a tale may be detected when the desire vividly to represent the thing outweighs discretion or shame. "Lost the 1st Instant, a Snuff Box about the Bigness and Shape of a Mango, with a Stalk on the Lid, it being a West-India Bean of a reddish Colour, and like Shagreen; the End of the Stalk tipped with Silver, opens with a Hinge, and the Inside lined with Lead. Whoever brings it to Toms Coffee-House Cornhill, shall have a guinea Reward, and no questions asked; it being three times the Worth of the Silver." The writer of this notice in the *Daily Courant* (10 January 1718) is so absorbed in representing the fashion of the thing that the narrative (how it was first acquired, how it was lost, why it is valued) begins to be audible in spite of himself. It is the human that wishes to give solely the appearance of the thing. It is the thing that would talk of a journey from the Caribbean to London, of a Creole's misadventures, of exotic tastes ill gratified, such as one would find decades later in popular plays such as Richard Cumberland's *The West-Indian* (1771) and James Townley's *High Life below Stairs* (1759).

Mandeville hints that the charitable familiarity that develops between thieves and the owners of lost property has another aspect besides the desire to retrieve what is one's own. He says the trade of redemption depends upon those neglectful people who, whether out of carelessness, debauchery, or incontinence, fail to mind their property as they ought (Mandeville 1725: 11). According to Wild, Charles Hitchin was suspended from his job as city marshal for trying to cash in on the imputed shortcomings of owners by writing threatening letters in which he accused them of having lost their goods while consorting with prostitutes (Wild 1718: 27). And it is true that many things go astray in coaches, inns, or streets in the vicinity of Drury Lane, as Moll Flanders demonstrates after she pillages a drunken libertine and then briefly drives a trade in redemption. A narrative of similar libertinage is to be found in the fashion of this snuff-box and the circumstances of its loss: "Lost out of a Gentleman's Pocket coming out of the Old Play-house in Drury Lane, on Thursday Night the 17th last an Oval Ivory Snuff-box, studded with Gold on both Sides, in the Shape of a Scallop, with a Gold Hinge, and a Picture on the Lid representing a Fryar whipping a Nun" (*Daily Courant*, 19 January 1717; see also Lawrence Lewis 1909: 145–6). The *Gentleman's Magazine* reprints a "Remarkable Advertisement" because it tells the same kind of story:

> Lost or Mislaid, one Pair of large Brilliant Diamond Ear-Rings, with Drops of the first Water, and 1 odd Night Ear-Ring, with 3 Brilliant Diamonds; three large Bars for the Breast, set with Rose Diamonds. If offered to be sold, pawn'd or valu'd, pray stop 'em and the **PARTY, and give Notice to Mr. Drummond, Goldsmith at Charing Cross, and you shall receive 200 Guineas Reward for the same.

How lost? How mislaid? If the diamonds could speak, they would tell a tale perhaps of disgraceful weakness, of a goldsmith so fascinated by a

---

* Especially if it be a young Lady (*Gentleman's Magazine*, April 1731: 167)

woman's youth and good looks as imprudently to allow her to wear and then walk off with his stock in trade.

When things such as jewels and sofas deliver the narratives that these advertisements begin to outline, they placard the folly, vice, and inhumanity of human beings. Diderot's jewels tell one scandalous story after another of hidden weakness in high society; and when they sing out high society's secrets in ribald ballads at the opera, their owners are struck dumb with shame (Diderot 1993: 42). In it-narratives, the transfer of moral initiative and speech from humans to things coincides almost always with the charge of inhumanity. In Gildon's *The Golden Spy*, as I have already pointed out, the guinea has to edit its tale of human depravity "for fear the Sense of Things should destroy all Confidence betwixt Man and Man, and so put an End to human Society" (Gildon 1709: 116). It is clear that it-narratives such as the fourth book of *Gulliver's Travels* go beyond satire and any real desire of human amendment, turning instead to a bleak prospect of nonhuman experience where humanity (generally defined as sympathy for all manner of sensations and perceptions not one's own) no longer has a place. Those owners disgraced by the loquacity of Diderot's jewels are variously derided as animals and automata (Diderot 1993: 129–30). Jonathan Wild, perched on the fulcrum between things aspiring to voices and humans degenerating into silence, was himself divided between the human and the nonhuman (Smith 1726: 2); hence Hitchin's jeering reference to Wild in his heyday as "his Skittish and Baboonish Majesty" (Hitchin 1718: 6). The year after he died, an anonymous biographer reported, "He had Skin like a Mulatto, and in his Face the very Features of a Baboon" (Anon. 1726: 2). Dickens's Fagin, like Wild, takes up the same amphibious position. Until the evening before his own transformation on the gallows he has always relished the silence of men metamorphosed by the rope ("What a fine thing capital punishment is! Dead men never repent; dead men never bring awkward stories to light" [Dickens 1994: 74]), But in the condemned cell he is aghast, like Wild and Macheath before him, at the immediate prospect of his death ("how suddenly they changed, from strong and vigorous men to dangling heaps of clothes"). Then Fagin's ingenuity and his voice come to an end, and all he can do is look into the life of things and wonder about their stories: "Thus, even while he trembled, and turned burning hot and the idea of speedy death, he fell to counting the iron spikes before him, and wondering how the head of one had been broken off, and whether they would mend it, or leave it as it was" (1994: 498). The spikes stare back at him like the shoes and hats on Crusoe's beach, measuring his utter irrelevance to themselves.

So advertisements for lost property filled with close descriptions of things cannot be considered models of empirical observation; they are expressions of desire directed with varying degrees of intensity at what is now only imagined to be one's own. The law's guarantee that the absent item still belongs to the owner is of no use and no consolation. So the drift of such an appeal is intended to materialize a singular thing for the benefit of one solitary individual, or to promote the independence and voice of what is sought. In this respect, the advertisements I have been talking about are really an early form of the personal ad, the public address from a single writer-subject to a single reader-object which says in effect either, "I want from you what is missing from my life" ("Green-eyed professional woman seeks male counterpart. You are at least 55, honest, intelligent, professionally successful, nonsmoker, divorced or widowed, with a sense of humour" [*New York Review of Books*, 15 January 2004]); or, "I am what is missing from your life" ("Rakish charm and contagious, naughty laugh, compassionate heart and ease about life. Curious, creative, passionate Renaissance man, 63. Blue eyes that sparkle, sexy trim build, handsome face, lively sense of mischievousness. Also accomplished writer" [ibid.]). On this axis of desire, writers of personal ads straddle the extremes of crying and being cried, alternating between the roles of owner and object in an effort to persuade their imagined missing part to take shape, or to render the shape irresistible. Description is the weakest rhetoric of this desire. The tournament of value is a better option and has become a highly self-conscious genre in journals such as the *London Review of Books*. "Arch, fractious floaty F in need of TLC? Hello Mags, it's your husband. Since I know you read these, why not take notice of me for the first time in years at box no 03/15" (*LRB* 7 February 2002). Archness can become super-arch in the effort to attract exactly the right attention: "Please help, I am a serious personal ad trapped inside the London Review of Books [sic]. I wanted to be in the Guardian [sic] but couldn't afford it. Now I've forgotten what it's like to be centre Left-wing and own a portfolio of shares. I don't laugh at Matthew Norman's hilarious diaries anymore. And really I don't care what the next Harry Potter book is like" (*LRB* 23 August 2001). Finally, there is the mini-narrative that verges on mad self-sufficiency, transcending the cause of its writing, or at least any cause that includes desirable portions of the world at large. Here is an example that exhibits a fierce alternation between dumbness and speech, beastliness and humanity, in a proto-narrative already familiar in those eighteenth-century advertisements where things overturn standards of humanity and start to tell tales on their owners:

Lothian, January 1937. Darkness descends through a mist that has permeated the boughs and moors for three weeks. A scream echoes through the wintry air. The peal of a new born. The song of the damned. The first sound to invade the lethal silence of centuries. The years pass and the child grows. He learns words—gutteral insistences—and he blunders into a twisted adolescence of cold, muted thought. A man, the streets are no haven for him. He exists in the shadow, the rats are his friends; the bare, indifferent moon is his lover. Children restless at night with dreams of a wandering golem cry in their parents' arms. Slowly, as deliberate and as corrosive as the soft stroke of wave upon the sand, the whisper of the townsfolk becomes a cry—a yell, a blistered demand unto the night—kill the monster! Kill! Kill! An escape over frosted expanse of cracked grass, the golem finally finds sanctuary. She has a name he cannot speak—that sound of dread. She utters evils, blasphemies—his ears bleed at her noise. And she gets a good lawyer. More expensive than his. And a satanic judge awards her the house, the car and the kids. But after therapy and tablets he is alright. Come, easy now, join hands with me and fly into that blackened, heartless sky. (*LRB* 7 February 2002).

The narrative ad does not preclude archness: "It came to him in a cocaine rush as he took the Langley exit that if Aldrich had told Filipov about Hancock only Tulgengian could have known that the photograph which Wagner had shown to Maximov on the jolting S-Bahn was not the photograph of Kessler that Bradford had found in the dark, sinister house in the Schillerstrasse" (*LRB* 1 April 2004).

In the eighteenth century, personal ads were geared fairly strictly to issues of age, money, and looks in that order, with maybe a glance at religion, whether it was a man or a woman advertising. The horrid Sir John Dinely, "The Windsor Advertiser," sets out attributes and prices on a heartless sliding scale (BM Satirical Prints 9446, 23 October 1799). These ads could easily modulate into dubious requests for female company, or the opposite; and it was evidently common for young gentlemen to make joke advertisements ("my person is far from disagreeable, my skin smooth and shining, my forehead high and polished, my eyes sharp tho' small; my nose long and aquiline, my mouth wide, and what teeth I have perfectly sound" (*Matrimonial Advertisements*, n.d. BL 11(a)). Because it was never plain who or what was the person of the advertiser, the bulletins were braced with the same promises of secrecy as the requests for the return of stolen goods: "Secresy may be depended on"; "Honour and the Greatest Secresy are desired"; "NB No Person whatever, except one, is privy to this Advertisement, nor is the Situation of his Affairs at present known, or suspected" (*Matrimonial Advertisements*, n.d. BL 10(a), 10 (1), 10 (2)). Still, there was room for tournaments of value too, such as this example: "A Gentleman was pleased last Sunday to advise and enjoin a young Lady to a Concession by the 4th of May, under Penalty of being esteem'd (after that Day) as out of her Senses, which she deems a fine Compliment to his own Worth, and 'tis a Pity such great Worth could have no greater Influence; but since that is the Case, 'tis requested of him to leave the Lady to her Insensibility; which, according to his own Opinion, this Day takes place" (ibid. 11 (2)). There is in this collection one remarkable example of a narrative personal ad, which may well have been a joke. It involves an advertiser Mr. A, who pays his attentions to the plain but worthy Miss B, approved by her father C and mother D. The day of marriage arrives and so does a gentleman E whom father D announces is to marry B instead of A. A looks aghast, B faints five times and is sent to her room to learn obedience. Not wishing to cause her further pain, A is now advertising for her replacement, "And though A's love for B is very remote from being lukewarm, and that quitting his claim so tamely must be daggers to his heart, yet as he has not a fortune to keep her as she has been reared, it would be ungenerous to the last degree to bring her to distress" (*Matrimonial Advertisements* 13 (2)). It is hard to find any real pathos in the story, but, like the best narrative ads in the *London Review of Books*, it places the advertiser between the positions of subject and object, lover of B but the discarded surplus of C and D (Benedict 2007: 194). Operating between those two points, his ad is both a signal of availability and an indictment of a venal family. It is also a schematic fable of the paradox of possession: B was to be his entirely, but now is entirely someone else's; and he is left with no option but to make the tale of his destitution the occasion of some sort of remedy. He is like the owner of a lost thing crying for its replacement; and he is like the thing that has been lost, crying the vileness of those that lost him.

The Beggar's Opera, as well as deriving its characters and plot from Jonathan Wild's career, was a generic hybrid, apparently a satire but one which deliberately thwarted its own lesson. It was cited by Swift as an anatomy of courts and ministers that never trespassed beyond the general outlines of human nature, "wherein [Mr. Gay] hath by a Turn of Humour, entirely New, placed Vices of all Kinds in the strongest and most odious Light; and thereby done eminent Service, both to Religion and Morality" (Swift 1962: 264). But Johnson found it so intensely contradictory ("a labefactation of all principles"), he thought it injurious to public morality; bordering in effect on the moral nihilism of Gildon's guineas and the bulk of it-narratives (Boswell 1980: 629). Having experimented in the language of things in his *Fables*, where amongst the speeches of animals he includes the history of pin, told by itself, Gay was already familiar with both sides of the isthmus that divides humans from nonhumans, and he was practiced in impersonating the voices of creatures that make the passage from one side to the other. I want to end this chapter by considering how advertisement and the crying of lost things contribute to Gay's rewriting of the history of Jonathan Wild.

The redemption of stolen goods is only briefly mentioned in the play. For the most part the fabrics (colored handkerchiefs, blacks, mantoes, scarfs, and petticoats) are destined for resale down the river at Rotherhithe or among the brothels toured by Mrs. Trapes. Only a repeating watch and a silver-hilted sword (both temporarily on loan to a prostitute and a thief) are intended to be returned to their owners (Gay 1961: 1.9.121). Otherwise it is people who are priced, either for the booty they bring in, or for the revenue arising from the sale of their bodies, or for the £40 payable for their impeachment. The play is remarkable for the degree of sententious implacability governing relations between owners of property and the people who are property in this play, hapless pawns who are owned, desired, disowned, and disposed of by turns. To operate outside this zone of commonsense exploitation is to be passionate and particular. Lucy says to Polly, "Love is so very whimsical in both sexes, that it is impossible to be lasting. But my heart is particular, and contradicts my own observation" (Gay 1961: 3.8.152). When Polly rejects parental wisdom in favor of love ("Can love be controlled by advice?"), her mother shouts, "What! Is the fool in love in earnest then? I hate thee for being particular (1.10.123). By and large, sententious implacability governs a series of stories that begin with profit and end with death. Peachum is never so fond of a thing that he would let it compromise his right to that kind of narrative. Love, on the other hand, is particular because it cannot be generalized: it aims at uncontrollable possession and never presumes to judge of what it cannot know.

Now the kind of particular love Polly stands up for at first is that of uncontrollable possession. The song she sings after having confessed to her parents that she is married to Macheath concludes, "O joy beyond expression!/ Thus safe ashore/ I ask no more;/ My all is in my possession" (Gay 1961; 1.8, 120). If the sententious language of the play bespeaks the circulation of human property ("Hang your husband, and be dutiful" [1.10, 123]) and the circulation of human money ("A wife's like a guinea in gold" [1.5, 116]), then particularity refers to the condition of those forlorn believers in absolute possession that Wild identified in his clients, characters who are mocked in this play by whores, highwaymen, and fences alike as romantic fools. And of course the test that Wild applies to the fantasy of absolute possession is going to be applied to Polly by her father, who means to put Macheath out of the way.

Nevertheless, when favorite ideas concerning love, hedonism, honor, or self-interest are assaulted, particularity overtakes everyone, even the most sententious cynics. Then the logic of the market gives way to the singularity and vocality of the human thing. In the quarrels between Peachum and Lockit, or between Polly and Lucy, or between Macheath and various women, the insult is always the same: a human has become something other than human. Peachum calls Lockit a dog, Lockit calls Lucy a spaniel, Lucy calls Macheath a brute, and Macheath calls the prostitutes beasts. Depending on the degree of rage, these epithets are more or less particular. Lockit gives a speech full of platitudes about humans as animals of prey, but when he calls Peachum a dog, he means something different (2.20.137). When Lucy compares the imprisoned Macheath to a rat, she is feeling more particular than sententious; but when Macheath greets Polly as a parrot, "O pretty, pretty Poll!" (1.13.124), he is fairly secure in his worldly opinion of women. But when someone is called out of his or her species in a particular way, this signals a rise in the level of passion which eventually floats the insulter and the insulted alike over the bar of the human into a zone of thinghood.

There are songs which represent lovers as animals or birds that are sung neither in the spirit of sententious wisdom nor in a fit of indignation or resentment. In these, the loss of a thing is addressed in a mood of deep uncertainty. In Polly's air, "The Turtle thus with plaintive crying," she imagines what it will be like to lose her lover, and it is the same song that attracts her mother's contempt for particularity. It is followed by Polly's most moving song, "O, what pain it is to part," which does not even draw a parallel between animals and humans because it is so focused on the contradiction of a love that can kill. This paradox comes home to Polly not as one of Peachum's or Lockit's Hobbesian generalizations, but as a personal agony. She anticipates the double torment of choosing to part with something she thought was uncontrollably hers which then will fly away on its own account—a pang she subsequently compares to the boy who sets his untamed sparrow at liberty—by figuring it both as the principled shedding *and* wanton desertion of something of one's own that will never be heard of again. Indeed, the original Scottish air is a tender acknowledgment of the fantasy of full ownership, interspersed with a mere hypothesis of satisfied love: "Gin thou wert mine e'ne Thing/ I wou'd Love thee I wou'd Love thee/ Gin thou wert my e'ne Thing/ So Dearly wou'd I Love thee" (Schultz 1923: 316). In Polly's song, the action of parting is equally divided between the owner and the owned, each moving away from the other in a mutual sacrifice needed to prevent the extinction of the thing. It is a personal ad back to front trying as hard as it can to reverse the sententious narrative of death.

> But lest death my love should thwart,
> And bring thee to the fatal cart,
> Thus I tear thee from by bleeding heart,
> Fly hence, and let me leave thee.

Mandeville could conceive of the same contradiction attending the relinquishment and flight of stolen goods, when an honest property-owner, disdaining advertisement and obeying the letter of the law, asserts title by letting things go that have already gone, and saying goodbye to that which will never respond. The element of advertisement in Polly's song— the intense desire for something of her own that she herself is both part- ing from and appealing to—is the measure of the pathos that can attend this contradiction.

A song of similar intensity and particularity is sung by Lucy on the same theme, the missing Macheath:

> I like the fox shall grieve,
> Whose mate hath left her side;
> Whom hounds, from morn to eve,
> Chase o'er the country wide.
>
> Where can my lover hide?
> Where cheat the wary pack?
> If love be not his guide,
> He never will come back.

(2.15.143)

Like Polly's, this song examines the dangers of bringing evasive things home, and probes the uncertainty of ownership of which advertised de- tailed description, I have argued, is the chief index. Why does particu- larity in *The Beggar's Opera* encourage no description, unless it comes within the verge of fatal possession ("Methinks I see him already in the cart (1.12.124))? Its absence is owing I think to the volition of the miss- ing thing and the savagery of the brokers who might intercept it. So the thing is credited with a will and a voice of its own to which the singer appeals as the sole motive of home-coming, and which she prizes as the sole virtue of the home-comer: "If love be not his guide,/ He never will come back." This puts a narrative question mark where a description might once have stood, and replaces the price of a commodity with the free will of the thing. So, although Lucy's lament belongs to the rhetoric of advertisement, whose aim is to influence the passage of the valued object toward its possessor, she is also uttering a very particular cry to a desiderated thing which she acknowledges will move according to its own exigencies and impulses, most probably away from her. And the particularity of the cry can be measured by the animal example, which according to all sententious standards makes no sense at all, for accord- ing to what precedent in fable or emblem is a fox expert in grief? The parallel between the forsaken women and the animal is so singular, so unparalleled, so contradictory, that it sustains particularity at an utterly unexemplary level of passion.

I have suggested that the logic governing Polly's and Lucy's songs is that of the narrative personal advertisement: not the personal advertise- ment that sets a cash price on one of a number of possible objects; nor that which draws a hypothetical lover by means of a tournament of value into a common judgment of taste; it is the advertisement of a self so far deficient in discretion and shame that it puts the crier outside the bounds of civil society, whence she engages exclusively in discourse with a singular thing whose absence has expelled all positive notions of home, identity, belonging, and perhaps even of species, leaving a vacuum penetrable only by the outline of an impossible narrative of escape. The singer sings of this before an audience whose interest in the song derives from its own utter remoteness from the particular case it opens. Such a song is a personal ad the wrong way round, as I have said, for instead of supposing that an extraordinary thing might have a being, and calling upon it to manifest itself, it acknowledges its actual existence and the reason why it must stay hidden. And in knowing this it knows also why a woman is uniquely like a fox, and a man specifically like a sparrow; and under what particular circumstances such hybrid things might break into speech.

In Gay's split ending of the play, there is evidently an attempt to place Macheath where these songs place him, between execution and redemption, with the same enigmatic status as stolen goods before they are either destroyed or returned. But it cannot sustain at the level of action the powerful ambiguity of these songs to a missing lover. The player has a choice either to obey the law and sacrifice his mute hero, or to redeem him at the cost of poetic justice and let him sing a song: to let him go and hear of him no more, or to buy him back, declare him not quite legally his own, and let him borrow a weak form of sententiousness for his last ditty. In effect, the play stays with a descriptive, not a narrative, regime, showing Macheath once again as the property of other people, not as a fox, sparrow, or rat, with things to say and a unique tale to tell of human fallibility.

CHAPTER 3

Making Babies in the South Seas

During his first visit to TAHITI, James Cook did something uncharacteristic. He gave a doll to Purea, an important woman in the region of Matavai Bay. "To Obariea for such is this womans name I gave several things but what seem'd to please her most was a childs Doll which I made her understand was the Picter of my Wife, as soon as we came a shore she fastened it to her breast took me in her hand and draged me first this way and then that the people all the while crowding about us to get a sight of the Doll" (Cook 1955: 526). What is even more surprising than this trivial gesture of a famous mariner is the white lie that goes with it—that this figure stands for someone else: Mrs. Cook. It is so unlike the commitment to the literal that we associate with Cook's accounts of his voyages. I want to argue that there is a link between Cook's fleeting and surreptitious interest in figurative representation and the events leading to his death. But first I want to establish what is at stake when a commitment to giving a factual account is infiltrated by things which are made like idols to stand (as St. Paul says) really for nothing at all.

There was no body of people more committed to the united priorities of property and narrative than the lords of the Admiralty who sent Cook three times into the South Seas. They believed in the absolute ownership of the king's property, and they believed that the experience of its being held and used by the king's commissioned officers could be owned exactly in a public narrative. In each of his voyages, Cook commanded vessels loaded with naval stores such as spars, rope, sails, tar, and munitions, together with food, liquor, and trade goods, all intended to last for two years. Unlike naval ships on station or active duty, Cook's were intended as platforms for scientific experiments and cartographical investigations, so on top of the storage of supplies, as much space as possible was set aside for specialized equipment and for the specimens and curiosities that were expected to be gathered in hitherto unnavigated parts of the globe. Cook was responsible for all of these things, for he had no purser on either the *Endeavour* or the *Resolution*, just a single clerk for each voyage. As well as accounting for the use or loss of every item of naval property, he had to provide a full narrative of the expedition, showing how punctually he had followed his orders and giving a full account of all his discoveries of lands, peoples, and novelties.

His instructions read as follows:

> You are, by all opportunities to send to our Secretary, for our information, Accounts of your Proceedings, and Copies of the Surveys and Drawings you shall have made; and upon your arrival in England, you are immediately to repair to this Office in order to lay before us a full Account of your Proceedings in the whole course of your Voyage; taking care before you leave the Sloop to demand from the Officers & Petty Officers the Log Books & Journals they may have kept, & to seal them up for our Inspection. (Cook 1955: ccxxiii–iv)

The accounts of Cook's three voyages provide a test case of narrative integrity, because it was exceptionally closely defined and it was tested to the extreme. Every single thing in his possession had to be told, and told again. Officially there was no room for anything that was not literally what it was: no dolls, no idols, no gods. After the liberties taken with his journal of the *Endeavour* voyage by John Hawkesworth, Cook clearly understood what was expected of him, and begins his narrative of the second as follows: "The Public must not expect from me the elegance of a fine writer, or the plausibility of a professed book-maker; but will, I hope, consider me as a plain man, zealously exerting himself in the service of his Country, and determined to give the best account he is able of his proceedings." He presents himself distinctly as a person, not as an author, someone acting on behalf of a higher authority; and according to the letter of the "full Account" expected of him, and the "best account" he is determined to give, he takes the reader into the history of the hull of the *Resolution* and its contents. "Before I begin my narrative of the expedition entrusted to my care, it will be necessary to add here some account of its equipment, and of some other matters equally interesting" (Cook 1777: 1.xxxvi, xxiii). He tells us how the *Resolution* and *Adventure* were purchased at Hull from William Hammond, he lists their displacements, describes their shape and behavior in shallow water, how they were sent to Deptford, and what they were filled with in preparation for the voyage. He is already aware that the narrative of spectacular discoveries is based on inventories of banal and technical facts like these.

But we all know that in the course of his third voyage, Cook died soon after his induction into a different system of authority, when he was named and anointed as a god at Kealakekua Bay in Hawai'i in February 1779. Twice he ascended a sort of altar and, flanked by idols, allowed himself to be adored. Evidently a breakdown occurred in the procedure of owning things with which he had formerly been so strongly identified. Somehow or other, he loosened himself from the restrictions of personhood and full accounting and entered into a different relation to property. Things that once belonged in his inventory assumed an importance derived from their adjacency to the sacred. This caused them to congregate and to move according to principles that had nothing to do with exchange or delegated power, encouraging the kind of idolatry that Hobbes defined as the worship of the material form of nothing. What had happened to change these things from facts into idols?

❦

Property of the Crown was supplied to the ship by warrant from the Navy Board via several other boards or agencies: medicines and surgical items were ordered through the Sick and Hurt Board; cordage, sails, and spars through the office of the shipyard (in this case Deptford), guns and ammunition from the Ordnance Office, food and liquor through the Victualling Board. The commander was responsible for a proper audit of all this material. Surgeons, gunners, cooks, and carpenters prepared accounts of stores expended, countersigned by the commander. There were over sixty separate accounts that had to be accepted by the Navy Board before a captain was paid off (Rodger 2005: 105; 320). Cook's task was made even more difficult insofar as his voyages were dangerous and experimental. When the *Endeavour* got stuck on the Great Barrier Reef, for example, a great deal of material was thrown hastily overboard in order to save the ship; yet everything lost would have to be accounted for in the end. Besides this, Cook was obliged to produce a report on the functioning of the reflecting telescope and the azimuth compass during the measurement of the transit of Venus (the first job at Tahiti on the first voyage). Well aware of the curse of scurvy in the Pacific, the Victualling Board had supplied him with a battery of alleged antiscorbutics which he was expected to test and to assess. So he was obliged to account in the sense of compile, and account in the sense of assess. This added dimension of his responsibilities is evident in a note from the Victualling Board at the end of his voyage, dated 19 July 1771: "Lieut. James Cook Endeavour Bark, Downes 12th, owing an account of the Sour Krout which he took on board the said Ship in the Year 1768 . . . Send copy thereof to Mr. Stephens for the information of the Right Honble the Lords Commissioners of the Admiralty" (Cook 1955: 634). So he and William Perry the surgeon, "owing an account," had to own the story of the consumption of sauerkraut, besides malt wort, lemon juice, portable soup, beans, and other remedies for scurvy, including comparative judgments of their efficacy.

In the end, all of Cook's accounts of the *Endeavour* voyage were accepted: "The Lords took into consideration several Letters from Lieut.

Cook . . . giving an account of his late voyage, and enclosing several Journals and Charts relative thereto. Resolved that he be acquainted the Board extremely well approve of the whole of his Proceedings" (Cook 1955: 635). His handling of property—its storage, consumption, and wastage—was vindicated, and his story of how and where things had gone, and what had been done and what had been seen, although these had often taken place during emergencies in distant seas and strange lands, was found acceptable and true. For his assessment of the antiscorbutic value of malt wort, he was awarded the Copley Medal by the Royal Society. In this respect Cook resembles Robinson Crusoe, who owns exactly what he did with the contents and appurtenances of a ship on a remote desert island—cables, spars, shovels, tongs, brass kettles, a copper pot, a gridiron (Defoe 1983: 96)—all of which add up to "a full Account" of things and "some little Account of my self" (Defoe 1983: 62) that his readers found entirely acceptable and often mistook for the truth. Crusoe finds himself growing from a solitaire in a state of nature, or a Hobbesian author, into the person of his island's governor as he assembles this collection of artifacts into an account of his life, formally handing it over to his first audience just as Cook hands his over to the Admiralty: "I left them my Fire Arms. . . . I gave them a Description of the Way I manag'd the Goats. . . . In a Word I gave them every Part of my own Story" (277). At all points but the very final one, Cook is aware of himself as the king's representative, operating "in Pursuance of his Majesty's Pleasure," carrying a commission that binds him to act as a person, operating "in the Name of the King of Great Britain" (cclxxxii–iii). In the *Endeavour* and *Resolution*, Cook carried trade goods and trinkets destined to be exchanged for supplies and goodwill; he also had aboard the seeds of fruits and vegetables, and breeding pairs of domestic animals and fowls, intended to supply the islands of the Pacific (and their visitors) with a rich source of food in the years to come. These gifts he offered on behalf of King George III, who took a great interest in these voyages. Nicholas Thomas has argued that Cook identified powerfully with this act of royal benevolence, and felt his reputation with posterity depended upon the successful acclimatization of these species (Thomas 2004: 287). That is to say he took his role as the king's person very seriously.

Sadly for Cook, there was no more perilous testing ground of the dual function of property and narrative than the South Seas. The first European landing on an inhabited island in the Pacific (Guam in 1521) was made in pursuit of stolen property. Magellan sent forty men ashore who burned upwards of forty houses and boats, killing seven men, in order to recover his skiff. He named what is now known as the Marianas the Ladrones (Thieves), in commemoration of the theft. From his first arrival in Tahiti, Cook was incessantly aware of the danger to property. He reported, "The

Natives Flock'd around us in great Numbers and in as friendly a Manner as we could wish, only that they shew'd a great inclination to pick our pockets" (1955: 78). Within a few minutes a snuff box and a telescope had disappeared, and these were followed some days later by the loss of an iron rake, a musket, a pair of pistols belonging to Joseph Banks, and (worst of all) the new quadrant made by Mr. Bird especially for the measurement of the transit of Venus. Nails, ironwork, books, clothing, weapons, buoys, boats, and animals fell victim to ingenious robberies committed by the Polynesians, which they then triumphantly re-enacted to the huge amusement of the local people (Salmond 2003: 208). William Anderson wrote, "The only crime we know they have a propensity to is theft, to which all sexes and ages are addicted in an uncommon degree . . . it seems to arise solely from an intense curiosity or desire to posess [sic] something which they see belongs to a sort of people so different from themselves, that if it were possible a set of beings seeming as superior in our judgment should appear amongst us, I doubt whether our natural regard to justice would be able to restrain many from falling into the same error" (Cook 1967: 2.929).

Whatever the motive for these thefts, Cook decided from the start to treat leniently the purloining of private property, but to make every effort to retrieve things belonging to the Crown, seizing canoes or taking hostages until the missing things were returned. In Tonga (The Friendly Isles), Paulaho was taken hostage until a turkey was given back. Poeatua (Poedua), the beautiful daughter of a Ra'iatean chief whose portrait was painted by John Webber, was ransomed with the restoration of two deserters. Cook was trying to take prisoner the paramount Hawai'ian chief Kalani'opu'u in order to regain the *Discovery*'s cutter when he was knocked down and killed. But personal items, especially if they were lost in equivocal circumstances, did not belong to the sovereign and did not signify (see Cook 1955: 101; and 1967: 2.1062). Banks's waistcoat and pistols, Dr. Monkhouse's snuff box, Lieutenant Williamson's fancy gun, even Cook's own stockings were stolen without fuss; but anything marked with the broad arrow of the Crown, as literally the cutter and effectually the turkey were, required the utmost exertion to secure. Accordingly, ships' stores and equipment were defended by Cook, sometimes savagely. No matter how curious he was about local customs, Cook's anthropology was mortgaged to this impermeable difference between royal *meum* and Polynesian *tuum*. And given the multitude of things both present and absent, still in store or already lost or used, for which he was accountable, it was perhaps excusable for Cook to be so agitated by their unexplained disappearance. After all, these were as much the material of his narrative as the discovery of new lands and the taking possession of them.

But it is worth noting just how agitated he could become. In mockery of Cook's ethnographic researches, the crew called it "tipping a *heiva*," referring to the loud rhythmic stamping of feet or clashing of canoe blades accompanying the war-chants of the Maori. James Trevenen recalled how he once angered his captain: "Of course I had a *heiva* of the old boy … violent motions and stampings on the deck … paroxysms of passion, into which he often threw himself upon the slightest occasion" (Cook 1967: 1.cliii). Even David Samwell, who wrote an account of Cook's death to acquit him of the charge of imprudence, was forced to admit that he had a hasty temper (Samwell 2007: 82). In his last days his crew thought him possessed, exhibiting "a degree of infatuation … which rendered him deaf to everything," "an infatuation altogether unaccountable" (Cook 1967: 1.537n. 2; Ellis 1969: 108).

It has long been a reproach to Cook's reputation that his reactions to the theft of naval equipment became increasingly bizarre. The man who stole the turkey for which the Tongan chief Paulaho was taken hostage was punished by having his arms sliced to the bone. On Huahine, the man who took a sextant had his hair and ears cropped. On Mo'orea, Cook destroyed great numbers of houses and canoes in reprisal for the loss of a goat. In his unofficial account of the voyage, John Rickman reported that two hostages taken at Mo'orea apparently were prepared for a hideous death: "Large ropes were carried upon the main deck and made fast fore and aft; axes, chains, and instruments of torture were placed upon the quarter deck in the sight of the young men" (cited in Williams 2008: 17–18). This contentious issue has not gone away. J. C. Beaglehole, Cook's most respectful biographer, was uneasily aware of the growing eccentricities in his hero's conduct, particularly in defense of property, and referred these to an inner tiredness, deepening toward the end of his ten years of dangerous and nerve-wracking service. Sir James Watt suggested subsequently there might be a medical explanation in the roundworm infestation Cook suffered during the second voyage, resulting possibly in pellagra and the violent personality changes associated with that disease (Watt 1979: 155). This diagnosis attracted the derision of Marshall Sahlins, one of Cook's most well informed and least sympathetic critics: "Worms done him in. Really there is something faintly heroic in the idea" (Sahlins 1985: 109). In the latest reassessments of Cook's career, it has been necessary to revisit the question of inner tiredness, either to explain it or dismiss it. Anne Salmond chooses to explain it, Nicholas Thomas more or less to dismiss it. She traces the origin of Cook's increasingly capricious and cruel behavior to the Grass Cove massacre, or rather to his refusal to avenge it. At Grass Cove, in New Zealand's Queen Charlotte's Sound, the crew of the *Adventure*'s cutter were slain, jointed, cooked, and partly eaten. On his third voyage, Cook entertained the perpetrator

Kahura on board the *Resolution*, inspiring the contempt of the Maori for failing to exact revenge (*utu*), and earning the reproaches of his own crew for not executing a murderer. Increasingly isolated from the norms both of the Polynesians and the British, Salmond argues that Cook grew cynical and barbarous to Polynesians and Europeans alike, ordering torturous punishments for native thieves, and more than doubling the number of floggings of his own crew.

Nicholas Thomas mentions Cook's failure to explore Fiji, Borabora, or Samoa by way of suggesting a set of priorities that emerged from Cook's conception of himself as the guardian of public property and the deputy or person of the king. At Niue (Savage Island) and Vanuatu (Erromango and Malekula), for example, he encountered hostile populations that he had no inclination to soften or civilize, and about which he felt no curiosity (Thomas 2004: 236–40). He was principally concerned with those islands of the Tahitian, Tongan, New Zealand, and Hawai'ian groups whose cultures had evolved rituals and customs he found interesting, and which he wanted to understand. And he wanted to understand them because he felt he had something to offer that would benefit them considerably. The subsequent extravagance of Cook's behavior, for instance his wholesale destruction of houses and canoes at Mo'orea in an effort to recover a single small goat, is intelligible, Thomas suggests, only if we consider the vastness of Cook's enterprise from his own point of view. He saw himself as the benevolent agent of a generous monarch, stocking the islands of the South Seas with vegetables, fruits, and animals. He was aiming to solve the problem of their lack of property. The theft of breeding pairs was peculiarly irritating to him because they were crimes that would perpetuate the privation in which lay the temptation to commit more. Any impediment to the royal scheme of benevolence was to be removed with maximum force (Thomas 2004: 287). But naval property had to be protected too: it was part of the account. Thus it was that Cook perished after two days spent in pursuit of items that had gone missing on the beach: the armorer's tongs, the lid of a water-cask, a chisel, a midshipman's cap, bits of the *Discovery*'s pinnace, and all of her cutter.

The clue followed by Thomas is consistent with the duty of owning of an account of property that Hobbes and Locke assign the person in civil society, and which Cook as commander was explicitly assigned by the Admiralty. Add to that the investment Cook made in his own reputation as the agent of a benevolent prince, and his irrational and passionate behavior becomes slightly more intelligible than the melancholy isolation supposed by Salmond. However badly he was acting, he was trying to redeem the things that would make the narrative of his voyage acceptable. But should the delegate or person of the king become cruel in pursuit of benevolent ends, behave unaccountably in his attempt to produce a true account, and become infatuated in the course of securing property, then the rationale of accounting no longer shapes his conduct even if it remains the ostensible end or purpose of it. Various descriptions have been given of Cook on the day before his death, making wild and undignified traverses of the beach in pursuit of a missing pair of tongs and a chisel, like Robinson Crusoe in his first frenzy on the shore of his island. The question raised by such extravagance is whether Cook did in fact retain some weird fidelity to his mission, or whether his relation to things and the accounts that may be given of them had begun to change.

Glyndwr Williams has shone a strong light on the moment in Cook's career when he appears either deliberately to have stopped writing his account, or to have written such strange or scandalous things that his editor John Douglas was induced (with strong encouragement from the Admiralty) to destroy the evidence and rewrite the narrative of the circumstances surrounding his death. Cook's holograph journal ends on 6 January 1779, two-thirds down the page, while Cook was still at sea, more than a week away from the landing at Kealakekua Bay. His holograph log ends on 17 January, three-quarters down the page and midway through the first day's events on the beach, which include the ceremony where he was wrapped in a red cloak and worshipped as Lono. Cook merely records that he was taken to the *heiau* or "Morai" of Hikiau, but no more. Assuming that Cook kept a daily log, but wrote up the journal intermittently, the missing pages of the log are the chief enigma. We are left to assume either that Cook, neglecting one of the most cardinal rules of the service, chose to stop making entries the day after his first taste of divinity, or that he kept it on separate leaves which no longer exist. It seems that Douglas received three packets of Cook's manuscripts, and at least one of these packets went missing. In any event, it is certain that there are now no traces of Cook's own firsthand impressions, in his own hand, from 18 January until the day of his death, 14 February. The question Williams is trying to answer really does for both of his alternatives. What was it Cook wrote which justified such censorship; or what was it he didn't write which explains his silence? (see Williams 2008: 49–60). Either way it defines negatively his role, not as a person of George III but as an author of his very own actions and feelings.

An answer to that question would need to embrace the three aspects of Cook's non-heroic actions. These are his passionate and undignified response to disobedience and in particular to theft; the disproportionate and inhuman punishments he was prepared to inflict, especially on thieves; and the readiness with which he seems to have accepted his elevation to the position of Lono. It is hard to find any consistency in them, for on the one hand his zeal to defend a European idea of the sanctity of property leads to his exorbitance; and on the other, it is his curiosity about local customs, and his sensitivity to other forms of belief, that inclines him to join in rituals which mystify him but which he longs to understand. Yet, no matter how sensitive on this front, his punishments of theft (everyone agreed) were tyrannical and disproportionate. If, however, we were to allow that theft represented a terrifying and potentially fatal interruption to the continuity of Cook's voyage and the symmetry of his account, of the order of Hume's convulsions in nature, prodigies, or miracles, which leave the causes of events unknown and unaccountable, then we have an explanation that ties the tumult of Cook's passions to his familiarity with idols and false gods, and at the same time offers a reason for actions which are less than human. "Madness, fury, rage, and an inflamed imagination, though they sink men nearest to the level of beasts, are, for a like reason, often supposed to be the only dispositions, in which we can have any immediate communication with the Deity" (Hume 1956: 42). Let us see if we can follow this line of enquiry further.

Here are two fables about the subversion of an accountable relation to maritime property. In Richard Hughes's pirate story, *A High Wind in Jamaica* (1929), questions of narrative order and of property become tangled up in the mysterious death of a ship's captain. In this strangely incoherent tale of a group of children on the Spanish Main, we find the linked difficulties of owning things and giving the story of them dramatized in a context of general theft, as ships are seized, their holds rifled and things and people are "changed," as the children put it. Two of them, Rachel and Emily, are dimly aware that the integrity of property is important, and they are standing by to own the truth of owning things. Rachel collects oakum, mop-heads, marlinspikes, and bits of rag, calling them her own babies and housing them in various parts of the ship. As for Emily, she simulates the owning of things by setting loose strings of words, "a sort of narrative noise" the narrator calls it, as if she were preparing herself for the arrival of real narrative substance (Hughes 1999: 184). Neither she nor her sister succeeds in owning anything, however, for things keep getting lost or escaping in a manner that is not (at least from their point of view) ownable or accountable. The marlinspike falls out of Rachel's grasp while she is nursing it in the rigging and it wounds Emily in the leg. While Emily is recovering, a knife comes into her hands which stabs and kills a tied-up Dutch skipper, an event which no public narrative is destined ever to frame. There is no ownership of these things, the marlinspike and the knife, and in their self-activity as babies they prove dangerous and even fatal to the human beings who come within their ambit.

The narrator says of Rachel's collections of babies, "To parody Hobbes, she claimed as her own whatever she had mixed her imagination with; and the greater part of her time was spent in angry or tearful assertions of her property-rights" (Hughes 1999: 156). It is not Hobbes of course but Locke who makes this claim for property, obtained not by imagination but by labor. "Whatsoever [a man] removes out of the State that Nature hath provided, and left it in, he hath mixed his Labour with, and joined to it something that is his own, and thereby makes it his Property"(Locke 1963: 329). Hobbes, however, acknowledges the enormous power of imagination over things, especially images and idols, "And whereas a man can fancy Shapes he never saw; making up a Figure out of the parts of divers creatures; as the Poets make their Centaures, Chimaeras, and other Monsters never seen: So can he also give Matter to those Shapes, and make them in Wood, Clay or Metall. And these are also called Images, not for the resemblance of any corporeall thing, but for the resemblance of some Phantasticall Inhabitants of the Brain of the Maker" (Hobbes 1996: 448). Although we have seen how widely Hobbes and Locke differ about the origin of property, and how it is kept, they agree about the close and necessary relation between owning things in the sense of possessing them and owning things in the sense of giving an account of them. It is evident from the way Hughes frames Rachel's and Emily's attitudes to things that this sort of property and this sort of narrative integrity is what they desire. But not possessing them, they are left with babies that strongly resemble Hobbes's images and idols, and the doll that Cook gave to Purea.

In *Mardi*, that strange fantasia on the theme of Polynesia, Melville describes the habits of Annatoo, a woman so addicted to theft she cannot resist stealing equipment from the wretched craft on which she is stranded. She raids it for booty which she has no other means of securing than in the ship itself. She is a sort of Robinson Crusoe with a wreck but no island: "No small portion of the hull seemed like a mine of stolen goods, stolen out of its bowels. I found a jaunty shore-cap of the captain's hidden away in the hollow heart of a coil of rigging . . . and nearby, in a breaker, discovered several pieces of calico." In a bizarre attempt to find a means of stowage independent of the hull, she steals the log-line, and tows behind the vessel a box filled with knives and axe-blades (Melville 1849: 123, 137). These are Annatoo's small babies for whom she finds beds and houses, just like Rachel; but unlike Rachel, and very like the Polynesians mentioned by Cook and Anderson, she has no attachment at all to the idea of property defined by Hobbes and Locke. Already these redistributed artifacts are idols, hers by virtue of the force of her imagination, the *lares* and *penates* of a foundering vessel. She is an author; they are things.

Is there any equivalent to such babies in Cook's experience prior to Kealakekua Bay? Well, there is the doll he gave to Purea. A gift made to provoke her imagination, it left his own unmoved, since he knew it bore not the least resemblance to his wife. Confident in that knowledge, he was unable to see however that the glamour of what he gave his host was inseparable from his own appearance as an *atua* or god, with babies in his belly reached by a pocket. "There were doors in their sides for property—doors which went far into their bodies, into which they thrust their hands, and drew out knives, iron, beads, cloth, nails, and everything else" (Jarves 1843: 110). While he was at Tahiti, perhaps remembering what Cook had done, William Bligh had a hairdresser's dummy painted and curled and put on a stick, with a body made of cloth:

> One half of them realy beleived [sic] it was an English Lady and asked if it was my Wife, and one Woman ran with a basket of Breadfruit and a peice [sic] of Cloth and presented [them] as a present; but they were all delighted with it even when they knew it was not real. Tyna and other Cheifs [sic] were mad after it . . . some joined Noses with it and others kissed it. (Bligh 1937: 1.386)

Cook observed an equal degree of excitement in his own men when they were collecting curiosities. In Tonga, his people were wild to obtain local artifacts such as tapa cloth, weapons, and tools, and would offer the clothes off their back or the nails out of the ship to barter for them. Cook was never pleased by the passion for curiosities (or for sex), because it inflated the market, particularly the market for food, and lowered the value of the red baize and axes he had for exchange. On one occasion a small boy toured the scene with a turd on the end of a stick, as if to hint that in such extreme circumstances, value could be found in everything. Cook disapproved of collecting curiosities for this very reason, that it replaced exchange value with an imagined and ephemeral standard of taste:

> Such was the prevailing Passion for curiosities, . . . the reader will think the Ship must be full of such articles by this time, [but] he will be mistaken, for nothing is more Common than to give away what has been collected at one Island for any thing new at a Nother. . . . This together with what is distroyed [sic] on board after the owners are tired with looking at them, prevents any considerable increase. (quoted in Thomas 2004: 244)

Notice that the suspect novelty of these things does not qualify Cook's disapproval for owners who fail to treat property as property. As objects of taste, curiosities have been impetuously obtained, often with pieces of His Majesty's ship, and then absentmindedly relinquished when the fit was over. What this carelessness destroys (Cook appears to say) is the continuity that curiosities might have sustained had they been treated as legitimate possessions with a factual place in the corporate story of the ship. Notice again that it is the reader, alias the Admiralty and finally the public, whom Cook alerts to this infidelity of his men toward things and thereby to the accounts that can be given of them for others to read.

Curiosities, for which Cook has such contempt, nevertheless raise for him a serious question of value when their faithful collection as something like facts bears upon a public narrative of the voyage. But instead of their serving an ethnographic or museological purpose, he finds them being used in the same way as Rachel's babies and Annatoo's stolen treasures. Caprice and imagination cause them to be collected in the first place, and then the same fantastic inconstancy is responsible for their tendency to scatter and vanish.

As Cook blames his men for their failure to treat things as property, it is no surprise that he should proceed to blame them further for a breach in the laws of narrative: they are as deficient as owners of stories as they are of things. Here he imagines what might be said in the press about the miseries suffered by the *Endeavour* while docked in Batavia (where incidentally a third of the complement died of dysentery and other intestinal maladies):

> Their sufferings . . . will very probable [*sic*] be mentioned in every News paper, and what is not unlikely with many additional hardships we never experienced; for such are the disposission [*sic*] of men in general in these Voyages that they are seldom content with the hardships and dangers which will naturally occur, but they must add others which hardly ever had existence but in their imaginations, by magnifying the most trifling accidents and Circumstances to the greatest hardships, and unsurmountable dangers. (Cook 1955: 461)

Under the pressure of imminent public disclosure, facts of the first voyage metamorphose into fictions just as curiosities in the third might have metamorphosed under the right conditions into facts. In both cases, Cook wants simultaneously to admit and deny the value of what he is talking about. Hardships as hardships should be faithfully reported, but hardships masquerading as "greatest hardships" are unnatural and false, the children of imagination, and ought never to be mentioned. Meanwhile, curiosities should not be collected, but if they are, they ought to be preserved for the record. What is he trying to say?—that things tell true stories provided the tastes and passions of those who "own" them in the sense of bargaining for them and narrating them, do not corrupt or alienate what now belongs to the navy and the public? It is as if Cook were entertaining an impossible ideal of a disembodied story, one that could speak for itself as long as all the things in it were fully and exactly inventoried, unsullied by the traces of their heedless and emotional owners. As soon as things are owned privately by individuals with no loyalty to authority, owned that is to say by *authors* rather than *persons*, they are contaminated by pleasure and imagination. Property turns into babies and the accounts of them become lies.

These issues were uncomfortably present to Cook's mind during the second voyage. In his two great loops toward the Antarctic, he was staggered by the emptiness of the seas and, when he came to Tierra del Fuego, by the sterility of the shore. "I never made a passage, any where of such length, or even much shorter, where so few interesting circumstances occurred" (Cook 1777: 2.170). His only amusement was to consider the fantastic shapes of icebergs, and the exquisite effect of transparent ice on the rigging, but whenever he thought of what this beauty betokened in terms of danger to his ship, he recoiled from it (1.33, 36). When he finally made landfall in southern Patagonia he reported, "The whole country is a barren rock, doomed by Nature to everlasting sterility" (2.179). Later he was fond of labeling spurious French discoveries as non-existent ice islands or proving the continent claimed by Kerguelen to be nothing but a barren waste. Repelled by the emptiness of ocean or shore, he wanted to accuse these pseudo-discoverers of deceit and mendacity because their reports had nothing, literally nothing, in them. He turned away bitterly from the birds and floating weed, usually sure signs of the vicinity of land, as meaningless. Of penguins he says, "We had now been so often deceived by these birds, that we could no longer look upon them, nor indeed upon any other oceanic birds, which frequent high latitudes, as sure signs of the vicinity of land" (Cook 1777: 1.53). With no trustworthy signs of a shore, with nothing to possess or report that was not desolate and barren in the last degree, he even suspects his own accuracy, for when he finally made landfall in Dusky Bay he recorded, "We now saw it under so many disadvantageous circumstances, that the less I say about it, the fewer mistakes I shall make" (1.68).

In the third voyage, the shimmer of unreality was compounded by the maps he was using, which were utterly unreliable, particularly Staehlin's map of the Alaskan coast, which not only bore no resemblance to the actual tending of the land to the west and south, but also falsely promised a large inlet into Hudson's Bay. Cook spent valuable time exploring one of the largest of these, only to find it terminating in an unnavigable river. He called the river Turnagain, in reference to his predicament, and he took possession of the shore; but the inlet he could not even be bothered to name, and it eventually became known as Cook's Inlet (Cook 1967: 1. 367 and n.1; see Williams 2002: 318–19). He concludes that "Mr Staehlins Map and account [are] either exceeding erroneous even in latitude or else a mere fiction ... made without the least regard to truth" (Cook 1967: 1.414, 456). Along with deceitful cartographers, he includes "closet-studdying Philosiphers" and "other people" (that is, his own lieutenant, John Gore), as persons wedded to a belief in the existence of improbabilities and devoted to the circulation of fictions which honest mariners were risking their lives to expose (Cook 1967: 1.cxxxv, 361).

But Cook himself was incapable of meeting the high standard of accountability these vituperations imply. In a distant world where the value of things was unpredictable, where artifacts moved about the beach with disconcerting rapidity, and the looming of land was hard to distinguish from cloud and ice, nothing was easy to keep and no story was easy to tell. It was hard to predict what would happen next, or to say what had happened. Cook's death took place, according to William Ellis, within "a chain of events which could no more be foreseen than prevented." Alexander Home said of the circumstances in Kealakekua Bay that it was "a hard matter to collect certainty . . . or to write any Account of it at all" (cited in Sahlins 1985: 104). It must have been clear to Cook in the weeks before he was killed that certain passages in his personal history—stripping to the waist in order to join the *inasi* ceremony in Tonga, for example, or acting the part of Lono in Hawai'i and being anointed by priests of the god—were not easily assimilated to a naval history. To some extent, Cook was conscious of being divided between the pressure of his feelings (let us say, his overwhelming curiosity about local ritual which Nicholas Thomas has recently characterized as "rapacious" [Samwell 2007: 44]) and his duty of making formal naval reports, a division that was exacerbated by his experiences on the beach, where his passions could so quickly and furiously get the better of him.

He was never prone to talk about private or domestic matters and seldom does he mention his feelings about anything, but after nearly losing the *Endeavour* on the Great Barrier Reef, he writes, "Was it not for the pleasure which naturly [sic] results to a Man from being the first discoverer, even if it was nothing more than Sands and Shoals, this service would be insupportable especially in far distant parts, like this, short of Provisions and almost every other necessary" (Cook 1955: 380). Beaglehole comments, "There is no more interesting and significant passage in all Cook than this." He adds, "It is not, really, a public utterance at all" (Cook 1955: clvii). This is one of the very few occasions when Cook not only lets slip the difference between his personal and official self, distinguished as his relationship to pleasure on the one hand and to the duty of accounting on the other, but also where he emphasizes that difference instead of concealing it. When he tries to bridge the gap, there is a quiver in his prose. "I must own," he confesses of his navigation off the Australian coast, "I have ingaged [sic] more among the Islands and Shoals, . . . but if I had not we should not have been able to give any better account . . . than if we had never seen it" (Cook1955: 380). What is owned between that defensive "I" and that equivocal "we" is very little better than nothing from a public point of view, although it may hint volumes about the pleasures of discovery ("even if it was nothing more than Sands and Shoals"). One of the reasons Cook found John Hawkesworth's redaction of his first voyage so painful to read was its dramatization of the conflict between the private impulse behind the Poverty Bay killings and the public account of it—one that Cook himself had blurred by claiming without any justification that he acted in self-defense. "I am conscious that the feeling of every reader of humanity," confessed Hawkesworth, writing as Cook in the first person, "will censure me for having fired upon these unhappy people, and it is impossible that, upon a calm review, I should approve it myself. . . . Yet in such situations, when the command to fire has been given, no man can restrain its excess, or prescribe its effect" (Hawkesworth 1773: 2.290). Hawkesworth presents Cook (reasonably enough given the bare bones of the scene) as someone unable to reconcile the emotions of the moment, signaled by four corpses, with the duties of humanity embodied in a reader—the same reader that Cook was fond of appealing to when trying to account for the inconstancy of his crew.

Alfred Gell points out, "Children do not 'play' with dolls but actually make a cult of them, or worship them. . . . [They are] not at play, but at work. They are serious" (Gell 1998: 134). As for the products of such labor, he mentions two potent examples from the South Seas. One is A'a, the fractal god of Ruruta, who pullulates from himself or, as Gell says, "the surface [of the idol] consists of amalgamated replications of itself . . . a succession of budding protuberances"—each identical with what it protrudes from (139) (figures 1 and 2). There is perhaps no finer image of a personification, performing on its own body the magic of self-creation. The other is the Tahitian *to'o*, (figure 3) a species of idol made of wood and sennit that refers only to the potentiality of form (the pillars of sky) without actually *representing* anything, for the *to'o* subsists in a state prior to the creation of the earth and the sky: "The to'o are are wholly iconic and wholly aniconic at the same time" (110). Having already offered Oberea an idol that referred to Mrs. Cook but did not represent her, closely imitated by Bligh who delighted the Tahitians with a dummy they knew was not real, Cook was alert to these issues, and about to become more so when he attended the installation festival in Tonga called the *inasi*.

As always, Cook was eager to find out what was going on, but this time his desire to see what was happening was evidently uncontrollable—rapacious—and despite warnings and the unmistakable gestures of the guards on the perimeter. he pushed his way through to the center of the event (figure 4).

> I had resolved to peep no longer from behind the Curtin, but to make one of the number in the Ceremony . . . with this in View I stole out of the Plantation. . . . I was several times desired to go away, and at last when they found I would not stir, they, after some seeming consultation,

Fig. 1. A'a, Ruruta, front view. © Trustees of the British Museum

desired I would bare my shoulders as they were, with this I complied. (Cook 1967: 1.151)

Williamson sourly observed, "We who were on ye outside were not a lit-tle surprised at seeing Capt Cook in ye procession of the Chiefs, with his hair hanging loose & and his body naked down to ye waist. . . . I do not pretend to dispute the propriety of Captn Cook's conduct, but I cannot help thinking he rather let himself down" (151 n.1). But there was hardly any indignity to which Cook would not submit to get close to the heart of the mystery, sitting with the other chiefs cross-legged "in the most humble posture with downcast eyes and hands locked together"—demure as a maid, as he says (154, 151). The concessions made in respect of dress and

Fig. 2. A'a, back view. © Trustees of the British Museum

gesture have only one purpose, to get a clear view of the ritual and to gratify his curiosity. At first Cook squints through holes cut in the fence then, being resolved to peep no longer, he makes his way to the middle of the area, but still is not allowed the free use of his eyes, being forced to sit with them downcast. When he moves to get a clearer sight he finds his view blocked by the people (152). At all points in this strangely excited story of the *inasi*, artifice (dressing up, acting a part, peeping from behind a curtain to witness an elaborate and mysterious display) is allegedly in service of ethnographic eyewitnessing. But corresponding to the difficulty of finding a clear sight-line is the enigma of what is finally revealed. "We endeavoured in vain to find out the meaning not only of the whole but

Fig. 3. To'o, Tahiti. © Trustees of the British Museum

different parts of the ceremony, we seldom got any other answers to our enquiries than *Tabu*" (1.153). He reports various offerings made of fruit and fish, and suggestions of eventual human sacrifice (the pole-bearers affect to stagger under the weight of their burdens, as if each was equal to the weight of a human body [1.147]), but with the exception of the fish these things are, as Cook himself puts it, emblematic. When he is allowed the unrestricted use of his eyes he finds that the poles and sticks with yams attached are not what they seemed. "After the assembly broke up I went and examined them and found that to the middle of each was tied two or three small sticks as has been related, yet we had been repeatedly told by those about us that they were young yams, insomuch that some of our gentlemen beleived [sic] them rather than their own eyes, whereas it is clear we ought to have understood them that they were only the representation of these roots" (149).

His split judgment of this affair is no different from his estimates of curiosities, hardships, and private discoveries of shoals and reefs: the

Fig. 4. Inasi Ceremony, Tonga

duty of sober inquiry into facts is in conflict with the emotional and imaginative investment in the matter at hand. Cook wants to arrange the products of imagination so that they will fit a factual report; at the same time, he is tempted to treat facts in a manner agreeable to the imagination. In the case of the *inasi*, the latter tendency is very strong; so strong it causes him no surprise to find that the facts before his eyes are fictions, bits of stick that represent yams as Starveling represents Moonshine in *A Midsummer Night's Dream*; or as Rachel represents marlinspikes as babies in *A High Wind in Jamaica*; or as the doll Cook gave to Purea represented his wife. "The small pieces of sticks that were tyed to the others we were told were yams, so that probably they were to represent this root emblematically" (147). That is what he wants to understand, the representation of one thing for another, but the representation has no value as a sign, for he cannot understand what it means; so the pleasure gained from the sight of the yam-stick must derive from its ambiguity: the yam that was formerly a stick, but is still a stick, iconic and aniconic at the same time. On the second day he observes "a number of small bundles or parcels made up of Cocoanut leaves, and tied to sticks made into the form of hand barrows, all the information I could get of them was that they were *Tabu*" (151). He wants to rebuke those who will not believe the evidence of their own eyes, but what can eyes report but that things like wheelbarrows are not what they seem. What he pretended to do with Purea, mixing his imagination with "picter" of his wife, he is now much more seriously engaged in, and it is a form of idolatry. "And these are also called Images, not for the resemblance of any corporeall thing, but for the resemblance of some Phantasticall Inhabitants of the Brain of the Maker" (Hobbes 1996: 448).

There is no position from which to authenticate these things or "picters"—babies let us say again—whose purposes and referents are all in doubt. But their attractive power and the pleasure they excite are immediate. There is no hint that Cook is disappointed in an inconclusive outcome. He says when it was all over, "I now went and examined the several Baskets which had been brought in, a thing I was not allowed to do before because every thing was then *Tabu*, but the ceremony being over they became simply what they realy [sic] were, viz. empty baskets, so that whatever they were supposed to Contain was emblematically represented, and so indeed was every other thing they brought in except the fish" (153). Whatever it was he wanted from the *inasi*, he seems to have obtained: the discovery of something whose artificiality was calibrated to considerable visual pleasure, a theater of representations of which he could give no account; a sort of bottomless dream. Bligh observed the same state of mind in the Tahitians to whom he showed his doll: "They were all delighted with it even when they knew it was not real" (Bligh 1937: 1.386).

The name Cook learns to give this pleasure is *tabu*, or *tapu*. In Polynesian systems of belief, *tapu* is the opposite of *noa*. All indifferent things are *noa*, and all things affected by the power of the sacred—such as the *mana* of chiefs, the mobility of gifts, the business of war, the uncleanness of corpses, or the presence of the *atua*—are *tapu*. We saw in the second chapter how things affected by *tapu* have a life and spirit of their own, the *hau* of the gift, for example. The wooden gods of the Hawai'ians required careful wrapping because they released such a terrible energy that sometimes they would shake and tremble of their own accord, a phenomenon known as *futefute*. The weapons of powerful chiefly lineages would do the same, and their food was poison to those not of a rank to eat it. Frederick Maning reported that a Maori slave who unwittingly ate the remains of a chiefly meal dropped down dead when he discovered what he had done, a story subsequently reported by Frazer and Freud (Maning 1863: 112). At his first landfall at Kealakekua Bay, Cook experienced the benefit of *tapu*, both his ships and the encampment on shore were protected by it, and nothing was stolen. King reported, "We enjoyd a tranquility about our Dwelling that was the very reverse to other places in these Sea's" (Cook 1967: 1.508). But when the British packed up to leave, the immunity ceased, "the Charm of Tabooed Ground was now broke & they [the local people] all rushd in, searching eagerly about the place . . . in hopes of finding something" (1.519). Nor was the *tapu* restored when they came back to the bay with a broken mast. Clerke remarked on the difference, "Ever since our arrival here upon this our second visit we have observ'd in the Natives a stronger propensity to theft then [sic] we had reason to complain of during our former stay; every day produc'd more numerous and more audacious depredeations [sic]" (1.531).

At the point in his ethnographic career when he understood the united pleasures and advantages of *tapu*, Cook arrived not altogether consciously at the state of intense curiosity" Anderson identified in the Polynesians who robbed his ships. In Tonga, he had spied artifacts connected with a god or at least with "something of divinity" (Cook 1967: 2.1162), and he observed them with increasing fascination. Although he tried to disguise this pleasurable absorption as a quest for knowledge, strict enquiry was no longer what he was engaged in, any more than he was when he mapped sands and shoals for an account no one but himself could find worthwhile, or when he tried to persuade himself that a catalogue of curiosities gathered solely for pleasure was no different from a catalogue of facts gathered for the account. By the time he reached Hawai'i and was hailed as Lono, he was aware that he and everything he possessed—all the property of the ship as well as everything about his person—had been mixed with imagination and transformed into more than the sum of their material parts, and were fit to be treated in a manner diametrically different from the objects that went missing in Tahiti on the first voyage. That is to say, they could not be owned as they were before; they were not accountable. They were idols, and like Rachel's babies or the emblems of the *inasi*, they set in train events for which there was no adequate narrative model.

Whether he was greeted as Lono the incarnate divinity and antagonist of the war-god Ku, or Lono-ka-makahiki, a personification or idol representing the god—a god-doll—or Lono-ma-i-kanaka, a resurrected scion of Lono's chiefly line, it is impossible to judge; but it is fair to say that the distance Cook was trying to lessen in the *inasi* was entirely closed in the *makahiki*, the festival in honor of Lono that coincided with his arrival in Hawai'i. He was stripped, awarded "the Title and Dignity of Orono" (Cook 1967: 2.1161–2)), and he was introduced to the important gods of the *Hikiau* temple, one of whom he kissed, as the Tahitians were to kiss Bligh's doll. He was at the dead center of ritual power, and in the last entry in his log, he described being anointed by the priest Keli'ikea, adored by hundreds of prostrate worshippers, protected by the chiefs, and presented with huge offerings of food in the most sacred precincts of the bay. His conduct at these ceremonies of installation as described by King is a curious blend of the feminized and the mesmerized: the degree zero of absorption. "Koah led him to different images, said something to each but in a very ludicrous and Slighting tone, except to the Center image . . . to this he prostrated himself, & and afterwards kiss'd, & desird

Fig. 5. Cook's Installation as Lono

the Captn to do the same, who was quite passive, & suffered Koah to do with him as he chose" (Cook 1967: 1.505–6). In this nation of "great Idolaters" (2.1185), Cook is adored as a god, and adores another in turn, in an act of homage as blasphemous as his own assumption of divinity, so thought William Cowper.

Like the *tapu*, this worship was not to be renewed on Cook's return to the bay. Although some of the priests tried as hard as ever to supply Cook with goods and devotion, his triumph was at an end, and the ritual sequel of conflict and death was about to be played out as reality according to the usurpational logic of *kali'i*, a Polynesian pun meaning to make a chief and to undo him (Sahlins 1985: 118). After a period of eclipse, Ku would defeat Lono, likewise Kalani'opu'u would defeat Cook. A series of blunders by his men alienated what was left of chiefly goodwill in the bay; all were committed in efforts to retrieve or defend property: the lid of the cask, the tongs, the chisel, the cap and so on. The important question to be asked is how the assault on property figured now in Cook's imagination. Was he standing up for naval equipment, the material element of his public account, and the proof of his duty as the king's commissioned officer; or was he reacting to the destruction of a dream in which he himself owned everything that was worth owning? It hardly seems likely that Cook would have entered willingly into the realms of godhead if he was still committed to a full naval narrative, and the interruption or censorship of his journal at the very point of his installation seems proof of it. If being Lono was a synonym for pure pleasure, then all things from food to the ship's fittings expressed that pleasure in the same way as the discovery of sands, shoals, false yams, and emblematic baskets. These were his babies, "picters" or idols: emptiness in its most voluptuous form and proof of his authorship. But when they were reconstituted as mere things—nothing but what they really were, viz. tongs, chisels, and caps—they caused an iconoclastic shock that recalled Cook to all the turbulent difficulties of sorting out public accounts from private ones, inflaming his passions in a painful way, causing him to act in a manner that was from the point of view of his people not rational or personate, nor (from his own point of view) authorial.

In the immediate wake of Cook's death, this state of affairs wore a face which no narrative could fully describe. King's journal turns into Chinese boxes of supplementary accounts as the search for a satisfactory public narrative comes to an indeterminate close. King yields to Edgar and Vancouver. Clerke yields to Phillips. Then Rickman, Ledyard, Zimmerman, and Ellis give their versions, and Douglas's official version is contradicted by Samwell's memoir. Nobody seems capable of owning an event which William Ellis said could no more be foreseen than prevented, and which Alexander Home said was impossible to relate. And so it goes on in a savage series of replies and rejoinders between Sahlins and Obeyesekere and in the more temperate disagreements between Salmond and Thomas over the details of the death and the reasons for it. As for personal property, that came home to the minds of the failed narrators at Kealakekua Bay in its most gruesome form. Locke says that our first property is our own body, and Cook's was distributed all over the place, a gruesome literalization of his own failed search for a coherent account. His head went to a chief called Kekuhaipio; his legs, thighs, and arms to Kalani'opu'u; his hair to Kamehameha; they were all destined become the focus of cults, babies of a potent kind. Cook ended up on the Polynesian side of the beach as a kind of A'a, breeding gods from his dead body. His hands, scalp, skull, thigh- and arm-bones went to the ship, and thence to the ocean, vanishing from the account like curiosities or mistaken facts.

CHAPTER 4

The Growth of Idols

> This idol which you term Virginity,
> Is neither essence, subject to the eye—
> No, nor to any one exterior sense,
> Nor hath it any place of residence,
> Nor is't of earth or mold celestial,
> Or capable of any form at all.
> Of that which hath no being do not boast:
> Things that are not at all are never lost.
>
> —Christopher Marlowe, *Hero and Leander*

Things gain independence when their owners desire to possess them uncontrollably; and this provokes a state of affairs ripe with paradox. Possession as the action of owning property slides into quite a contrary condition where not only does a thing cease to be owned, but possession itself is redefined as transport, not what you own but what possesses you, and passion is experienced as the impression of the sense of things, the irresistible "power of some external cause compared with our own" (Spinoza 1993: 146). In this chapter, I want to examine more closely examples of unauthorized personhood and the power of things. We have seen how deodands are recognized as criminal instruments by the law when human action turns into accident, and things must be personified because passion demands a manifest agent of injury, even if it is inanimate. We have seen also how things that have been owned, and are wanted back, gain independence in proportion to the strength of that desire, and get to tell their own stories. Corresponding to the deodand and lost thing, there is a species of fictional person that Hobbes names *idol*, an empty figure fashioned from matter and representing nothing. In spite of its nullity the idol is the focus of energy and emotion, and it raises a question about the authority of things vis-à-vis themselves. I want to start with Hobbes's use of the theater to define the difference between authorized and unauthorized personation; then I shall turn to *A Midsummer Night's Dream* to show how idols get a footing in the world of that play; and then I want to come back to Gay and one of the more startling pieces of theatrical nonsense performed in the eighteenth century, *The What D'Ye Call It*. Despite the anachronistic arrangement of these examples, I hope to show that personation generates a force capable of traversing not just the frontiers of authority and action, but also those of genre and species. It points out a distinctive route to the lives of things and the function of the gods; that is, from personation to personification.

In his commentary on the sixteenth chapter of *Leviathan*, "Of Persons, Authors, and Things Personated," Quentin Skinner invokes *A Midsummer Night's Dream* to explain the system of representation that constitutes Hobbes's commonwealth. The idea that the state presents the person of the people (Hobbes 1996: 120), and that a sovereign in turn bears or carries the person of the state (121), is taken from Roman models of oratory and advocacy, but the terms in which that idea are expressed—presenting, bearing, or carrying persons—are taken (as Hobbes himself observes) from the stage. Skinner turns to the Athenian tradesmen of Shakespeare's play for an illustration. Their dramatization of the story of Pyramus and Thisbe involves an elaborate demonstration of the presentation of persons, both inanimate and human. Thus, the players are required to "present the person of Moonshine" and to "present Wall" (Skinner 2002, 181–2). For his part, Bottom the weaver, who plays the hero, plans to explain to the audience that he merely bears the person of Pyramus, and that "I, Pyramus, am not Pyramus" (Shakespeare 1994, 178). By turning to the stage, Hobbes and Skinner are able more fully to explore the degrees of artifice which divide a "Naturall Person" (whose words and actions are considered as his own) from "a Feigned or Artificiall person" (whose words and actions represent someone or something else) (Hobbes 1996: 111).

It is clear from Hobbes's three-tiered notion of the state that the artificial person authorized by the people—the commonwealth or "Mortall God" (120)—proceeds to create another called the sovereign. Although authority for this double transformation derives ultimately from the natural right of each individual, it is sieved and refashioned as each successive artificial person spawns others to represent it, for in descent from the artificial person of the sovereign there are delegates such as governors, magistrates, officers, and priests. These in turn "personate," or are personated by others, including inanimate things. Indeed, it is when he gets to the issue of personating things, such as churches, hospitals, and bridges, that Hobbes reveals the limitless potential of the network of personation. "There are few things, that are uncapable of being represented by Fiction" (113). Two different multitudes stand either side of the focal point of the Mortall God: a host of natural persons who have authored it, and a host of artificial creatures (including things) who variously bear its person or have their persons borne by it.

"There are few things, that are uncapable of being represented by Fiction." It is not a phrase to Skinner's mind. He is unhappy with it because it implies an attenuation of real political rights into total artifice. He prefers the Latin version of *Leviathan*, where Hobbes wrote, "paucae res sunt, quarum non possunt esse personae," or, "there are few things incapable of being persons" (Skinner 2002: 195). Neither he nor Hobbes wants the reader to believe that a person represented by a fiction is not duly authorized. Authorization means that the original natural right belonging to an *author* has been successively covenanted away to *actors*, those who represent or personate the author. No authority is lost in this process. The owning of actions by authors, which is immediately evident in the deeds of natural persons, still occurs seriatim in the case of artificial ones. There is no action undertaken in the commonwealth which no one owns. But it is different among the tribes of Israel and in the Roman Republic, where things are personated which have no basis in natural right or reality. These are idols, shapes that represent mere figments, ideal forms "without place, habitation, motion, or existence, but in the motions of the Brain" (Hobbes 1996: 446). "An idol," says Hobbes on the authority of Saint Paul's first letter to the Corinthians (8:4), "is nothing" (114).

It is worth pursuing a little further the difference between a foreign idol and an English church, hospital, or bridge. The idol is nothing, represents nothing, and derives from nothing; but in Rome it was a fiction with legal status, being personated by someone recognized by the state as fit to act for the god, holding on his or her behalf "Possessions, and other Goods, and Rights" (113). Such gods owned property and owned the actions attributed to them, all mediated by an official delegate. As well as property, then, the god owned a history in the form of myth or fable. But it would be impossible to trace this ownership to an original right possessed by a natural person. The priest or vicar of the god had authority to represent it solely by means of fiction or belief, a motion of the brain. The god's right to property and narrative came from nowhere else but the mind, out of whose confusion "did arise the greatest part of the Religion of the Gentiles in time past, that worshipped Satyres, Faunes, Nymphs, and the like; and now adates the opinion that rude people have of Fayries, Ghosts and Goblins; and of the power of Witches" (18). Nor is it much different with a bridge. "Things Inanimate cannot be Authors, nor therefore give Authority to their Actors" (113). The actors—that is to say their overseers or trustees—get their authority from "those that are Owners, or Governours of those things." It is not clear why these owners or governors are any different from the overseer who personates the bridge. Each owns a fiction, a person that never existed as anything but stones and mortar, and one whose representation can never emerge from the trap of fictionality. The actor-overseer has no author but the actor-governor, who is in effect another actor authorized by a sovereign, himself a person of a person of the people. Yet this is no impediment to the civil life of the bridge or that of the Roman god; both possess endowments and the rights that go with them. The same is true of fools and madmen, to whom the state assigns guardians whose duty is to personate them; but actually what they personate is as inchoate as the ideas in which idols originate, mere motions of the brain severed from reality (446). On account of this confusion, fools and madmen are judged (like gods and bridges) incapable of authorship. But their estates and property are administered in their names.

The issue is brought back to the theater by Hobbes in *De Homine*, where he uses the example of Agamemnon to show how a purely artificial entity may be personated. His argument is that the mask or *prosopon* of the ancient theater was always supposed to divide the actor from the figure he personated, and that even when the literal mask disappeared from the performance, the audience acknowledged that Agamemnon was distinct from the fiction by which his actions reached them. Skinner puts it like this:

> If I play the part of Agamemnon on the stage, the actions I perform in the persona of Agamemnon will be taken by the audience to be Agamemnon's actions rather than mine. They will not "truly" be taken to be Agamemnon's actions, however, but only "by fiction," since the audience will remain aware of the fact that (as we put it in a knowingly ambiguous phrase) I am only playing. This will especially be the case, Hobbes implies, if I follow the convention of explicitly pointing out that I am merely engaged in a performance. For then it will be clear that I am only pretending to be an imaginary character, that there is no other person whom I am "truly" representing, and thus that there is no one else to whom my actions can validly be attributed. (Skinner 2002: 193)

In a curious move, Skinner replaces a scene of representation, where the person of the actor represents the deeds and speech of an original "author," with one where the possibility of a "true" representation entirely disappears, and the actor is at liberty to do or say anything as Agamemnon because it is all pretense. In order to rebut Hanna Pitkin's point, namely that actors embodying a fiction on these terms occupy the stage as purely artificial persons destitute of all authority (Pitkin 1967: 23–5), Skinner points out that plays were licensed by the Master of the Revels. The actor in the role of Agamemnon stands in the same relation to the actual Greek king as an overseer to a bridge, or a guardian to a lunatic, as someone vested with authority to personate them by an officer of the state. But Pitkin's point seems good, since the authorization of a performance by the Master of the Revels or, at a later date, the Lord Chamberlain, restores no link between the person of the actor and he whom he represents, the historical or traditional Agamemnon in this case, only between one fiction (the performance) and another (the playscript).

A Midsummer Night's Dream covers all these bases, being a play exclusively concerned with the invention of fictions and their personation. At the center of the play about the marriage of Theseus and Hippolyta is another play called *Pyramus and Thisbe*, based on Ovid's *Metamorphoses*, dealing with the transformative effects of lovers' passion and its tendency to blur the boundaries of fiction and truth. Curling around this embedded fiction is another, promoted by the fairy powers (themselves agitated and deceived by passion), which causes the aristocratic characters to wander in a wood, mistaking the objects of their true love. In all three of these nested dramas, love has caused a radical change of affection: Theseus loves the woman who was his enemy; Lysander and Demetrius stop loving Hermia and love Helena instead; and Titania turns from her lovely Indian boy to dote on a monster. The justification of dramatic art—its representation of the truth in a fiction—comes under strain because here, densely thematized, are examples of the reverse, a layer of fictions displacing a "real" state of the case which itself was owing to the metamorphic effects of love. The spell which causes Demetrius to fall in love with Helena is never lifted. The question is to what degree these theatrical representations can vindicate a fixed and reliable point of judgment.

Helena and Bottom both experience the representational vertigo caused by the loss of this fixed point. When Lysander and Demetrius declare their love for her, Helena is denied the character of forlorn maiden that had been hers up until then, for now she has one more lover than she needs. To sustain her role she must believe herself conscripted into an impromptu plot hatched by these two men to mock her misery. She can only find some semblance of stability and continuity for herself, that is to say, if she adds another layer of fiction to the world in which she is acting. Her plight is mirrored in Bottom's metamorphosis, which moves him from the play of *Pyramus and Thisbe* into another where he must take the part of the bemused object of Titania's improbable passion. It is by no means an unpleasant interlude, but it convinces him of three things; first, that his life has become a dream; second, that it could well be represented in a ballad; and third, that its fictionality is bottomless, that is, non-referential. From different sides, certainly from different orders of society, and with different sensations, Helena and Bottom find out what it is like to become purely artificial persons, creatures of fancies outside the realm of the nature of things, figments of a "dream and fruitless vision" (3.2.371). In effect they experience what it is like to be Agamemnon when there is no authority to limit the representation of what he is like, enveloped in a performance where anything can happen and in which it is pointless to assert, "I am Helena" or "I am Bottom. Thus the caveat of the *prosopon*: "I, Pyramus, am not Pyramus," opens a trapdoor into nothing.

Responsibility for their lodgment in sheer fiction is claimed by Oberon and Robin, but Oberon is to some extent the victim of his own passion and Robin, for all his magic, makes mistakes. Neither is perfectly certain of what he is doing, or why. Behind them shimmers the mind of the poet, whose imaginative power seems to set at an even greater distance the possibility of distinguishing a stable point of reference. A relationship between the poet, the lovers, and the actors of Pyramus and Thisbe is supposed by Theseus to exist, but it is not one in which he has much faith. Of Bottom and his company he observes, "The best in this kind are but shadows, and the worst are no worse if imagination mend them" (5.1.210–11). Of lovers and the mad he says they are seduced by their imaginations to believe in demons and paragons; as for the poet's mind, it gives body to nothing and to things unknown (5.1.15). Imagination, he concludes, is a personifying force, "that if it would but apprehend some joy/ It comprehends the bringer of that joy" (5.1.20). But then, as a lover, who is he to say? Does the love he feels for Hippolyta have its source in his own heart and action or in Love, the figure of the passion? If the poet gives a habitation and a name to "airy nothing" (5.1.16) by personifying the motions of his brain as fairy gods and their elfin agents, is he their creator or their creature? Certainly they proceed to recruit human actors as the persons of their fantasies, performers who are partly aware that they are "just playing" (as Theseus pretends to be playing when he analyzes the illusion in which he appears) but who are mostly absorbed and altered by fictions bred of fiction. Either way, there is no reality principle and no source of authority. The poet embodies figments to see if they will yield order, legislation, and harmony, or whether they will crumble into nothing. If that is the poet's gamble, to test sheer invention against the unity and power of experience itself, Hobbes promotes the political equivalent. He wagers that the almost illimitable capacity of fiction to represent the constituent parts of the commonwealth can be demonstrated to work when licensed fancies operate as the channels of political power and make things happen. He guarantees these fictions free from "gloriation of mind," when phantasms "without place, habitation, motion, or existence" masquerade as real events and natural persons; but like the poet, he seeks his proof in the efficacy of fiction, not in the authority of truth (Hobbes 1651: 90; 1996: 446).

The acid test of this experiment in the play is the performance of *Pyramus and Thisbe*. The restored Bottom takes the leading part, playing to an audience of partially restored lovers (Demetrius is still under the influence Robin's magic juice) who, to their shame, are unaware how closely the performance points at them. "It is nothing, nothing in the world," says Egeus, and they agree (5.1.78). The tradesmen's best efforts at bearing the persons of those whom they would represent are devoted oddly enough to nonhuman objects. Once the play begins, there is no mask or *prosopon* for the actors playing the lovers. Quince says briefly, "This man is Pyramus . . . this beauteous lady Thisbe is" (5.1.128–9). But he explains that Wall is represented by a man, and that another will represent Moonshine. Snout duly announces himself as the person who will act the part of Wall, and Snug introduces himself by name as the one who is to play the part of Lion. Starveling is most particular in his imitation of Moonshine, for he carries a lantern to present the moon, and he shows himself, with his thorn bush and dog, as the man in the moon—as it were a personation inside a personation, prompting Theseus to exclaim, "the man should be put into the lantern. How is it else the man i'th'moon?'" (5.1.241–2). Quince anticipated this double artifice when he said during the rehearsal that the actor must say he comes "to present the person of Moonshine" (180), that is, to seem to be the man who makes a person of the moon. Perhaps disoriented by these *mises en abyme* and by the audience's wit, Starveling attempts an extempore distinction between fiction and action, his artificial and natural persons, by telling the quibblers, "The lantern is the moon, I the man i'th'moon, and this thorn bush my thorn bush, and this dog my dog" (5.1.252–4). But whether these are the properties of the moon, or the man in the moon, or the actor who plays that man, is left in the dark.

What began as a courtesy to verisimilitude—human scenery—and an insurance against its more alarming effects—a lion that can calm an audience by saying he is not really a lion—has turned into something else. The rhetoric of the play is largely devoted to reinforcing these representations and personations by addressing them in high-strained apostrophes: "O wall, O sweet, O lovely wall . . . O wicked wall . . . I thank thee, Moon . . . O wherefore Nature didst thou lions frame?" Quince began the play by affirming the importance of these three characters ("Let Lion, Moonshine, Wall . . . at large discourse" [5.1.149–50]), and at the end Theseus notes, with Wall down, "Moonshine and Lion are left to bury the dead" (5.1.342). Starveling, Snout, and Quince had been going to play the parts of the lovers' parents, but they have been written out. The displacement of the human by the nonhuman shapes the argument as well as the action, for according to Quince's prologue it is not Thisbe but her mantle which is slain (5.1.144). The importance of inanimate or nonhuman things as rhetorical tennis balls was evident in the insults of the lovers, who in the whirlwinds of their passion variously assailed each other with the names of dog, burr, dwarf, cat, maypole, puppet (3.2). In Ovid's story of Pyramus and Thisbe, the precedent is set of addressing the inanimate as persons: "O wall . . . O all ye lions . . . O tree," and so on (Ovid 1999:1.183–9). When Psyche's lamp drops oil upon her lover in *The Golden Ass*, another important source for *A Midsummer Night's Dream*, she exclaims, "O rash and bolde lampe … how darest thou bee so bold as to burne the god of all fire?" (Apuleius 1923: 111). Peter Holland points out how Shakespeare parodies the extravagant exclamations of Gascoigne's *Jocasta* and even of the Nurse in his own *Romeo and Juliet* (Shakespeare 1994: 240 n.). But in this demotic Pyramus and Thisbe, the physical intimacy as well as the rhetorical prominence of the thing personified is extraordinary. Thisbe confesses to Wall, "My cherry lips have often kissed thy stones,/ Thy stones with lime and hair knit up in thee." And when Pyramus demands a kiss, she laments, "I kiss the wall's hole, not your lips at all" (5.1.189–90; 200).

The broad humor emphasizes the interposition of the actual stuff of Wall in what amounts to (in Hobbes's terms) an accidental idolatry. He says:

> To worship an Image, is voluntarily to doe those externall acts, which are signes of honoring either the matter of the Image, which is Wood, Stone, Metall, or some other visible creature; or the Phantasme of the brain, for the resemblance, or representation whereof, the matter was formed and figured; or both together, as one animate Body, composed of the matter and the Phantasme, as of a Body and Soule. (Hobbes 1996: 449)

Hobbes gives the example of the throne (which he also calls the stool) of a prince that is reverenced on account of the power and authority it represents. "But if hee that doth it, should suppose the Soule of the Prince to be in the Stool, or should present a Petition to the Stool, it were … Idolatry" (449). Within the representational system of Leviathan, however, the succession of images does not vitiate the reality of power and authority, "So an earthly Soveraign may be called the Image of God: And an inferiour Magistrate the Image of an earthly Soveraign" (448). This is the standard distinction in iconoclastic discourse between a prototype or *eidolon* and a similitude or simulacrum, the difference between an image consubstantial with what it represents from one which represents a separate or absent being. Both Hobbes and Carlo Ginzburg regard the former as "intrinsically meaningless signs" (Ginzburg 2001: 107), but Hobbes concedes that an idol is the material form of a fantastic idea. He puts it as follows: "But in these Idols, as they are originally in the Brain, and as they are painted, carved, moulded, or moulten in matter, there is a similitude of the one to the other, for which the Materiall Body made by Art, may be said to be the Image of the Phantasticall Idoll made by Nature" (448). The image does not represent the idea but manifest or embody it. Answerable to the multitude of human figures enclosed within the body of Leviathan on the title page of his book, the idol encloses a multitude of fancies within the extraordinary shape of wrought matter; the difference is they bear analogy with nothing else. Hobbes's example is the centaur, the mixture of horse and human, "a Figure [made up] out of the parts of divers creatures" (448) and found nowhere else but among the motions of the brain.

John Locke observes that fantastic ideas are those "made up of such Collections of simple Ideas, as were really never united, never were found together in any Substance; v.g. a rational Creature, consisting of a Horse's Head, joined to a body of humane shape" (Locke 1975: 374). In his essay on idols, Ginzburg cites Origen's attack on all the fantastic combinations of bodies, heads, and species to be found in idols, a chaos which Aquinas exemplified as the head of a horse joined to a human body (Ginzburg 2001; 105). Lucretius spends time showing the impossibility of a creature framed half of a horse's body and half of man's, "I say this that you may not believe that Centaurs can be formed or be, composed of man and the seed of the burden-bearing horse" (Lucretius 1997: 449 [5.890–1]). This most potent image of the idol, idol-ness itself, is achieved in Bottom's metamorphosis. The correspondence between the multifarious contents of the brain of the poet and all its various personations on the stage, actors authored out of thin air, is concentrated in this hybrid figure. Titania worships it idolatrously, enthralled by its shape, smitten by its properties, its fair ears, sleek head, and amiable cheeks. She adores it just as other idolaters fall down before wrought metal, wood, and stone, touching stuff they believe to be consubstantial with the divinity.

Titania's fondness for this idol, deriving from the lewd interlude of Apuleius's The Golden Ass where a noblewoman falls in love with Lucius and copulates with him while he is still in the shape of a beast, is nevertheless rendered in verse of transcendent sweetness, as of a god to a mortal, although here Titania plays the mortal's part: "Come, sit thee down upon this flow'ry bed,/ While I thy amiable cheeks do coy,/ And stick musk-roses in thy sleek smooth head,/ And kiss thy fair large ears, my gentle joy" (4.1.1–3). The mistaken object of passion so lusciously accosted glances in the direction of Wall, with its properties of stones, lime, and hair on which Thisbe lavishes her kisses, and also toward the remarkable episode of Psyche's vision of Cupid in Apuleius's story. When she finally beholds her invisible spouse, Psyche is enthralled with the details of his body, "his haires of gold . . . his neck more white than milk, his purple cheeks . . . his tender plume feathers, dispersed upon his sholders like shining flours, & trembling hither & thither" (Apuleius 1923: 111). The passion of a woman for a lover of doubtful shape, undimmed by proof that he is not human, attaches itself to the specific properties of his being, or what Hobbes calls "the visible creature." The referent of these instances of misprision is a thing so diversely compounded of the material outworks of imaginative effort that it provokes and deserves the emotion being spent on it. Bottom's ass's head is more easily idolized than the bodies of Hermia, Helena, Demetrius, and Lysander, whose physical properties are never so compelling as to prevent their feelings for each other from bursting into impatience and vituperation. This is where Bottom and his company have the edge over their audience. Their exuberant apostrophes to personate things, including the details of their texture and color, indicate how important they are, and how necessary that they be properly addressed if passion and political trouble are not to supervene.

Even in the domain of things thus prudently represented, it is not always easy to assign the property of the material part. Thisbe wishes she could kiss Pyramus's lips instead of wall's roughcast, stone, lime, and hair. Starveling is not sure where to place dog and thornbush in the presentation of Moonshine. Snug is still worried that his personation of lion will terrify the ladies. Notwithstanding such punctual divisions between what is represented and the things that represent it, things thus personified have an active life and are addressed as personified agents, without definite or indefinite articles. That is to say they are personifications both in the sense of having their persons borne by someone else, and in the sense of being greeted as causes of their own effects, as Moonshine is of light at night, Lion of mayhem, Wall of illicit communication. As Theseus says, when we apprehend joy we suppose the bringer of that joy, namely Joy (5.1.233). So the things of this play act simultaneously as names and as propertied entities, like Hobbes's Roman gods or the stool of a prince. Under this idolatrous regime, it is when a thing is most fictional that it enjoys the maximum degree of physical presence; similarly, a god is never so much a god as when he or she is incarnated in wood, stone, metal, or even flesh. Psyche is a mortal god, a virgin of surpassing beauty presenting Venus's majesty on earth, "the Vicar of [her] name" (Apuleius 1923: 97, 114); accordingly, she is worshipped as a thing, "Every one marveled at her divine beauty, as it were some Image well painted and set out" (98). It is also true that in this state of maximum visibility and tactility the god attracts the most powerful feelings of its devotees. Psyche's cult is so popular that Venus's altars are deserted, her ceremonies neglected. Bottom metamorphosed sits between the two positions of abstraction and materiality. On one hand, he incarnates and expresses the myriad figments of the poetic brain; and on the other, he exhibits physical attributes so unique they command the eyes, lips, and fingers of his lover. To this extent it is never certain whether he is the product of imagination or its trigger.

It is hard to say exactly how Bottom occupies his role as the idol of imagination. The recursive puns upon his transformation ("Man is but an ass if he go about to expound this dream" [4.1.203]) are strangely insistent upon the stark division between the intoxicating limitlessness of the dream and the narrowness of human faculties, between the sensations of being in it and recalling what its passages actually looked like. The vision he has enjoyed is "past the wit of man . . . man is but an ass . . . no man can tell what . . . man is but a patched fool . . . the eye of man hath not heard" and so on. Bottom treasures the uninterpretable uniqueness of the experience, which belonged to what he was when he had it, namely, not a man. To announce this in words he is obliged to dismantle links with the species—man—that would mistake what he was by translating it back into anthropomorphic terms. At the same time, he pictures that mistake as the core of his dream: man turned to ass. So he fashions a sort of hollow defined by negatives, a place where no man can say what he was, nor no ass either.

In trying to put this inexpressibility into words, Bottom garbles two texts that represent extreme and opposite positions on the value of testimony: Lucretius on the irrefutable truth of empirical observation, and Saint Paul on the triumph of faith. "Will the ear be able to convict the eye, or the touch the ear?" demands Lucretius, "Will the taste of the mouth again refute the touch, will the nose confound it, or the eye disprove it?" (Lucretius 1992: 315 [4.486–89]), citing the impossible synaesthetic collisions Bottom actually broaches as typical of his case: "The eye of man hath not heard, the ear of man hath not seen, man's hand is not able to taste, his tongue to conceive, nor his heart to report what my dream was" (4.1.207–10). He is misremembering Paul, who in the Authorized Version writes to the Corinthians, "Eye hath not seen, nor ear heard, neither have entered into the heart of man, the things which God hath prepared for them that love him" (1 Corinthians, 2: 9). In setting aside the importance of empirical observation in order to make way for a more imperative truth, Paul himself confounds the accusative case belonging to the things eye cannot see or ear hear, and the dative case governing the action of the things that will enter the heart of man (and maybe the eye and ear) (Holford-Strevens 2009: 26). Instead of things appearing as objects by virtue of the action of personified faculties (Eye and Ear), agency is quite reversed, and it is things, impelled by spirit, that will strike the human sensorium. The impressive power of things will register the degree of intimacy between what is divine and what is mortal, according to Paul. The same state of affairs is evident in the story of Cupid and Psyche, when a human deserted by her own kind and by the gods (Eye having seen by means of Lamp what it had no right to look at), is saved by Reed, Water, Tower, and Eagle, who step in to disperse Trouble, Sadness, Sleep, and Mortality.

In the end, there is not such a great difference between Lucretius's materialism and the pressure of the Pauline spirit, for he says it is not by its own virtue that eyes see things: "There is seen to be in images a cause of vision, and without these nothing can be seen." Like the things that are going to strike the heart, the films flying from the surfaces of things "strike our eyes and excite vision" (Lucretius 1992: 295 [4.238; 217]). Whether the primary impulse comes from the nature of atoms, spirit, gods, or God, things are the agents of it, and humans the patients: they impinge and we feel them. The ballad Bottom thinks Peter Quince may write of his dream would include this disturbing and passionate relation of humankind to things typical of Robin Goodfellow's practical jokes ("Their sense thus weak . . . made senseless things begin to do them wrong" [3.2.27–8]). Paul's idea of the transports to come differs not in the strength of the passions caused by things, only in the degree of exaltation they will confirm. So Bottom's ballad in some form or another would comprehend an occult impulse, an active thing and a human transported and possibly metamorphosed by passion.

Robin Goodfellow says the state of suspended ownership caused by his magic, during which Jack does not have Jill and the man is still bereft of his mare, is strictly preposterous: "Those things do best please me/ That befall prepost'rously" (3.2.121, 7–28. In a far more tragic vein, Philomel says to Tereus that the rape of his sister-in-law has turned every social law and cultural affinity upside down ("omnia turbasti"), and that she will sing of his offense to the rocks and the trees, since it is impossible for a human audience to make sense of it. Like Niobe or Myrrha, she feels to their fullest extent the passions aroused by preposterous arrangements of things such as those that cause Thrasileon the bandit in *The Golden Ass*, once he is dressed in a bearskin, to fight and die only as a bear, or Plutarch's Gryllus to praise his life as one of Circe's swine. Similarly, Bottom's loyalty to his incarnation as an ass-idol is absolute; he defends it against the wit that might remove, transpose, interpret, or otherwise diminish it. Like Wall he has that within him which, while it represents nothing, makes him an author instead of an actor, endowed with virtues more than nominal. In Lucretius's theater, where there is neither play nor actors and nothing is represented, the preposterous scene is formed out of streams of light as the yellow, red, and purple awnings flash their colors, so rapidly that "fixed outlines of shapes and of finest texture . . . flit about everywhere, but singly and separately cannot be seen" (Lucretius 1997: 283 [4.75–77]). He calls it a flood of beauty, and Pope remembers it when he describes the iridescent outlines of the sylphs as they rise and fall above the Thames. Thisbe pays distracted testimony to Pyramus's manifold qualities in the kaleidoscope of misplaced colors and similes out of which she fashions the memorial of his face, a speech whose passionate improprieties operate like Bottom's synaesthesias in demonstrating how the spirit expresses itself in sheer chromatic diversity: "These lily lips,/ This cherry nose,/ These yellow cowslip cheeks" (5.1.324–5).

The passion that veers around things that are utterly their own can make instant idols of them. With the loss of a favorite possession such as a snuff-box or a pen-knife, the owner, says Adam Smith, "is vexed out of all proportion to the value of the damage." Contrariwise, "We are angry, for a moment, even at the stone that hurts us. A child beats it, a dog barks at it, a choleric man is apt to curse it" (Smith 1976: 94). What we feel for such things is equal to the independence of action of which we suppose them capable. This has nothing at all to do with empirical judgments of their worth; it is primarily a matter of passion and its correlate in matter. As Shakespeare's rustics go about to perform a play of "very tragical mirth," persons of things are constructed out of willing human bodies, and made available for passionate apostrophes that are by no means merely comic. Passion is most powerfully expressed toward things or in the presence of things, chiefly by actors who have borne the persons of things or briefly been a thing. And in the condition of a thing, Bottom has been passionately addressed by a fairy in the same language that he has used to apostrophize Wall and Moon. Starveling's pedantic apportionment of propriety in his presentation of Moonshine may be understood as deference toward the visible creature of what is to all intents and purposes an idol; likewise Snout's presentation of Wall, with such careful attention paid to the hollow defined by its loam, stone, roughcast, and mortar, shows how precisely its material attributes carry him beyond personation into the kind of personification answerable to the passions generated when the definite article goes missing. Titania is obsessed with the hair and skin of her lover because it is in their very texture that her passion is excited and lodged. These things are treated with the same extremes of reverence and expostulation reserved for the material forms of other gods. The passion is proportionate to the belief that matter may be the proper dwelling place of divinity, with energy to blast the sense of things into our hearts. So there are no passionate encounters in this play that do not require things actively to be confronting humans or the imputed transformation of humans into things. This is faithful to the Ovidian original of the story, where the blood of the lovers is preserved forever in the reddened fruit of the mulberry tree. It is also faithful to Hobbes's belief that on the stage "not truth, but Image, maketh passion" (Hobbes 1994: 68). The mortal god of his commonwealth operates on such a stage, transacting between the multitude of fictions that sustains the illusion of represented unity, and the multitude of subjects forced to yield to it until such time that they discover the secret of self-authorization.

In the preface to his play within a play, *The What D'Ye Call It* (1715), John Gay cites *A Midsummer Night's Dream* to justify his use of actors who bear the persons of other persons and other things (or semi-things), such as a chorus of Sighs and Groans and the ghost of an embryo. "Shakespeare hath some characters of this sort, as a *speaking wall*, and *Moonshine*" (Gay 1923, 1.35). The loose resemblance of Gay's piece to Pyramus and Thisbe in *A Midsummer Night's Dream*—both involve tragicomic performances mounted by the poor in order to entertain the rich and powerful—was no accident. He had collaborated with Richard Leveridge who (clearly under the influence of *The What D'Ye Call It*) wrote *The Comic Masque of Pyramus and Thisbe* the following year (1716). In his preface, Leveridge plunders Gay's, demanding the reason why "I may not turn Moonshine into a Minstrel, the Lion and Stone Wall into Songsters; and make them as Diverting as a Dance of Chairs and Butterflies have been in one of our most Celebrated British Entertainments?" (Leveridge 1716: [ii]). Referring to his *Wonders in the Sun; or, The Kingdom of the Birds* (1706), Gay had written, "Mr D'Urfey of our own nation has given all the fowls of the air the faculty of speech equal with the parrot. Swans and elbow-chairs in the Opera of Dioclesian have danced upon the English Stage with good success. Shakespear hath . . . a speaking wall' (Gay 1923: 34). Evidently there was a vogue for this kind of thing. In Buckingham's *The Rehearsal*, all inventions come piping hot from Mr. Bayes's fancy, including dead men that dance, along with Earth, Sun, and Moon, who "come out upon the Stage, and dance the Hey" (Villiers 2000: 2.5.10–15; 5.1.360). In fact, personated things do not take a very large part in Gay's play, but things themselves have an importance arising from unauthorized persecution, the force of passion, and the generic indeterminacy of the piece.

This latter novelty seems to engross Gay's attention, his invention of the first "tragic-comi-pastoral farce." This owes something to Peter Quince's description of his play as "The Most Lamentable Comedy" (1.2.11), and his subsequent promise of "very tragical mirth" (5.1.57). In Gay's opinion, his own handling of the mixture is distinguished from tragi-comedy by the impossibility of identifying the constituent generic parts. The four ingredients cannot be "distinguished or separated," he says (Gay 1923: 31). So the prologue promises that the play will give the audience a variety of opportunities for response, it "may make you laugh, or cry . . . move with distress, or tickle you with satyr" (41). This indeterminate play of affect is aided, and possibly controlled, by Gay's use (on Bossu's authority) of concealed sentences or morals, otherwise irony. But in this case irony is supposed not to be inimical to the passions possible to be represented in a burlesque format (any more than it is in Gay's mock-pastoral *The Shepherds' Week*, written the year before). So the complicated relation between the novelty of the poet's inventions and their clownish exemplification on a rural stage are referred, like Bottom's, to warnings against too easy an interpretation of the action or too lordly a response to the representation of passion in a lowly dress.

To give further weight to these strictures, Gay issued in the same year *A Complete Key to the last New Farce The What D'Ye Call It*. It is a mock-negotiation between the apparent irregularities of the action and what were the likely motives of the author in inventing them, "these odd Fancies in the [poet's] Brain" (Gay 1715: [i]). It aims to spot all the satirical allusions to heroic tragedy that are allegedly quilted together in a production that only pretends to be naive. The critical mind Gay is impersonating here cannot admit that anything in the play is there for its own sake; it must be a parody of Rowe, Dryden, Addison, or Otway. Thus, in the execution scene many allusions are found to *Venice Preserved*, and the writer of the *Key* remarks, "The Solemnity of parting with dying Friends, which has so often drawn Tears ... is here made a Subject of Merriment" (18). If every incidental phrase or scene in the farce recalls distinctly a tragic parallel, emphasizing its incongruity in order to fetch a laugh, not much would survive of the effects the poet claims for his new genre in the Preface. Why would we feel distress at the mockery of distress; or laugh at the absurd trace of pathos? The author of the *Key*, however, has no other point to make: "The Application of a fine well-work'd Passion to a mean Object certainly makes it Ridiculous ... and the most moving Passages in all the Antients ... may by this means be sunk into Contempt" ([iv]). How might Gay's irony have infiltrated such an obtuse argument?

Like *A Midsummer Night's Dream* the matter at hand is the presentation of persons. In this story of two peasants—Thomas Filbert forced to enlist because Dorcas falsely claims he is the father of her child, and Timothy Peascod about to be shot for desertion—the descent of authority through the various persons who stand for the arch-person of the sovereign instigates the action on two levels. Within the play itself, recruitment for the army has principally been organized by magistrates such as Sir Roger, Sir Humphrey, and the Justice, who have sent generations of men off to Flanders to be killed or maimed as punishment for poaching fish and game, as well as for fornication. They cite "his gracious Majesty" as their authority (42), and a train of ghosts and a chorus of Sighs and Groans rise up to accuse their inhumanity. However, the law issues a reprieve for Peascod at the very moment that the Sergeant who was arranging for his execution is arrested for stealing a horse. Peascod is naturally pleased with this outcome, and tries to express his pleasure by running changes on the statute that subordinates human life to the ownership of a horse: "He shall be hang'd that steals a mare" (55). The play itself has been commissioned by Sir Roger, lord of the manor and a real magistrate, presumably with the idea of affording a Christmas entertainment that exemplifies the mercy as well as the awfulness of the law.

So rather than love, which dominates the action of Pyramus and Thisbe as well as the context of its rehearsal and performance, the law is principal mover in *The What D'Ye Call It*, with love in second place, as it is again in Gay's masterpiece *The Beggar's Opera*, whose germ is clearly visible here. So when he surveys the cast, Sir Roger sees very little difference between the persons presented in the play, and the tenants who do the presenting. He says, "We have so fitted the parts of my tenants, that every man talks in his own way!—and then we have made just three justices in the play, to be play'd by us three justices of the Quorum" (39). For their part it is true, they play themselves smoking and drinking and passing sentence; but it is different with the tenants. Filbert is played by Sir Roger's son Thomas, who is the father not of Dorcas's child but Kitty's, the steward's daughter, who plays the part of the innocent virgin Kitty Carrot to whom Filbert is eventually married—really married, as it happens, by a ruse of the steward, who has a genuine curate perform the ceremony in the play. So the smooth parallel between the two sorts of persons supposed by Sir Roger—personations deriving from sovereign authority twinned with personations deriving from his own—breaks down, together with the system of obedience it upholds. The clergyman, a person of authority who only pretends to be a presented person in the performance, marries two people who are on the stage only pretending to talk as tenants "in their own way," while secretly settling their business. Thus, the three of them snatch some justice from a Justice who otherwise would not easily have parted with it.

This state of affairs is signaled by an insistent use of doublets, chiefly by Sir Roger, intended to affirm the solidity of theatrical presentations. "Why neighbours, you know, experience, experience," he says, alluding to his thorough knowledge of the world and the stage, before announcing, "The Prologue, the Prologue" (39–40), his introduction to a performance indistinguishable from real life. Of Othello he recalls, "and he would put out the light, and put out the light so cleverly" (40), gesturing at the same equivalence between the actor and author of a deed that lets his tenants perform what they already are, or that allows him and his colleagues to "sit and smoak at the same time we act"—that is, to sit and smoke while they "sit and smoak." When he defends having a parson play the part of a parson he calls it "an innocent thing . . . an innocent thing" (59). But when the innocent thing proves less than innocent and more than mere performance, incredulously he echoes his son Thomas's phrase, "If I be a husband, if I be a husband!" (61), only to have it confirmed by the steward, who points out that the names of the actors who were married are identical with the real couple, Thomas and Katherine, and that the marriage is good in law. "Good in law," exclaims Sir Humphrey, instantly seconded by Justice Statute, "good in law" (61). Now the repetitions indicate a rupture in the supposed symmetry of representation as Sir Roger finds out that what is good in law is not in this case good for him. In Hobbes's terms, the system of artificial persons on which the law depends has been invaded by a special kind of artificial person (the curate) acting in the service of a fiction, which is nevertheless promoted and confirmed by a deed that only a delegate of the sovereign can perform. The fiction serves the interests of two natural persons, Thomas and Kitty, but undercuts the authority the play commissioned by Sir Roger was meant to illustrate and enforce.

Gay uses genre to deal with this complexity. Comedy defines the play Sir Roger thought he was involved in, where the real experience of his tenants was to be represented in a manner congenial to them and to the order of things. Tragedy offers a fund of expressions apt for the failure of that harmony, as when the law menaces lovers with separation or death. Pastoral, as he says in the Preface, abounds with sentiments that put the lowest country people on a level with the greatest: "their thoughts are almost the same, and they only differ as the same thought is attended with a meanness of pomp of diction, or receives a different light from the circumstances each character is conversant with" (32). Farce consists of "absurdities and incongruities" such as ghosts, Sighs and Groans, speaking walls, and Moonshine. The *Key* limits all judgments of the piece to its imperfect pursuit of tragic-comedy, noticing pastoral only as a symptom of its failure—"a Milk-Maid raving with the strains of a despairing Empress" (Gay 1715: [iv])—and farce as the unintended outcome of undisciplined ridicule ("It seems impossible for mortal Eyes to distinguish the Person represented, unless the Ghosts are so kind as to inform them who they are" [11]). Gay's priorities are the reverse of the *Key*'s. The recent author of *The Shepherd's Week* incorporates bits of "Wednesday" (Sparabella's options for suicide) into Kitty's mad scene (Gay 1974: 1.108; 1923: 55). But if he was to persuade his audience that the pathos of common life was not just an opportunity for literary condescension, he needed to show pastoral and farce functioning independently of burlesque alliances of high and low, with its shadowed forms of authority that are never really meant to be mocked.

One way of doing this was to incorporate the ballad into the generic mixture, a technique he was to perfect in *The Beggar's Opera*. In *The What D'Ye Call It*, Kitty's friends sing a song just before she runs mad, "'Twas when the seas were roaring," set to music by Handel. Cowper thought it an extraordinary exhibition of the strengths of the ballad, "a species of poetry, I believe, peculiar to this country, equally adapted to the drollest and the most tragical subjects" (Cowper 1981: 2.155). It must have operated on the play's early audiences like Polly's "O ponder well" in *The Beggar's Opera*, crystallizing an emotion from the incongruous elements of the scene that induced them to take it seriously on Kitty's terms. I have tried to suggest in the second chapter that Polly's later song, "O what pain it is to part," turns the paradox of absolute possession the same way, developing a pathos out of all proportion to the circumstances in which it is sung. If we consider that a ballad is the only vehicle identified by Bottom as apt for his sense of how powerfully things not empirically observed can enter the heart, then the parallel between these two interludes grows stronger.

As for farce, Gay makes it plain he had *Pyramus and Thisbe* in mind, particularly its personations of figures whose pure fictionality carries them outside the system of authorized representation, such as his ghosts who inform the audience who they are, and then accuse the three personations of sovereign power of injustice. We have seen how, in Shakespeare's play, farce (or what Gay would label as such) builds a bridge between the motions of the poet's brain and the material circumstances in which the characters find themselves, fostering the personification of incidental things (Wall) that attracts and concentrates the loose affect of a scene ("O Wall!"). The same is true of Gay's. The "odd Fancies in the Brain" are located in things that carry the freight of emotion, such as Kitty's rake. When she promises to go off to the wars with Filbert, he asks, "O Kitty, Kitty, canst thou quit the rake?" using a synecdoche of rural labor that is subsequently transformed into a prosopopeia, as Kitty's passions rise and she addresses it as a companion: "On thee I lean'd, forgetful of my work,/ While Tom gaz'd on me, propt upon his fork" (Gay 1923: 55). The lovers' passionate exclamations, "Ah!" and "Oh!" appear as the personified Sighs and Groans, disconsolate ejaculations disconsolately ejaculating, "Ah! Oh! poor soul! alack! and well a day!" (56).

At this stage, the material elements of this rural world start to move around too. Lots of property changes hands as token or keepsake: "Take you my 'bacco-box—my neckcloth, you./ To our kind Vicar send this bottle skrew./ But wear these breeches, Tom; they're quite bran-new" (53). The country folk try to seduce the cruel Sergeant into compassion by offers of things that are not so much bribes as materializations of pathos: "And take my fourteen-pence . . . and my cramp-ring . . . take my box of copper . . . and my wife's thimble . . . and this 'bacco-stopper" (50). The preposterous correspondence between this heterogeneous accumulation of things and the powerful surge of local sympathy it expresses teaches the audience to appreciate how the odd fancies of Kitty's distracted brain provoke a similar mixture of incongruous items, rolling around the border of her temporary metamorphosis:

> Hah!—I am turned a stream—look all below.
> It flows, flows, and will forever flow.
> The meads are all afloat—the haycocks swim.
> Hah! who comes here?—my Filbert! Drown not him.
> Bagpipes in butter, flocks in fleecy fountains,
> Churns, sheep-hooks, seas of milk, and honey.
>
> (58)

The *Key* finds sources for these wild associations in Nourmahal (*Aurengzebe*) and Belvidera (*Venice Preserved*). It seems more like Ovid's deluge crossed with Swift's *A City Shower*, with touches of the Land of Cockaigne. Jane Austen remembered it when she wrote the mad scene in *Love and Freindship*. It bears comparison with the Arcimboldo effect Thisbe produces out of her lover's countenance when she is too overcome by grief to get the tints and similitudes in the right order.

Before he is to be shot, Timothy Peascod is handed a copy of Bunyan's *The Pilgrim's Progress*, whose title page he reads out loud, stuttering with passion and with Jonas Dock's speech impediment: "Eighth edition—London—printed—for—Ni-ch-olas Boddington: with new ad-di-tions never made before." He cannot go on, "Oh!, 'tis so moving, I can read no more" (Gay 1923: 49). The author of the *Key* gets very cross about this, which he takes as a slight to Addison's *Cato* and that moment where the hero picks up a book of sentences to confirm him in his resolution to die, reading it and then conceding, "It must be so,—Plato thou reason'st well" (Gay 1715: 16). Plainly, Peascod's reading of Bunyan has nothing to do with either reason or the sentiments of the story, for he never gets into it. Instead, his mind dwells on a random series of print-data contained on the first page of the wonderful thing in his hands, which acts not at all as a summary of the contents but rather as the lodging of feelings so strong they would otherwise have none. It is a wild and idolatrous way to treat print, to be sure, but it establishes a semi-iconic role for it in a scene that in many other respects exploits the insignificant clutter of things pictured in mid-seventeenth-century Dutch still lifes. In Joseph de Bray's *In Praise of Herring* (1657), for instance, an open book is set inside a frame formed of smoked and sliced fish, a ewer, a chest, a glass, a flower, and some onions. In Peascod's scene, a book open at the title page is shown in a prospect of a tobacco-box, a neck-cloth, a corkscrew, and a pair of breeches, contributing to a sense of words not as messages but as viewable things (Alpers 1983: xxv). The printed words in still lifes are legible but detextualized, as barren of meaning as the artifacts arrayed around them, which somehow ought to have been emblems but are not. They are there, as Alpers says, to "give us more to look at" (187): aniconic traces of ink delivered to the eye as images, examples of the paradoxical iconoclasm of this branch of art which prefers to present things solely as they are, seldom as what they represent. What remains in the picture is the cause of visual pleasure: the play of light on surfaces of different tints and textures. What animates the page of Bunyan's book are names of a man Peascod doesn't know and a place he has never visited, each acting as foci of his passion. In a moment of desperation equally intense, the woman of Berlin tried to scratch her way toward the substance of the words she read on the page of her romance. In moments like these, Hume detects the origin of polytheism:

> By degrees, the active imagination of man, uneasy in [the] abstract conception of objects, about which it is incessantly employed, begins to render them more particular, and to clothe them in shapes more suitable to its natural comprehension. (Hume 1957: 47)

And hence what Ernst Bloch calls "this uncanny pathos derived from the vitalization of the inorganic" (Bloch 1996: 92).

CHAPTER 5

The Rape of the Lock as Still Life

> Partout la volupté marque sa trace, et bientôt l'idole res-
> semble à la victime. [Lust leaves its traces everywhere, and
> soon the idol resembles a victim]
>
> —Vivant Denon, *Point de lendemain*

In the prologue, I mentioned the Quixote effect as the tendency of print culture to foster the re-circulation of ancient genres such as fable and romance. Under the stress of feelings incident to modernity, Swift's Author turns to fairy stories, Lucy Lockit and Bernard Mandeville to animal fables, and Charlotte Lennox's Arabella to salon romance. In modern dress these genres shed any fidelity they might have had to an ulterior cause, bringing whatever it is in which they consist to the surface. Lucy will grieve like a fox not according to some well-established lore of distress but immediately and impulsively, animal-like, just as Hecuba barks like a dog. Arabella approaches romance as a witness to the pure un-mixed truth of things as they are, a rigorous adherent to "the imperative of excessiveness and the claim to totality" (Luhmann 1986: 71). In *The What D'Ye Call It*, print is directly addressed in the company of things that have stopped being objects, and takes its place in the assemblage as a thing too. I ended the last chapter trying to suggest that still life along with fable and romance emphasizes this rise to the surface as a commitment to things not as symbols but as shapes, shadows, and colors that directly strike the eye. The strangely iconoclastic result is a picture confounded with what it reflects, a pleonasm of "thing" and thing, a shimmer announcing if not quite fully demonstrating the immediate visual equivalence of those two phenomena Hobbes believed to be distinct: the image and its cause. It is the pictorial equivalent of the echo-game in the play: "the experience, the experience" or "an innocent thing, an innocent thing."

I have been discussing this equivalence as a kind of accidental idolatry that takes place when persons, the products of a system of political representation, shed their civil function and engage with things more passionately and directly, personifying them and treating them as causes of their own effects. When for whatever reason the rules of representation on which persons depend are set aside, and what was owned may no longer be accounted for as property, then there is nothing so trivial or superficial that it cannot bid for the kind of singularity that distinguishes things capable of personification—whether it is a hay-rake, a cramp-ring, a tobacco box, breeches ("quite bran new"), or any of those other odd items that congregate around the condemned Peascod in *The What D'ye Call It*. In Gay's subsequent experiment with that kind of crisis in *The Beggar's Opera*, where everyone exists under the shadow of the gallows, persons are transformed into the measure of things, and consider themselves as fabular animals or birds whose mates are other creatures. Experience ceases to be what they shape for themselves, and emerges instead from the activity of things—literally the things—that at first surround them and then appear to happen to them. Similarly, when Captain Cook decided to quit his account of things that kept going missing in Polynesia—the chisel and the midshipman's hat—and chose instead to slake his curiosity on the mysteries of *tapu* and *mana*, he found himself inside the same zone of agency already occupied by European artifacts in the eyes of his hosts, who then worshipped him as a god before killing him.

I want to argue now that *The Rape of the Lock* moves in a similar direction by setting a clutter of things alongside a human figure that is treated from various angles as a thing too: the sum of her ornaments, the creature of cosmetic art, the synecdoche of her hair, or a candidate for neurasthenic transmogrification into a teapot, bottle, or pie. But from the start, Belinda is conceived also as an incarnate divinity whose visible tokens are present not just in the phials and boxes on her altar or even in the outlines of a handsome body, but more gloriously in the colors glancing from her clothes, skin, and eyes. Not just a creature of accidents, then, she is for a while personified and enjoys the triumph of self-coincidence, the hallmark alike of personified things and idols.

Pope's poem is filled with echoes of the *Metamorphoses*, and it is worth considering briefly the evolution of Ovidian metamorphosis from the early modern period to the Enlightenment—that is, from tales conveniently moralized into much more anarchic collisions of power and art—and comparing it with parallel developments in animal fable and still life. The less easily fable yielded to the schematic morals and often partisan reflections pinned underneath them, and the more daringly its exponents sifted the Machiavellian subtleties couched beneath its homely anecdotes, the more extraordinarily detailed its illustrations became, some accurate enough to be used for natural histories of plants, birds, and animals, as in the work of Wenceslaus Hollar, Francis Barlow, and William Bewick. The great illustrators of the nineteenth century, Gustave Doré and John Tenniel, cut their teeth on fables, and often harked back to these remarkable designs. Over the same period, still life escaped from the eschatological constraints of death, judgment, heaven, and hell which it had originally served to illustrate—cherries standing for paradise, strawberries for salvation, redcurrants for the incarnation of Christ, and gooseberries for his sufferings (Ebert-Schifferer 1999: 87)—and its exponents began to dwell instead on the evanescence of a peach's bloom, the dust on a plum, or the gleam of a dead animal's fur, as if the whole point of the exercise was to let the thing be seen as if for the first time in that particular shape and light, as if it had just happened. In the case of fables and still lifes, exquisite attention to detail does not refer to an antecedent reality or a socially valuable truth; it makes no serious allegorical claims at all, not even in a vanitas. It aims instead to capture the viewer's eye in the moment of being viewed. Often in the *Metamorphoses* this capture takes place in an oscillation between a figure and its reflection (Perseus and the Gorgon), or a struggle between one eye and another (Diana and Actaeon). In the story of Narcissus an eye observes itself, an image in the pool no different from that it prints upon the retina, at once what sees and what is seen. In *The Golden Ass*, Apuleius dramatizes the importance of sight, both as a pleasure and a danger, when Cupid looks at Psyche and wounds himself with one of his own arrows, self-cupidinizing, and Psyche, having gazed at him in the lamplight, does the same: cupidinized.

There is an oil and water-color sketch by Paul Klee of 1920 called *Die Büchse der Pandora als Stilleben* (figure 6). It shows a vase (the original "box") filled with flowers. On the side of the vase, a genital ornament or crack seems to emit a black vapor that curls into a rebus of pubic hair. It is also possible that the vase and the table on which it is standing function as the schematic outline of a woman's head and shoulders, in which case the pubic hair rises into what is merely hair, adjacent to the handles of the vase, now coiled either side of it, also like hair. Vase and hair, boxes and vanities, ornamental outsides and potentially shocking insides, all keyed to a notion of the feminine as trouble on a grand scale, is summed up by Klee as still life, a genre not notorious for its misogyny although certainly hospitable to certain kinds of fetish, as Laura Mulvey points out when talking of this very picture (Mulvey 1996: 54–6). What is happening in Klee's still life? Is something secret or uncanny being disclosed; is the box being opened, or opening itself? Is a woman turning into a thing? In fact, part of the contents of the vase-box is already on display as an arrangement of flowers. The vapor or hair blots out the central bloom by extending the genital design from which it originates, so that the trace of one inside (if that is what it is) is laid over another. The relation of hair to hair suggests also a link between the perfunctory signs of hair already framing the vaginal divide and this larger plume, as if to emphasize that the container and what it holds occupy not only the same physiological area but also the same plane. This is no smoky token of occult evil, then, but a game played upon the surface. As for the woman's head, it is part

Fig. 6. Paul Klee, *Pandora's Box as Still Life,* oil and watercolor on paper, 1920. Photo by Jens Ziehe; with permission from Nationalgalerie, Museum Berggruen, Staatliche Museen, Berlin, Germany

of the same game, obliterating the difference between what is to be seen and what pretends to be hidden. In Klee's picture, hair is an ornament on what can only ever be a surface. Any move in the direction of depth creates only the sprouting of more hair—not hair as sign or hair's referent— as one surface (the vase) merges with another, the paper on which it is represented. It is the oscillation between these two possibilities, of a surface conveyed to the eye both as an image and a material fact, that leads Klee to assign the name of still life to his picture.

The parallels between Klee's still life and Pope's *The Rape of the Lock* are strong, for in the poem too a woman's hair, confounded with her pubic hair, is implicated in a world of vanities that is continuous with the charming and fragile superficies of vases. So there is room to ask what further resemblances might bind the poem to what Svetlana Alpers calls this "benchmark genre" of painting, which she says is capable of rendering even history painting, landscape, and portraiture in the manner of still life (Alpers 2005: 33). Helen Deutsch has shrewdly noted how closely the sheer superficiality of Pope's poem resembles the *trompe l'oeil* effect of some still lifes (Deutsch 1996: 118). Along the same lines, I want to suggest that the oscillation of the eye between the view of a thing and the view of that view, between the image as reflection and the image as experience, is typical of generic still life and its optical counterpart, the camera obscura, and that it plays an important part in the arrangement of surfaces and the hollowing out of centers in *The Rape of the Lock*—so much so that scant basis remains for a satiric or commonsense commentary on things so superficial as to seem (as Baudrillard puts it) insolent in their insignificance (Baudrillard 1988: 54). It is all a matter of the eye's relation to what it sees. When a probed surface yields only more surface, and the heart itself is revealed as a "moving Toy-shop," its rhythm keeping time to the rotations of trivia in the world at large (1.100), there is no ulterior duty which levity neglects, and no hidden deficiency which vanity betrays: "If to her share some Female Errors fall,/ Look on her Face, and you'll forget 'em all" [2.17–18]). The only mistake to be made in this kind of world, and it is an egregious error, is to suppose that a thing or an idol contains a secret different from its outside, or that there is an occult meaning to which it silently gestures, when really there is nothing there but what is visible. Viewers of the interpreting stripe, like the baron, are really crude iconoclasts in disguise, bent on disfiguring the image in order to possess or destroy whatever hidden value they believe it contains. They are just the reverse of still life artists, who experiment with iconoclasm—stripping images of their coatings of liturgical or allegorical meanings until they are hollow, like their churches—in order to fashion idols whose sole content is the material and visible creature of which they are made (figure 7).

There is a semi-still life by Jan Weenix, called *Port de Mer*, that rehearses the temptations leading to the baron's mistake. It shows a lady standing between two men near a dockside (figure 8). One of the men is a huckster offering her trinkets for sale. She has turned away from him toward a gentleman-lover who holds up a mirror in which her reflection can be seen, and from that too the lady seems inclined to turn away. Caught between two temptations to vanity, the woman has nowhere to turn but the foreground, where a still life of fruits and game is laid out. Weenix's picture is a compendium of the issues raised by Pope in *The Rape of the Lock*, where the contents of a woman's dressing table, filled with ephemera and cosmetics, and topped by a mirror, become of concern to the men as well as the women of the poem. The men would like to see an easy transition from one sort of female vanity to another. First comes the consumption of the alluring commodities of worldwide trade ("all that Land and Sea afford" [1.11]) which deck out a female for the marriage market. These are followed by the lover's compliments, a ritual indulgence which precedes the removal of the woman from the protection of her father to

Fig. 7. Jan De Heem, *Still Life with Oysters and Grapes*, oil on panel, 1653. Museum Associates / LACMA, gift of The Ahmanson Foundation

that of her husband. Thus, she enters the market to purchase one sort of commodity in order that she might be purchased in turn as another.

Like Weenix's lady, however, Belinda has no inclination to regard her dressing table as this sort of trade route to marriage. But in turning aside from the proffered flatteries of trade and courtship and the narrative they jointly imply, her options are limited to the things that contingently fall within her purview. In *Port de Mer*, these are to be found in the clutter of the still life. Similarly, on the dressing table Belinda sees a muddle, "Puffs, Powders, Patches, Bibles, Billets-doux," and in the world at large she spots a disorderly mixture of kinds: "Men, Monkies, Lap-dogs, Parrots" (4.120). These medleys, which largely comprise the scenes of *The Rape of the Lock*, offer themselves to the female eye in the same way as the still life in *Port de Mer*. They present themselves as accidental variety, pleasing in its diversity and totally uninterpretable. Nothing in these clusters is differentiated by moral, economic, or practical value, and no meaning is attached to the relation between indifferent objects. Bibles are flanked by patches and billets-doux without any arch judgment being made: they are like the writing that is shown not to be read but to be viewed in *trompe l'oeil* paintings. Jews may kiss the cross that hangs on

Fig. 8. Jan Weenix, *Port de Mer*, oil on canvas. Photo credit: Réunion des Mu-sées Nationaux / Art Resource, NY

Belinda's neck, and infidels adore it, because its symbolic value is nil. Like the rarities which are collected, as Shaftesbury observed, for rarity's sake, these various things have gathered together solely for the sake of variety.

Weenix and Pope raise the possibility of value-free visual pleasure in a world where the prevailing assumptions are all on the side of trade, calculation, and marriage à la mode. They show how things and women may subsist without the government of prices, morals, husbands, and other instruments of intelligibility and social control, and how they may even obtain power for themselves by adapting their bodies to variations of fabric, color, and light. That this more eligible insignificance is not significant at some higher level is evident in the failure of the vanitas, at one time the focus of still lifes in the shape of the skull that measured the ephemerality of the material world against eternity. Introduced first by Clarissa and then the poet as a reminder to Belinda of the passage of time and her own mortality, these lessons are shown to be inapplicable to her view of her circumstances. Thalestris despises them and Belinda ignores them. Frail china jars are not icons of mutability, commodities for exchange, or storage containers. On their painted surface lies their charm, and the pleasure of the eye is all that they afford. Similarly, still life artists emphasized the surface of the thing and the surface of the work, turning even the vanitas into an occasion for superb technique, and letting the exquisite mottling of the skull, like the dimples in the glaze of a jar, identify a sensuous variation that is interesting for its own sake. Cornelis Gysbrecht painted pictures of the backs of pictures, demonstrating the thinness of painted illusion in another illusion just as thin (figure 9). When Pepys saw a flower-piece by Simon Verelst, he kept touching it to test its depth, and finding that it had none he was so far from being disappointed, he declared: "I was forced again and again to put my finger to it to feel whether my eyes were deceived or no. . . . I was never so pleased and surprised with any picture" (quoted in Chong and Kloek 1999: 262, 66). Svetlana Alpers says, "The sharpness of these depictions involves a kind of denial, an avoidance, a lack of interest in what lies beneath the surface of the paint" (Alpers 2005: 241). All that remains of the old vanitas in these pictures is the hint of disquiet or shock that qualifies the pleasurable experience of their viewers. Things emerge into the light from an intense darkness, charged with a radiance that corresponds to emptiness. "Is vitality or mortality the sovereign principle here?" asks Simon Schama of still life, without offering an answer (Schama 1993: 483). Hal Foster chracterises *trompe l'oeil* still lifes as "not alive, not dead, not useful, not useless . . . the pictorial effect is often one of deathly suspension or . . . eerie animation" (Foster 1993: 257).

In his *Remarks on Mr Pope's Rape of the Lock* (1728), John Dennis points astutely if impatiently to those aspects of the poem which most strongly resemble the distinctive qualities of still life. Although Pope claims to have a literary model for his piece in heroic poetry, Dennis argues that in fact it has none, for the heroine lacks any leading traits ("a Chimera, not a Character" [Dennis 1728: 11]), and there are no incidents of note save the cutting of the lock, which is then lost. The poem is filled with descriptions instead of episodes and ends with nothing resolved (9–10), so any resemblance it may have to epic action is arbitrary and unconvincing. Although the poet promises to treat general themes appropriate to heroic poetry (such as love and conflict), he deals in nothing but frivolous particulars (31). The machinery introduced so ceremoniously in the expanded five-canto version of the poem fails to organize a dramatic conflict or to promote an outcome, for these little gods are denied foreknowledge and, to make things worse, they desert their protégée at her moment of greatest danger (24–5). Dennis goes on to complain that occult lore is deployed as a kind of microscope ("the false Opticks of a

Fig. 9. Cornelius Gysbrechts, *Back of a Picture*, reverse side of framed painting—trompe l'oeil. Statens Museum for Kunst, Copenhagen, Denmark. Photo credit: Erich Lessing / Art Resource, NY

Rosicrucian Understanding") in order to exalt trifles to a specious importance (28). He points out that the extension of the machinery into the personifications of the allegory of the Cave of Spleen makes no sense and confounds the sequence of cause and effect (45). Since the little world of the poem lacks solid antecedents and a definite closure, he declares it to be deficient in the two articles of neoclassical verisimilitude, namely, the narrative (or "fable") and the moral. "It is a very <u>empty Trifle</u>, without any Solidity or *sensible Meaning*" (6). Dennis returns again and again to the theme of its emptiness. Pope, he says, "seems to take pains to bring *something* into a Conjunction Copulative with *nothing*, in order to beget *nothing*" (53). He sounds like Leontes, another impatient student of female idols, "Nor nothing have these nothings" (Shakespeare 1976: 22 [I.ii, 295]).

He contrasts *The Rape of the Lock* with Boileau's *Le Lutrin*, a mockepic of the travails of a pulpit to which Swift's *A Tale of a Tub* and *The Battle of the Books* are both indebted. Boileau's satire has a narrative filled with incidents. Dennis cites the midnight sortie to the vestry made by Lamour, Brontin, and Boirude, armed with tools to repair the wrecked pulpit. An owl that has roosted there makes them think that the pulpit has learned to speak; but when the bird flies off they resume their task and carry off the pulpit to the body of the church. While they are engaged in this work, their enemy the prelate has a dream in which the pulpit has become alive, and is rampant in his choir stall. The point about the dream and the mistake about the owl is that they are shown indisputably to be delusions. Pulpits are made by human labor and their placement affects passions and politics—human nature, in short—ensuring that the narrative has a human origin and a human end. The thing itself can never act or speak on its own behalf. In the ensuing battle in the bookshop, volumes turn into missiles because human feelings have become engaged, not because of any impetus found in calfskin and paper. If we needed a painterly parallel with *Le Lutrin*, we would find it in Rembrandt's *The Flayed Ox* (figure 10), where the subordination of the thing to human needs and human perceptions is expressed by the signs of the labor expended on it, both in the resemblance between the carcass and the frame in which it is suspended, and in the broad and undisguised brushstrokes with which the resemblance is achieved. The still life artist Johannes Torrentius, on the other hand, collected by Charles II, was so skillful at disguising his brushstrokes that he was imprisoned on a charge of sorcery (Chong and Kloek 1999: 132). In Pope's poem, this degree of art distinguishes what the eye can worship from what it can't. In the Cave of Spleen, the distinction is made grotesquely obvious, with former goddesses decayed into effigies and emblems of what they were, like the skulls in early still lifes.

Dennis is troubled by it. Belinda's beauty, he notices, is owing entirely to her toilette; as for her lock of hair it is almost totally artificial, the result of the application of bodkin, comb, essence, paper, curling tongs, and lead fillets. A natural beauty, Dennis affirms, "wants neither *Flounce*, nor *Furbelow*, nor *torturing Irons*, nor *Paper Durance*" (14). He cannot understand why Belinda, young and beautiful, is presented by Pope as if she were a kind of Lady Wishfort ("a decay'd superannuated Beauty" [13]) who (we remember) culls so many advantages from her dressing table that the slightest symptom of emotion threatens to shatter her appearance. "Paint, paint, paint," she cries after a rash frown has made her peel, "Thou must repair me, Foible . . . or I shall never keep up to my picture" (Congreve 1993: 1936 [3.6]). With nothing more substantial to Belinda than the supplements that color her face and mold her form, Dennis calls her "*an artificial daubing Jilt*" (18).

I think it is hard to disagree with Dennis on any score, for if one were to base the standard of good poetry on its attention to the deeply incised and ineradicable marks of character, one would find little to approve of here. Of the three leading duties of poets and artists—a proper regard to moral, character, and coloring in that order—Pope has concentrated

Fig. 10. Rembrandt, *Flayed Ox*, oil on wood, 1655, Louvre, Paris. Photo credit: Réunion des Musées Nationaux / Art Resource, NY

exclusively on the last. Consequently, in Belinda's world there is nothing to distinguish people from things except degrees of adoration: husbands and lapdogs, women and china vases, belles and barges compete to be viewed and adored. All accidents are measured on a plane defined by what is seen: even lost chastity is classed as a superficial impediment to the social whirl, equivalent to a coffee stain. Whether at the level of earth, hell, or heaven, there is no imperative preference to be made between angels, humans, and things, or any final judgment between the quality of their agency. In this miniature cosmogony, caskets unlock themselves, patchboxes fall without being touched, pins extend themselves in rows, fans clap, boxes breathe, gowns plait themselves, and sleeves are self-folding. In the preparation of coffee, berries crackle and mills turn round on their own to produce a liquid which, when drunk, acts on human beings by putting ideas into their heads. At all points, sylphs and people are confounded with things in their single-minded struggle to be seen. They all inhabit a space

> Where Wigs with Wigs, with Sword-knots Sword-knots strive,
> Beaus banish Beaus, and Coaches Coaches drive.
>
> (1.101-2)

Unlike the heroic synecdoches from which this couplet is derived ('Now Shield with Shield, with Helmet Helmet clos'd' (Tillotson 1962: 152 n.), these ones confound the difference between accoutrements and the men who wear them. Humans and things compete on the same ground, and the sylphs embody the luck of the competitors. In the underworld, the process is completed when people are so far affected by things they actually turn into things themselves. The Cave of Spleen is populated by bodies transformed into bottles and jars; while in the upper sphere of the moon, passions and intentions are preserved as useless remnants, *trompe l'oeils* of performative words that never worked:

> There broken Vows, and Death-bed Alms are found,
> And Lovers' Hearts with Ends of Riband bound;
> The Courtier's Promises, and Sick Man's Pray'rs,
> The Smiles of Harlots, and the Tears of Heirs.
>
> (5.117-20)

At all three levels, humankind is shown to be impotent if it relies only on its own faculties of will and speech. Vitality depends upon the experience of things mediated by semi-visible apparitions, and unless persons exchange or absorb the attributes of the artifacts around them, they have no salience in the scene and cannot take part in it. In Swift's *A Tale of a Tub* a fashionable person cries, "That Fellow has no Soul; where is his Shoulder-knot?" (Swift 1920: 82).

Hence the importance of the dressing table. With her cosmetics and instruments to hand, her servant by her side, Belinda as priestess beholds her image in the glass, an idol she worships more fervently with each offering made to it from the jars in front of her. According to Dennis she is Lady Wishfort, repairing herself by keeping up to her picture, composing an artificial image in the glass by adding paint to her face, and using jewels and crimped hair to frame it. In a parallel scene in *The Winter's Tale*, where Paulina acts as the priestess and Hermione as the idol, this is how the work of the artist is described: "He so near to Hermione hath done Hermione, that they say one would speak to her and stand in hope of answer" (V, ii, 99–101). When the painted statue fulfils these expectations by coming alive, however, art is no longer the ape of nature, it is identical with it; or, to use Paulina's word, the phenomenon it reveals is "singular," resembling nothing but itself. Pope plays with these alternatives by combining two Ovidian motifs: art as supplement and art as metamorphosis. Ovid's *The Art of Beauty* is really a georgic, with recipes for washes and rouge, interspersed with warnings of Narcissus's fate,

> For when the conscious maid her glass explores,
> And finds she's handsome, she herself adores.
> (Garth 1815: 661; ll. 44–5)

This is a genial example of those less attractive "remedies of love" that take the poet into ladies' dressing rooms to explore the secrets that makeup, perfumes, and dress all conspire to hide. The *ne plus ultra* of this genre is Swift's "A Beautiful Young Nymph going to Bed," a dreadful experiment in reverse makeup as each device and prosthesis falls away to reveal what is wrong with the woman's body, or missing from it. On the other hand, the story of Pygmalion's statue records how the visible creature of an image turns from stone into flesh not in imitation of a living model but by virtue of its own beauty. Indeed, the work is conceived and executed as different from all other female figures, singular and like nothing but itself, and its agency as a living being simply confirms its uniqueness.

For her part, Belinda is described both as repairing herself, and calling forth the wonders of her face; but the emphasis falls on the strangeness of what she looks at. In this regard her self-inspection is the reverse of Narcissus's. He eventually understands that the exquisite creature he sees in the pool is really his own reflection, whereas Belinda finds that the longer she gazes at the glass, the more wonderful and independent the image appears. The consummation of the ritual of self-adoration by means of paint is not a mask; it is a surface so intensely like her own that like a flask or an oyster in a still life it outglows (to borrow the phrase of Fielding's Parson Tickletext) what it resembles. A blush made of Spanish red is superior to the real thing, "purer," like eyes made "keener" by belladonna. The real face is manifest because its charms have been made to rise, not because its flaws have been found out underneath. Of Willem Kalf's *pronkstilleven* (still lifes of exquisite and expensive artifacts), Norman Bryson says they outdo the appeal and, as it happened, the price of the things they show—the Chinese porcelain, the nautilus shell goblet, the Venice glass, an oriental rug—by means of a virtuosity that makes the painted thing in every phenomenal sense richer than its actual counterpart (Bryson 1990: 126).

Belinda is herself just such a painter as Kalf, adapting the benchmark genre of still life to the self-portrait. And her dressing table is her studio. Alpers sees the studio as the central theater of operations in any variant of the genre of still life. There, a portion of the world can be transported and viewed experimentally. The conditions of the experiment are closely monitored by the artist, who displays the things to be observed on a table and directs the angle of the light that will illuminate them (figure 11). These things are not portable property under the absolute dominion of an owner. As Alpers puts it, "the objects . . . put pressure on or exact something from the painter who has retired there. . . . I refer to the possibility of the painter representing the perception of a thing . . . in such a way as to encourage the mind to dwell on . . . the painter's experience of an object as coming into its own" (Alpers 2005: 27). Thus, Cezanne's still life of a landscape is reported by him as the experience of a landscape that "reflects on itself, is humanized, thinks itself in me. I objectify it, project it" (Paul Cezanne, quoted in Alpers 2005: 44). Alpers cites Peter Galison's example of transformational experimental science, namely, Charles Wilson's cloud chamber experiment at the Cavendish Laboratory, which not only contrived to imitate the action of clouds in the real world, "the really beautiful appearance of these clouds," but produced real things which had never been seen before: wonderful subatomic particles that behaved equally like matter and like light (Alpers 42–3; Galison 1997: 105–13). In Belinda's case, the reflection of her face runs parallel with the clouds, and the idol she worships runs parallel with the mysterious particles. Her studio experiment produces an icon that comes into its own not because it is looked at, but because it looks back at its model looking at it, and enjoys the shimmer of difference.

The experimental machine most apt for illustrating still life in general and benchmarked landscape in particular is the camera obscura, for it brings a portion of the living world into a studio space for inspection and introduces the possibility of its coming into its own. When John Gay thought of the camera obscura, he did not imagine it like this. In his poem *The Fan*, a fable about virtue and common sense finding a way through the dazzling perplexities of the fashionable world, the fan is conceived

Fig. 11. Jan De Heem and David Teniers, Artist in his Studio, oil on oak panel, 1643. Museum Associates / LACMA, gift of H. F. Ahmanson and Company in memory of Howard A. Ahmanson

by Venus as a machine, "this fantastic engine" (Gay 1974: 1.44) whose purpose is not to multiply the artifice of patches, pulville, pins, and paint, but to focus and limit it. Minerva agrees with Venus, and compares the fan-machine to another engine, the camera obscura, whose virtue is to show the world exactly as it is:

> Thus have I seen woods, hills, and dales appear,
> Flocks graze the plains, birds wing the silent air.
> In darken'd rooms, where light can only pass
> Through the small circle of a convex glass.

(iii. 15–20)

The fan as camera obscura will show the authentic and tragic outcomes of vanity, pride, and self-love.

> Let vain Narcissus warn each female breast,
> That beauty's but a transient good at best,

> Like flow'rs it withers with th'advancing year,
> And age like winter robs the blooming fair.
>
> (ii. 127–30)

Strephon gives Corinna this fan, a portable hybrid of a camera obscura and a vanitas, whereupon she corrects the errors of her heart, and they get married. The truth of the fable has to be a moral one—for Gay as well as for Dennis—and the art of composition and synthesis which provides the vehicle of the moral brings the indiscipline of social art into symmetry with natural order ("woods, hills, and dales"). The particulars of modern life must yield to this sort of synthesis, or the picture will scatter into unrelated fragments, like a broken China vase.

It is clear that Pope's notion of the realism of the camera obscura is far more extensive and less convenient than Gay's. Twice in the course of his poem he introduces a moral similar to Minerva's, first with Clarissa's commentary on the rape, then in the Ovidian compliment to Belinda at the end. Like Minerva's, they are variations on the vanitas and warn the heroine of her own mortality. Clarissa recites what Dennis would have expected to be the moral of the poem, actually a sentiment from Ovid's *The Art of Beauty*, slightly expanded:

> But since, alas! frail Beauty must decay,
> Curl'd or uncurl'd, since Locks will turn to grey.
> Since painted, or not painted, all shall fade,
> And she who scorns a Man, must die a Maid;
> What then remains, but well our Pow'r to use,
> And keep good Humour still whate'er we lose?
>
> (5.25–30; see *Art of Beauty* ll. 62–3)

That the poem will not sustain this level of moral realism is an index of the degree of "pictorial ambiguity" (Alpers 2005: 27) in the composition. It begins with Belinda in front of the glass, studying her face as she makes it up into an idol. I have said this is not narcissism, nor is it the disguise or discovery of female weakness. To be faithful to the model of dressing table as studio, and painting as still life, her cosmetic art has to be construed as interplay between the real and the artificial in which the artificial acquires a material reality of its own, even though it may have begun by offering to imitate the other. Thus, in Galison's example of the Cavendish experiment there are clouds *and* particles, the reproduction and a new phenomenon; in Kalf's *pronkstilleven* there is paint like priceless things and things rendered in priceless paint. "[It] seemd the waves were into yvory;/ Or yvory into the waves were sent," wrote Spenser of the carved gate of the Bower of Bliss, no friend to such effects (Spenser 1993: 2.12.45, ll. 399–400). Belinda's face experimentally displayed in the frame of the mirror exacts from her as artist a still life painted on skin that doubles as the original of the image in the glass and as the canvas on which that image is laid. It is a species of pictorial ambiguity that begs comparison with Gysbrecht's pictures of the backs of pictures, where the stuff that lies behind the picture comes to the surface of it, and vice versa, in a painterly *tour de force*. Let us say then that the sight of Belinda's image in the glass at the dressing table puts pressure on her to make it up, to paint an image of that image capable of coming into its own.

The distancing effect of such a reflection resembles Roxana's experience in front of a mirror. After the prince has fastened a necklace of diamonds around her neck, she remembers: "I was all on fire with the Sight, and began to wonder what it was that was coming to me," as if her reflection were another person with a momentum of its own (Defoe 1981: 73). The closest analogy in materialist philosophy is Lucretius's idea of the film, rind or skin of things, simulacra of real things infinitesimally thin, which fly out from them in a steady stream, literally striking the eyes of the viewer, so that experience is formed from the successive blows of an endless stream of images. Belinda's image has this force. When it is darted at her spectators, they receive the impression as an impact or a blow. Her eyes, made up to flash more brilliantly than the originals, do not *meet* the eyes of her spectators, they *strike* them like the sun (2.13). "Therefore it happens that where we turn our sight, there all things strike upon it with shape and colour" (Lucretius 1997: 297 [4.243]). According to Lucretius, we see an image not because its shadow passes through the portal of the eye to an internal receptor, but because the eye, being constantly struck upon its surface by the material films thrown from the image, is compelled to see it; and without those blows, it would see nothing. Swift was thinking of this process when he imagined the flappers in Laputa, who strike the ears and eyes of their clients that they might hear and see.

Alfred Gell uses Lucretius's doctrine of physical emanations to account for the energy radiating from Polynesian gods, who need very careful wrapping and unwrapping (*pa'iatua*) if their worshippers are to be best served and not harmed. Similarly, the gods of Egypt began their day at their toilet, being prepared for public display by being ritually wrapped in cloths of white, green, red, and brown, and their features carefully painted green and black (Gell 1998: 104, 11, 134). As for the self-identity of personifications and gods, the quality of singularity which makes them solely like themselves, it is variously observed: for instance, in the god A'a of the Austral Islands who is revealed sprouting miniature images of himself all over his surface, and in the *vierges ouvrantes* of Europe, figures of Mary and the infant Jesus that opened up to reveal God, the Son and the Holy Ghost inside: "the Trinity in their abdomen, as if [it] assumed flesh in the Virgin" (142). It is notable that these images who wear their self-similarity so clearly on their surfaces attracted iconoclastic violence. Very few of the *vierges ouvrantes* remain in existence, having been thought to encourage idolatry and even necromancy; as for A'a's fellow deities, they were destroyed by agents of the London Missionary Society (137). However, their capacity for self-reproduction, which Gell compares with the replications of fractal geometry, is distinctly non-symbolic. Gell says, "The essence of idolatry is that it permits real physical interactions to take place between persons and divinities. To treat such interactions as symbolic is to miss the point" (135).

Belinda's image takes to the outdoors not like the wigs, sword-knots, and coaches that promiscuously throng the public walks, haphazardly striving for the advantage of being seen; she is conducted in a vehicle or ark that Hobbes names the *ferculum* (Hobbes 1996: 456). Pope puns on the relationship between the container and its content, as if to emphasize the self-identity of glorious nothing as Belinda is launched upon the Thames: "But now secure the painted Vessel glides" (2.46). Apart from that pun, there is no figurative play on "painted Vessel." The world of the poem allows no natural coign of vantage from which it may be called a "painted" vessel or a painted "vessel," or for that matter "a 'painted vessel.'" There are no whited sepulchres or daubing jilts here. Pope means literally what Gay offers only ironically when he writes of a china jar and a woman, "How white, how polish'd is their skin,/ And valu'd most when only seen!" (Gay 1974: 1.293 [l. 37–8]). When Garth draws this sort of parallel between a female and a thing in *The Dispensary*, comparing a grieving woman with an animate jewel, for example—"How lately did this celebrated Thing, Blaze in the Box, and sparkle in the Ring" (Garth 1699: 88)—her superficiality is reproached with a thingness edging in a humiliating way toward the genital. This is more explicit when Etherege disparages the ornaments of an Austrian countess:

> The Thing that wears this glitt'ring Pomp
> Is but a tawdry ill-bred Ramp.
>
> (Etherege in Dryden 1702: 225)

There is a large vein of misogynist satire in the 1690s which tackles female artifice in the harshest terms as a Pandora's box, as in this paraphrase of Virgil's fourth eclogue published in Dryden's *Sylvae*:

> Pomatums, Washes, Paints, Perfumes they use,
> And never think they can be too profuse.
> False Shapes, false colour'd Locks they wear,
> False Smiles, and Looks more false than is their Hair.

> Thus they, like Actors 'till the Play is done,
> Have nothing on that they can call their own.
>
> (Dryden 1702: 221)

Shaftesbury directly equates women's devotion to the false appearances of fashion with the effeminacy of men who delight in still lifes, "So that whilst we look on paintings with the same eyes as we view commonly the rich stuffs and coloured silks worn by our Ladys ... we must of necessity be effeminate in our Taste and utterly set wrong as to all Judgment and Knowledge in the kind" (cited in Bryson 1990: 177). Presumably he refers to viewers of pictures who are struck with such a stream of simulacra that they are overwhelmed by it, and whose experience is therefore feminine because it is passive.

Pope's view differs widely from Shaftesbury's, and for that matter Swift's in the section on madness in *A Tale of a Tub*, where he praises with grave irony the optical effects of reflecting surfaces. It is evident in Pope's treatment of light, to whose effects he is remarkably susceptible, particularly when its beams are disheveled and breaking out in iridescent gleams, that he is entranced by rainbow colors. This is the element in which the sylphs flourish, those minor deities who are the force behind the subatomic effects in Pope's beautiful clouds, half light and half form, their job to redeem the painted vessel from the least hint that it might be jejune:

> Loose to the Wind their airy Garments flew,
> Thin glitt'ring Textures of the filmy Dew;
> Dipt in the richest Tincture of the Skies,
> Where Light disports in ever-mingling Dies,
> While ev'ry Beam new transient Colours flings,
> Colours that change whene'er they wave their Wings.
>
> (Pope 1963: 2.63–68)

Descriptions like these invite the reader to observe that Pope's camera obscura works equally well as a kaleidoscope or a magic lantern to the extent it reflects nothing that is not already made up, and that what it composes is already the stuff of composition. In Pope's hands, the image is always in the process of coming into its own, and its movements betray no trace of unaccommodated nature or of time, just the self-activity of things that are no longer property. Except for the failed attempts at a vanitas by Clarissa and the poet, no space is made in his camera obscura for the implied observer of the image, capable critically of distinguishing art from nature and the observer from the world (see Crary 1992: 38). The metaphor of the *Epistle to Burlington* that has nature painting as the landscape artist plants (l.64) is literalized in *The Rape of the Lock* in respect of colors that are laid on the surface of a moving image, starting in the dressing room. All nature then becomes a toilette. The sky is a rotating prism or a paintbox, the earth a palette. The iridescence of vapor, like the spontaneity of a blush or the lightning darting from an eye, has already been appropriated by art, and improved into an autonomy that looks natural. The spectrum of colors visible for an instant in the spume blown from the surface of the river is reflected through "the false Opticks" of the sylph machines, rebounded from a rainbow and repeated by the flowers. Alpers says that in his bare interiors of Dutch churches, Pieter Saenredam gives us not views of architecture, but views of architecture viewed; so Pope gives us paintings of pictures being painted.

By a means of such improvements in art, everything is brought to the surface and all things are moved by *cosmetic* power. The process begins at the dressing table, where Belinda paints her own portrait on her skin. Then come the sylphs who add paint to paint, drawing "fresh Colours from the vernal Flow'rs" and borrowing tints from "Rainbows ere they drop in Show'rs" (2.94–5). Finally, there is the poet's painting of the painters of paint, the amazing description of airy things whose fluid bodies are "half-dissolv'd in Light" (2.62). At every stage in these successive applications of paint, the result is beautiful: Belinda's face, her clothes, the light that sparkles from her ornaments and glows in her skin. The effect may be compared with Kalf's *pronkstilleven* inasmuch as the brilliance of the image entirely supplants its model, leaving a hollow where the flesh-and-blood Belinda might once have stood (Bryson 1990: 126). Roland Barthes says of Saenredam's butterscotch churches, "Never has nothingness been so confident" (Barthes 1988: 106; also, see figure 12). The same sensation provoked Dennis to accuse Pope of coupling everything with nothing in his poem. Hazlitt felt this too, but with more delight: "The Rape of the Lock is the most exquisite specimen of filigree work ever invented. It is admirable in proportion as it is made of nothing" (Hazlitt 1902: 5.72; Deutsch 1996: 67).

Addison describes the experiment of the camera obscura and gives some hints on how its images are to be viewed. "The prettiest Landskip I ever saw, was one drawn on the Walls of a dark Room, which stood opposite on one side to a navigable River, and on the other to a Park . . . I must confess, the Novelty of such a Sight may be one occasion of its Pleasantness to the Imagination, but certainly the chief Reason is its near Resemblance to Nature, as it does not only, like other Pictures, give the Colour and Figure, but the Motion of the Things it represents" (*Spectator* 414). He compares this effect to accidental landscapes found in veins of marble, and says that our pleasure in them arises from a double principle: "the Effect of Design in what we call the Works of Chance" (ibid.). Later in the century, Horace Walpole coined the word serendipity to denote a

Fig. 12. Pieter Saenredam, *Interior of the Mariakerk*, Utrecht, oil on panel,
1651. Museum Associates / LACMA, Gift of Mr. and Mrs. Edward W. Carter

variant of the double principle, "making discoveries, by accident and sagacity, of things which [one was] not in quest of" (Walpole 1937–83: 20: 407). Addison was fascinated by the binocular possibilities of accident combined with sagacity. In his notes on Ovid he applies it to the picture of the rape of Europa described in the story of Arachne, where in his opinion the scene appears to better advantage than when it is first told at the end of the second book of the *Metamorphoses*. It is typical of the Roman poets, he says, "to take hold of all opportunities to describe the picture of any place or action, which they generally do better than they could the place of action itself; because in the description of a picture you have a double subject before you, either to describe the picture itself, or what is represented in it" (Addison 1765: 1.284). The camera obscura comes closest to turning all of nature into a picture, where everything can be viewed as real and as painted, just as the haha was a device that represented the whole landscape to Walpole's eye as a garden and as nature.

It is clear that Addison's double principle is adapted from *ekphrases* such as the two *xenia* or still lifes given by the elder Philostratus in his *Imagines*, where figs are forever bursting and apples never stop blushing, and the viewer is poised between visual experiences which seem to derive equally from the actuality of real things and the techniques of the brush (Philostratus 2000: 11.31; 2.26; Bryson 1990: 17ff.). Bryson draws two important and related conclusions from Philostratus. The first is that the fruits in the *xenia* seem self-impelled ("You will say that their redness has not been put on from outside, but has bloomed from within" [Philostratus 2000 1.31; 125]), rather like the fruits that snare the poet's feet in Marvell's *The Garden*. The second is that this is a genre at the furthest remove from narrative. Nothing happens in the picture, the picture happens to us. It is very difficult to sustain the balance required for this degree of pictorial ambiguity, evident from Homer's *ekphrasis* of Achilles's shield, or Keats's of the Grecian urn, because a picture of frozen time always tempts the viewer to insert the human interest and finish the story, at the same time changing the tense from the present historic to the past. The same difficulties confront God in *Paradise Lost* when treating his creation simultaneously as a perfect thing suspended in eternity and as an imperfect one traveling through time. The issue is advertised at the beginning of the second canto, "But now secure the painted vessel glides" (2.47). Now, but not always.

Before advancing further on that line, I want to return to the idol of Belinda. Having been made up as an image, coming into its own and moving through the world in its vehicle or ferculum, what was Belinda—a person responsible for her own story, or a character in someone else's—is now a cosmetic film subsisting in its own media of vapor, pigment, and light. The "own" this idol comes into has nothing to do with property or identity, rather with the aura and glamour of an apparition or living picture. If we claim an interest in the world in which that film keeps projecting itself, striking our eyes and making us see it, that is a matter of no concern to the idol. Its radiance is indifferent to what its spectators desire ("Favours to none, to all she Smiles extends, Oft She rejects, but never once offends./ Bright as the Sun, her Eyes the Gazers strike,/ And, like the Sun, they shine on all alike"[2.2.13–14]). They experience it, it doesn't experience them. Addison says, "The Intention of the Idol . . . is quite contrary to the wishes of the Idolater; as the one desires to confine the Idol to himself, the whole Business and Ambition of the other is to multiply Adorers" (Addison 1909: 1.278; *Spectator* 73).

Writing about this poem, Charles Gildon, otherwise so alert to the sense of things, became irked by this example of thingly independence, and was impatient with its ambiguity. Comparing Pope with modern authors and grotesque painters, he lumped them together as literalists and nonsense-mongers: "To find a Likeness in their Works, is to find the greatest Fault imaginable. A Natural Connexion is a Slur, a Coherence, a Design, a meaning, is against their Purpose, and destroys the very Spirit and Genius of their Workmanship" (Gildon 1714: 4–5). It is clear that he finds the cosmetic layering of the poem to be its prime defect, since it prevents a judgment based on nature, or the real, and assigns all value to art, or what Mandeville called with equal contempt the fashion of a thing. Gildon's reaction is to spoil the surface of the poem by proclaiming what he believes lies beneath it: "Thus a Friend of mine has lately, with an admirable Address, made Arabebella F—m—r prefer the Locks of her Poll, to her Locks of another more sacred and secret Part." And he ends with a lewd variation of the drinking-club toast to the best in Christendom: "Here's a Health to the Lock least sight" (Gildon 1714: 43, 48). Similarly, when Polixenes confronts the puzzling perfection of Perdita in *The Winter's Tale*, his immediate reaction is to have her flayed and show the world what lies beneath, a popular mode of torture in this play: "I'll have thy beauty scratch'd with briers" (IV, iv, 426).

Gildon is never tempted into idolatry, but otherwise his iconoclasm is very similar to the baron's. He and Clarissa refuse to regard a painted surface simply as a treat for the eye. They want to know what it represents and what it means. It is evident from the baron's hecatomb of gloves and garters that he regards the lock as a trophy of sexual triumph, even before he cuts it off. Regardless of whether the triumph has actually taken place, or whether he likes looking at the lock, or whether he likes Belinda, to wear it on his finger would be to have the world understand it as an authentic sign of his prowess, the emblem of the genital "thing." Even Thalestris believes this to be the case. All the destructive impulses in the poem arise from this desire to symbolize and to interpret things—locks, motions, looks, and eyes. Such idolatry stands in contrast to the still life iconoclasm of Belinda and the sylphs, who set up no images on the whirligig of fashion that signify or represent any occult intention or meaning. Pope travestied the tendency to read these images as signs when, as Esdras Barnivelt, he published *A Key to the Lock*. The sparkling cross on a white breast alludes, Barnivelt says, "to the Ancient Name of Albion, from her white Cliffs, and to the Cross, which is the Ensign of England" (Pope 1723: 13). Later he contradicts himself, arguing that Belinda represents the Whore of Babylon, and the cross on her breast, "the Ensign of Popery" (30). But her dressing table is worst of all, as it figures a Catholic altar and "plainly denotes Image Worship"' (29).

The history of still life shows how likely it is that an art founded in iconoclasm will attract the charge of idolatry, partly because its exponents were so alert to the equivocal status of images in the culture around them, and partly because the very modesty of their enterprise of representing things just as they are struck critics as an extravagant and portentous literalism. Michelangelo said, "In Flanders they paint with a view to external exactness . . . and all this, though it pleases some persons, is done without reason or art" (cited in Alpers 1983: xxiii). For his part, Pieter Saenredam publicly mocked the discovery in Haarlem of Catholic icons in the bolls of rotten trees, and felt most confident contemplating the interiors of churches largely empty of visual aids to worship (Alpers 1983: 80–81). Marinus van Reymerswael, a brilliant painter of velvet and brocade, eventually took revenge on images for coming into their own, and started to destroy them (Schama 1993: 485). The "enabling void" left in the naves of churches during the Reformation in northern Europe, where altars were stripped to leave an "unadorned nowhere," were the forerunners of the bare tables on which fruit, flowers, and fish are set in the still life artist's studio (Koerner 2004: 84, 88). That blank background of the table and the darkness behind it, from which all still life emerges, lit only from the left, suggests to many viewers a disquieting absence not just of symbols and allegories but of the human itself. Bryson says these pictures have "the look of the world before our entry into it or after our departure from it" (Bryson 1990: 143). This is the authentic response to an image that has come into its own and strikes our eyes. A Roman Catholic writing a poem about members of the Catholic aristocracy, Pope knew the risks he took of having cynosures interpreted as symbols. Dennis's discovery of the emptiness of the poem was really Pope's vindication. It kept its primary idol within the pale of Hobbes's definition: the material form of the imagination, but of nothing else (Hobbes 1996: 445). It taught Pope a valuable lesson first broached by Andreas Karlstadt, author of a book called *On the Removal of Images*, where he wrote, "What good things could the laity learn from images? Certainly you must say that one learns from them nothing but the life and the suffering of the flesh and that they do not lead further than the flesh. More they cannot do" (Koerner 2004: 138).

Bruno Latour has invented the word "iconoclash" to name the curious resemblance between those who build images and those who tear them down. He is fascinated by the equivocal fables to be found in Aesop and La Fontaine where formerly inert idols take revenge on their destroyers, or where they are found to be worth worshipping only after they have been broken up as useless lumber (Latour and Weibel 2002: 23). Joseph Koerner shows an anonymous crucifixion (*St Bernard embracing the Crucifix*, c. 1340) where the blood comes from Christ's body in such copious gouts and streams they seem to be canceling the image of which they are a part. On the other hand, *The Allegory of Iconoclasm* by Marcus Gheeraets the Elder (1566) shows a procession of people climbing up a road winding round a mountain, breaking images as they go; but the whole composition forms itself into the picture of a howling monk, thus (as Koerner says) performing and undoing defacement at the same time (Koerner 2002: 201; 2004: 113). It is evident that some iconoclasts understood the difference between the view of an image and the view of the view. The assailant of Master Seewald's *Mass of St Gregory* left the images shown within the picture whole, damaging only the eyes of the figures looking at them (Koerner 2004: 101).

Perhaps Addison was responding to the implied correspondence between his double principle and the paradox of the iconoclash when he selected Ovid's second attempt at representing the rape of Europa as a particularly good example of it. The story of Arachne's tapestry, where the episode is shown not as an event but an image, allows him (he says) to consider the scene either as a moment in a narrative or as a picture, or as both together. But of course the story concludes with the account of the destruction of the image by Minerva, outraged at the effrontery of a mortal female who has dared not only to represent this undignified passage in Jove's long history of adultery, but to do it so well that Minerva's own picture in honor of the gods, woven at the same time, is put in the shade. So she tears Arachne's work into pieces, wounds her face with a weaver's comb, and then transforms her into a spider. Setting aside the chagrin of the goddess, it is possible to see that Arachne's crime is to have made such a fine image that it reverses her relation to the gods, who appear now as her creatures, the product of her own invention and the work of her own hands and not (as indeed Minerva was in the art of weaving) her model. The story of the rape of a mortal is turned around too, for with Europa, Jove had the initiative and worked as an artist on himself ("His hornes were small, but yet so fine as that ye would have thought/ They had been made by cunning hand or out of waxe bene wrought" [Ovid 2000:

2.1069–70; 59–60]). Now under Arachne's hands he is the object of a finer art ("A swimming Bull, a swelling Sea, so lively had she wrought,/ That Bull and Sea in very deede ye might them well have thought" [Golding 2000: 6. 128–9; 139]). As Latour says, "either you make, or you are made" (Latour and Weibel 2002: 23). Addison considers the presentation of this scene typical of another habit of Roman poets who, when they describe pictures, "bring together two such thwarting ideas, by making one part of their descriptions to relate to the representation, and the other to the thing that is represented" (Addison 1765: 1.287–8). I think he means that something represented as very fine is actually treated as something very terrible. This could refer to the aesthetic triumph of Arachne's picture and the violent deed it represents; or it might instead embrace the picture itself, regardless of what it shows, along with the spiteful act of a goddess displeased by its fineness and the pride of its maker; or Addison might be standing farther back and uniting the ideas of an impious artistic genius and the punishment it is bound to call down, "*rupit pictas, caelestia crimina*" (Ovid 1999: 6.131; Addison 1765: 1.288).

Velázquez's painting of the contest between Arachne and Minerva, *Las Hilanderas*, turns this metamorphosis back on itself once again. Svetlana Alpers has offered an extraordinary reading of this picture which is centered, like Pope's poem, upon a rape; and which again, like the poem, places the heroic dimension in the background so that women's work can come to the front, a theme well represented in Velázquez's work (figure 13). She shows how he has ordered the composition into four artificially lit interiors or stages, each inside the other, anticipating some of the effects of Philippe de Loutherbourg's eidophysikon. At the farthest point from the viewer is a scene of the rape of Europa. It is a tapestry represented inside a tapestry showing Minerva confronting Arachne, who is standing in front of her work. Arachne's picture is based by Velázquez on Rubens's copy of Titian's painting, *The Rape of Europa*, but the scene enclosing it is a copy of Rubens's own *Minerva and Arachne*, showing the goddess armed and about to strike the offending artist. In front of this, three court ladies are standing, one of whom seems to be modeling for an invisible painter the figure of Arachne as she appears in the picture. The fourth and final frame includes five women, two (*las hilanderas*) actively engaged in spinning and reeling the threads destined for tapestrywork, with three others busy at ancillary tasks (carding, gathering hanks of spun wool, bearing yarn to the dyer). Simplified, the arrangement is like a mirror, with five working women over against five heroic, courtly, or divine women. Alpers leaves open the possibility of whether parallels can be drawn between the woman in the foreground at the spinning wheel and Minerva in the background, and between her companion reeling the thread and Arachne. She is more fascinated by the loosening

Fig. 13. Diego Velasquez, *Las Hilanderas*, canvas, 1657. Museo del Prado, Madrid, Spain. Photo credit: Erich Lessing / Art Resource, NY

of Velázquez's style as his attention moves from the deepest part of the picture to the last frame, nearest the surface as it were, where his brushwork is free of all imitative constraints, spontaneous and voluptuous, and the unconstrained gestures of the women (particularly she who holds the thread) respond to the freedom of the artist (Alpers 2005: 158). Altogether the effect, says Alpers, is one of peculiarly vivid over-painting, "and instead of making art out of life, [Velázquez] draws life out of art" (177). As for Arachne, she is redeemed from her Ovidian fate. Out of the unfolding scenes of her punishment and humiliation the materials and skills of her art are reassembled, and once again the colored thread is ready for the loom, in which tapestries of divinities maltreating mortal women have already been shown and will be shown again. In this sense, Titian and Rubens help figure the three levels of metamorphosis: Jove into bull, Arachne into spider, spider into woman.

Belinda's dressing table, situated between the social world on one hand and the iridescent sylphs on the other, provokes a different sequence of metamorphoses: woman into image, image into goddess, and goddess into woman. Pope's finds it more difficult than Velázquez to work his way back to the freedom of the studio where those who have struck the eyes of the gazers with their eyes, and then been assaulted by a spectator, can recover the initiative and come into their own again. When the poet tells Belinda that she will die, but that her consolation must be the translation of her lost lock of hair to the heavenly body, it is generally understood as an extravagant compliment designed to ease the pain of being returned from still life to a narrative where she is subordinate to a greater power, and subject to lessons of morality and mortality. But if Velázquez's investment in paint is equal to Arachne's in colored thread, so is Pope's investment in words equal to Belinda's in cosmetics. To transform the circumstances of disfigurement into occasions of fresh triumphs of representation is the common cause of idols and those who make them up. The enemy defined by the sylphs is "MAN," both in the sense of a masculine agent and a representative of the species. The antithesis of the rape inflicted on women by iconoclastic MAN is painting, and the antithesis of MAN the false idolater is a lock of woman's hair, a thing that comes into its own purely as its own, and which cannot be symbolized or possessed without entirely disappearing. The lock is the fractal repetition of an idol that disintegrates as soon as ever it is supposed to be more than what it is; but if it can be restored to divinity by being transposed to the heavens in a poetic gesture as lavish as it is pointless, no less can the image on whose self-similarity the lock depended. To that extent it resembles Bottom's ass's head, the idol of all the iconic pairings of incongruous ideas of which the poetic imagination is capable, and of which no one may speak long without becoming preposterous.

PART TWO

Persons and Fictions

CHAPTER 6

Locke's Wild Fancies

> Thought ... expresses exactly what is, precisely because
> what is is never quite as thought expresses it. Essential to it
> is an element of exaggeration, of overshooting the object,
> of self-detachment from the weight of the factual.... Thus
> every thought resembles play ... as soon as thought repudi-
> ates its inviolable distance and tries with a thousand subtle
> arguments to prove its literal correctness, it founders.
>
> —Theodor Adorno, *Minima Moralia*

The Baconian roots of experimental science thrived upon an accumulation of real data, obtained in a set of controlled circumstances and communicated to the mind by means of sensations. No matter how partial
or private these sense-impressions may have seemed at the outset of the
work, by being properly assembled and arranged, they emerged as empirical knowledge which promised not only an accurate contemplation
of God's creation but also effective action within it. Once the calendars
of learning were properly distributed and inventoried nothing, even immortality itself, was held by Bacon to be impossible. The experimental
pioneers would mine for causes, and the smiths would hammer out the
effects. So Bacon cautions his reader, "I would not have such knowledges
... to be thought things imaginative or in the air ... but things of bulk
and mass" (Bacon 1965: 202).

At all points in their program, Bacon and his followers sought to distinguish between the legitimate ambitions of experimental knowledge and
"high and vaporous imaginations" (101). He compares degenerate natural magic with Arthurian romance, and solid learning with Caesar's *Commentaries* (100). He named each of the four chief errors in science *idols* in
order to underline their lack of solidity. In his dedication of *Micrographia*
to the Royal Society, Robert Hooke set strength of imagination to one
side in favor of "a sincere Hand, and a faithful Eye," for (he added), "The
Truth is, the Science of Nature has been already too long made only a
work of the Brain and the Fancy" (Hooke 2003: [iv–v]). Yet it is the case
that the boundaries of the real were habitually traversed and negotiated
by imagination. When the unaccountable passages of the experimental
process itself failed of explanations, the nature and movement of "things

of bulk and mass" were referred to the provisional assumptions eyewitnesses were forced to make, often cast in the form of nonhuman agents. Bacon himself read the Greek myths as allegorical summaries of knowledge, and warned his reader against the corruptions of vaporous learning by reciting the fable of Ixion, who coupled with a cloud instead of Juno, bringing forth chimerae and monsters. Given the incomplete state of knowledge, credible fictions were the only defense against vaporous fancies. One had to imagine what one could not see or demonstrate; and probability, not certainty, was the guide.

I want to argue that even in the zone of experimental science, the desire for the absolute possession of a thing—in this case the knowledge of its corpuscular reality—sends the enquirer into a world that can only be reported as a sort of romance: alien, magical, and wild where things move according to strange impulses toward outcomes that were never predictable. Searching for absolute cognitive possession of a thing, the scientist discovers the very opposite, namely, its autonomous movement under influences he cannot account for. The same paradox has been explored in the sphere of illicit exchange in the second chapter and was advertised in the first, where the immanence of perception and the activity of things (taught by Bacon among others) reveal the thinness of the human subject and the thingliness of what it seeks. In the three examples of idols supplied by Captain Cook, Bottom, and Belinda, the ratio of imagination to real knowledge determines the likelihood of a metamorphosis of the human into the nonhuman, and of the thing into something active and intelligent.

John Locke thought the best method of controlling such anarchy and limiting the damage it did to human identity was to have a firm grasp upon (or perhaps firmly to be grasped by) an agent of the self he called the person, a figure capable of organizing the irregular products of experience into a credible semblance of identity and reality. This chapter aims to uncover the seeds of imagination in the production of knowledge, and to trace from that a forking model of identity that will dominate the discussions of the remaining chapters of this book. One prong of the fork points out a personate relation of the self to the real favored by Locke and, under a rather different rubric, by Hobbes too. The other locates a much more isolated individual whose experience under certain circumstances resembles the serene and absolute certainty of the Cartesian soul, and under others the stress of a labile and inarticulate singleton trying to survive in an uncomfortable state of nature. If to the relative uniformity of the first kind of identity we assign the name of *person*, the title of the social artifact needed for the structure of delegation on which civil society depends, then the isolation and unpredictability of the second kind is better named an *author*, also called by Hobbes the natural person, a figure unaligned with any civil obligation. From these two branches of a personate and a nonpersonate self emerge on the one hand the novel, in which imagination serves only to disclose or even to shape the real, and on the other a clutch of disparate genres—fable, oriental tale, pornography, "spy" literature, secular biography, and the it-narrative—which I shall discuss in more detail in the seventh and ninth chapters, but may here be characterized as skeptical or hostile accounts of social persons delivered by private individuals who stand outside the limits of sociable life.

The novel's principle of verisimilitude rests on an imagined but credible picture of things derived directly from the empirical function of the person, whose perceptions are represented as continuous eyewitnessing that is easily narrativized. That is to say, the lapses and elisions incident to the experience of an actual brain are stitched up into a factitious unity that nevertheless is offered and treated as reliable testimony; and the novel develops the same technique, framing fragments of invented experience into a useful fiction, a lesson compendiously if ironically taught in *Northanger Abbey*. The nonpersonate memoir is quite different, exhibiting a mode of being that is neither social nor necessarily human. But no matter how isolated, it emerges from a numerically identical entity capable of directly expressing itself in a manner that has nothing in common with the artificial representation of persons. The reality and truth of its manifestations are tested repetitively and aggressively against the specious hypocrisy of the rest of the world, especially humans who have no humanity. Necessarily the expressive force of such candour, combined with the clarity and simplicity of the soul impelling it, leave the reader in an oblique and disturbing relation to both.

❦

The inheritors of Bacon's program were committed to the rigors of experimental practice, but they were much less confident than he about the discovery of causes. Newton refused to hypothesize a cause of gravity, for example, for fear of making the absence of real knowledge the site of an occult force. In their disagreements about the air-pump, Boyle and Hobbes, though they were both mechanists committed to the impossibility of self-moving matter, accused each other of alleging motion in matter without a cause. Boyle's belief in the "spring of air," the upward pressure of the atmosphere which was supposed to stick two moist marble discs together, failed of vindication when the two discs didn't separate in a vacuum; and this was seized on by Hobbes as a causeless fact and an impossible concession, namely "that something can be moved by itself" (Shapin and Schaffer 1985: 48, 204). Contrariwise, Hobbes's assaults on the physical integrity of Boyle's air-pump became so obsessive that Boyle accused him of personifying it and wishing "to be revenged on an engine that has destroyed several of his opinions." "These exchanges," observe Steven Shapin and Simon Schaffer, "illustrate the difficulty of identifying, so to speak, the 'real' position of each author" (205).

The real position was defined by Newton as mathematical demonstration, in which ideas are communicated directly as thought, without the obscurity caused by figurative language. It was defined by Boyle as a proper relation of the witness to the experiment: a credible person working with reliable equipment and good materials, delivering the result of the work in a narrative or relation, not a prescription (Boyle 1999: 2.209). Hooke thought it depended on the supplements of the evidence of the senses provided by "Mechanical Inventions" such as his microscope. But Hooke was forced to confess that objects magnified multiplied instead of reducing their mysteries (Hook 2003: [viii]; 8). Even without such instruments, there were mysteries in practical chemistry that nothing could elucidate. Boyle was especially puzzled by compounds that could not be reduced to their original ingredients. "I know there may be a Distinction betwixt Matter Immanent, when the material Parts remain and retain their own Nature in the things materiated," says Carneades in *The Sceptical Chymist*, "and Transient, which in the materiated thing is so alter'd as to receive a new Forme, without being capable of re-admitting again the Old" (Boyle 1999: 2.273). Boyle chooses the passive mood in order to set aside the question of agency, but it lurks around the phrase "the materiated thing is so alter'd," for if it is not the chemist, his materials, or his procedure that are responsible for this change, then it must be something else which is not known and cannot be named. In his essay on the language of experimental science, "The Rhetoric of the Passive," J. M. Coetzee points out how difficult Newton found it to talk of gravitation outside the realm of mathematics. Lacking in Latin or English a language that collapsed the distinction between agents and instruments, Newton was haunted by figures, especially personifications. He resorted to the short passive mood as the one least liable to be mistaken. Here the effects of forces can be described without specifying an agent such as gravity which, if so specified, is inevitably personified as Gravity. But there was always a danger that the short passive would simply make room for a personified object. Thus, water in a centrifuge, "shows its endeavour to recede from the axis of its motion" (cited in Coetzee 1992: 189). The cause of motion is shifted from Gravity to the liquid itself, acting on its own behalf as Water, and like Boyle's spring of air or transient matter, it appears to possess the faculty of moving and changing itself.

Caught between his ignorance of a cause and the error of self-moving matter, Boyle desiderates a means of experimental accuracy that would solve the problem: "The acute Eyes of a Lynx, whose perfecter Sight would discerne the Elements," and by these means understand how they are joined (Boyle 1999: 2.267). With such piercing vision the observer might discover the secret of transient matter. This desideratum had already been partly supplied in the early seventeenth century by a group of scientists and artists working under the direction of Federico Cesi in Rome. Known as the Linceans for their lynx-eyed attentiveness to the smallest details, they perfected the arts of close observation, dissection, anatomy, microscopy, and telescopy. Exploiting the talents of Dutch still-life artists living in Italy, they produced extraordinary sets of specimen drawings. Perhaps because they were operating outside the limits of scholastic authority and doctrinal orthodoxy, the Linceans became attracted to the anomalous, the deranged, and the exorbitant. They were fascinated by fungi, sunspots, and misshapen fruit, such as lemons with fingerlike growths on their skin, and oranges with nacreous warts. They showed hydrocephalic heads and hermaphroditic rats (Freedberg 2002: 50, 241–3). Although they were initially dedicated to an empirical taxonomy, they were seduced by the multifarious appearances of nature, things "bizarre, digitated, pregnant or cancroid" (Freedberg 2002: 399). Bacon's plan for the advancement of learning inadvertently encouraged this tendency, for it depended on a mind unbiased by the allure of harmony and uniformity, "broken to contrary motions" as he puts it, and sensitive to natural diversity (Bacon 1965: 162). Citing Machiavelli's *Discourses* as experimentally sound in this regard, he said, "For knowledge drawn freshly . . . out of particulars, knoweth the best way to particulars again" (186). The trouble with Cesi and his group was that the search for particulars was never resolved into general terms or systems and always dug itself deeper into particulars. They isolated phenomena that traversed the boundaries between kinds and species, and showed mixtures and metamorphoses demonstrating not a system but merely (like Boyle's irreversible compounds) a power of alteration without a known source (Freedberg 2002: 367). And the effort to express this particularity as vividly and exactly as possible in drawings and watercolors succeeded only in emphasizing, like Newton's short passives, the mystery of the force capable of producing such strange effects.

Hooke developed a similarly compromised relation to things by means of his microscope. Although it was designed for the "strict examination of the reality, constancy, and certainty of the Particulars that we admit" (Hooke 2003: [iii]), it revealed the surface of a fly's eye in different lights as lattice, golden nails, pyramids, cones, "and in other postures of quite other shapes" ([xxiv]). In his study of tiny creatures such as ants and fleas, Hooke was hard put to it to get images of living things sufficiently immobile to let him draw them. But when he did, all the force of imagination was needed to express their beauty, and magnification takes on the meaning not only of enlargement, but also praise. Of the flea he wrote, "the Microscope manifests it to be all over adorn'd with a curiously polish'd suit of sable Armour, neatly jointed, and beset with multitudes of sharp pins" (210). These chivalric similes are extended into a witty allegory of the traitor-louse, "so busie, and so impudent, that it will be intruding it self in every ones company, and so proud and aspiring withal, that it fears not to trample on the best, and affects nothing so much as a Crown . . . and will never be quiet until it has drawn blood" (211). Although the experimental ideal may require of things that they be "moveless" (204), what they suggest to the expanded eye is not a determinate sum of particulars, but a phenomenon abounding in variety, beauty, motion, and initiative.

Citing the local mystery of the spring of air in the context of the general mystery of the cause of gravitation, Locke took the opportunity in his *Essay Concerning Human Understanding* to define the limits of Boyle's experimental "real position," both in respect of the ingredients of the experiment and the eyewitness of it. He wrote:

> How clear an Idea soever we think we have of the Extension of Body, which is nothing but the cohesion of solid parts, he that shall well consider it in his Mind, may have reason to conclude, That 'tis as *easie* for him to have a clear Idea, *how the Soul thinks, as how the Body is extended*. For since Body is no farther, nor otherwise extended, than by the union and cohesion of its solid parts, we shall very ill comprehend the extension of Body, without understanding wherein consists the union and cohesion of its parts, which seems to me as incomprehensible, as the manner of Thinking, and how it is performed. (Locke 1979: 309 [II, xxiii, 24])

Here Locke places ignorance of the process of material union squarely within our overarching ignorance of the means by which we reflect upon it. How might it be possible even for the most candid eyewitness to testify to the truth of an experiment when the act of testimony itself is not to be accounted for? He says, "When the Mind would look beyond those original Ideas we have from Sensation and Reflection, and penetrate into their Causes, and manner of production, we find it still discovers nothing but its own short-sightedness" (312 [II, xxiii, 28]). So of the substance of solid things and thinking things we are equally ignorant, "not knowing the real Essence of a Peble, or a Fly, or of our own selves" (315 [II, xxiii. 34]). To try to proceed further is to fall "presently into Darkness and Obscurity, Perplexedness and Difficulties" (314 [II, xxiii, 32]). Locke notices, however, that the language we use banishes this ignorance, often describing effects as if they were causes of actions. "And when a Countryman says, the Cold freezes Water, though the word Freezing seems to import some Action, yet truly it signifies nothing, but the effect" (294 [II, xxii, 11]). Newton is adverting to the common sense of such effects when he says, in the common language, "The force which retains the moon in its orbit is that very force which we commonly call gravity" (Newton in Coetzee 1992: 189). Just as Newton transfers the power of gravity to the object of centrifugal water in an effort not to personify an unknown agent, so Locke translates the countryman's prosopopeia into the statement, "Water, that was before fluid, is become hard and consistent" (294). It remains a question, however, whether water has suffered or caused a change in its state, and the virtue that provoked the change, lodged either in the liquid or its surroundings, remains undefined.

Throughout the sections on mixed modes and complex ideas of substances, Locke traverses the ground between causes and effects in an effort to diminish the authority of causes, and to assert the value of the minimal knowledge provided by effects. Whatever qualities we observe in things such as the sun ("Bright, Hot, Roundish, having a constant regular motion, at a certain distance"), we suppose "a Substratum as gives as it were support to those Qualities," and then we ascribe to the substrate the power of producing the effects collocated under its name (298 [II, xxiii, 6]). By means of these transfers it is possible to imagine that an extended thing is inhabited by an essence and that in a thinking thing there dwells an immaterial spirit. Our ideas of angels and God himself depend ultimately upon the same transfer of effects into causes. The corrective to such thinking, which is to accept that the power of fire or gold, for example, consists only in "the power of communication of Motion by impulse ... wherein as much Motion is lost to one Body, as is got to the other" (311 [II, xxiii, 28]), introduces the heterodoxy of which Hobbes accused Boyle; namely, matter in motion without a known cause: "a *thing* that is extended, figured, and capable of Motion ... a *thing* capable of thinking" (297 [II, xxiii, 3]). Locke's "real position" here is that all knowledge supposes an unknowable extra factor, a power supposed to inhere in things, "something besides ... observable ideas, though we know not what it is" (297 [II, xxiii, 3). He teaches his reader to resist the appeal made by ignorance to the imagination, and to conquer those common habits of speech that award agency to unknown causes and inexplicable effects.

What if we were to know what it was that lay beyond the range of observable ideas? Like Boyle, Locke imagines a state of affairs where our finer sight might supply us with what is missing—an advantage Hooke believed he already possessed with his microscope. He imagines what it would be like to need no imagination, to have eyes that could identify the finest corpuscles of matter and examine how they are joined together. We would cease to have ideas of yellow in the case of gold, for instead we should see "an admirable Texture of parts of a certain Size and Figure."

Blood would no longer be perceived as a red liquid, nor a hair as brown or black, nor sand as opaque; they would all be as clear as glass (301–2 [II, xxiii, 11]). The experience of the corpuscular reality of matter would lead in the same direction as the specialist studies of the Linceans: so remote from common ideas of things that the objects would no longer fit into the categories of class, species, or kind. Consequently, "the appearance and outward Scheme of things would have quite another Face to us," and we would dwell in a different world from other people, one so outrageously particular that "nothing would appear the same" (302–3 [II, xxiiii, 12]).

As a reporter from such a world, Hooke had been forced upon his imagination to express the uniqueness of its contents. When Swift invented another such a reporter, he found it best to deliver the microscopic and macroscopic marvels of Gulliver's various worlds in the authentic language of the Royal Society—particular, literal, and exact—but this was the measure of how far his imagination exceeded such limits. For his own part Locke embarks upon "an extravagant conjecture" concerning angelic creatures capable of inhabiting bodies with senses apt for whatever purpose they might require, such as tracing the circulation of the blood or the evolution of one of their own ideas; and then he asks the reader's pardon for indulging "so wild a Fancy" (304 [II, xxiii, 13]). God, he says, keeps us in a state of ignorance relative to our needs and duties. Pope emphasizes this lesson of a middle state in his *Essay on Man*, when he warns us against the enhancement of our senses, for the smell of a rose could prove fatal, and we might start seeing tiny insects as insects see them, centaurs in their dragon world. This suggests that Locke's real position is not as real as one might have expected; and what we mistake for reality is what is not in fact there, or what we cannot know is there. The world we move in is like Arthurian romance, filled with phantom qualities—red blood, congealed water—hinting at forces we know nothing about, such as the irresistible motive power of things. As for the *real* real world, it can be reached only by the operation of fancy, supplemented here and there by data from machines like microscopes; and were we really to inhabit such a sphere of truth, the reports we would give of its particulars would be treated by everyone else as outlandish and improbable fictions, such as the achievements of Hooke's treacherous Mr. Louse.

The thing whose motions are of most concern to Locke is the self. It sits at the heart of his political philosophy as that thinking thing which must at all costs be preserved—by instinct, duty, and right. In the sphere of empirical knowledge it is the receiver of the impressions of things, the source of volition, and the seat of memory. However, it is clear that Locke believes the self and its hidden principle of union are no more exempt from the limitations of real knowledge than matter itself, "not knowing the real Essence of a Peble, or a Fly, or of our own selves" (315 [II, xxiii, 34]). At all points the self is immersed in matter and can do nothing without it. The challenge facing Locke is to argue for its identity, the proof that it is "the same with it self and no other" (328 [II, xxvii, 1]) without falling into the trap of essences and immaterial substances, which would involve him in supposing on the basis of a few sensible ideas that its identity belongs to an immanent and independent spirit capable of action and life beyond the body.

To accomplish the limited task of locating identity among embodied ideas and thoughts, he claims three underlying unities in the constitution of the self. These are the unities of substance, man, and person. Substance here comprehends a living organized body composed of particles of matter that may change over time, but whose structure is constant until death dissolves it. Man refers to the specific shape and make of such a body, common to other creatures that bear the name of human. And person refers to reflection, the capacity of a self to be conscious of itself as a self and to examine and declare the continuity of its own experience. Each of these unities is defined negatively by means of a wild fancy. While discussing the relative coherence of bodily substance, Locke tackles the question of amputation, first of all as a loss which makes no difference to personal identity, "though the Limbs, which but now were a part of it, be cut off" (337 [II, xxvii, 11). Then for a joke he supposes the very opposite, that consciousness might migrate with the divided body part, a little finger, in which case it would be evident that "the little Finger would be the Person, the same Person; and self then would have nothing to do with the rest of the Body" (341 [II, xxvii, 17]). Hobbes had already handled the absurdity of a little finger with a soul in it (Hobbes 1996: 466), a scholastic absurdity developed further in Sterne's tale of Slawkenbergius, where it is disputed whether a man falls off his nose, or the nose falls off the man (Sterne 1983: 207). To buttress his idea of the unity of kind, Locke, who denies himself the reality of species, resorts instead to the long quotation from Sir William Temple about the vocal Brazilian parrot that talked so wittily with its human company of its job of minding chickens (Locke1975: 334 [II, xxvii, 8]). Among the several motives he has for telling this tale, chief among them is his sense of the absurdity of mistaking a parrot, even this rational fowl, for a creature endowed with the properties of a man, including something like a soul. His mockery of metempsychosis is persistent, and informs his subsequent distinction between the unities of man and person, where he wildly fancies the soul of a prince occupying the body of a cobbler. Under such circumstances the cobbler would no longer be the same man, at least from his own point of view, having been absorbed into the person of the prince and now answerable for his actions (Locke 1975: 340 [II, xxvii, 15]).

The tendency of these examples is not as self-evident as Locke appears to think, and the uncertainty of their point is exacerbated by the extravagance of the hypothesis or, in the case of the parrot, the anecdote. It is likely that he wishes to emphasize the improbability of the supposed case in order to contrast the usualness and familiarity of the "real" one, which as far as he is concerned is summed up in the axiom that two things cannot have one beginning, or two persons one body. But in view of the vulnerability of the "real position" in these empirical inquiries, there is a risk that his contrasts might be less vivid than planned. When Locke carries a conjecture about self and personhood as far as it will naturally go without the aid of wild fancies, it ends up as an unmanageable series of possibilities fenced around with negative qualifications. Here is the problem of the prince and the cobbler stripped of fiction:

> Why one intellectual Substance may not have represented to it, as done by it self, what it never did, and was perhaps done by some other Agent, why I say such a representation may not possibly be without reality of Matter of Fact, as well as several representations in Dreams are, which yet, whilst dreaming, we take for true, will be difficult to conclude from the Nature of things. (338 [II, xxvii, 13])

It may be that wild fancies are a way of sidestepping the painfully small degree of certitude entrenched behind this barrage of negatives, which leaves standing only the exiguous proposition that the representation of one agent by another is not demonstrably untrue. At all events, the importance of the function of the person, which Locke sharply distinguishes from person-as-body and person-as-man, lies in its reflective power of self-recognition and self-remembering, and in the forensic responsibility it takes for the transactions in different times and places that can publicly be called its own. The person represents the self inwardly to the self, and outwardly to the world, as an accountable agent. This means it cannot reasonably or legally be usurped. Considering the self in relation to the person, Locke says, "That which the consciousness of this present thinking thing can join it self, makes the same Person, and is one self with it, and with nothing else; and so attributes to it self, and owns all the Actions of that thing, as its own, as far as the consciousness reaches, and no farther" (341 [II, xxvii, 17]). This is a sentence that deserves close attention, for although the subject of it appears to be "this present thinking thing" or the self, it is actually that to which the conscious self attaches itself in order that it might be represented—that is, the person. So what the sentence means is that none other than the person makes the identity of the person and then issues the narrative of what we call the conscious thinking thing, or self, as its own. That is to say, the person is the means of delivering a history of the self's experience while at the same time acting as its impulse. It is the "owner" of it, both in the sense of claiming it and of narrating it. Consciousness merely marks the temporal boundaries, and self the referential limits, of its operations; but agency belongs to the person. In this regard, Locke's owner-person behaves exactly like Boyle's author when he says of credible eyewitness reports of experiments, that they must be vouched for by a named "Author or Authors" (Boyle 1999: 209). Hobbes means much the same thing when he says, "For that which in speaking of goods and possessions is called an Owner . . . speaking of Actions is called an Author . . . he that owneth his words and actions, is the AUTHOR" (Hobbes 1991: 112; see Blackwell 2006, 77–94). But the author in this case is the person.

Locke does not use the term "author," only person, a term which includes the power of representing the self and the actual representation of it, both the cause and the effect. Whatever it is we don't know and cannot know about thinking things, namely their essence, is compounded for by means of a formal representational function, adumbrated by wild fancies, which assures us of one certainty, namely that its representation of the self is coherent within the limits of probability, unique in relation to other persons, and hence that it can be substituted by no other *person* (such as a prince, a parrot, or a finger). We arrive at the authority associated with an author, in Hobbes's and Boyle's use of the word, not by invoking some original act of covenanting or witnessing, but by replacing an essence with a social and legal entity known to itself and to others by means of the narrative of its experience. If we were to transpose this process into Hobbes's terms, we would say that the self is the true author, whose authority is useless unless it is transferred, and that the person is authorized by representing or "bearing the person" of the self (hence the distinction between person and man) and acting in its name (Hobbes 1991: 112). Locke's person is in effect an imagined thing whose virtue and justification, from his point of view, is the very narrow range of its function. But if this person were to bear the persons of other selves, either by migrating into other bodies, or by claiming to represent more than one self in a single body, then representation would turn into sheer fiction, the stuff of wild fancy, and its forensic value be reduced to nil.

Nevertheless, it is impossible not to conclude that Locke's person is itself a fiction of some sort insofar as it stands for a thing which in itself it is not, and speaks as if it were that thing. A person constitutes no absolute distinction between a true authority and the wild fancy of (say) a conversational parrot, only one of degree: it is more like the owner of the truth of identity than the extravagant alternative. Hume, for example, treats the terms self, person, soul interchangeably as fictions of continuity. He says, "The identity which we ascribe to the mind of man is only a fictitious one" (Hume 1978: 259) based on ideas associated by means of the appearance of resemblance and causation (260). Everything Locke labors so hard to define as personal identity in the *Essay*, he sets aside as "some fiction or imaginary principle of union" (262).

It is worth briefly rehearsing the reception of Locke's theory of personal identity in the terms proposed by Hume. Even today it is not agreed among his critics whether with the word *person* Locke is referring to a mode or a substance; that is, to an abstraction formed by the mind's reflections upon its own operations and as demonstrable as a mathematical truth, or to an empirical fact drawn from the residues of experience, necessarily imperfect and supplemented by imagination. For those who assume he is talking about a mode, such as Leibniz, it seems ridiculous that Locke should trouble the issue by supposing a difference between a real and an apparent personal identity: real identity is all that counts. "What makes the same human individual is not 'a parcel of matter' ... nor is it what we call *I*, it is the soul" (Leibniz 1996: 241). Joseph Butler assumed that Locke was committed to substance, and had wrecked his notion of personal identity on the concession that mental substance is not identical over time, hence his having to wrestle with the impossibility of asserting the numerical identity of a conscious action now with one made in the past because the substances are different. Butler's answer to that difficulty is that consciousness, in presupposing personal identity, cannot in any way constitute it, for it is "a mode of being" known "by our natural sense of things" (Butler 1902: 330, 332). So the person is a red herring, and what is really important is being, or self-existence. A century later, Thomas Brown allotted the same fundamental importance to being, arguing that the substance of the mind may be altered by circumstances, but that this change cannot affect its "corpuscular identity" or "absolute identity," in which we intuitively believe with a force that is "universal, irresistible, immediate" (Brown 1851: 1.335). Even Edmund Law, who argued powerfully on Locke's side, recurred implicitly to the mode-substance division, for while explaining that Locke's person had nothing to do with being, or soul, or the irreducible identity of the mind, being "solely a creature of society," and "no part of the natural constitution of a thing" (Law 1769: 10, 20), he made it out to be a mode, "an abstract consideration of man" and "not the man himself" (10, 40; see Martin and Barresi 2000: 12–79).

Hume's idea of fiction seems to evade these extremes of mode and substance by triangulating a self whose consciousness of experience is discontinuous with a public that requires accountability for the actions of each individual and a person representing the imperfect self in the form of a narrative sufficient for all the forensic purposes of public life. For Hume, the impenetrability of the self is no different from the obscure corpuscular reality of things, which can never fully be known and were best not to be so if we are to talk about them—and it—intelligibly to people whose faculties are as limited as our own. By coming thus creatively to terms with our own ignorance, we establish by means of imagination and an instrumental fiction the groundwork of common social experience on which a non-philosophical reality may take shape and thrive. Under this regime of fiction, the person is neither an abstraction, or mode, nor a corpuscular phenomenon, or substance. It is more like a figure in rhetoric.

In owning the history of the self, the person needs to attend solely to the criterion of verisimilitude. In this respect, Locke's person opens up at least for Hume what Catherine Gallagher calls "the conceptual space of fictionality" (Gallagher 2006: 1.340) before the novel has been invented. In her argument the distinction between a *realist* fiction such as *Robinson Crusoe* and a realist *fiction* such as *Joseph Andrews* lies in the purpose of its referential precision, whether it is to solicit belief in the truth of what it asserts, or merely to reinforce the probability of what has been imagined, its likeness to life (344). She points out that the novel belonged to a period when "no enterprise could profit without some degree of imaginative play" (346), a state of affairs in which an expedient fictionality assigns to opinion, credit, money, and moral virtue a kind of coherence that real knowledge cannot supply (346). In this whirlpool of representations, where paper money may stand in for gold, belief for value, and vice for virtue, the merit of realist *fiction* is discovered in the constraint under which it is imagined, "locked inside the confines of the credible" (337). It is not hard to see the parallels between this constraint and the rational ends served by imagined unity in Locke's theory of the empirical self. With neither the novel nor the person is the "real position" represented; rather, a collection of ideas that sorts with common sense and with whatever reality may emerge from that community.

Locke is by no means the only seventeenth-century thinker to consider truth as a credible representation of what our limited senses allow us to experience. Boyle talks of virtual witnesses who derive their authority from "the Relations of some credible person" (209), that is, a virtual self. Hobbes's world is a vast system of delegation, where real authors long ago gave up their rights to those authorized to act in their names, and where everyone either bears a person or is borne by one. This means that any witness is a virtual one, that truth itself is virtual, and that there are no true authors left. "They that have already Instituted a Commonwealth, bound by Covenant to own the Actions and Judgements of one [ie the king], cannot make a new Covenant . . . they are bound every man to every man, to Own, and be reputed Author of all, that he that already is their Sovereigne, shall do" (Hobbes 1991: 122). As for children, fools, and madmen, not to mention inanimate things, they can be personated just like a citizen, for "there are few things, that are uncapable of being represented by Fiction" (113).

Hobbes is no more daunted by the multiplication of persons in a commonwealth, which itself is one vast artificial person or Leviathan, than he is by persons—even persons of churches and bridges—authorized by fictions. Within the pale of civil society, all forms of acting and personation are possible provided they are authorized. But of course the authority is only another person: the person of the commonwealth, or the person of that person, the sovereign. Locke treats such extensive personations as wild fancy. To be bound to own as an author whatever a king might do is all one with the madness of his acquaintance who thought his body contained the soul of Socrates, or of the prince whose soul migrated to the body of a cobbler. That a church or a bridge might have a civic personality through the person of its representative is as absurd in Locke's opinion as believing that a person can find lodging in a parrot or a dead finger. Yet Locke's person is self-generated, a representation armed with the power of representing, just like Leviathan, delivering to the public the figure of a natural self whose authenticity is presumed but never empirically to be known—precisely what Hobbes too would call a person. Its unity consists not in a summary of all that constitutes a self, but in a collection of those ideas filtered by our imperfect senses which are "considered as united in one thing" (305 [II, xxiii, 14]). A person acts as if such a summary had been made on good grounds, and claims it as its own unity.

Consider that the difference between a self doubled by fiction—an intellectual substance represented as doing by itself, what it never did—differs from the truth only in respect of what is represented, not the representation: An intellectual substance may have represented to it, as done by it self, what it really did, or appeared to do. And how would it know that? Because "a present representation of a past Action" (337) would be confirmed by recollection, the memory's image of the same event (345). That is to say, one representation would keep another in countenance. Locke's person represents to the self its little residue of knowledge as a unity of which it, the person, is both the originator and the instance. The same tautology governs the power of water and fire, in whose effects alone are identified the traces of their agency. There is no solid criterion to be applied here, only the relative wildness and extravagance of alternative representations, or what Gallagher would call a standard of probability. Locke touches on the predicament of relative fictions when talking about the most usual method we have for making mixed modes, that is, "By explaining the names of Actions we never saw, or Notions we cannot see; and by enumerating, and thereby, as it were, setting before our Imaginations all those Ideas which go to the making them up, and are the constituent parts of them" (292 [II, xxii, 9]). The phrasing of this definition of mixed modes anticipates with surprising clarity Fielding's of romance (records "of persons who never were, or will be, and facts which never did nor possibly can happen" [Fielding 1977: 184]), and, if applied to a person emancipated from the limitations of time and space, might do for a conscious finger or a humanized parrot. As Paul de Man says of this aspect of Locke's thought, "Properties, it seems, do not properly totalise, or, rather, they totalize in a haphazard and unreliable way. It is not a question of ontology, of things as they are, but of authority, of things as they are decreed to be" (De Man 1978: 19)

Locke's person performs rather like Boyle's transient matter and Hobbes's commonwealth insofar as it gathers a multitude of discrete ideas into a compendious and stable shape. The self without the person would be like those compounds that can decay into their original parts, or like Hobbes's crowds that come together briefly and then break up again. It would be haunted, like the Lincean rarities, with the spectacle of its lonely particularity. It is typical of this shift from a collection to an alleged unity (or what elsewhere Locke calls a "precise multitude" (289 [II, xxii, 4]) that the person steps into the space of agency left by the passive mood. Our specific ideas of substances, says Locke, "are nothing else but a Collection of a certain number of simple Ideas, considered as united in one thing" (305 [II, xxiii, 14]). Considered by whom? By a thinking thing that does not know what thought is? By God? Or by a representation of that thinking thing which itself is the fruit of such a unity? The question posed of the relation of the self to its representations is put in the passive, "Why one intellectual Substance may not have represented to it, as done by it self, what it never did" (338). The cause of the representation is set aside, although nobody but the person could possibly be responsible for it, being a representation endowed with the power to represent. In this sense, Locke's person is no different from Hobbes's self-authoring Leviathan, a fiction so powerful it becomes a mortal god, generating the historical reality of the unity for which it stands.

Although he allowed it great latitude in his commonwealth, Hobbes was as much alive to the dangers of personification as anyone else. Of the seven causes of absurdity, the second is "the giving of names of *bodies*, to *accidents*, and of *accidents*, to *bodies*; as they do, that say, *Faith is infused*, or inspired; when nothing can be *powred* or *breathed* into any thing, but body; and *extension* is *body*" (Hobbes 1991: 34). Similarly, in dreams he notices that effects such as heat associated with certain states of mind, such as lust, become their causes. The linguistic, or sixth cause, of absurdity is personification. "For though it be lawfull to say, (for example) in common speech, *the way goeth, or leadeth hither*, or *thither*, The Proverb says this or that (whereas wayes cannot go, nor Proverbs speak;) yet in reckoning and seeking of truth, such speeches are not to be admitted" (35). More specifically, he challenges those such as Locke and later Smith who try to give a shape and agency to the results of their ignorance, "As when they say, Fortune is the cause of things contingent; that is, of things whereof they know no cause" (Hobbes 1996: 468). But he talks of Leviathan and of the persons of churches and bridges with no sense of contradiction because within the system of representation that constitutes civil society these fictions are derived by authority and serve a purpose. Bruno Latour believes that he and Boyle never really mistook each other's real position because they were both equally committed to a parliament of mute things. He says,

> Boyle's descendants had defined a parliament of mutes, the laboratory, where scientists, mere intermediaries, spoke all by themselves in the name of things. What did these representatives say? Nothing but what the things would have said on their own, had they been able to speak. Outside the laboratory, Hobbes's descendants had defined the Republic in which naked citizens, unable to speak all at once, arranged to have themselves represented by one of their number, the Sovereign. . . . What did this representative say? Nothing but what the citizens would have said had they all been able to speak. (Latour 1993: 142–3)

Latour defines the full extent of such representation and the obedience of those things and selves personated by it. The real and alarming activity of things always happens on the other side of parliamentary muteness, in a state of war, or in fits of idolatry, or in an outrageous "Fiction of the mind" (Hobbes 1991: 16). When Gulliver is identified as an animate non-human in Brobdingnag, variously treated as a small animal, a clockwork toy, and an amusing monster, his nondescript status is never so sinister as when he talks of the unauthorized power he commands. Despite their broad disagreements regarding what persons can legitimately own, Locke and Hobbes are of one mind about the subordination of things to persons—persons whose authority rests either on a system of civil delegation or on a common standard of the probable.

Mutatis mutandis the persons emerging from *Leviathan* and the *Essay* are, as Latour points out, cognate with ideas of civil society based on a right of self-preservation, each defended by its own system of representation. At the level of the state, what would have been a crowd fractured by competing claims for power and goods, is figured as a unity; and at the level of the individual, the mutable substance and discontinuous ideas of the mind are brought before the public as a coherent history of a responsible agent. It doesn't matter that the crowd is not actually a single body, or that the essence of the self remains unknowable: it is the representation that counts. However, it is notable that in the sphere of politics and personal identity alike, representation is self-authoring. Leviathan can only come about when the guarantee it is to embody (namely, that contracts will be enforced by sovereign power) already exists. Similarly, Locke's person is an effect of self-consciousness that pretends to originate that identical self-consciousness, functioning as effect and cause of the same phenomenon. In both cases, the act of representation is required to precede the inauguration of representation, a circular arrangement that leaves the person functioning exactly like a personification, something that *is* what it *does*. This is precisely the tautology Newton tried to avoid when talking about gravity, Boyle when talking about irreversible compounds, and Locke when talking about the freezing of water. It is the same habit of mind and speech Hobbes's deprecated in common discourse when, without authority, inanimate things such as roads are credited with mobility, and proverbs with speech.

The autonomy of a state or a person which takes place as a result of its own power is a problem I now want to solve: is a person the same as a personification, and if not, why not? But I shall begin by emphasizing how little the person has to do with the feats of the "author" or singleton. Although the category of person can be distributed very widely, and comprehend (as far as Hobbes is concerned) things which are not human, neither he nor Locke confounds the representation of persons with the migration or coalescence of them. Perhaps it is the self-authoring capacity of the person that has inclined Locke's readers to suppose that there is no limit to such a power, and that his wild fancies were not extreme and unacceptable alternatives to probable fictions but likely or even inevitable outcomes of its exercise. Samuel Clarke charged Locke's apologist, the materialist Anthony Collins, with defending an imaginary figure whose existence within the mutable substance of the brain could only be supposed real if it were transferable from the old matter to the new: "He cannot be *really and truly* the same Person, unless the same individual numerical Consciousness can be transferred from one Subject to another" (Clarke [1738] 1928: 844; cited in Martin and Barresi 2004: 35). It is a misunderstanding that is still current, for example when Dror Wahrman explains that "the thrust of Locke's argument, in short, was that personhood, or selfhood, can in certain cases roam away from the man, move to another man, or be superseded by another self—within the same man" (Wahrman 2004: 197). Undoubtedly such delusions occurred (in the mind of the mayor of Queenborough, for instance, who believed he was also Socrates), but they are never presented by Locke as other than pathological or ridiculous. Edmund Law felt called upon to reprove critics who understood them to be necessary consequences of Locke's argument, pointing out that it is solely in their own conjectures that such improbabilities are to be found:

> To dwell upon those surprising consequences that might attend the transferring the same consciousness to different Beings, or giving the same Being very different ones, is merely puzzling and perplexing the point, by introducing such confusions as never really existed, and would not alter the true state of the question, if they did. Such Fairy tales and Arabian transformations . . . can only serve to amuse the fancy. (Law 1769: 35)

More to the point, he stated concisely that the purpose of Locke's wild fancies was mockery. "These flights of mere imagination, Mr Locke generally avoids, though he was here tempted to indulge a few such, in playing with the wild suppositions of his adversaries, [v.g. a change of souls between Socrates and the mayor of Queenborough] probably to enliven a dry subject" (36).

Chief among these adversaries as far as Locke was concerned stood Descartes, whose notion of the self or rational soul comported as closely with an absolutist politics as Locke's person did with a representative one. The certain knowledge of being arising from the fact of thinking leaves the Cartesian soul like a monarch, seated on its throne of the pineal gland, attentive to the notices and pleas sent in from the vassal senses but immune to any passion save that of self-delight, when its inclination to self-esteem, as Descartes puts it, "renders us like God" (Descartes 1989: 102). How a sheer act of reflection, or what Ralph Cudworth the neo-Platonist named the *hegemonicon* ("the soul as comprehending itself . . . and holding itself, as it were, in its own hand, as if redoubled upon itself" [Cudworth 1838: 36]), could yield any certainty at all, much less one of such colossal pretensions, was beyond Locke to conceive, unless the soul, like the inherent ideas that were its companions, had a life in the ether that rendered all empirical knowledge at best theatrical and at worst fantastic. So his wild fancies are variations played upon the theme of metempsychosis, which he understands to be everywhere implicit in the Cartesian scheme of knowledge. If the immaterial substance of identity is not limited or influenced by the body, then clearly it has entered its physical host en route from another and will repeat the migration after death. And need there be any restriction on what kind of body is inhabited, such as a finger, a sheep, a pig, or a parrot? Sir William Temple's story of the Brazilian parrot that could hold conversations with human company was transcribed directly from the testimony of Prince Maurits of Nassau-Siegen, formerly governor of the Dutch possessions in Brazil and the nephew of the man Descartes called his "patron saint" (Toulmin 1996: 138).

The idea of using one form of fiction to embarrass another was doubt-less taken by Locke from Descartes himself, who had deployed extreme conjectural techniques to come at the truth of his own being. In his *Meditations on the First Philosophy*, he begins by listing some of the delusions that inadequate ideas drawn from mere empirical knowledge cannot contradict, such as people who believe themselves to be made of earthenware, pumpkins, or glass. Rather than dismiss such delusions, however, Descartes gives a broad welcome to them, and resolves them into the following experiment: namely, to assume that all evidence of the senses is a deceit or fiction composed by a wicked author, until such time as he can alight upon a demonstrable truth.

> I shall then suppose ... that ... some evil genius not less powerful than deceitful, has employed his whole energies in deceiving me; I shall consider that the heavens, the earth, colours, figures, sound, and all other external things are naught but the illusions and dreams of which this genius has availed himself in order to lay traps for my credulity; I shall consider myself as having no hands, no eyes, no flesh, no blood, nor any senses, yet falsely believing myself to possess all these things. (Descartes 1996: 62)

He records the moments of cognitive dissonance this weird fiction supplies: "What do I see from the window but hats and coats which may cover automatic machines?" (Descartes 1996: 59–69). The need to feign the fictions of an evil genius comes to an end when he grasps the certain truth of his own existence as a real thinking thing (65). The empirical reality of the whole world is made a sacrifice to that single reflexive mental act, upon which the structure of Cartesian dualism is raised, together with its enduring suspicion of the value of all sense impressions. So we have Descartes deploying an instrumental fiction for the sake of an inaugural moment of self-recognition, and likewise Locke using probable and wild fictions to establish the basis of a consistent first person. But there is a difference, for when Descartes has drawn from his grand delusion the one truth he needed, he sets it aside; while Locke, who likewise needed imagination to provide the unity of his person, is obliged to maintain his loyalty to this probable fiction if the structure of his reality is not to collapse. Descartes' plan conforms roughly to Gallagher's *realist* fiction, insofar as it is intended, by means of what is not truth, to disclose a real truth; whereas Locke's is closer to realist *fiction*, arriving via imagined or represented cases at a probable representation of what the truth might be, or might become. I want to examine this distinction further, to see if it is not possible to specify the nature of Cartesian fiction in such a way as to begin an elucidation of authored as opposed to personate narratives. I mean to do so by approaching one of the most popular it-narratives of the eighteenth and nineteenth centuries, Charles Johnstone's *Chrysal, or Adventures of a Guinea* (1760, followed by multiple editions), in which Locke is enlisted as the authority for adventures which follow, namely, the migrations of the soul of gold into the various bodies of its owners.

The story begins with an alchemist extracting the spirit of the gold in his crucible, an entity called Chrysal who tells him that she has the power of entering the mind of anyone who possesses her body, "and there reading all the secrets of their lives" (Johnstone 1785: 1.5). Her first encounter is with a man called Traffic who, for his many crimes in pursuit of riches, has been sent a slave into the mines of Peru. He greets gold with a savage prosopopeia, and Chrysal flies up into his brain, entering into a conversation with the "Self" of Traffic, who is busily reviewing the traces of ideas that are visible there. Self says she has to do this, or "a man would no longer continue the same person; for in [what] . . . is called consciousness, does all personal identity consist" (1.8). The footnote marked at this point says simply, "Locke." So what seems to have happened is that Chrysal has entered Traffic's brain as his person, a technique she means to follow with all her human owners whether these are stock characters such as Traffic and the Miser, or real historical figures such as John Wilkes and Charles Churchill. Once someone seizes the gold in which she is lodged, she will enter their consciousness and declare what she finds there. But she will not own it herself, for in most cases there is a disparity between what she discovers and what each individual has claimed was there. She surveys each mind like a person while refusing to function as one; in fact, she remains loyal to what she is, the personification of Gold.

This was a metal in which Locke and Newton took a great interest as the prime incarnation of labor and value. At the same time, it was the means of circulating, alienating, and possessing things that once bore an imprint of the self's identity. It was only after the invention of the use of gold as money that fancy was formally introduced to the owning of a thing and the transfer of ownership: "Gold, Silver, and Diamonds, are things, that Fancy or Agreement hath put the Value on . . . And thus came in the use of Money, some lasting thing that Men might keep without spoiling, and that by mutual consent Men would take in exchange for the truly useful but perishable Supports of Life" (Locke 1960: 343). The empirical effects of gold Locke finds peculiarly arresting. Gold has the power of being melted, but not decaying; of being dissolved in *aqua regia* and of being recovered from the solution; of producing the sensation of yellowness in those who look at it, but of actually not being yellow at all (301 [II, xxiii, 10]). Against its multifarious qualities of malleability, fusibility, solubility, ductility, weight, and yellowness, gold preserves a mystery: "something besides the Extension, Figure, Solidity, Motion . . . or other observable Ideas, though we know not what it is" (297 [II, xxiii,

3]). And it is to that invisible quality we attach the collection of our ideas of the thing we call gold. To know the secret of gold, namely, the corpuscular bonds that make it what it is, is not possible; but out of that impossibility three conjectures emerge: First, that we might know the reality of gold and dwell in the strange Lincean world of its true constitution, incommunicado amidst a set of ideas so unique they are like no one else's. Second, that a substrate of our sensible ideas of gold has let us think of a unity called gold that permits us all to use it effectively and talk of it intelligibly and probably. Third, that gold has convinced us that its mystery is really an agency, Gold, like Cold and Water and Hooke's Mr. Louse, capable of causing its own effects, such as our perception of its yellowness, and generally declaring what it is in everything it does. The first conjecture is the fiction of real knowledge, the forerunner of the Cartesian version of *realist* fiction, for Descartes said of stone that it cannot exist "unless it has been produced by something which possesses within itself . . . all that enters into the composition of the stone" (75). The second is Locke's fiction of effective knowledge, the forerunner of realist *fiction*, where the probability of what is imagined makes current a set of incomplete ideas that stand successfully for a general notion of what is the case. The third appears to be the fiction of wild fancy, where persons enter strange bodies, such as little fingers and parrots, and talk as if they belonged there. If Edmund Law is right, and Locke invented such fictions to embarrass his adversaries, then it is likely that what Johnstone himself invented was not a fiction based on what Locke really thought about personal identity, but a blend of the first and third conjectures in which the spirit of Gold is a personification of the virtue of the metal, something which can only be known by such as enter into the secrets of its composition, and which then can migrate into other bodies.

Along these lines there are plenty of narratives of Gold's agency. Take a standard satire of venality and corruption such as Pope's *Epistle to Bathurst*. In some detail it enforces the proposition, cast in the short passive, to the effect that, "While exchanging goods and money human beings are corrupted and enslaved." In the sequel, it is clear that this corruption may be calibrated to the sophistication of money and its instruments: the more compendious and abstract it becomes, that is the more like a personification, the easier it is for men and women to be adversely affected by it. The lighter and swifter the bribe, the more vividly they begin to live unlike themselves, to borrow a loaded phrase from the poem. No matter in what form it appears, however, a long passive can be built out of its achievements: "Gold is the reason that people are corrupted and enslaved." This happens not because they incorporate gold, or smell it, but because they handle it. This is what leads Sir Balaam from the life of a yeoman to the death of a traitor. So Gold is like the Gravity that Newton could not explain, and the frozen water that was a mystery to Locke's countryman: impenetrable to empirical science, and to any moral science that depends on empirical procedures. On the other hand, those Cartesians acquainted with the certainty of their own existence can possess within themselves all that composes a stone or a metal, and in the mood of self-sufficient delight such reflections bring, compare themselves with God, the author of these truths. The personification of Gold is a standard against which all that is not truth is revealed and humiliated. Gold is like Descartes in the moment of his certitude of self-existence, the proof that everything which is not consubstantial with the truth of being is dispensable as fiction. Basically this is the standard that Johnstone's Chrysal applies, again and again, in order to show that even the best of humans are corrupted, if not actually by gold then by means of the comparison with it. Gold needs no alibi to warrant this judgment, being both author and object of everything that happens. The difference then between her function as a personification and Locke's person is that she represents nothing and nobody, not even herself (she points out that everything she says is immediate), and in every adventure proclaims her glorious indifference to the world she beholds. The sole job of Locke's person is to arrange a public around each individual by means of representation. That is what a person is, that is what it does. This leaves novelists of it-narratives of gold, such as Gildon and Johnstone, in a strangely servile relation to the products of their own imaginations, impelled by the fidelity of their impersonation of a personified thing to take part in what is effectually a war with human beings.

CHAPTER 7

Fictionality and the Representation of Persons

> A group's knowledge or belief cannot be ultimate or
> irreducible—it must ultimately be individuals who are in
> such states, and, to speak of the knowledge of a group, or of
> society's representation of reality, must involve some kind of
> fiction.
>
> —Bernard Williams, *Descartes: The Project of Pure Enquiry*

Deidre Lynch cites Samuel Person, an imitator of Theophrastus who (perhaps ambitious to unite his name with his theme) blended the meanings of "character" and "person." According to Person, character expresses both typical and individual qualities and is stamped not only with the "*signatura rerum* but also *personarum*" (Lynch 1998: 47). As far as Lynch is concerned, Person makes a blunder which has been duplicated in all theories of personal identity and in all treatments of the novel which assume that the particularization of character results in a person, allowing character and person to be used as interchangeable terms. Thus, Anthony Damasio lists the constituent elements "that characterize a person," and Ian Watt talks of "presenting character as a particular person" (Damasio 1989: 17; Watt 1957: 18). There is no need for this confusion, Lynch explains, assigning to character a vast repertoire of manifestations. Its many "strokes" and "colours" include the testimony of coins and printed paper, not to mention first-person narratives of creatures and things, as well as invented stories of named but nonexistent human beings. Although character may expand "in an inward direction," it can equally well remain on the surface, barely particularized at all: round or flat, just as you please.

Aside from the use of the word person to denote the physical properties of a man or a woman, it seems to have been quite common in the eighteenth century to find the ideas of character and person rightly or wrongly adjacent. Eliza Haywood's Fantomina adopts a set of disguises she indifferently refers to as persons and characters: she hires persons to impose on a person whose person she adores, and all this she performs in an assumed character (Haywood 2006: 2575–80). Similarly, Adam Smith uses the words synonymously: the "person and character" of those with whom we sympathize (Smith 1976 (1982): 317). In his Preface to his translation of Homer's *Iliad*, Pope announces, "We come now to the characters of his persons," as if to reverse Person's equation between person and particularized character by suggesting that a person outlines what a character fills in (Pope 1959: ix). In *Spectator* 262, Addison proclaims that nothing he writes is aimed "at private Persons": "For this Reason when I draw any faulty Character I consider all those Persons to whom the Malice of the World may possibly apply it, and take care to dash it with such particular Circumstances as may prevent all such ill-natured Applications" (Addison and Steele 1907: 2.41). Here the particularization of a fictional character serves to protect the actual person from any confusion with it. However, the reverse seems to be the case in *A Sicilian Romance*, where the Marchioness is terrified of scandal and determined to eject from her castle "the person to whom her character was committed" (Radcliffe 2008: 102). After Roxana's lover the Prince has asked leave "to lay aside my Character" she says, "I gave myself up to a Person who, tho' a Man of high Dignity, was yet the most tempting and obliging, that I ever met with." She tells him that "a Person of his rank . . . cou'd not be withstood," and she tells the reader, "I can go no farther in the Particulars" (Defoe 1981: 62–5). Evidently his person grows more interesting, as far as she is concerned, amidst the accumulation of particulars privately noted, leaving the world at large (where she seldom trespasses) and the publishable portion of her tale as the spheres where characters are seen to move.

It seems generally agreed that characters, whether particularized or not, scandalized or preserved, are public, while persons, if they are really set on privacy, tend toward a narrower role and ultimately an inaccessible particularity, at which point they become something else altogether. Crusoe traces these degrees of difference while dealing with the mutiny on the English ship. He reports, "The Captain knew the Persons and Characters of all the Men in the Boat, of whom he said, that there were three very honest Fellows" (Defoe 1983: 260). We can be fairly sure these three honest men are characters, while those of more doubtful loyalty are persons, obliged to re-establish their credentials: "They promis'd faithfully to bear their Confinement with Patience" (261). At the extreme of disobedience are found outrageous and desperate men like the boatswain, enemies of civil society beyond any kind of contractual remedy. These are termed "the Authors of all the Mutiny on the ship" (256) and are shown no mercy. They are authors in the same sense used by Milton's God when accusing Adam and Eve of culpable free will, "authors to themselves in all" (III, 122). This kind of authorship, non-civil and perversely independent, is productive of a kind of originality that all authors take some kind of interest in, whether as the attribute of someone of whom the story is told, or of the teller of the story, or of the book in which it is inscribed.

It is in this larger province that Lynch locates the versatility of character and its currency as fiction. If there is any point in the history of character, she declares, it will be reached when that history "will become unthinkable apart from the history of fiction and the fictive" (Lynch 1998: 84). She makes the same claim for the fictionality of character that Catherine Gallagher makes for fiction generally when she says that the question we ought to pose about the rise of the novel is "not why the novel became the preferred form of fiction, but why fiction became the preferred form of narrative" (Gallagher 1994: 164). Like Lynch, she steers well away from the confusion of character with person. A particularized character is not a person but "nobody *in particular*"—that is, a character so heavily freighted with traits and properties, including a proper name, that the reader, far from being allured to think of it as a real person, is disposed on the contrary to relish its fictionality precisely on account of these multifarious elements: "Readers attach themselves to characters because of, not despite, their fictionality," she says (Gallagher 2006: 351). Nobody's attractions arise not from the gullibility of a sympathizing reader, then, but from the emphasis on the difference between them: "The very specificity and particularity of realist representation ... should be viewed as confirmation ... of fiction" (Gallagher 1994: 173).

By sticking to character and jettisoning persons from their histories of the novel, Lynch and Gallagher have been able to emancipate early fiction from what they take to be its servile relation to empiricism and individualism. Supposed at one time simply to reflect the Cartesian unity of the self on the one hand and the experimental basis of knowledge on the other, the novel they offer us is freed from this kind of referentiality, and has struck out on its own, exploiting a set of generic possibilities that enlarge the diversity of character by way of imaginative virtuosity, not empirical knowledge. With a slightly different emphasis from theirs on character, April Alliston shows nevertheless how much character has contributed to the development of formal realism, but in a manner subversive of the empiricist assumptions on which it was based. Instead of knowledge, she argues, character gestures toward an enigma that is not easily handled outside of romance; so that fictionality acts as the gravitational field of this mystery, not the means of disclosing it (Alliston forthcoming). On the other, hand Julie Park has suggested that it is the very transparency of character, as handled in the medium of free indirect discourse, that exhibits its artifactual and even mechanical origins within the world of exchange, just like the coins, vehicles, and other objects that circulate as part of the legion of characters in Lynch's general economy (Park forthcoming). Then there are the literary characters discussed by Candace Vogler, whose traits put them in company with

Gallagher's nobodies insofar as no reader would wish to be "knowable in the way that any literary character worth repeated readings is knowable" (Vogler 2007: 15). However, it is precisely from the gap between what is known on the page and what is secret in the heart of the reader that an ethical challenge springs and which makes reading worthwhile (19). So, on the one hand stand those who interpret characters as signs in a global text, with a meaning and a function we all understand, and on the other are those who locate in character some kind of mystery on which the function of fiction depends. The mystery, as I take it, is the clue that leads from character to person, then from person to author: what is not disclosed at the outset, and may well remain a secret at the end.

The recovery of fictionality has been an important step in a debate that began with Michael McKeon's *Origins of the English Novel*, where he showed how intimately the protocols of historical narrative mingle with those of romance in the novels of the eighteenth century. Recently he has returned to the debate, arguing that a parallel dialectic between the actuality of individual experience and the virtuality of the public realm is in fact controlled by "the unprecedentedly normative force of empirical actuality" (McKeon 2005: 109). He goes on, "Only through the modern valorization of the actual—of the factual, the empirical, the historical—does the ancient and equivocal whole of 'fiction' become resolvable into separate and unequivocal parts: falsehood and fiction, deceit and the aesthetic mode of truth, what is made up and what is made" (ibid.).

By drawing a boundary of empirical actuality around fictionality, McKeon seems to reverse the propositions of Lynch and Gallagher, and to restore the primacy of experimental and sensationist criteria in judgments about fiction. On the other hand, it may well be that he is raising the possibility of the relative independence of the rhetoric of probability within the novel, along the same lines as Gallagher when she emphasizes the correspondence between particularity and fictionality. In any event, he poses an important question about referentiality and particularization which needs an answer. If the credibility of fiction and the currency of its characters are to be measured by degrees of particularization—more or less—then to what would these particulars refer if not the experimental procedures and rhetorical austerities that define the production of facts among scientists, navigators, virtuosos, and historians of the seventeenth century? And how would we know that such particulars were probable and more worthy of the suspension of disbelief that any other form of amplification? Alliston's answer is to say that probability in fiction is indeed defined by these gendered aims—male factuality devoted to the business of disclosure, female secrets preserved by codes of romance—but that what is intended to be discovered by probable means (say, the core traits of character) is always resisted by its counterpart. Gallagher, on the other hand, supposes that credibility in fiction of all sorts, from romance to the tragic novel, requires a narrowing of referentiality sometimes to zero; and that this non-referentiality will be particular in the cause of sheer singularity, governed by some non-general "idea of truth" as opposed to a system of knowledge (Gallagher 2007: 1.337, 341, 344). I suggest that the difficulties of supposing that the language of reference can somehow supersede what it has referred to are overcome only if probability is detached from a history of the real and installed instead within the instrumental function of imagination, or what Sir Philip Sidney called in reference to fiction its "fore-conceit": "For any understanding knoweth the skill of [the] artificer standeth in that idea or fore-conceit of the work, and not in the work itself" [Sidney 2006: 957]). Reference is made then not to what is real, or has been real, but what may become so. Here fiction may not only command belief, it can bring about what is believed.

When McKeon talks of the virtuality of civil society and emphasizes the "manifest fiction of the state of nature" (2005: 12), he points to a solution to the problem of referentiality that is embedded in the historical crisis dating from the onset of the discourse of rights, when fictionality of the modern sort might have been said to have had its birth. Why it did so and what strange alliances it then fostered between the fields of politics, property, and poetics has been the theme of Victoria Kahn's *Wayward Contracts*. In this chapter I mean to use Kahn's insights to show that fictionality could not have taken root or extended its effects by relying on character. Fiction became the preferred form of narrative because it depended heavily on the idea and function of the person, while at the same time making room for a figure who was neither a character nor a person, nor yet quite a nobody. The definition that comes closest to this anomalous fictional category is to be found in the idea of the *author* already furnished by Milton and Defoe, and elaborated by Thomas Hobbes when he names the singular figure in a mere state of nature an *author*, unattached either to the cycles of exchange that define a character, or to the fictions of representation that define a person. I mean to illustrate the difference between characters, persons, and authors by contrasting two of Defoe's novels, *Robinson Crusoe* and *Roxana*, and by considering briefly, with reference of Charlotte Lennox's *The Female Quixote*, what might be termed the Cartesian strategy of mock-romance.

But first I want to explain what I mean by fictions of representation and the persons who embody them. The abolition of feudal tenures in 1646 followed three years later by the trial and execution of Charles I were events coincident with ideas about history, narrative, justice, and property radically different from what went before. These two decisive interruptions of legal and dynastic continuity inclined many people to believe that history had evolved not from an immemorial ancient constitution or the dateless prerogatives of sovereignty, but from their own consent: that it was made by them, not providentially dispensed or absolutely disposed. Sir Edward Dering understood this change in narrative terms, although he did not approve of it. Of the Grand Remonstrance he said, "I did not dream that we should remonstrate downwards, and tell stories to the People, and talk of the King as of a third person" (cited in McKeon 2005: 5). But others *had* dreamed it, and told stories of it until it had taken place as an historical fact. Now that the course of history had changed so radically, no one was under any illusion about the power of imagination to supply, under the right conditions, the historical evidence that would justify such a rupture. The sudden shift from a narrative of obligation to one of mutual agreement, from a story the king had been telling to one that was told of him and was in fact fatally happening to him, was experienced as a narrative event, a different way of telling a story that was responsible for an alteration in the consciousness of the people. The event was naturalized by the fiction of the original contract, involving the joint inventions of the state of nature and the covenant which brought it to an end: how we emerged from the one and entered the other when a multitude of individuals consented to have their unity represented by what Hobbes called the person of Leviathan and the person of that person, the sovereign. Hobbes himself proclaimed the fiction—"It may peradventure be thought, there never was such a time, nor condition of warre as this; and I believe it was never generally so" (Hobbes 1996: 89)—but he dared his opponents to challenge the reality of its consequences.

Why did Hobbes talk of Leviathan as a person and not as a character? One powerful reason was the dynastic and historical weight of the latter word. Hume defined it as "our reputation ... our name" (Hume 1978: 316) and gave the characters in his *History of England* only after their lives, generally royal ones, were complete and their reputations secure. Characters are settled and well known; people rely on them for the truth of reports, and trade on them in pursuit of profit. Olaudah Equiano says that Robert King decided to buy him "on account of my good character" (Equiano 1995: 99). Persons, on the other hand, last only as long as they live, and lose all their belongings at their death. Their medium is always passing time, not the past, leaving a person always in a provisional state of being, and effectually in a subjunctive mode of self-identification (Baier 1991: 188 and 1985: 85). The province of character is not only the extent of the world, it is more importantly the history of what has already happened in it; and Leviathan was putting a decisive end to the dominion of that kind of history. Victoria Kahn explains that Hobbes and his fellow political philosophers "were rewriting traditional accounts of obligation as a story that 'could have been otherwise.'... [They] revealed their awareness that the power of contract to construct new social and political relations was inseparable from the power of imagination" (Kahn 2004: 85). There was now an instrumental analogy between political action and poetic fiction, she explains, "a radically new poetics of the subject and the state" (15, 1).

All authority in this new alliance of poetics with politics was first imagined and then represented; it had no previous referent in the real. Hobbes's "author" or natural person, the individual who is allegedly antecedent to the "actor" or artificial civil person, dwells in a state of nature that never was. Subsequent political unity, justice, and personal identity relied entirely upon representation, by whose means a person not only replaced the entity for which it stood, it lodged that entity in the fiction which replaced prehistory. The real itself was represented by the consequences of keeping faith with that fiction. Even those who objected to this turn of events, like Sir Edward Dering, acknowledged the terms in which they were couched. They knew that what had been imagined, dreamt, and uttered—political fictionality—was now shaping their reality. Some years later Lord Shaftesbury could not understand why 'the wit of man should so puzzle this cause as to make civil government and society appear a kind of invention and creature of art' (Shaftesbury 1999: 1.52). In civil society, what was not invented or created by art? The referent of its fictions lay not in the procedures of knowing things, or even in some abstract idea of truth, but rather, as Sir Philip Sidney put it, "in that idea or fore-conceit of the work, and not in the work itself" (Sidney 2006: 957).

Hobbes fetched his notion of person from the stage and the law courts, and he saw no limit to its efficacy, declaring, "There are few things, that are uncapable of being represented by a Fiction" (Hobbes 1996: 113). Even inanimate things could have their persons, churches, roads, and hospitals, playing their parts in a vast network of power distributed through delegates, vicars, deputies, and officers, all acting their parts on behalf of one another. Locke drew his person solely from the law, not the theater, and he considered its job to be forensic, accounting for actions for which one is morally and legally responsible. If Hobbes's person contributes to a public history, Locke's gives a narrative of a consistent self. However, it is clear from the section on personal identity in the *Essay* discussed in the previous chapter that terms such as man, self, consciousness, thinking thing, and person are by no means synonymous and that the person, the result of the combined activities of the self and consciousness, provides a narrative version of the self, not the self itself. Considering the self in relation to the person, Locke says, "That which the consciousness of this present thinking thing can join it self, makes the same Person, and is one self with it, and with nothing else; and so attributes to it self, and owns all the Actions of that thing, as its own, as far as the consciousness reaches, and no farther" (341 [II, xxvii, 17]). The difficulty of the sentence is owing to its disguised subject, which is really the person, not the self. It is the person that makes the person, nothing else; and then the person represents the self within the time-frame set by consciousness.

This led Locke into a hypothesis of representation that many of his critics were to comment upon: "Why one intellectual Substance may not have represented to it, as done by it self, what it never did, and was perhaps done by some other Agent, why I say such a representation may not possibly be without reality of Matter of Fact, as well as several representations in Dreams are, which yet, whilst dreaming, we take for true, will be difficult to conclude from the Nature of things" (338 [II, xxvii, 13]) . Bishop Butler's answer to this enigma was to assert that not the most ardent of Lockeans could maintain that the person really coincides with the self, and that this representation of the one by the other operates solely "in a fictitious sense" (Butler 1852: 322; cited in Martin and Barresi 2004: 40). It is not clear that this was what Locke was intending to claim, but for Hume it made no difference, because the confusion was inevitable given the actual discontinuity of our experience: "For when we attribute identity, in an improper sense, to variable or interrupted objects, our mistake is not confined to the expression, but is commonly attended with a fiction, either of something invariable . . . or of something mysterious . . . or at least with a propensity to such fictions" (Hume 1978: 255).

We need go no further than this in order to begin revising our ideas of the effect of fiction on the representation of the lives of individuals or nations, and to assess its importance in the rise of the novel. Traditionally, the novel is closely linked to the protocols of truth-claims made during the seventeenth century, whether in respect of Cartesian skepticism, Lockean sensationism, experimental science, journals, catalogues, voyage literature, antiquarian research, or certain genres of pictorial art. The assumption fostered by the link is that the novel came about as a modification of these reflections of the reality of experience. But in the views of the private and the public domains I have just outlined, the conditions which prevailed were not hospitable to a direct encounter with the empirical truth of things. Quite the contrary, the modern systems of political unity, justice, and personal identity, no less than experimental science, relied entirely upon representation (Latour 1993: 142–3), in which a person replaced the entity for which it stood, an entity that had no recognizable existence outside the form of this substitution, and in which the fiction of an original contract replaced prehistory. It has often been noted that Hobbes's sovereign, the person of Leviathan, must first endorse the contract which brings him into being: he is the *sine qua non* and the creature of the same event. The same paradox applies to Locke's person. Allegedly it comes about by the combined actions of self and consciousness, but this is just a way of saying that the person was made by the person and that what it pretends to represent are its own original deeds: what *it* accomplished and what *it* is answerable for. Persons were widely understood to be fictions to a greater or lesser extent, invented for the production of truth insofar as the orderly conduct of political life and the continuity of an individual's memory contribute to that end. At the same time it could not be denied that the fictionality of persons, no matter how useful, introduced an artificial element into the owning of history and property, and a preposterous relation of cause to effect.

So, rather than supposing the formal realism of the novel to be a celebration of the real experience of individuals rendered in probable pictures that reflected the common sense of things, it is more useful to view it as part of what Hume calls the propensity to fiction. In which case, what is represented is not a picture of reality achieved by the bringing home objects in all their concrete particularity (Watt 1957: 29), so much as the power of imagination itself to create the materialities and propel the continuities upon which the sense of identity or nationality is founded, those selves and communities that are productive of events which we call solid and real. It is not reality itself which is disclosed, then, but fidelity to the consequences of an imagined beginning. Novels in this light are an element of that imaginative work, and the reading of them is congruent with the experience of other fictions which do not mirror a given reality but wholly constitute our sense of how things actually are. Here is where McKeon's distinction between what is made and what is made up—or Hobbes's between civil fictions and Quixotic romance—is best applied. As part of the broad propensity to fiction, novels are constructed according to the same preposterous principles and accomplish the same ends as one of Hobbes's or Locke's persons. It is a matter of keeping faith with the probable results of imaginative work. Like a person, the novel will, if it is judged credible, that is, if it is consonant with our passions and desires, vindicate its invention in the symmetry and reality of its effects, effects which then look like causes.

Let me go back to the original contract. As there was no material trace of such a thing, nor any evidence of an actual state of nature, the history of civil society had to be construed not just as a fiction of origin but as a continuing struggle between rival narratives, each claiming more legitimacy and power than its competitor. The verisimilitude of the fiction of consent was tested finally not by prior standards of authenticity (they were not to be found, "not written on parchment, nor yet on the barks of trees" [Hume 1985: 471]) but by the falling out of events themselves. The happiness or otherwise of the historian's flights of fancy was determined, as Catherine Morland and Dr. Johnson both surmised, by the proportion of accidents to the predictability of life. In civil society, as we all have recently rediscovered, the law of unintended consequences dominates the future. We may know what we do, but not what that doing does, as Foucault says. Once Catherine wonders what it would have been like to be Mrs. Tilney, she is destined to learn that the consequences of imagining things are very real indeed, capable of triggering events of which she could have no inkling. She has no idea that she has committed herself to a train of circumstances in which she will find out exactly what it is like to bear that name and to be that person.

The temporal extension and flexibility necessary for the functioning of a person is not possible for a character. An individual's character is, to coin Hobbes on the topic of honor, its price, what it is worth; and this will not change without its being altered and destroyed (Hobbes 1996: 63). That is why, according to Lynch's model of the market network, characters are signs whose value, even if it is a fictional value, is constant: only with that guarantee may they circulate. Persons on the other hand never know fully who they are because they are always finding out more about themselves. That is why they keep diaries and wonder what the future will hold. The tragic novels of the eighteenth century, such as *Clarissa*, *Camilla*, or *The Memoirs of Miss Sidney Bidulph*, fully exploit this uncertainty by recording the unintentional but disastrous consequences of actions taken in all innocence, or on the best of motives. More than any other branch of fiction these narratives probe the possibility on which civil society is founded, namely, that stories may be represented otherwise than as they were supposed to be. Instead of being told, the story starts happening to those involved in telling it. Then the measure of a person is found in the degree to which he or she adapts to what was entirely unforeseen and takes responsibility for what was never meant to happen—something a character could never attempt (Macpherson 2010). But persons, themselves creatures of the preposterous relation of cause to effect, are much better placed to do this.

❦

Premonitions in Defoe's fiction generally act as guarantees of happy outcomes. When Robinson Crusoe is getting down to the business of forging contracts on his island, he pauses to note an action of the mutineers he had correctly anticipated, saying, "I imagin'd it to be as it really was" (Defoe 1983: 264). He says the same thing when he finds that the envisaged inlet in which he is to unload his booty from the ship is actually there when he needs it, on the other side of the promontory: "As I imagined it, so it was" (51). Having already dreamt Friday's arrival before it happens, distinguishing with peculiar fidelity the insignificant point at which imagination parts company with the facts ("I did not let my Dream come to pass in that Part, viz. That he came into my Grove for Shelter"

[Defoe 1983: 205]), Crusoe experiences with astonishing immediacy the back-to-front factuality of a history framed by the imagination. To compare the bare journal account of his stripping of the wreck—"All these Days entirely spent in many several Voyages to get all I could out of the Ship, which I brought on Shore, every Tide of Flood, upon Rafts" (Defoe 1983: 70)—with the ten pages of vivid description given earlier, containing some of the most memorable scenes of his island sojourn, describing how liquor, ironwork, tools, weapons, rope, biscuit, lead, powder, spars, and even money were taken from the ship, how they were ferried ashore to become the means of his self-preservation, how overjoyed he was to be handling them and how lovingly he arranged them in his dwelling, is to understand the difference between a simple summary of facts in the present tense and the rich supplement provided by imagination as it looks forward or backward to inspect the results of its own activity. J. M. Coetzee considers this the foundation of Defoe's realism. "Crusoe alone on his island ... is Defoe at his best. ... It is a matter of pure writerly attentiveness, pure submission to the exigencies of [a] world which ... becomes transfigured, real (Coetzee 2001: 23). What has been imagined becomes real because not a single consequence of imagining it is set aside: each thing is weighed, considered, and put in its place until the coherence of the narrative is undeniable. When on the rare occasions the act of imagining is imperfect, for example in the case of the cedar trunk Crusoe carves so painfully into the shape of an immobile boat, the fore-conceit parts company with the work, so the outcome is pointless and has no place in the story except as a joke or a nightmare.

The importance of imagination is emphasized when the hero makes his transition from a solitary to a social life. His idyll of use-value comes to an end when he spies a footprint in the sand that is not his own, and he has to start calculating his relationship with the other human beings who visit his island, some of whom will shortly settle on it. In anticipation of these events his imagination is hugely excited, forming plans for all kinds of violent exigencies. He mentions how on one night in particular a great multitude of thoughts "whirl'd through that great thorow-fare of the Brain, the Memory" (196). This is the first of several times he tells his own story: "I run over the whole History of my Life in Miniature, or by Abridgment." This narrative puts him in a position where he can connect the past to the future, and he does so by means of the dream which predicts in every detail but one his rescue of Friday from the savages. So when the mutineers arrive at his island, Crusoe has himself introduced indirectly, first as "the Person the Governor had order'd to look after them," and then as the Governor: "so I now appear'd as another Person" (271). These appearances as a person, and even as the person of that person, are he admits "all a Fiction" (268), but they define the public and contractual side of his self which has been nascent throughout his story as the self who watches or guards the other self, as in phrases like these: "I frequently stood still to look at myself" (149); or "I employed my self several Days to find out proper places to put my self"(169). Pure spontaneous authorship is seen by him now as a dangerous novelty. The mutineers as we have seen are "the Authors of all the Mutiny on the ship" (256), just as he was once the disobedient author of all his life as a solitaire. Now he formally and deliberately places himself at one remove from his self, personating and representing it as an actor or storyteller, an artificial person whose story is imagined before it happens.

In *Roxana*, the assumption of personhood never takes place, although it is attempted, and as a consequence the fiction—the narrative and the transfiguration of imagination into the real it was supposed to be representing—fails. Roxana never stands still to consider herself, or to expostulate with herself as Crusoe is so fond of doing. On two notable occasions she is brought in front of a mirror, and she is mesmerized by the sight of her image. When on the second occasion the prince puts a diamond necklace round her throat and leads her to pier-glass, she remembers how she blushed, how the sight of her rising color set her on fire again, and how she began "to wonder what it was that was coming to me" (73). It is a scene remarkable for the absence of reflexivity. As David Marshall says, it is "as if she were looking at someone else" (Marshall 1986: 138).

When as an exceedingly rich woman Roxana tries to answer her query, "Why should I be a Whore now?" the best answer she can come up with is that she has been the creature of circumstances, a receptacle of "the Sence of things" (200), and that the importunity of her sensations and impressions has helped "fortifie my Mind against all Reflection" (201). Having put this question to herself several times, she admits that it is a futile exercise, for it "made no Impressions upon me of that Kind which might be expected from a Reflection of so important a Nature" (203). What she is talking of is a reflection in the sense of a critical self-estimate, the sort of self-examination which forges a person out of a self, and makes an abridged history out of the chaos of one's memories. What she prefers is a different kind of reflection: her image in the mirror, or her relationship with Amy, or her feelings for the prince when she calls him her deity and herself his idol (70, namely, an engagement with an image of herself that excites a peculiarly absorbed and uncritical attention. For instance, when she puts Amy naked into her own lover's bed, and watches as they copulate, she obtains a satisfaction she can explain to no one, not even herself; but undoubtedly what she is doing is studying her own reflection. Her reflection-as-image makes the same impression upon her as "the Sence of things," fortifying her mind against the other sort of reflection (that is, self-reproach). She calls such a luscious sense of things a lethargy of the soul, the stupidity of her intellectual part (69). That is to say, she never seriously represents herself to herself as a person; rather, she views herself in the mirror as a phenomenon directly seen but not recognized, like Eve or Narcissus when they find themselves fascinated by images they do not yet know are their own, an impulse Lord Kames calls "an act of intuition, in which reflection enters not" (Kames 2005: 1.68). It is an experience that Hobbes's natural person or author would enjoy, sheer sensation without perception, seeing but not seeing that one is seeing. Adam Smith imagined that this was Crusoe's experience on the island, but it is much more typical of Roxana's when she enjoys what she calls the "fullness of Humane Delight" (Defoe 1981: 68):

> External bodies which either pleased or hurt him would occupy his whole attention. The passions themselves, the desires or aversions, the joys or sorrows which these objects excited ... would scarce be the objects of his thoughts. (Smith 1982: 110)

Roxana's habit of experiencing herself as a reflected thing, and not as a person consciously representing her own history, puts insuperable difficulties in her way when she confronts in her daughter Susan the objective form of her own self ("for she was my own Name"—presumably Susan de Beleau [205]). Soon it is plain that Susan means to assemble the details of her secretive mother's story, and then to make it public. Roxana has no intention of owning her past, or of having it owned ("It was my Business to be what I was, and conceal what I had been" [301]). The whole point of her adultery with the Dutchman, as she explains to him, is that it is a transaction without a history, for the reproach "drops out of Knowledge, and dies; the Man goes one-way, and the Woman another ... and ... the Folly is heard no more of" (152). The girl bitterly asks why she should be denied a past and a future. "What have I done that you won't own me?" (267). "She is my mother," she tells the Quaker, "and she does not own me" (304). The explanation for such neglect has to lie in the fact that the daughter is trying to own the mother by personating her—Susan de Beleau with a history—and the mother will have none of it. In the rewritten *Roxana* of 1740, one of the children greets his mother with this question, "Are you, Madam, the Person to whom I owe my being?" (Anon. 1740: 440). The original Roxana would deny it on at least three counts: her need for secrecy, the absolute importance of not owing anyone anything that she has not owned herself, and her unreflective and non-representational cast of mind.

If we were to ask Roxana what use fiction was in her enterprise she would say, "This was my Plot to be more completely conceal'd" (213). She owns none of her story to her daughter, and certainly not very much to the reader, both of whom are more or less excluded from the private passages of her life. What she has told is a bad fiction—shapeless, implausible and "dirty" as she calls it—revealing how little in her life has been shaped by imagination and how seriously she has been dedicated to concealing the fullness of the delight she has taken in the "Sence of things." Her addiction to that kind of pleasure she keeps secret while clamorously repenting the sin of whoredom. Persistently she invokes the power of evil—"I was now become the Devil's Agent" (48), "All still manag'd by the Evil Spirit" (201), "These were my Baits, these the Chains by which the Devil held me bound" (202)—in order to disguise her very satisfying sensations of tranquility, peace, and delight. Why use bad fiction to disfigure what is really important to her? The simplest explanation is that, not being a person but something else, she does not possess the means of representing (otherwise than in a mirror) sensations that were experienced as full and immediate. A supplementary line of enquiry is opened by Alliston when she suggests that fiction of all sorts, including these bad fictions of Roxana's, deploy one way or another a model of empirical enquiry adumbrating a mystery whose natural home is romance, not the novel. Terry Castle has hazarded a guess at what this mystery might be when she says of *Roxana*, "We receive . . . this history as transformed by the persistent presence of another, alternate self, indeed—in Roxana's case—an ideal self" (Castle 1979: 83–4). Castle imagines this ideal self as an enchanted princess: "She lies asleep at the centre of the fiction" (89).

In his novel *Foe*, J. M. Coetzee blends *Robinson Crusoe* and *Roxana* in order to tell the story of how Susan Barton's memories of being cast away on a desert island inhabited by two people called Cruso and Friday will not make a story. When she talks to Mr. Foe about the stunted bushes, the monkeys, the thorns underfoot, the incessant wind, the building of terraces by the inscrutable Cruso, and Friday's strange custom of casting flower petals on the waters of the bay, it is plain there is plenty of journal but no narrative, and he tempts her to make one by imagining that muskets had been brought ashore from the wrecked ship, and that cannibals visited the island. Susan resists these suggestions, so Foe switches the narrative angle, and suggests instead that her missing daughter ought to be the focus of the story; and no sooner does he make the suggestion than someone claiming to be this very daughter begins to haunt the house where she is living. Among other things, Coetzee is playing with this hypothesis: what if Roxana had been Robinson Crusoe? The answer is that she would allow no place in her story for imagination, and none to anyone who offered to supplement it with imagined additions. In refusing to represent herself, or be represented, as a fiction worth reading, she retreats to the same kind of anonymity and pointless authenticity of her solitary original, whose only company was kept with images of herself.

In both of these novels, Defoe was assigning room to the activity of spirits and demons. Roxana blames the devil again and again for her sinful career, and even before he sets off on his fatal journey, she has a second sight of her jeweler husband's murder. As the formal role of Providence gets weaker in *Robinson Crusoe*, so the secret hints and notices of a "Converse of Spirits" get stronger: "And if the Tendency of them seems to be to warn us of Danger, why should we not suppose they are from some friendly Agent, whether supreme, or inferior . . . and that they are given for our Good?" (Defoe 1983: 250). In his *The Secrets of the Invisible World Disclos'd; or, An Universal History of Apparitions* (1729), published under the pseudonym of Andrew Morton, Defoe offered to demonstrate the reality of agents in themselves invisible and imperceptible. He calls them angels and spirits whose function is to transmit useful hints and notices to mortals, sometimes invisibly and sometimes in the shape of a person. In *Robinson Crusoe* it is made clear, despite the bald empiricism for which Defoe is renowned, that they are real presences, not illusions formed by false projections of the imagination (Defoe 1735: 327). Not that he is heedless of the many counterfeit examples of similar events "made by the Invention of Story-makers" (Defoe 1735: 224); but unlike Descartes, who sets evidence of an immaterial substance against the general multitude of fictions produced by the senses, Defoe means to distinguish between lies and probable stories, for it is by virtue of the latter that evidence of spiritual activity comes to light in sensible form. So half of his job is to discredit evidence of ghosts, specters, and wraiths; but the other is to show that unaccountable pressures and premonitions affecting our lives are revealed in narratives so coherently structured and so replete with important details, that they constitute undeniable proof of the action of a benign immaterial intelligence. In his arrangement of these three categories—what is insensibly true; what is palpably false; and what is probably related—his *History of Apparitions* may be read as Defoe's contribution to a theory of fiction, specifically personate fiction.

For example, all stories of ghosts and revenants wishing to impart secrets to the living, or to redress injuries, or to exact revenge, are utterly improbable. The souls of the dead are above such earthly concerns. Nor is it likely that persons about to expire have time to send their souls on journeys to distant friends in order to alert them to their fatal emergency. It is possible that the devil comes in such shapes to tempt mortals, but it is more likely that gullible people mistake an idle fancy of their own brains for a spiritual presence, as "when the Eye sees double, and Imagination makes it self a Telescope to the Soul, not to show Realities, but to . . . show things as in being which are not" (Defoe 1735: 327). The truth of the matter is that the converse of spirits is conducted in its purest form as pressure between two intelligences, "Soul conversing with Soul, Spirit communicating to Spirit, one intellectual Being to another . . . by secret Conveyances." These pressures and hints are capable of affecting the recipient imagination with "Impulses, Forebodings, Misgivings, and other imperceptible Communications" (56, 59). Now it may well be that for the surer transfer of its message, the spirit will transform an invisible into a visible medium by adopting as its person another recently disembodied soul, and speaking in its first person. Thus, James Haddock returned to earth to ensure his son was not disinherited, but it was "Haddock" who did this, not the real Haddock's ghost, that is, a benevolent spirit acting and speaking in his person. The story of the Duke of Buckingham, warned to abandon his dissolute career by the specter of his father, is another case in point, for "the Shape assumed was the most likely to give weight to the Errand . . . the Figure . . . as it were aptest to enforce the Message . . . [a] Surface or Outside . . . put on like a Masquerade Habit" (290). This explains among other things why spirits in role dislike being asked who they are (278).

The personate spirit operating on the imagination of a human patient, issuing hints and notices by sympathy while dressed in the first person of someone else, has another important task to perform, and that the rebuttal of false stories being told on earth by humans or by other alleged spirits. A woman misled by the lies of her lover is kept from harm by the advice of a spirit, for she tells the story of this intervention so steadily and consistently that her deceiver submits to her narrative, and withdraws his own (150–51). Whenever the gold standard of secret converse is set against mere invention, the truth is instantly distinguishable from the lie. That the soul of a dead merchant should go to London to inform his wife and maid of a host of impertinent details, "This, I say, has to me no Consistency in it, no Coherence, it does not hang together in my Opinion at all, nor can I make any common Sense of it; no, not if I was to come to the old poetick Fiction of Charon and his Ferry-Boat. . . . 'Tis founded wholly in the Imagination; and though the Imagination may not in this Case form the Apparition, yet 'tis evident the Imagination only appropriates it to the Person, that is to the Soul of the Person, who has really no Share in the Operation" (272). Tales like these, "I take not to be imaginary but fictitious, and made or supplied out of the Invention of the Relator, in order to dish up the Story" (273). If the reader compares Aubrey's account of the Duke of Buckingham's apparition with Clarendon's, it is plain that Clarendon's works as a credible story, whereas Aubrey's belongs to the fictions "of the very very many Relators, or who have called themselves Relators, of that Story" (273). Finally, it is not only the coherence of the true story, as opposed to the inchoate tale hatched out of sheer invention, that makes a difference; it is also the fact that true communications from the spirit world to the human imagination always have a good effect. The point of the story is not simply to charm an audience with its coherence and probability. The telling of it is an important event: it contradicts and discredits an opinion or tale that should never have been broadcast and at the same time gets something done, changes the circumstances of those that hear it, or changes them, for the better. This is the purpose of his early pamphlet, *A True Relation of the Apparition of Mrs Veal* (1705), where Mrs. Bargrave is made to understand by the figure of someone already dead that Mrs. Veal's brother is failing to execute her will. In his opening of his *History of Apparitions*, Defoe vindicates his claim to marry invisible phenomena to "the Reality of the thing it self," and to set "things in a true light, between Imagination and solid Foundation" ([iii], [ii]) by showing that what we imagine is often a fuse between two realities, an invisible and a visible.

If we put all of this together, we can see how closely *Robinson Crusoe* follows the pattern laid down: an imagination alerted by hints and notices of spiritual converse frames a story that then transpires as a reality—an allegory transformed into a history, a shrewd intuition that becomes transfigured, real, affirming the truth-value of the preposterous relation of cause to effect implied in the proposition, "as I imagined it, so it was." So accustomed is he to being acted on in this way, the hero finally personates a specter on his own account when he comes to give useful hints and notices to the victims of the mutiny— "Is it a real Man, or an Angel!" they cry (Defoe 1983: 254). Although he denies he is the person of a secret minister, effectually he is both the creature and agent of such ministry; and as Crusoe starts telling his story to people who find it credible not least because it has come to pass around them, they themselves blend into the fabric of what is told. Behind these narratives are to be found not only the secret admonitions that have taught Crusoe's imagination how to shape his world, but also the editor—and indeed the author—whose imaginations must be supposed to have been acted on the same way, for if the stories they deliver are credible, are they not also proof of the reality of the invisible influences they represent? An undulating thread, now seen and now unseen, stitches the immaterial to the material so that we readers cannot tell the difference between a dream and a fact, an excited imagination and an imagined excitement, stories told and the tale of their telling, or finally between Robinson Crusoe and "Robinson Crusoe." The fiction resulting from that personation is as true and real, and as virtuous in its outcome, as James Haddock's when he is personated by an angel called "James Haddock."

How poorly *Roxana* measures up against this standard is easily seen. Told by a "Relator," a term reserved for the cheats whose clumsy lies serve only to dish up a story, Roxana's is incoherent in every way. If nothing else were needed to convict the narrative of improbability, the apparition of the jeweler would do it. She sees him as a bloody specter at the very moment he is taking leave of her, hours before his murder (Defoe 1981: 53). If this were the communication of soul to soul, the jeweler himself would have received the notice, not Roxana; and if, after his death, the vision had appeared to her, one would have had to ask what advice it was conveying to her through the person of her consort. After his actual murder she specifies what she saw in that scene before it occurred, and it makes no sense. She says she sees him first as a skeleton "rotten and wasted"; then as a corpse freshly killed, his face covered with gore; and finally as a heap of blood-stained clothes (55). We are left to conclude either that this was a temptation from the devil (for immediately afterward she possesses herself illegally of the man's large fortune in gems and money, thereafter to be the foundation of her own); or that it was made up, "a Fiction, a Cheat . . . only a Story made by the Invention of Story-makers . . . [with] no reality in it" (Defoe 1735: 274). Roxana's "Relator" tries hard but hopelessly to give these incoherences a virtuous turn, planting signs and tokens of repentance at all junctures, none of which is vindicated by events, each one of which is ornamented with some reference to the devil, a sure sign either of an editorial lie or a narrative framed by evil intentions. There is nothing told in this story that has a virtuous tendency: nothing therefore to signal the beneficent effect of spirit upon imagination, or imagination upon reality.

Assuming that Defoe did not deliberately sit down to write an improbable novel where the imperfections of the heroine are matched by the incompetence of her Relator, we come back to the question of what was he trying to achieve. It is as if Defoe had conceived of his heroine as Rousseau conceives himself in *Reveries of a Solitary Walker*, as someone cast out from society: misunderstood, forsaken, scandalized, and alone, protected by none of the usual consolations friends provide, finding comfort only in those delicious pauses of empirical existence when, as Rousseau puts it, "a feeling . . . fills our soul entirely . . . with a sufficient, complete and perfect happiness which leaves no emptiness" (Rousseau 2004: 88). Roxana finds it very hard to exchange sentiments out of her own sphere—an impossibility occasioned not so much by the scandal of her life as from the difficulty of imparting the weight and flavor of the "Sence of Things" and the fullness of human delight. The final interruption of her story is one more occasion when it is not convenient to pretend that the story of her life is designed for public view. Not a character and, even when she dances as Roxana, not a person, Roxana presents the outlines of the author, half in the public eye, half out of it, consumed with assembling the concrete negative evidence of the certain existence of her private self.

Here is Samuel Johnson, summarizing an experience of reading biography which I imagine is quite the opposite of what most readers have when reading *Roxana*:

> All joy or sorrow for the happiness or calamities of others is produced by an act of the imagination, that realizes the event however fictitious, or approximates it however remote, by placing us, for a time, in the condition of him whose fortune we contemplate; so that we feel, while the deception lasts, whatever motions would be excited by the same good or evil happening to ourselves. (*Rambler* 60)

In the sequence Johnson traces from an act of imagination to the production of a fiction that puts us in the place of another person, a substitution constituting an event which happens to us, and of whose reality we cannot be in any doubt for the few moments the substitution lasts, he follows a path very similar to Defoe's in *Robinson Crusoe* and *The History of Apparitions*. It is a path that Adam Smith also hews to closely in *The Theory of Moral Sentiments*, when he makes a claim for sympathy as an act of imagination:

> But though sympathy is very properly said to arise from an imaginary change of situations with the person principally concerned, yet this imaginary change is not supposed to happen to me in my own person and character, but in that of the person with whom I sympathize. When I condole with you . . . in order to enter into your grief I do not consider what I . . . should suffer . . . but I consider what I should suffer if I was really you, and I not only change circumstances with you, but I change persons and characters. (Smith 1976 (1982): 317)

Setting aside Smith's loose use of the word character, we see that imagination does the same work described by Johnson of putting a person in the situation of another person, in fact of the person of that person, and sinking him so deeply in the fiction that it is as if the circumstances of grief or joy were really happening to him in the person of the other person. However, the fiction takes complete effect when I bring "your case home to myself" and restore the balance between your account and my own (317). Smith uses this phrase often, "bringing the case home to our own breast" (18); "we bring home in this manner the case to our own bosoms" (71); "we bring the case home to ourselves" (73). Imagination acts on us like a real event and metamorphoses us into another person, but the moral value of the change is known in the end by an agent conscious of what has been performed, and of what belongs to whom.

If the resumption of propriety achieved by the fetching of the fiction home were not to occur, what then? Smith mentions early in the *Theory* how imagination can exceed the bounds of an imaginary change, and inhabit a fiction that is not easily reversed and impossible to domesticate. He gives the example of sympathy with the dead, when we stun ourselves with the predicament of mortality by putting ourselves into the situations of cadavers which no longer have persons. The result is a terrible collision between the social and temporal properties of our persons and the permanent unconscious isolation of the figure with whom we sympathize. "It is from this very illusion of the imagination, that the foresight of our dissolution is so terrible to us, and that the idea of those circumstances, which undoubtedly can give us no pain when we are dead, makes us miserable while we are alive" (Smith 1976 (1982): 13). This is when imagination produces a bad fiction from which nothing useful or benevolent can emerge. Terry Castle and April Allison call it romance, and so does Defoe (Defoe 1981: 72).

If we put the two hints together—an ideal self masked by bad fiction that conforms in some way with romance—it is possible to place Roxana next door to another female hero who is immersed in sensations, passions, and stories that have nothing to do with probable representation? Charlotte Lennox's Arabella, as Catherine Gallagher has pointed out, does not believe that romance is fiction; it is history. She has no time for facts that are not true, and she finds an abundance of true facts in the punctual and impartial chronicles of the French salon romancers such as Scudéry and La Calprenède. As Gallagher explains, the importance of history for Arabella lies in its non-textual nature, into which she immerses herself not as a reader but as an active participant, using to the full the non-reflective intuition that Kames assigns to the illusion of "ideal presence," when history lives and breathes around a fascinated eyewitness (Kames 2005: 1.68). What Arabella finds there are "historical exempla of the eternally real" (Gallagher 1994: 189), each set out with all the demonstrable force of a theorem. She is a witness to "pure unmix'd Truth," mathematical in the severity of its propositions and in the force of its conclusions. By virtue of this demonstrable truth, quite the opposite of empirical knowledge, she acquires what she calls her glory, a faculty she exercises in the extensive and lawless empire of Love (Lennox 1989: 106, 171, 320). The empire of love is like a highly formalized state of nature in which no character or person could possibly be preserved:

> Arabella ... went on to prove the independent Sovereignty of Love, which, said she, may be collected from all the Words and Actions of those Heroes who were inspir'd by this Passion. We see it in them, pursued she, triumphing not only over all natural and avow'd Allegiance, but superior even to Friendship, Duty, and Honour itself. (321)

Such glorious anarchy of mind Hobbes had already identified as the chief lie of romance. He named Don Quixote its most notable exemplar, who claimed to have done what he never did while announcing himself as someone whom he was not (Hobbes 1994: 50; 1996: 16). And all this was achieved by taking romances for histories, and descriptions for actual events, in contempt of common sense and the law of the land. But it is intriguing that defenders of individual glory, all the way from an ingenious madman like Quixote to a philosopher like Descartes, use fiction, imperfect fiction, as the bulwark of an ideal self, and as an experiment in bringing referentiality to its zero degree. Remember that in the *Meditations*, Descartes invents the improbable fiction of an evil genie in order to mock the evidence of the senses: "I shall consider that the heavens, the earth, colours, figures, sound, and all other external things are naught but . . . illusions and dreams . . . I shall consider myself as having no hands, no eyes, no flesh, no blood, nor any senses, yet falsely believe myself to possess all these things" (1996: 62). Traces of the same mockery of empirical actuality may be found in Quixote's enchanters, whose transformations of authentic chivalry into squalid particularity dramatize the implausibility of any referent but that of glory. The genie and the enchanters are cousins of Roxana's devils, who provide the lurid scenes of temptation behind which her "Sence of things" can thrive in peace. As for Arabella, the fiction she resists is very much like Descartes', including as it does all the contingent details of the phenomenal world, and all systems of arranging and judging them. Only when she is forced into a forensic conjecture by her clergyman-preceptor, conceding for the sake of argument that history itself might be fiction, is she overwhelmed by instrumental untruth. Then she loses her glory and her *estate*, a word Gallagher allows to resonate with heroic pathos (Gallagher 1994: 195).

The empire of love, the recovery of the golden world, the privacy of delight, and the radical first personality of Descartes' skepticism conspire to define worlds of single individuals whose intuitive and demonstrable truths are unmodified by any active principle of common sense. Roxana's is perhaps the grimmest and most literal of these insofar as it introduces the likely fact of infanticide, Hobbes's most decisive proof of the ancient dominion of women, and the limit case of the gendered mystery of romance:

> The question lyeth now in the state of meer Nature; where there are supposed no lawes of Matrimony; no lawes for the Education of Children; but the Law of Nature, and the naturall inclination of the Sexes one to another, and to their Children. In this condition of meer Nature, either the Parents between themselves dispose of the dominion over the Child by Contract, or do not dispose thereof at all. . . . If there be no Contract, the Dominion is in the Mother. For in the condition of meer Nature, where there are no Matrimoniall lawes, it cannot be known

who is the Father, unlesse it be declared by the Mother. . . . Again, seeing the Infant is first in the power of the Mother, so as she may either
nourish, or expose it. (Hobbes 1996: 140)

The mere state of nature, where the natural right of a woman to call fictions truths sits alongside that of nourishing or neglecting children, and
of coupling without contract, pretty well describes the state in which
Roxana conceals her glory and secretly pursues the satisfactions of what
Hobbes would call an author. Gallagher finds it useful to explore the
analogy between the lawlessness of romance and the literal state of authorship, finding in both a core of absolute freedom that is non-textual
and unrepresentable. It is located in the brief interlude when a Hobbesian
author and a female writer can enjoy their estate. Thanks to the Copyright Act of 1710, the author of an original text—let us say Charlotte Lennox with the manuscript of *The Female Quixote* in her hand—enjoyed
dominion over something that was entirely her own and which came
to her not by virtue of distributive justice and the law, nor by her labor
expended upon the stuff of nature, but solely from herself. Authors like
her were "their own people and original owners of their copyrights"—
original in the full and primitive meaning of the word (Gallagher 1994:
157). Not until they chose, or were compelled by necessity, to enter the
market, and sell the copyright for fourteen years, was that original and
limitless dominion lost. But when it was, the author was dispossessed of
something that had never before been in the market, and even now was
only equivocally a commodity. When Arabella gives up resisting fiction
and loses her estate, the same authorial loss is sustained: "As long as
Arabella refuses fiction and resists the suppositional, she owns her estate,
but when she capitulates to textuality . . . she understands her 'real-life'
function as a representation, as a means of transferring and preserving
the property [of her estate] by giving herself away" (195). In short, she
takes her place alongside her author as a person in a system of contracts
and representational politics.

Foucault has suggested that Descartes' notable contribution to modernity was to define a relation of the self to truth (as opposed to knowledge)
outside the ethos of virtue (Foucault 1997: 278). You do not have to be
good to find it out; nor is it proved by its successful communication to
other people. That is to say, it is not arrived at by empirical means, nor
yet by virtuous ones. If this is the beginning of the radical independence
of the author from the practices of characters and persons, then it precipitates a new kind of isolated nondescript—the spy, the unowned thing, the
slave, the idol, the mad traveler, the still life—and the kind of fiction this
book is trying to contextualize.

PART THREE

Authors and Nonpersons

CHAPTER 8

'Me and My Ink'

> Self-acting ink, that 'ere, it's wrote your mark upon the wall,
> old gen'lm'n.
>
> —Charles Dickens, *The Pickwick Papers*

There is a genre of writing in which the delivery of the self makes way for more immediate notices of its sense of things, and which is therefore more suitable to the idea of the "author" I am trying now to specify. Michel Foucault has traced a history of what he calls self-writing running from Epictetus to Descartes in which the work of inscription is not to record what happened to the self; rather, it is to provide a mirror similar to Roxana's in whose reflection is found, Narcissus-like, the event that brings the self into focus: "a means of establishing a relationship of oneself with oneself" (Foucault 1997: 211). An inheritor of this tradition, Montaigne explains that he is not fashioning himself for public esteem, being sufficient even in his ignorance, for "a sufficient Man is sufficient throughout" (Montaigne 1711: 3.24 ["Of Repentance"]). On this account Montaigne is hardy enough to write "purposely of nothing but nothing" (3.381 ["Of Physiognomy"]). More like a spiritual exercise or meditation, writing the self has no other object and no other audience than the self; nor is it reached by dividing the self into the portion that represents and that which inspects. An author is not adorning the self for social activity or for public or even private applause, nor is she framing a narrative that will represent the self as a character or a person. When in his *Meditations* Descartes considers his ideas of the world as those of an isolated "thinking thing," he says they are exclusively his own concern, "To these it is certainly not necessary that I should attribute any author than myself" (Descartes 1996: 77). Hobbes's author has this at least in common with Descartes', namely, that neither is concerned to disclose traits of which the world might judge, being engaged entirely in the discovery of what is important to a single individual.

The incompleteness of Roxana's story therefore dramatizes a conflict not between a woman's shame and its public acknowledgment, which is what her "Relator" wishes to suggest, but between the private memoranda of self-writing and print. In the Preface, he circles the issue, wanting to say that the story is a transparent delivery of the lady's words, a history that speaks for itself; but at the same time he concedes that some of it is suppressed. While claiming that this is a necessary step taken by himself to prevent scandal, it is clear that what he chooses not to print is far exceeded by what she refused to say, or have said, in public. His phrase "Buried in the Dark" (Defoe 1981: 1) leaves undetermined the nature of what is not published, but if the Cartesian aspect of Roxana's authorial self-idealization is plausible, then there is something more substantial than rumor that has not seen the light: something more like the journal ("full of many dull things" [Defoe 1983: 69]) that Crusoe abandons for want of interest and ink. In *Foe*, J. M. Coetzee's conflation of Defoe's two novels, the nature of writing and materiality of ink is important. The Roxana figure is forced to act like Crusoe, badly impeded by a narrative that is too much like a journal and by her mute companion Friday, who cannot or will not utter the extra details she believes will make her story complete. Susan Barton tries to teach the silent man how to write, and on his slate he chalks the same figure over and over again, legions of hieroglyphs looking like the letter O with legs. It is an enigma comparable with *mass-klo*, the word that Primo Levi hears coming out of the mouth of Hurbinek, the mute child in Auschwitz (Agamben 2002: 38), except that it is written. Barton ends her narrative with a vision of Friday under water, apparently drowned, and out of his mouth is flowing a stream of sepia liquid, a rebus of inky silence, keeping the sense of things buried in the dark.

In earlier chapters, the difference between personate representation and authorial writing was dramatized not in the handling of pen and ink but in emergencies where the familiar use of print is made strange: Ernst Jünger in a bombardment, the woman of Berlin surviving the Russian occupation, Thomas Peascod about to be shot. Bewildered parties to events which form no intelligible narrative, they confront a disconcerting world where things move around without any human direction. A peculiarity common to each of them is the proximity of the undone person to printed pages—Jünger comes across a fine edition of *Don Quixote* in a ruined house; the Berlin woman tries to scratch a meal out of a sentence in a popular novel; Peascod is overwhelmed by the pathos of the title page of an edition of *Pilgrim's Progress*. Reduced to a condition below or to one side of personhood, these people are involved in an intense physical and emotional relation to print. In it they spot some quality they have never seen before: beauty, a faithless promise of supply, immense sadness. Crusoe briefly finds something like the same radiance in the pages of his bible when, having fallen into despair on his desert island, he opens it at random for a timely sentence whose significance is to last no longer than his ink. In these four cases what is felt in the vicinity of a book is close to nostalgia, a longing for what is behind or antecedent to the bland arrangement of type on a page. They share a flavor of the property of the self lodged in ink prior to its alienation by the book trade, when the estate and glory of it was entirely one's own. The memory of this mood is itself preserved in written form. We would not know what print meant to Crusoe, Jünger, or the Berlin woman under extreme circumstances had they not jotted down memorials of their encounters with it. In the more dismal of the two endings supplied by Godwin for *Caleb Williams*, the hero records the extent of his moral and physical destitution, and the extremity of his solitude:

> If I could once again be thoroughly myself, I should tell such tales! . . . But I never shall—never—never!—I sit in a chair in a corner, and never move hand or foot—I am like a log—I know all that very well, but I cannot help it!—I wonder which is the man, I or my chair. (Godwin 1982: 334)

With no more sense than that of a thing—a log or a stone—he alludes to the secrets he will never tell, but he does so by writing it all down in a letter to Mr. Collins. No matter how distant from the amenities of character and person, or how immobile, Caleb still has the resource of being able to set down as in a diary the extremity of his condition. At the same time, it is clear that writing does not preserve a minimal community of two; it is the legend over the gateway into the life of a thinking thing.

There are two important investigations of writing's relation to print produced in the early eighteenth century, and both refer constantly, almost obsessively, to the name, function, and status of the author. These are Swift's *A Tale of a Tub* (1704) and Shaftesbury's "Soliloquy; or, Advice to an Author," published in *Characterstics of Men, Manners, Opinions, Times* (1711). Each text explores in detail what is at stake in the production of the self by means of pen and ink in a culture where the sanction of print confirms the value of what one has done, thought, or indeed what one is. Each has a counter-text that complicates even further the relation of writing to print, and of secrecy to publicity. In the case of Swift's *A Tale of a Tub*, it is "An Apology" written by the "Author" and prefixed to the 1710 edition; while Shaftesbury's "Soliloquy" has its prototype in a manuscript of meditations written several years before the *Characteristics* and never intended for publication, eventually seeing the light of day in 1900 in an edition by Benjamin Rand entitled *The Philosophical Regimen* (1900). Between them, Swift and Shaftesbury provide an exhaustive coverage of the strains and paradoxes of self-writing, and of the troubled sequence that transforms a penned sheet into a printed one. They offer an insight into the secular autobiographies of authors such as Francis Kirkman, John Dunton, and Charles Gildon; and later, of Rousseau and Sterne. Swift from the point of view of a modern Author and Shaftesbury from the point of view of an ancient Stoic confront the problem of a self detached from all influences except its own activity, as if it were nothing more or less than Descartes' thinking thing. From now on in this chapter, I shall distinguish the writing thing as Author, and all false claimants to that title as "Author."

❦

Swift's references to Locke are few and insignificant, but Hobbes's *Leviathan* and *De Cive* made a bigger impression. The picture of the commonwealth as a congregation of little persons making up one large person, represented in the iconic figure shown in Abraham Bosse's frontispiece for *Leviathan* (Bredekamp 2006: 31–51), piqued his fancy. It suggested a parallel between Hobbes's idea of the structure of the state and Lucretius's account of the mind as a congeries of minute particles, "exceedingly small, smooth and round" (Lucretius 1992: 203; 3.177–80). Swift brings it up whenever he is thinking of the imperfect unity of bodies of people, especially authors, which usually he ascribes to the incoherence of their thoughts. The artificial person of the commonwealth, bearing the persons of all those little individuals and itself borne in turn by the sovereign, and thereafter by all the magistrates and office-holders that bear *his* person, represents for Swift a peculiarly fallible political bond. For him it exhibits the opposite of what Hobbes offers as a coherent distribution of intensive and extensive authority; instead, it fosters the perpetual threat of isolation and conflict. Swift judges Leviathan to be just another name for mob, and sees everyone inside that kind of whale professing an authority that never can be vindicated and owning actions that are not theirs. A brain formed on the same principle of union is liable to extreme unsteadiness edging into madness.

In the Preface of *A Tale of a Tub*, the Author explains rather awkwardly the allegory behind the title of his work. Like the tubs thrown overboard by mariners to divert the violence of whales, his performance is intended to distract the attention of pamphleteers from making attacks on the institutions of church and state. The whale in this case is Hobbes's Leviathan, "which tosses and plays with all schemes of Religion and Government," and the ship is the state or commonwealth. His diversionary tactic will "prevent these Leviathans from tossing and sporting with the Commonwealth (which of itself is too apt to fluctuate)" (Swift 1920: 40). Far from providing the energy that fuses the state together, the actions of the whale are, in his reading, potentially fatal to it. The whale is not the person of the commonwealth at all, it is its adversary. Hobbes's *Leviathan* is deployed for another analogy in *A Discourse on the Mechanical Operation of the Spirit*, where the image of a multitude of small creatures

formed into a column is applied to the brain, "a Crowd of little Animals
... [which] cling together in the Contexture we behold, like the Picture
of Hobbes's Leviathan, or like Bees in perpendicular swarm upon a Tree"
(279). In both examples of union—of the state and of the mind—Swift's
modern Author mistakes Leviathan-as-Commonwealth for a crowd, ig-
noring the unity which Hobbes's "artificiall Man" is supposed to embody.
The factional pamphleteers inside the whale endanger the state not because they are a rival body but because they are inchoate and represent
nothing but each warring individual. As for the little creatures, the bites
of whose teeth cause us to think and feel, they are like Mandeville's un-
regenerate bees, each engaged on its own particular business with no
thought for the ultimate end or meaning of its activity. Of the union of
bees Hobbes had this to say, "Yet their swarms are still not *common-
wealths* [*civitates*], and so the animals themselves should not be called
political; for their government is only an accord, or many wills with one
object, not (as a commonwealth needs) one will" (Hobbes 1998: 71).

Hobbes explained the difference between a crowd and Leviathan in his
De Cive as follows:

> What actually is a Crowd of men? ... they are not a single entity but a
> number of men, each of whom has his own will and his own judgement
> about every proposal ...There will be nothing about which the whole
> crowd, as a person distinct from every individual, can rightly say, this is
> mine more than another's. Nor is there any action which should be at-
> tributed to the crowd as their action ... For this reason a crowd is not
> a natural person. But if the same crowd individually agree that the will
> of some one man or the consenting wills of a majority of themselves
> is to be taken as the will of all, that number then becomes one person.
> (Hobbes 1998: 75–6)

Once the crowd is represented by a person, it is transformed into Leviathan, a creature incapable of menacing the state because it is fundamental
to the representational structure that renders the commonwealth a gov-
ernable unity: one person, an artificial man, a mortal god, the body of the
king, sovereign power, and so on through a series of personate substitutions. But while it is still a crowd, each atom of it dwells in a miniature
state of nature where property cannot be held, authority is limited to each
solitary individual, and the preservation of the self is perpetually at risk.

Swift's Author acts as just such an individual in a crowd and cannot
conceive of a figure fit to represent his relation to it, although he tries very
hard. He talks boastfully of the vast number of his fellow writers, the immense bales of paper they use, the ten thousand ways their works go out
of the world never to be seen again, the multifarious symptoms of madness, the innumerable followers of zealous Jack, and so on, as if he were

about to synthesize them all. But he is dogged by particularity, confessing that it is as hard "to get quit of Number as of Hell" (55). Unassimilated particularity makes his Leviathan a personification of anarchy, the shape of shapelessness, like Milton's Death. It exhibits none of the symmetry of a corporate entity; and having confused this crowd with a person, it is clear that the Author lacks any real idea of how to represent a body of individuals, either as an image or as a constituency. Without such a body behind him, he has access neither to a system of justice, nor to the property it guarantees. Defining "the Republick of Dogs" as "an Institution of the Many" where rights of possession lie in common and where everyone is in a "State of War, of every Citizen against every Citizen," the author of *The Battle of the Books* reduces politics from a commonwealth to the state of nature, and authorship from the study of literature to combat (218–19). The nature of this combat is specified in *A Tale of a Tub* as the use of gun-quills for firing ink at sheets of paper, which then confront other sheets in a perpetual strife of ink and print. This warfare originates in a quarrel over property that cannot be arbitrated, namely: who owns Parnassus.

From this original attempt at pillage and violent occupation it follows that all titles to authorship among the Moderns (whether they are assumed or alleged) remain suspect and contestable, and any system of representation to which they pretend is correspondingly dubious. *The Battle of the Books*, and the dispute about ancient and modern learning on which it is based, began with Richard Bentley's and William Wotton's challenge to Sir William Temple's attribution of authorship of Aesop's fables to Aesop and of Phalaris's letters to Phalaris. These are really the names of a succession of editors and interpolators, argued Bentley, who was satisfied with the authenticity of no writer who was not fully annotated by himself, as Bentley's Horace, Bentley's Milton, and so on. From the pro-Ancient point of view, this sort of editorship was not a judicious assignment of property, just a more elaborate form of theft. The ladder at the gallows—the favorite oratorical machine among the British—stands so eminent because it institutionalizes the relationship between theft and authorship, being ascended only by those remarkable for confounding the distinction between *meum* and *tuum* (63). Bentley's Milton is no longer Milton, therefore, but Bentley garnished with bits of Milton. The ladder is not so much the penalty for literary felony as it is the necessary circumstance of modern authorship, for without usurpation and theft there would be nothing to write, nothing falsely to claim, and no position from which to make announcements. Swift's definition of a commonplace book as a supplemental memory in his *A Letter of Advice to a Young Poet* sums up the modern position, for "there you enter not only your own original thoughts . . . but such of other men as you think fit to make your own" (Swift 1803: 8.71). For his part, the modern author of *A Tale of a Tub* owns that none of the "Seven Hundred Thirty Eight Flowers and shining Hints" in his commonplace book in fact belongs to him (209). Yet it is solely on the basis of these borrowings that he has set up as author. He pretends to authorship on the basis of what he has seized, in a world at war where everyone is doing the same.

The corollary is that no one owns any thing, no one shares a common cause with another, no artificial person represents groups of individuals, no one has a continuous relation to time, and no one makes any sense. In the war with the Ancients, the Author notices even in his own cohort widespread defections to the enemy, "and our nearest Friends begin to stand aloof, as if they were half-ashamed to own Us" (65). Authors have challenged "Authors, as unworthy their established Post in the Commonwealth" (64). And as if Authors were not already acting in a sufficiently perplexed, fantastic, and futile relation to one another, he adds implausibly, "This is the utmost I am authorized to say upon so ungrateful and melancholy a Subject" (64–65), speaking as usual in the voice of the pseudo-person of this non-community. Similarly, in his address to Prince Posterity, where the Author wishes once more to cite copiousness of literary production as proof of the existence of his commonwealth and of its permanence, he can produce no evidence because what his associates have written is not owned, nor is it kept. There is in modernity, as in Hobbes's state of nature, no account of time (Hobbes 1996: 89), so no sooner does a modern work of wit emerge than instantly it turns to waste, and is consigned to the "Abyss of Things" (32) where it is heard of no more. The latest writer is the only writer visible. On a broad front the Author stands vindicated by nothing but his bare assertions, which are necessarily spurious ("I my Self, the Author . . . am a Person" [180]). Even what he confesses (owning that his flowers and shining hints are not his own) dramatizes the paradox of the Cretan liar. Like Gulliver, he is forced to say only the thing which is not, and to affirm that which is neither ownable nor evident, because he keeps no company but with himself, an atom in a mob of other atoms.

Notwithstanding the problems he faces in establishing himself the person or vicar of "the Institution of the Many" (218), the Author persistently refers to himself as a representative of communities. At different times he writes on behalf of "a vast flourishing Body" and "a Legion" of authors, as a member of the "illustrious Fraternity" of Grub Street and secretary of "our Corporation of Poets" (33, 99, 73); he mentions too that he is the official agent of a Grand Committee and the sponsor of "a large Academy" (40–41). His most valiant attempt in this regard is to speak for the inhabitants of Bedlam, "that honourable Society, whereof I had some Time the Happiness to be an unworthy Member" (176). Here the analogy between crowds and brains is perfected as reciprocal disorder, and the only authority the Author can muster for representing the insane—those who, like children and fools according to Hobbes (Hobbes 1996: 113), are incapable of conferring authority—is the fact of his own insanity.

These so-called associations, academies, and fraternities are miniatures of the state itself, the shapeless Leviathan in whose service has been sacrificed "Me and my Ink" (71). It is plain that the structure of the Author's brain is fully as weak as the social bond he claims to represent. The person he inhabits is as evanescent as the cloud he points to while explaining to Prince Posterity the metamorphoses of a modern community—now a bear, now an ass, now a dragon. His Leviathan is just such a shifting image, and there is no authority by which he can represent it, no continuity that would give it a history, and no symmetry that might allow it to be embodied in a single will and person. The authority of this Author is defined by a series of failures to own anything, to identify a reader he can trust, or to set his writing credibly within any system of meaning. All he can do is write, and all he can affirm is that, from moment to moment, he is writing. His testimony amounts to no more than the trail of his ink.

This is no impediment to the grandeur of the authorial illusion. The aim is the universal benefit of mankind, to be achieved by means of the advancement of universal knowledge, first enlarged to all spheres of learning and then distilled into a universal system (180, 106, 126). His cabbalistic and alchemical agendas are aspects of a mystical cult of unity and abridgement—the *Iliad* in a nutshell—that Michel de Certeau finds typical of all mystical and proto-modernist enterprises in the seventeenth century, when coalitions of menacing and violent circumstances throughout Europe weakened or removed traditional sources of authority, tempting isolated egos to invent utopian dialectics of "the nothing and the all" (De Certeau 1992: 156). Although this dialectics was pitched at the conjunction of knowledge and practice, or what Bacon called the union of contemplation and action, its novelty necessarily divided it from institutional norms and received forms of expression, leading to exaggerations, improprieties, and barbarisms, particularly in usage (119, 133). De Certeau points out that mystics were notorious not only for their pseudo-synthetic programs of knowledge, but also for the jargon and obscurity of their universal languages, and for the extravagance of their metaphors and tropes (113–19). Our Author refers to this modern state of nonsense and glossolalia when he complains that his enemy Time ("Author of this universal Ruin'") has obliterated the works of Authors who could not write English: "Unhappy Infants, many of them barbarously destroyed, before they have so much as learnt their Mother-Tongue to beg for Pity" (32–33). Similarly, in *The Mechanical Operation of the Spirit*, he notices that the rhetoric of the modern saints issues as "insignificant Words, Incoherences, and Repetition" and sometimes just as noise—sighs and humming (290).

The gulf separating a universal system from mere noise is analogous to that dividing a true person from our modern Author in the *Tale*. On the one side is a representative of a body—of knowledge, people, or callings—and on the other is a purely singular individual with no audience and nothing of interest to say beyond himself. Swift finds another analogue for this difference in language. As a person is someone standing for other people, so a figure or metaphor is a word that stands for other words: Leviathan for the commonwealth, a swarm of bees for a crowd, for instance. And just as the proper language of a person would be figurative—eloquence and wit—so the natural language of the Author is purely literal, or what Crusoe would call "many dull things." His enterprise stems from misconstruing the metaphor of Leviathan as whale, and deciding that "tub" means simply *tub* (40). Driven to his wit's end by the ephemeral conditions of the literary marketplace, he assures Prince Posterity "that what I am going to say is literally true this minute I am writing" (36). The arc of his writing follows the line leading from clumsy figurative beginnings to inevitably literal endings. He starts his treatise by stating that all meaning lies hidden beneath occult figures and fables, and that all wisdom is shut up in allegories. His "Scheme of Oratorial Receptacles" is a vast plan of wit ("a Type, a Sign, an Emblem, a Shadow, a Symbol, bearing Analogy to the spacious Commonwealth of Writers" [61]). But because this commonwealth is no more substantial than Leviathan in the allegory of the tub, its signs and emblems are as incapable of representing a hidden meaning as the author is of representing the crowd of writers. He has no other relation to the institution of the many but that of an individual; so these figures have no other effectual relation to a body of ideas than single literal words. We observe the early metaphors of *A Tale* contradicting one another (wisdom is first a fox and then a hen) until they lose all buoyancy and fall into matter. The genealogy of the true critic dissolves into a haphazard collection of hieroglyphic possibilities—critic as ass, serpent, beggar, brass, rat, and dog—just like the clouds on a windy day that represented the modern commonwealth of authors successively as a bear, an ass, and a dragon. Eventually the Author determines to meddle with this kind of wit no longer, parting company with those whose converting imaginations "dispose them to reduce all Things into Types . . . whose peculiar Talent lies in fixing Tropes and Allegories to the Letter, and refining what is Literal into Figure and Mystery" (190).

Of course as much of the tale as is told is itself an allegory, a fable of parental authority that represents the history of the Christian Church. But even this contrives its own ruin, for "coats" end up as heterogeneous pieces of fabric, and the "will" is reduced to a material residue of words that is scraped from the surface of the document and swallowed. The allegory of the tale runs out of steam when finally there is no text left worth interpreting and no authority left to dispute. Then everything is literalized. Nothing remains of the tension between the story and its application that might preserve interest or suspense. At this point the Author finds his commonplace book empty and his stuff for digressions all used up, just like his fable. So he is driven to his last shift and commences to write upon nothing—owning in effect that his authority extends neither to the past nor the future, neither to allegory nor even to literal meaning, just to nonsense inscribed this very moment on a piece of paper. His treatise disintegrates into a special kind of noise, the sound of scratching made when "the Pen still move[s] on; by some called the Ghost of Wit" (208).

The material form of this nonsense is always the same: a dark and unpleasant liquid draining from the individuals that compose crowds. Whether a crowd is understood as a brain or a Leviathan, its particles yield phlegm, snot, sperm, poison—fluids that ultimately take the form of ink. The citizens of the little commonwealth of the brain, for instance, are subject to a looseness of the bowels that flows from the head as snot-verse and rheum-rhetoric, and can be improved by orators: "A Master Workman shall blow his Nose so powerfully as to pierce the Hearts of his People" (281). The war of all against all is fought with ink derived from the brains and gall of modern authors, seasoned with extra supplies from the teats of the goddess Criticism. In the introductory fable of the spider and the bee in *The Battle of the Books*, the odious self-sufficiency of the spider is explained by Aesop as an allegory of modern authors, whose originality is nothing but poison distilled from their own insides and shat or spat at the public as "Excrement and Venom" (232). No sooner is it received than it is returned in a perpetual cycle of projectile sewage. Thus, the Bedlam professor survives on ordure, expelling then re-ingesting it (178); and the Aeolist congregation join a circle, blowing each other up with wind that is then belched and farted into the mouths of the faithful (154). The serpent-critic "emit[s] a poisonous Juice whereof, whoever drinks, that Person's Brains fly out of his Nostrils" (100). The modern books in St. James's Library are in the same plight, either discharging this foul effluent or doused with it, the occasion and the means of their endless warfare. The "Author" of the Apology (not our Author but another) declares, perhaps too confidently, that his work is so much his own as never to suffer from this poisonous stream, proof against "Dirt-Pellets however envenom'd the Mouths may be that discharge them" (10).

The stream of effluent as ink has an important place in the Scriblerian imagination. In *The Letter of Advice*, Swift regards it as a danger to public health in Dublin to have no means of channeling the leakage from writers' brains. He praises the use of Grub Street as a common drain in which authorial purgings can be safely carried off. Pope returns to this image in the *Dunciad*, where the Fleet Ditch runs pitch-black with the dirt and venom of dunces into the Thames, like ink on to a fair sheet:

> The King of dykes! than whom no sluice of mud
> With deeper sable blots the silver flood.
>
> *(Dunciad* 2. ll. 273–4)

In the *Epistle to Arbuthnot*, Pope follows Swift in identifying the filthy self-sufficiency of the modern writer as spider-like, who out of himself spins a new self-pleasing thread for every one that gets snapped in the war of wit (*Epistle to Arbuthnot* ll. 89–92). As for madness, it spills directly from the disordered brain onto adjacent surfaces:

> Is there, who, locked from in and paper, scrawls
> With desperate charcoal round his darkened walls?
>
> (ll 19–20)

Swift's Author compares his own performance with an inky phlebotomy, and "since my Vein is once opened, I am content to exhaust it a Running" (184). Even the "Author" of the Apology insists on his work as handwritten stuff that has flowed from his pen, sheets "which he could easily have corrected with a very few Blots" (4).

The preferment of blotted lines to the sanction of print (210) is in the case of modern authors an unlucky one, for no sooner is their copy typeset, printed, and bound than Time, the author of modern literary ruin, sets about destroying it, leaving no trace. For a while loose papers may be found in lanterns, broken windows, bakers' shops, and privies, but very soon they are lost forever in the Abyss of Things. *The Battle of the Books* is the mock-epic account of this destruction, where authors more favored by Time join in committing what the Author in his complaint to Prince Posterity laments as an Herodian slaughter of the innocents. The only remedy for this state of affairs is to reverse the process of publication as fast as possible, and turn print back into script or liquid. Transcription into a commonplace book is one method of putting printed words back into handwriting; but the alchemical technique for distilling an elixir out of "fair correct Copies, well bound in Calf's Skin" is even better, for by taking three drops of it and "snuffing it strongly up your Nose" (126), ink gets back to its source in the brain, flying up the nostrils instead of out of them. Jack's and Peter's tricks for reducing their father's will into food, medicine, or pickle are variations on this theme.

If the spider is the type of modern authors, spinning out its excrement and then sucking it back in, then the idol of this crowd is not our Author, who is adored and followed by no one, but the goddess Criticism. She evinces spider-like habits, being a divinity who feeds her subaltern agents ("Noise and Impudence, Dulness and Vanity") from her spleen, which they suck like a breast, imbibing the black liquor that will foment the war of all against all. When Criticism enters the field of battle, she flings some of this liquid into Bentley's mouth, provoking such a disturbance in his brain that when he starts fighting, "an atramentous Quality, of most malignant Nature, was seen to distil from his Lips" (251). Like the circulation of unspent sperm in the Digression on Madness, which evaporates into clouds and then distills into madness, ink courses through the body, alternating between the status of physical excrement and a big idea, a private embarrassment and a public outrage, but never finally transcending its material form of waste or its tendency to sustain a state of war. In personifying this process, Criticism does not assemble it into a real Leviathan, nor does she act as its person. She preserves the accidents of crowds—their atomization, pugnacity, and disorder—literally by supplementing the circulation of ink. She is like the god worshipped by Jack's disciples, "a new Deity, who hath since met with a vast Number of Worshippers, by some called Babel, by others, Chaos" (194). Such deities embody incoherence by manipulating its most obvious physical attributes—noise, waste, and dirt. They are not representations, visible or audible, of a summary idea of disorder; nor are they projections of human qualities. Criticism comes about like the personifications of Death, Fate, History of War, a figure necessary to be invented when humans lose or abdicate control of their own affairs, and what they thought they were doing starts happening to them. She embodies the accidence of writing, the stream of ink that writers at once exploit and endure, the means of reporting and the event reported.

Swift had been reading *De Rerum natura* carefully as he was composing *A Tale*. Among other aspects of Lucretian materialism that caught his fancy was the neglect of the arts of music, drama, and painting in the poem. In Lucretius's theater there are no actors, no figures bearing the persons of others, just the vivid colors of the awnings dyeing the audience different colors as the films thrown from the surfaces of the colored fabrics strike their bodies (Lucretius 1992: 283; 4.71–89). He delivers a world of perpetual movement, of blows given by the films and bark of things as they collide with our eyes or skin ("the blows take effect upon our body exactly as if some object were striking us and giving us the feeling of its own body" [Lucretius 297; 4.262–64]). The powerful moments of the Digression on Madness are short hymns to the voluptuous turning away from representation, where always there is a medium between the skins of things and our skin—an actor hidden beneath a mask or a meaning hidden beneath a metaphor—toward the directness of the sheer surfaces of bodies, whose loveliness possesses us. "He that can with Epicurus content his Ideas with the Films and Images that fly off upon his Senses from the Superficies of Things; Such a Man, truly wise, creams off Nature, leaving the Sower and the Dregs, for Philosophy and Reason to lap up" (174). There is an evident difference between the bitterness of literary conflict and the condition he calls "the Possession of being well deceived" (174). And what exactly would this possession amount to? Well, it is not something that he can own because this sort of possession is what happens to him, not what he takes or seizes. In this sense it is like writing liberated from the War of Criticism, being the means and the substance of the same pleasant sensation. The Author comes closest to it by means of pen and ink when he experiments with writing on nothing, the nothing he can own because he alone has created it, a nullity achieved in the privacy of his garret with his mind idling, just he and his pen leaking and scratching. The shape made by emptiness is not the image of a thing nor is it the sign of any idea, merely the liquid film of the brain itself. This exudation is not like snot, phlegm, or faeces because it lacks even an ostensible business with the public, being destitute of a medium such as print and barren of any other social value. Should the Author be tempted to desert the simplicity of this state of possession for the literary strife of Leviathan, it would be then that he would catch sight of himself as "a little paultry Mortal, droning, and dreaming, and drivelling to a Multitude" (278). As it is, he is more like the bird of paradise, flying for flying's sake until death brings him to the ground.

In 1710, Swift added an "Author" to *A Tale* in the shape of an anonymous apologist who writes in order to distinguish firmly in the reader's mind between his own wit and the imbecile literalisms of the Author he has impersonated. The difference between the two is handled almost exclusively as a social one. The "Author" belongs to a club resembling the community of wit praised by Shaftesbury in his *Letter on the Freedom of Wit and Humour*. His community is as solid and real as his authorship, its members committed to the pursuit of good taste and a relish for what is just and proper, standards of which he is the competent public representative. He proclaims himself the urbane and ironical counterpart of William Wotton, so awkward in his attempts at vernacular wit, and of Richard Bentley, a man who has steeped himself in literature not in order to civilize and polish himself, but to become more brutal in his combat with other authors. The wit of the "Author," on the other hand, is always current; and he is aware not only that his ethos embraces the best minds of the age but also those of the future ("the Book seems calculated to live at least as long as our Language" [3]). Significantly his wit is printed, no longer inhabiting loose sheets, and it is in the form of a book that it comes before the public, warranting his importance as someone who commands an audience, a representative status, a past and a future. He is proof against dirt pellets because his wit, like Virgil's or Horace's in St. James's Library, is the *brutum hominis* or soul lodged in a bound volume which is strong enough to survive the ravages of time (Swift 1920: 222).

Here is a distinction between himself and the Author upon which he enlarges. He explains that it was not sufficient merely to describe the savage traits and ill language of the literary crowd; wit—specified as irony— was introduced to distinguish taste from prejudice, raillery from railing, and so on, by means of a person bearing the person of a Modern. Regardless of how well such irony has passed in the club, however, it has caused some confusion in the public mind, not least in Queen Anne's, who was so outraged that not the best apology could make a bishop out of Swift. In his attempt to justify himself, the "Author" is obliged to stand back from the person he represented in order to explain in his own voice the art of ventriloquism. Irony being a species of wit whose value lies solely in its self-evidence, an ironist forced to instance and explain his use of it destroys his figurative deeds with literal definitions. The "Author" finds that his impersonation of the Author has implicated him in the very same rhetoric he held up to scorn, namely, the *citation* of an authority he cannot *demonstrate*. With no further access to the criterion of the club than to say he did once possess wit and use irony, there is no certain difference between the "Author" apologizing and the Author writing. On what distinction can the former rely if the proof is not in the pudding but in his averring that formerly he tasted it? The further he gets from self-evidence, the further he is driven into the body of the whale; and the deeper he goes there, the more he sounds like a dunce.

In a strangely self-annihilating gesture, the "Author"'s last shift as an apologist of irony is aggressively to declare his own anonymity, the very badge of Grub Sreet authorship, daring anyone to own what he himself cannot put his name to. How differently he performs here from Swift on the occasion recalled by Samuel Johnson, when he was challenged by an arrogant lawyer to own himself the author of a piece attacking him: "Mr Bettesworth, I was in my youth acquainted with great lawyers, who knowing my disposition to satire, advised me, that if any scoundrel or blockhead whom I had lampooned should ask, 'Are you the author of this paper?' I should tell him that I was not the author; and therefore I tell you, Mr Bettesworth, that I am not the author of those lines" (Johnson 1791: 3.404). The "Author" performs so poorly in his Apology not only because he literalizes his wit, but because in trying to say what he is instead of what he is not, he does not take the necessary step of denying himself. In owning that he is impersonating an Author whose last experiment in nonsense is to write on nothing, what can the "Author" say that is not not? Irony is always a parasite on nothing—saying what you mean by not saying it—but in this case it comes along with the extra negative that turns the nothing of impersonation into the something of wit, but only as long as it doesn't own that this what it is doing. Another way of putting this is to say that it was not possible for the "Author" of print to betray the Author of ink without betraying himself.

In the "Soliloquy," Shaftesbury divides himself into two persons in order to disclose his "real Character" (Shaftesbury 1999: 1.87, 104), a collection of traits dignified with the prerogatives of magisterial and even royal authority (1.101, 114). This is by way of sharpening the distinction between august penmen like himself and the false "Author-Characters" who adopt any opinion and impersonate any figure provided they win public attention (1.90). Against these writers the familiar images of waste are deployed: They have been found "discharging frequently and vehemently in public," using a "Method of Evacuation" chosen only by those unable to find "wholesom manner of Relief in private; [so] 'tis no wonder if they appear with so much Froth and Scum in publick" (1.90). It is as if they had taken a purge in the public square, guilty of a filthy deed sponsored by the "Factor Booksellers" of the "Letter Trade" (90, 191). In Shaftesbury's opinion, the shabby metamorphoses of authors "turn'd and model'd . . . by the publick Relish and current Humour of the Times" (1.139) are signs of self-destruction. So pitifully eager to be worth his price, the writer delivers in exchange for it "a wrong self," the false image of "no certain Man; nor . . . any certain or genuine Character" (1. 161, 107).

Shaftesbury has a host of adjectives fit to characterize the right and certain self: it is "the Reality of the better Self" given by the "true and native Self," or "our real and genuine Self," the "better and nobler Self," the "genuine, true, and natural SELF" (1.147–8). What he says of characters based upon such solid foundations is also pretty direct: they are real when they are entirely our own, unalterable, just, and perfect; and they are recognized in "the Character of a Man of Breeding and Politeness" (1.167, 173, 174). Persons serve characters by facilitating self-dialogues, conducted in front of what Shaftesbury calls variously the "vocal Looking-Glass," the "Pocket-Mirror," and the "magical Glass" (1.94, 105). Such an attendant is "one and the same Person to day as yesterday, and to morrow as to day" (1.101). But should "the Passion or Humour of a known Person" change, then the person turns into an impostor, and the character suffers a revolution, no longer remaining "any certain or genuine Character" (1.148, 107). Character seems to be the self embodied in the public eye; but how embodied? Not in print, it seems.

"Practicing Authors" who are evacuated and discharged into the public domain as froth, puke, and scum rely entirely upon the press to reach the public, but this is not the route of the self-possessed magisterial author. "I am no-wise more an AUTHOR, for being in Print" (158), he declares; and it is of no concern to him, he goes on, how his private amusements reach the public, or what judgment is made of them. There is no preferment or sanction that comes of being published. "I am conscious of no additional Virtue, or dangerous Quality, from having laid at any time under the weight of that alphabetick Engine called the Press. I know no Conjuration in it" (1.158). He uses such an engine for one purpose only, which is to reproduce his handwriting in a legible form, like a pentagraph. His publisher is in this respect no different from a secretary or amanuensis. "'Tis requisite, that my Friends, who peruse these Advices, shou'd read 'em in better Characters than my own Hand-writing. And by good luck I have a very fair Hand offer'd, which may save me the trouble of re-copying, and can readily furnish me with as many handsom Copys as I wou'd desire, for my own and Friends Service" (1.158). If more of these copies are sold by the owner of the engine, then he has nothing to do with the sale or the profit: "'Tis a Traffick I have no share in" (1.158). Contrariwise his publisher has no share in Shaftesbury's title page, which gives a date but no place of publication, nor a publisher (1.xxix). John Darby's name and the real date of publication of the second edition (1715, not 1714) are listed only in the index (1.xxxi). It is consistent with his lordly approach to the alphabetic engine that Shaftesbury in the first edition of the *Characteristics* gave his name only in a letter code at the end of the Preface, shielding his identity from the world while confirming it to his friends: a method of going public in confidence, a paradox explored later in the century by Sterne's Tristram Shandy.

There is an obvious difference between Swift's and Shaftesbury's estimates of the value of print compared with writing in ink. Liquid scum and froth flows only in the form of print, according to Shaftesbury, because the press is the indiscriminate channel of evacuation chosen by the letter-trade. Imperfect Authors might write in ink as much as they please without creating this kind of sewage: the multiplying power of the alphabetic engine is to blame. Swift's opinion is the opposite. It is specifically spilled ink that links each driveling mortal to the goddess Criticism in *The Battle of the Books*, and it is only when such filth is printed that it is materialized in a form that can be expunged. Shaftesbury affects to rise above the difference, saying, "I can hardly think that the Quality of what is written can be alter'd by the Manner of Writing: or that there can be any harm in a quick way of copying fair . . . why a Man may not be permitted to write with Iron and well as Quill, I can't conceive" (158). But this is disingenuous, for he has availed himself of every advantage of the iron of the press while reserving for himself the unique glory of the noncommercial quill. The difference between him and a common Author lies in his fidelity to the physical circumstances of writing with his own pen in his own character in his own private space, a boast that no one writing for money would bother making. The emphasis he places on the native and genuine self, the unalterable person and the real character refers to what he understands as the necessary continuity between the individual writing and what is written. So why does he attempt to disguise it? The truth is that the printed work is not an ultimate destination: Writing in ink is a route to another place that is not public, where Shaftesbury's self is validated neither by being read nor even by being written. In the Platonic dialogues he so admires, the medium is the voice, the sense of whose purity erases all traces of writer, ink, and reader, "the Author is annihilated and the Reader, being no way apply'd to, stands for No-body" (1.108).

If this sounds a little like the nothing that the nameless Author tries writing in *A Tale of a Tub*, then the impression is strengthened when we compare Shaftesbury's truly private writing exercise, *The Philosophical Regimen*, with the "Soliloquy." He means these private papers to record a discovery of the self by writing which is congruent with a long tradition of memoranda of self-reflection. Epictetus, Marcus Aurelius, and Seneca used their pens to reconnoiter and neutralize the dangerous passions, stripping away all accidents to leave exposed in all its symmetry the core of being, "the thing which only *is*" as Shaftesbury calls it (Shaftesbury 1900: 133). As well as these Stoic models there are Christian ones too, such as Athanasius and Augustine, who placed the emphasis of self-writing not on *ascesis* but on the shame of self-examination and the difficulty of renouncing the pleasures of the flesh. And there is the purely technological dimension of writing, the *hypomnemata* or book of commonplaces in which fragments from all manner of sources were transcribed and then incorporated into the self, becoming its tissue and blood, as Seneca said (Foucault 1997: 211). The *Regimen* is filled with quotations drawn from Shaftesbury's favorite authors, and in many respects it combines the genres of journal and anthology. Finally, there is the prototype of the Cartesian philosophical meditation, where the writer learns to rinse the phenomena of the material world in the solvent of doubt, until nothing is left but the undeniable truth of the thing that thinks.

Shaftesbury sets out by writing to free himself of all the pointless appendages to life, things that cannot truly be called his own, such as real property, sympathetic feelings, and the appetent body. He refuses to consider himself an heir, the appurtenance of an estate or grange-house (126–27), and when he thinks of rural retirement in a charming small house with a garden, surrounded by "pictures, trees, fabrics, models, design, ordering," he spurs himself to resist these "bosom-snake" temptations, "Recover, resist, repel, strive, arm.—War! War!" (120, 109). Sympathy is even more dangerous, having led him already into difficulties that seem to have been erotic and shameful, "sympathising . . . and . . . covering it with those names of natural affection, and tenderness . . . sympathizing with them, and harmonizing in a wrong way" (128, 145). As for the body, it betrays him with "certain involuntary motion towards bed-time and in bed, dreams, waking, sudden starts, rejolts, bangs, eagerness, agony" (160). All of these attachments and mechanical transports are to be extinguished if "the author of his being" is to be revealed (158, 190). Property is easy to set aside, affording nothing but bastard joys (158). Seductive social feelings are degenerate, diseased: "Cut off tenderness of a certain kind; cut off familiarity, and sympathy of a wrong kind" (144). Bits of the body are set up for amputation too, "Let it be a limb. Off with it" (137). "Is the system of self . . . changed if a leg or arm be lost? Is the man a quarter less himself? A fifth, a sixth, or bit less himself than before?" (137). Of course not; these sordid fractions that pretend to be the sum of self can all be lost and, far from being diminished, the self is that much better for it.

The paring away of what is surplus to the self is performed by writing, as if the pen were the scalpel and the ink the blood. It discloses the real character as it were in the real character, the soul in manuscript. But in any enterprise so severely opposed to the carnal creature as this *Regimen*, a problem is bound to arise with inscription since it is a vehicle not of the same make as the immaterial substance in whose service it operates. David Marshall has pointed to those moments in the *Regimen* when Shaftesbury writes of his doubts about writing. Pen is put to paper to mock itself, "Why writing? Why this flourishing, drawing, figuring, over and over, the same still?" (Marshall 1986: 55; Shaftesbury 1900: 241). Even in the privacy of his study he has burned and crossed out his lines, purged them along with all the other corporeal traitors of the native self. He imagines how much finer it would be if his self-remonstrances were silent, "inwardly spoken and not aloud . . . in the closet or study" (Marshall 58; *Regimen* 202). "Why tell thy tale, why sing thy ditty?" (203–4) he demands, jeering at the non-spontaneity of script which necessarily redoubles the message, the messenger, and the audience, leaving more than a single self the theme and descant of the work. Writing is tactless, noisy, indiscreet, surplus to being; not quite as disgusting as the evacuations of print, but by no means perfect. If Shaftesbury is to follow his own advice ("recollect thyself wholly within thyself" [112]), the penman needs some extra privacy. He talks more than once of "the involuta, the shadow, the veil, the curtain" (205) as a recess within the recess of the closet, a resource he calls "soft irony" (192). Marshall comments: "Written as if in invisible ink, this writing would withdraw from reading" (Marshall

1985: 55). This is precisely the spiritualization of the author and the nul-
lification of the reader that Shaftesbury identifies as the excellence of
Platonic dialogue, where the form of intelligence carries the least flesh,
and the body, the "excrement in seed" (141), is rooted out.

By two radically different routes, one following the voluptuous de-
lights of Lucretian materialism and the other in pursuit of a Cartesian
ascesis, Swift's and Shaftesbury's Authors arrive almost at the same point.
Each pauses on the threshold dividing something from nothing, where
the eligible alternative is to write of nothing, or to turn writing into
nothing; to let the Author disappear into secrecy and to let the reader
stand for nobody. I have suggested that Swift's irony is a technique for
hovering over the paradox of nothing as a minimal presence, writing of
the thing which is not as if it were not just not, so that every limping
addition to a list, every digression and every string of asterisks figures
something that is not quite the entire absence of wit. And this works
splendidly until the "Author" literalizes his relation to the Author and
the implied superstructure collapses: "Those Passages in this Discourse,
which appear most liable to Objection are what they call Parodies, where
the Author personates the Style and Manner of other Writers, whom he
has a mind to expose" (Swift 1920: 7). The risks of paper-war and the
strange immediacy of ink are exchanged for personate critique, where everything is represented, everybody stands for somebody else, and it is all
in print.

Shaftesbury doesn't make this mistake because instead of adding literalism to literalism in a futile defense of irony, he parades in print traits
the very opposite of what writing had taught him about himself. This is
not to deny the truth or value of the lesson of self-writing, any more than
Roxana denies the importance to herself of what she doesn't say amidst
what she does, but irony— "soft irony"—lets him use print to claim attention to virtues none of which he would seriously recommend to himself in ink, privately in his own study. He comes on the stage in "the
Character of a Man of Breeding and Politeness" (1.174)—steady, repu-
table, of the right stock, sociable, and replete with *bienseance*; in short a
landed gentleman, a creature of his property, tastes, and company. The
first section of the *Characteristics*, "A Letter Concerning Enthusiasm,"
provides a good example of this character in action. He tackles the social
ills of excessive passion by impersonating the very thing he deprecates,
transposing the machine-like absurdities of the French prophets into an
easy and urbane hyperbole:

And now, my Lord, having after all, in some measure, justified enthusiasm and owned the word, if I appear extravagant in addressing to you

after the manner I have done, you must allow me to plead an impulse. You must suppose me (as with truth you may) most passionately yours. (1.33)

Shaftesbury alone knows what this soft irony veils—the unmanageable impulses of his own risen flesh, the wrong passions that insinuated themselves into his sympathetic friendships, the property that stood in the way of his owning anything truthfully about himself, and the shame that came with them all. Like Swift's irony, Shaftesbury's is appreciated by a club, but the full measure of what ironically is not being said is his secret, and the triumph of keeping it is purely his own. To manage this involution in a printed letter emphasizes—to him—how equivocally authorship and writing have carried him to the margin dividing the duplicities of a public character from the singularity of a thing that only is, bringing him to a position from which he can discourse volubly if indirectly about what was scarcely to be written, and certainly never to be published. In a public sort of way, Shaftesbury solved a conundrum framed by Mandeville specifically with Shaftesbury in mind. Mandeville said that if you are determined to improve yourself to the degree that you are no longer like yourself, of what benefit is the improvement to yourself? "That He itself, the Person wishing, must be destroy'd before the Change could be entire" (Mandeville 1924: 2.137). If we call the wishing self the "character" and the wished-for self the "thing," then Shaftesbury used the chief elements of his dismantled character to impersonate what it was that its destruction had achieved, and to celebrate the invisibility and silence of "the thing which only is" in an extravagant demonstration of what it is not.

A Tale of a Tub and "A Letter Concerning Enthusiasm" for a while were assumed to be the work of the same Author. Swift mentions the confusion in a marginal note to the Apology (6). Charles Gildon seems to have had them linked in his own mind, for he distinguishes A Tale in his first English it-narrative, The Golden Spy, with a prefatory letter to its Author from the bookseller. In his A New Rehearsal; or, Bays the Younger (1714), he quotes extensively from the "Soliloquy" against "Authors" ruled by humor and the fancy of the world: "In our Days the Audience makes the Poet, and the Bookseller the Author" (Gildon 1714: xvii). It is an impressive display of cheek on the part of Gildon, the venal penman of the Dunciad, to attach himself to two of the finest contemporary satires against writers like himself. Gildon writes too fast to be entirely coherent, but two ideas are associated in A New Rehearsal. The first is that dunce-Authors enjoy the physical act of writing ("Scribbling's the Diabetis of the Mind; and when a Man's infected with it, he can't help clapping Pen to Paper" [Gildon 1714: 10]). The second is that the modern stream of wit is fed by stories about things: "You must choose some odd out of the way Subject, some Trifle or other that wou'd surprise the Common Reader that any thing could be written upon it, as a Fan, a Lock of Hair, or the like" (42). Ink and things are given a Grub Street make-over, not quite Lucretian and certainly not Cartesian or Platonic, but expressive of an interest in the two topics that was shared by Gildon's own acquaintance on the street, of whom the most redoubtable was his occasional employer, John Dunton, singled out by Swift's Author as a bookseller eminent in the ladder-branch of publishing.

In *Before Novels*, J. Paul Hunter considered Dunton to be a prime example of an author working the border between knowledge and news, autobiography and self-invention. He noticed a difference between Dunton's "maggots" or willful nonsense and his perverse originality. The maggots were Dunton's version of the Author's drivel, but the curious emphasis he placed in his memoirs on the authenticity of his first-person testimony, no matter how incoherent and private, is more like the Author's experience of possession, in which Dunton too observes distinct Lucretian lineaments ("All matter is in motion, and therefore perpetually chang'd and alter'd") (Hunter 1990: 12–17 et passim; Dunton 1691: 1.27–8). Hunter thought Dunton the first exponent of this kind of self-exhibition in print, but Michael McKeon had already identified Francis Kirkman's *The Unlucky Citizen* (1673) as the precedent for unstable secular autobiography which is experienced by the reader as "approaching ever closer to the moment of writing" (McKeon 1987, 2002: 244). Kirkman was a melancholic scrivener who took to authorship to ease his mind, then published the results as a rambling autobiography, interspersed with a number of fabliaux ornamented with cuts.

Recently, Jody Greene has suggested that it was his appearance in print that was the truly recuperative exercise for Kirkman, carrying him from a state of distraction ("I was a very lump of Chaos or confusion to my self" [Kirkman 1673: Preface]) to what she calls "self-entitlement" where the book acts as his person, making him somebody in the eyes of the world (Greene 2006: 19). McKeon's account of this is more equivocal. While the growing market for print gave a published writer a degree of authority, and while the Copyright Act allowed for absolute possession of the text by the author until the point of sale, the validation of text as a public document was only possible when it was alienated: bought and sold and printed. "Once ideas can be owned, their value lies in disowning them by making them public" (McKeon 1987, 2002: 124). If Kirkman did rely on the alphabetic engine for entitlement and personhood, then he was going to lose something of his own by printing and parting with what he had written, unless his plan was in fact to repudiate the chaotic state of mind of his pre-published self and present himself in print as a person happily metamorphosed into a book. Kirkman admits that there was a risk in going to press, and that he ought to have kept some things secret, including his name; but he explains, "I was resolved to be plain and sincere, especially when taking a view of my Actions . . . I did resolve to write . . . the Truth, naked as she was" (Kirkman 1673: 6). At some point in the process of writing himself out, whether by quill or iron, Kirkman was committed to Shaftesbury's standard of candor.

Hunter, McKeon, and Greene are agreed that the originality of Kirkman and Dunton is owing in some way to their close association with the publishing trade, and that their experience of tribulation and isolation is, like Robinson Crusoe's, meant to be ameliorated by the solace of a printed book. I want to suggest that in Kirkman's case it is more complex, more like Jünger looking at the edition of *Don Quixote*, or the woman of Berlin raiding a line of print for food. When Kirkman says he wrote to relieve the troubles of his mind, it is evident that it was by writing with a pen (which after all was his trade) that he succeeded. It was the next step of getting himself published that threw him back into despondency. Twice he tells the story of how his printer died halfway through the print run, and how his widow stole the paper set aside for the rest of it; and as if that were not bad enough, how the printed sheets were seized in a judgment against the printer's estate (Kirkman 1673: sig.A 8; 289). Indeed, the last portion of his book bears witness to the truth of what he says, being set in a different typeface. So it is the attempt to use the alphabetic engine, to exchange iron for quill as Shaftesbury would say, that undoes all the good effect of putting pen to paper. Looking back on the miseries of the letter-trade, Kirkman testifies not only to his exasperation but also to his isolation: "the consideration whereof does so swell and rage, that it is like to over-flow the Banks of my Intellectuals to consider how many Storms I have been in, and how many times shipwrack'd . . . I think I have not any [Friends] in the world, for they are all dead, or so to me, *ungrateful*, will not own me, nor my Courtesies" (206–7). He is a citizen so unlucky he loses his society. Although it would be extravagant to claim any close alliance between the authorial practice of Kirkman and Shaftesbury, they have in common an ideal of candid penmanship that causes all kinds of emergencies through which still they write on, like Caleb Williams, as if there were a refuge quite opposite to publication that ink might disclose, or even make.

Dunton was a bookseller with an extensive business centered for many years on his best idea, the Wikipedia of the late seventeenth century, *The Athenian Mercury*, an achievement Swift gravely praised in an early ode. In the less gnomic of his autobiographies, *Life and Errors* (1705), he gives an account of his successes as a broker of print, together with his experience of the importunate "ITCH and Inclination, [as well as] Necessity of Writing" (1705: 239). It seems Dunton had a plan to reverse the market paradox of "disownment" by publishing his autobiographical volumes anonymously, aiming to retrieve from his copy something he could call his very own; and to do this he had to hide his identity. He sees a connection between the peculiarity of his narrative, utterly original, and the need to appear in front of the public as neither a character nor a person, but as an Author, like Swift in his confrontation with Mr. Bettesworth or Shaftesbury when he owns himself to Lord Somers "passionately yours." Dunton starts with the mystery of his intentions which, being perpetually thwarted by his bent for digression, never results in a consistent account of himself. "Perhaps I had never any mind you should know what I mean, nor what to make on it . . . to see a Man describ'd and not describ'd, playing Bo-peep with the World, and hiding himself behind his Fingers" (2.7). This is the limit of the amusement he means to afford his public, for then he moves to the valiant corollary of true authorship: "So great a Glory do I esteem it to be the Author of these Works, that I cannot . . . endure that any should own 'em who have nothing to do with `em" (2.19). It is possible that Dunton is simply proclaiming his dual function as writer and marketer of the book (it contains an advertisement for itself), but it is more likely that he is warning that the purchase and perusal of the book give no rights to the buyer, identified as "Mr. Reader." This forlorn person is further annihilated by Dunton's next feat of authorial superbia, which is to shield his sheer and indivisible identity as author behind an impenetrable veil of anonymity. "[No] other Person[s] yet named or suspected, are the real Authors of this Book, or the real Evander, but that I, and I only am he; and who I am, is yet, and ever shall be a Secret" (2.23). He alone can be the warrant of what he writes: "Whatever I deliver my self to be, provided it be such as I really am, I have my end" (3.32). That "whatever" is presumably the book, but its resemblance to the unknown I is an end the author keeps to himself, leaving Mr. Reader holding something that the Author is not letting him own by not owning it himself. The "ownness" of such a book is claimed absolutely and as absolutely renounced, suggesting that it subsists in the limbo of literary property where nothing can be owned in any sense, a sort of authorial state of nature resembling the isolation of Swift's Author when writing upon nothing, Shaftesbury's silence behind the veil of soft irony, and Kirkman's woe on the flooded banks of his intellectuals.

If that is a fair statement of the case, then it is worth considering how far Dunton's Epicureanism affects the production and consumption of the text. Throughout his *Voyage round the World*, not just the analogy but the continuity of movement and writing is insisted upon: "What his industrious Toes do tread, his ready Fingers do write, his thinking Head dictating" (1.9). He asks the reader not to read but chew and digest the book, incorporating it as "Life, Blood, and Nourishment" (1.8). In his rambles he mentions sneezing, or what he calls blasting his brains through his nostrils, that leaves traces of his thinking head on the foliage as he passes (1.15). Similarly in his writing, "I love to . . . sprinkle now and then some of that same in my writings which is so remarkable in my self— that people should miss what they expected, and find what they never lookt for" (1.108). They may have been expecting the picture of Dunton's self, but what he gives them are these streaks and splashes of his brain. He is fond of Sir Thomas Browne, and even fonder of Montaigne with whom he shares the ambition of writing a book consubstantial with its Author. In choosing sprinkling as the method of evacuating his brain onto the surface of paper, Dunton needs quills and ink to achieve what elsewhere he calls writing his guts out (1.7). The itch of writing is soothed by the flow of ink; but like other soliloquists he finds publication a menace: "I have usually started something that was New, whilst others, like Foot-pads, ply only about the High Roads, and . . . one way or other contriv'd [to steal] the very Life and Soul out of the Copy' (1705: 248). Like the other secular autobiographers we have been looking at, Dunton views with considerable alarm the attentions of the "Kind, Courteous, and Gentle Reader" (2.31) and is happiest when writing is solitary, his brains emerging from his nose or his pen as something a casual passerby might sense rather than know and understand. He plays the dual part of the publisher to the writer, you feel, to protect what is unique and unrepresentable in the empirical phenomenon of "this incomparable Author" (1.5).

The sort of Author exhibited in this strange line of wit is a ruined character or destroyed person, standing in an uneasy relation to society, feeling thwarted but capable of fits of mirth or self-satisfaction. The singular Author keeps cropping up in the eighteenth century. In Richard Savage's *An Author to be Lett* (1729), Smollett's *Humphry Clinker* (1771), and Thomas Holcroft's *Hugh Trevor* (1794), they are described in this marginal position, whether they are actively delinquent like Smollett's Tim Cropdale or Savage's Iscariot Hackney ("In short, I am a perfect Town Author: I hate all Mankind . . . [and] never stick at a mean Action, when . . . my own Interest in at stake" [Savage 1729: 11]); or passively abused, like Holcroft's Wilmot who, having tried to kill himself, leaves a note: "This body, if it ever should be found, was once a thing, which, by way of reproach among men, was called an author. It moved about the earth despised and unnoticed; and died indigent and unlamented" (Holcroft in Hazlitt 1902: 2.137). This is the plight in which Caleb Williams finds himself when, bereft of all social distinctions, he gives up all narrative ambitions because he cannot tell the difference between himself and a chair, a log, or a stone.

Authors are a kind of temporary and intermittent idols, and very vulnerable on that account. Instead of "Wood, Stone, Metall, or some other visible creature" (Hobbes 1996: p. 449), they are made of paper and ink. On a good day these materials shape what De Certeau calls a mansion of the soul. It is already clear that this dwelling does not represent its Author any more than Criticism represents writers, or the book she turns into represents her. Even among the Epicurean Authors such as Swift's and Dunton's, the material trace of ink on paper, or brain on foliage, does not represent anything: explicitly it is the proof of nothing taking shape. Shaftesbury spiritualizes the residue of his writing, but it emerges as the nothing which animates his soft irony. Humpty Dumpty, authentic heir of these early authors, always organizes his words in this manner, ensuring that they mean only what he says; for he is careful never to say what he means. It is a distinction on which the noisy extravagance of the modern manner of writing in authentic phrases is established. And there is never anything unequivocal about that kind of authenticity because it acknowledges only ironically a public standard by which it can be measured.

Rousseau's disastrous decision to concoct "the ink of sympathy" perfectly exemplifies the twin impulses toward publicity and secrecy in this sort of writing, for it was intended by Rousseau not only as the perfect vehicle for his limitless candor, a virtue that David Marshall compares in Shaftesbury's case to "writing as if in invisible ink" (Marshall 1985: 55), but also as a medium protective of secrets which were to be imparted only to those whose sincerity was equal to his own. Consisting chiefly of quicklime and sulphide of arsenic, the sympathetic ink blew up in his face while he was trying to bottle it and blinded him for six weeks (Rousseau 1953: 209; Marshall 1988: 172). Someone with a stronger professional motive for using the same invention was Edward Bancroft, an American naturalist who, during the War of Independence, spied on the Franco-American negotiations for the British. While in Guiana, he had learned the secret an invisible ink made from the fruit of the Mauna tree (*Gardenia Genipa*). Bright red, it quickly faded into invisibility, and the technique of reading it was left with his masters in London, who paid him handsomely for the private messages he left them in the Tuileries Garden cunningly disguised as love letters (Delbourgo 2009: 287–91). Candor, whose medium is literally transparent, and cunning that knows how to write what must not generally be known: these are two sides of the same sheet, with ink the common component.

A notable writer of himself, and someone who writes in confidence to the "world," Tristram Shandy is ever attentive to the quality of his pen and the consistency of his ink, and in between his numerous notices of how his sits at his desk, spurting his ink and spoiling fair sheets, he makes two confessions to his reader. The first concerns self-writing as the public revelation of the self by means of ink: "A man cannot dress, but his ideas get cloath'd at the same time ... so that he has nothing to do, but take his pen, and write like himself." The second concerns the impossibility of ever achieving such clarity of self-expression in a social dialogue, when he affirms that the relief obtained by writing in private never appears to the public eye wholesome, pure, or of any social utility whatsoever: "There was one single month in which I can make it appear, that I dirtied one and thirty shirts with clean writing" (Sterne 1983: 507). This is Tristram's version of Rousseau's ink of sympathy: invisible to the world, but very obvious to him.

CHAPTER 9

Things as Authors

The it-narrative—the story in which a thing functions as an actor or author, or both—may be compared with still life, Ovidian metamorphosis, and the Aesopian fable in this respect, that all four genres have at times been heavily moralized, commonly understood as bearing a meaning directly relevant to human affairs; and at others they have been read as celebrations of the nonhuman, of things and creatures indifferent or even hostile to the concerns of their readers. Perhaps the threat of their dissident insignificance has provoked in us humans a determination to make them morally valuable in spite of their teeth. A stopped watch in a vanitas, a hollow mask in a fable, a youth who falls hopelessly in love with his reflection and turns into a flower, these are easy to interpret if we want to. Thus, in Aphra Behn's *The Lover's Watch*, a forerunner of the it-narrative, the timepiece at the center of this elaborate protocol of longing calls out the hours for Damon's meditations upon his absent Iris, and should he falter in this discipline, the watch will stop (Behn 1751: 2.65). Like those still lifes of Cotan or Zurbaran, where cabbages and lemons hang in an eternal pause, the timepiece sitting at the center of this devotional arrangement helps the mind on to better things.

At a lower level, chapbook stories of pins and coins and small animals, all armed with sturdy morals of fair play and goodwill that survive into the nineteenth century, owe much to the tendentious collections of fables published by John Ogilby, Roger L'Estrange, and Samuel Croxall a hundred and fifty years before. Similarly, Hogarth's progresses and especially his remarkable exercise in the anti-sublime, *The Bathos*, are indebted to the genre paintings and to those still lifes such as Jan Steen's and Maerten de Stomme's that specialized in the iconography of things broken and upset. In all these stories the thing contributes directly to the moral benefit of humanity, functioning either as an emblem, a lesson, or a reproach. The author of *The Adventures of a Halfpenny* boasts of having "rewarded the labours of industry, and relieved the necessities of indigence" (Anon. 1835:14). The narrator of *The Gold-headed Cane* is proud of having accompanied a succession of physicians on their rounds, men of "compassionate and feeling heart[s]" devoted to the recovery of the sick (1828: 21). The hackney coach is fond of recommending to its reader figures remarkable for their humanity, such as a charitable mother, a faithful lover, and the ideal reader "whose eye swells with the invaluable tear of humanity," while holding up to scorn the inhumanity of sheriff's officers, heartless landlords, and Mr. Filch, a libertine (Anon. 1783: 104, 103, 107, 52). Rather more sardonically, the author of *Memoirs and Adventures of a Flea* observes, apropos the sparing of a litter of kittens that has been born overnight in Mr. Goodwill's hat, "The reader will here see that a truly compassionate mind shews itself in every particular" (1785: 2.104).

Even in these moralized tales it is possible to see tensions emerging between the demands of humanity and the interests of the narrator. Dorothy Kilner's late eighteenth-century it-narrative *The Life and Perambulations of a Mouse* (1783) sets out to be a tale designed to amuse and instruct its young audience, although it consists chiefly in scenes of cruelty to animals witnessed by a mouse and commented upon by a human narrator. When the boy Charles is caught by his father dangling a mouse in front of a cat, and his father says, "I promise you the smallest creature can feel as acutely as you" (53), he proves his point by horsewhipping the boy. This practical lesson in humanity and sympathy charts a route to moral virtue via cruelty and violence: for one reason or another you will know what it is like to be an animal only if you are in agony. Does this truth serve to point a moral for us; or are we finding out something about the lives of animals?

Mandeville's *The Fable of the Bees* (1724) brings up the same problem in a different key. Having cut his teeth on translations of La Fontaine, Mandeville had a sense of the ironic and even anarchic potential of animal fables, and how they might lead to a narrative point of view that had nothing directly to do with human experience. His Remark P dramatizes this possibility, especially vividly in the dialogue between the lion and the castaway merchant. However, the irony Mandeville is manipulating slips out of his hands. His intention in writing the poem and the commentary, which was not to expose vice but to make it intelligible, is tested by the poem itself. His motive for exhibiting the traffic between a public system justifying outcomes and a private one hiding motives was to underline the folly of Societies for the Reformation of Manners, whose methods of social engineering he found contemptibly superficial. But that is not where the fable stops. The oscillation between the paradoxes generated out of the productive cycle of commerce and the hypocrisies of self-interest—what the poet calls the "Shew" of the hive—comes to an end when the governing paradox of the poem (namely, that what you think you are doing is not what happens) starts to operate not only at the national level but also in the recesses of each individual consciousness. It turns out that the last weakness among vicious folk is a taste for moral virtue. At which point the entertaining social paradox of virtue sprung from vice dissolves,

for talk of virtue leads unaccountably and literally to virtue. The reno-
vated bees appear to enjoy a Spartan kind of happiness which the poem's
narrator is obliged explicitly to deny in "The Moral." Mandeville sets
this primitive felicity aside as a golden age fiction, "a vain EUTOPIA
seated in the Brain" (1.36). He will not allow the possibility of a national
reformation of manners to fit into his exposé of the law of unintended
consequences. This interruption to the story Mandeville thought he was
telling by another quite contrary to his drift replaces one kind of authorship with another. Who might the new author be: the poem itself? The
genre of fable? A real bee? Whoever or whatever it is, the poem gets to
say what it means, not what it was supposed to mean in "The Moral."

Hobbes and Mandeville are aware that ruin lies in wait for common-
wealths. They know that the prudent equilibrium of art and nature that
ensures the probability of the "Shew" or "Fiction" of civil society may
easily be overwhelmed by unpredictable coalitions of passions and circumstances. But they assume that even in such an event, the resulting
chaos is at least a human predicament, recognizable as society in a state
of ruin, when every civil plus turns into a savage minus. They discount as
improbable the fiction that things, creatures, or words themselves might
take advantage of such anarchy by bidding for authorship. If a hospital
or bridge may function as a person, or a hive of bees as a commonwealth,
what is to stop them in a natural state, where they are no longer held as
property, from functioning as themselves? Is there any prohibition except
human disbelief? If an it-narrative or a fable is to explore beyond the
narrow anthropomorphic range of human substitution, where things act
as probable representatives of our interests and passions, or we of theirs,
then the isolation and alienation of the author-position is what they will
exploit, and the story they will tell will be hostile to the fictionality that
defined their servitude to our concerns. "If you ask Fable, talk of civiliza-
tion is rot" (Henderson 2001: 186).

The first full-scale it-narrative, Charles Gildon's *The Golden Spy*
(1709), has at its core a secret held by money so devastating it threatens
the basis of civil society. Not fully to part with this secret but to have as
it were limned and adumbrated by the actions of human beings is the
narrative challenge Gildon sets himself, and later I shall try to show how
well he manages it. In the meantime, I want to probe the ideas he had
in mind while setting about to write such a book. In the eighth chapter
I have explored Swift's experiment in writing like a Grub Street dunce,
where he carries his impersonation beyond the limits of irony into the
unique satisfactions of Authorship, exhibited in the momentary flourishes of a pen where mind materializes as ink, where every word sheds its
figurative load and where the narrative itself yields all its symbolic pretensions to the actuality of the deed of putting pen to paper. In the Epistle

Nuncupatory that the "Bookseller" of Gildon's work writes to "The Author of a Tale of a Tub," he applauds the power wielded by anonymous Authors and the wonders they command, particularly the marvel of self-invention. He declares, "Authors can make Pedigrees, as well as any Herald," and on the title page we find Gildon's genealogy of *A Tale of a Tub* (Gildon 1709: [iv, vi]). It runs: *The Golden Spy: or, a Political Journal of the British Nights Entertainment of War and Peace and Love and Politics: Wherein are laid open The Secret Miraculous Power and Progress of Gold, in the Courts of Europe.* He is alluding to three other books that contribute to the idea of emancipated authorship. These are the *Arabian Nights Entertainment*, translated by Antoine Galland between 1704 and 1717, and translated into English between 1706 and 1721; *Letters Writ by a Turkish Spy*, attributed to Giovanni Paolo Marana and published in France in 1683, then in its first English translation by William Bradshaw in 1687; and *The Golden Ass* of Apuleius, translated in 1566 by William Adlington, and rather more loosely by Gildon himself the year before.

Although oriental tales and fables had been circulating in Europe for centuries, often blended with collections of Aesop's fables, the *Arabian Nights* was new in the West: a series of astonishing and improbable stories told by the wife of a sultan whose life depends upon their success. But the success has nothing to do with the effects of the moral tendency of the stories, for few of them exhibit any. It derives from the degree of wonder, suspense, and excitement each is capable of arousing; for if a single one should fail, the sultan's wife will die. Unlike the collections of tales of Bocaccio, Chaucer, or Margaret of Navarre, this one places the issue of the consumption of stories at the heart of their composition and delivery, rather as Cervantes does in the second part of *Don Quixote*. A large part of the appeal of the *Arabian Nights* for Gildon, a man living by his pen, would have lain in its thematization of novelty, where the story itself tells of an author who risks everything to fascinate her audience; and how skillfully she feeds its appetite, accomplishing by more versatile means the mastery that Swift's Author derives from placing "a Spur in the side, [a] Bridle in the Mouth, [a] Ring in the Nose, of a lazy, an impatient, and a grunting Reader" (Swift 1920: 203) . But in *The Golden Spy*, Gildon did not want to describe the consumption of books; he wanted to report secret histories of the courts of France, Italy, and England. And for this he used the format of *The Turkish Spy*, where a disguised alien secretly reports the customs and politics of a foreign nation. In this case the gold coins that hum and whisper at night in the author's ear are the spies, and they discover astonishing secrets, not all of which are communicated to the reader. By this means Gildon was able to unite the sinister ethnography of the spy (cognate with the invisible ink of Authors and of actual spies such as Edward Bancroft) with the quality of the marvelous in Scheherazade's narratives; and in choosing an inanimate source for these reports he could suppose a sort of absolute espionage, unlimited by the extenuations and compunction of a species looking obliquely at itself. He aims for a defamiliarization close to the sheer critique directed by Gulliver against humanity in his fourth voyage.

Gildon was the alleged author of an adaptation of Apuleius, *The New Metamorphosis* (1708) about Don Fantasio, a gentleman turned into a Bolognese lapdog. In this tale and in *The Golden Spy*, he constructs an angle on the human world that opens up, like Lucius's life as an ass in Apuleius's story, a spectacle of lust and venality. The animal offers an intimate and shocking picture of the actions of its successive owners. The technique of using a nonhuman witness of human passions had been explored anciently by Ovid and Plutarch, as well as in the eastern fables of Pilpay, Aesop, and Lokman. In the early modern period, painters such as Piero di Cosimo and Bosch, and poets such as Shakespeare and Dryden, experimented with it too. But it seems likely that Gildon was keenly aware, along with Mandeville and Defoe, of the division between facts and values forced by commerce upon an ambitious middle class, now competing with the court for political power. The scandalous mysteries of Machiavelli's *ragione di stato* descended to the counting house and the Exchange. Gildon's Roman coin teaches that it is better to be feared than loved, and that "Self-Interest [is] a much surer Tie than the airy Notions of Honour and Probity." All religion is hypocrisy, it explains, and false promises are current coin [Gildon 1709: 43–45, 106]). In its raw form, before it is transmuted by trade and manufacture into something resembling a confederacy of mutual love, self-interest cannot pretend to be exemplary. It imports into the allegedly polite world of economic exchange what Hobbes would call a condition of war. Machiavelli himself had written *L'Asino d'oro*, a poem conceived partly in imitation of Apuleius and partly of Plutarch, in which the hero is courted by a beautiful woman who keeps a menagerie of former humans. After his Circean hostess has made love to him, he thinks of history and the ruin of states by greed and ambition, how "Evil follows good; good, evil;/ And each is of the other the sole cause" (Machiavelli 1963: 80). Then he meets a pig who, like Plutarch's Gryllus, praises the fullness and happiness of the beastly state. Thinking once again of the disgrace of the human condition, Machiavelli's hero asks, "Why should I want to be a man again?" (100). Gildon's coins are close to posing the same question to their human audience, despite recommending (like Mandeville) the political realism that brings about the need to ask it.

Gildon had already used oriental reporters in order to exploit what Ros Ballaster calls "the reverse gaze" (Ballaster 2005: 149). He experimented with this device in *The Post-boy Rob'd of his Mail* (1706). Even in this ephemeral text Gildon goes a step beyond *The Turkish Spy* and its important descendents, such as Montesquieu's *Lettres persanes* (translated 1722) and Goldsmith's *Citizen of the World* (1762), in having the reverse gaze voice doubts about the eligibility of certain kinds of social life, doubts so serious they verge upon Machiavelli's and Gulliver's radical challenges to humanity. When Honan the Chinese narrator falls in love with a Spanish nun, he confesses that the chasm opened up by passion between oriental and western standards is so great that it has made ethnography and irony equally impossible: "The Bulwarks of Philosophy, with all the Pallizadoes of her Precepts, that us'd to guard me from the Follies and Knaveries of Mankind, are quite blown up, all the strong, regular Fortifications, rais'd by repeated and judicious Observations, are now dismantl'd" (Gildon 1706: 242). Although this might be mistaken for a lover's rhodomontade, the judgment is reinforced even by the skeptical wits who have intercepted his letters. One of them says, "Tho' we have the Advantage of Precepts ... yet we are much inferior ev'n to the Canibals of the Caribee Islands, in our Practice, and in all the Parts of Morality" (1706: 273). It is worth comparing this powerful intuition of the disintegration of moral virtue with the menace of the secret told by the coin of *The Golden Spy*: "In short, the Mysteries he reveal'd, are like those ... which are not to be exposed to unhallow'd Eyes, for fear the Sense of Things should destroy all Confidence betwixt Man and Man, and so put an End to human Society" (Gildon 1709: 116).

What further the *Arabian Nights* contributed to Gildon's experiments with the nonhuman is perhaps reflected in its opening stories, which were all that was available in English at the time. It begins where Machiavelli's and Gildon's tales leave off, with the profound disillusionment of the sultan Schahriar, who has discovered his wife's adultery with Masoud, her black slave. The bulwarks and palisadoes of his preceptual wisdom are so badly shattered that his only method of ensuring the constancy of future wives is to marry them for a night and execute them the following day. When Scheherazade dares to marry him because she believes her battery of stories will keep her alive long enough to convince the sultan of her constancy, it is clear she has no faith in the moral illumination of fables or parables themselves. Her father tells her the story of the merchant and his ass in order to dissuade her from risking her life in such a mad scheme, but it has no effect at all on her decision, any more than the last fable told by Aesop keeps the Delphians from killing him. The man to whom she will tell her tales has decided that it is impossible to preserve innocence by precept, ceremony, or vow; so she knows there is no chance of awakening his moral sentiments with a fiction. He inhabits a world where the absence of principle brought on by despair is supplied by his limitless prerogative, inclining him to a bleak and cruel realism.

The social breakdown Gildon advertises in the *Post-boy* and *The Golden Spy* has already taken place here in the *Arabian Nights*, then, and the only remaining guides for conduct are reasons of state. Precepts are anti-precepts: reward good with evil, and sacrifice the innocent rather than spare the guilty (Mack 1995: 31, 41). There are two notable consequences of this moral ruin. The first is the permeable boundary between humans and animals. It is always easy for the one to change into the other, and for either to understand the other's speech. Whether this state of affairs illustrates the animist doctrines of the east, where the spirit world extends all the way from genies to stones, or whether it is a measure of brutal degeneracy among humans, it is at least a valuable resource for a storyteller whose audience is to be compelled only by wonder, not by example or compunction. The second is the peculiar function of the fiction itself, which acts neither to enforce a lesson, nor to shape and finish the events it records. If fable was discarded as bad fiction, as Michel de Certeau suggests, for having "presumed to mask or to have mislaid the meaning it contains" (de Certeau 1992: 12), then Scheherazade resolves (like Roxana) to exploit the same fallibility of her vehicle. She tells stories in order to create the suspense whose sole purpose is to provide the occasion for another story. What is most improbable in them keeps up the narrative flow and preserves the narrator's life; and wonder, Schahriar's reaction to their astonishing pointlessness, stimulates his appetite for another story. So, rather than operating as the representations of real or imagined events, her stories supplant events. They are literally the sequent moments of Scheherazade's life, all that remains of her post-marital experience besides sex. There is in her no reserve and no ulterior motive but the desire to tell another story. In fact, the stories are not only what happen to their narrator, they are what happen to themselves, for the only thing occurring outside the improbabilities that propel the marvels of each tale is the telling of the next one, wonder making way for successive wonder.

A similar effect is achieved the *The Fables of Pilpay* where nested tales, told in a kind of narrative *mise en abime*, operate as a chain of stories-as-incidents, a journey from fable to fable, instead of from point to geographical point, adventure to meaning, and example to moral. Thus, when King Dabschelim travels to Serandib to visit the hermit Pilpay in order to learn wisdom, he hears a fable rather like *A Tale of a Tub*, the story of "The Merchant and his three Sons." Inside it is another, "The King and his two Sons," which breeds "The Ox and the Lion," a tale enclosing "The Carpenter and the Ape," whose counterpart is "The Two Travellers," and so on. In the tour of this landscape of fables, travel is denounced by travelers, fables by the characters inside them, or even by fables themselves (Pilpay 1775: 24, 122, 140, 213). Like the last section of *A Tale of a Tub* or the utopian outcome of *The Fable of the Bees*, these eastern stories evade the intentions of their tellers, who will find out what they mean—what the fables mean and what they mean by telling them—not by virtue of conscious and exemplary representation of the truth but by the confusing experience of telling, hearing, or reading them—what La Fontaine calls the conjuncture of places, persons, and times (La Fontaine 1865: 215). Serandib in Pilpay provides Horace Walpole with part of the idea for his neologism, *serendipity*, which he defined as accidental sagacity, the only kind of knowledge this branch of fiction supplies (Walpole 1937–1983: 20: 407–11).

The reason for such narrative autonomy in all three books is the abdication of human responsibility for equity and order in favor of the interplay of power and chance: in effect the replacement of social organization, or Hobbes's artificial man, with a condition Hume describes as perpetual disorder—convulsions, prodigies, miracles—where gods and animals come closer together as humans drift further apart, re-entering this new conjuncture only on terms of brutality and worship (Hume 1956: 42). Whatever degree of fictionality preceded this state of affairs, whether it was the representational personhood of people and things in Hobbes's Leviathan, or some other form suitable for Eastern or Roman models of government, it has now been intensified to the highest degree of passion where improbability will be embodied in the telling of a tale and do it no harm at all. Scheherazade's sheer fictions, her silent estimate of the world's moral incapacity, are just such an embodiment and her only resource. Obeying no principle of representation or of moral government, her tales are all she has; they are her last chance in a game with absolute and unpredictable power.

After Gildon's experiment, the it-narrative moved to France, developing the erotic possibilities of the oriental tale and of the *Arabian Nights* in particular. Crébillon's *Le Sopha* (1742) is derived from the latter source, beginning with a dialogue between Scheherazade's grandson, who is addicted to marvelous stories, and his wife, who despises them. Diderot's *Les Bijoux indiscrets* (1748) is set in Muslim Africa and begins with a genie's gift of a magic ring to Mangogul that makes women's jewels (that is, genitals) tell all their owners' secrets. Like the *Arabian Nights*, these erotic tales explore the modes of resistance to a world that doesn't make a great deal of sense, but which is not so extremely unaccountable as Scheherazade's. Instead of sheer fiction, the narrators explore the myriad devices used to disguise or silence the language of pure passion. The sofa and the jewel are situated between the private zone of satisfied desire and the public arena of reputation and honor; and binding the two together are probable fictions disguised as magic. The bulwarks and palisadoes of civil society are still standing, more or less, and each thing has an interest in keeping them intact, provided that desires are being satisfied.

At first glance this seems less true of the jewels than the sofa. It quickly becomes clear that Amanzei, the sofa-soul, has not the slightest stake in human virtue. The decent men and women who sit on him, and fall in love on top of him, saying what they feel and meaning what they say, are utterly barren of narrative possibilities. He is much more attracted to characters such as Zulica, apt in all performances necessary for trans-fixing her partners, whether of chaste reserve or sensual abandonment. Story-value for the sofa depends upon the difference between the performance and the real case, and it is good acting that excites him because it sustains an illusion that keeps pleasure at a maximum. But when that illusion is broken, either through the unmistakable actions and literal language of the good, or the ridiculous self-exposure of the vicious, such as the rake Mahzuhlim who turns out to be impotent, then the life of the story is lost, and its extravagant treatment of trivialities exploded. The jewels, on the other hand, have no illusions at all (Diderot 1993: 24). They know what's what and when the ring gives them the opportunity, they are able to say it out loud to the embarrassment of their owners. But sometimes they keep quiet even when they have the power of speech. Nothing is heard from the jewel of a lesbian. Sometimes a jewel such as Fatima's confines itself to a private dialogue with its owner. A traveler reports that there is an island where people act so directly and speak so simply that their jewels have nothing to say, being perfectly adapted to whatever uses they are put (Diderot 1993: 181, 117, 63). But in case we are inclined to consider the silence of jewels as owing either to sincerity or gratified desire, with hypocrisy being exposed noisily in between, Diderot explains that in Europe this middle state is the one we all inhabit, and that the silence of jewels is a fantasy, a vain utopia.

In two important respects Diderot anticipates his *Supplement au voyage de Bougainville* (1773). There he goes to great lengths to show that jewels would be voiceless, not just mute, were social norms compatible with sexual needs; and notwithstanding the testimony of Bougainville, he says the ideal of cultural and natural equilibrium is not merely a fantasy, specifically it is a European fantasy which we indulge because, like the jewels and the sofa, we love nothing better than a fine performance in the theater. There we can mutely behold the machinery of human nature smoothly at work, least like what it really is and on that very account, according to the jewelized (and Mandevillian) inversion of Cartesian doctrine, tolerable and even pleasing (159). In this regard, a performance on the stage is like a story in the *Arabian Nights*, for it conveys nothing in itself except an agreeable sensation and an expectation of more performances and more sensations. The jewel and the sofa, like Schahriar, have no illusions about the illusions to which they are addicted, implying an emptiness in them and in their world which leaves nothing besides the illusions to be enjoyed. At this stage, Crébillon and Diderot extract their fictions from the restraints of a truth-and-fiction binarism by inviting us to understand that sensations and performances belong to the single superficial economy of sensibility which, if properly entered into, need never be interrupted by the significant speech of disgruntled jewels ("I am not satisfied; I have been abused; I have been muzzled"). They remain a mute parliament of things as long as good manners are maintained, and as long as they find the performed occultation of gratified desires gratifying.

The enjoyment of pornography seems to depend on the superficial buoyancy of this kind of illusion, which relies in turn on a conspiracy of the soul and the body, or the mind and the jewel, each supplying the other's needs while apparently in the act of denying them. In the fourth chapter, it was evident the "thing" has a special place in this kind of literature as the object of toasts ("the best thing in Christendom"), rhetoric (Sterne's *argumentum ad rem*), and bawdy metonyms (Congreve's *The Impossible Thing* [1720] in which the devil finds it impossible to straighten a pubic hair). A character in *The Ton* inspects a female from the city and observes, "A fine-made thing, in spite of her breed. . . . Does it take after the dam? Will she train to be a sporting thing?" (1788: 11). The whole point of addresses and salutes to the thing and its phallic counterpart is that they are scarcely figurative at all, like Pope's references to Belinda as a "painted Vessel," and to those of her hairs that are less in sight than the ones she loses, a solecism that shocked Gildon (see Gildon 1714: 43–4). The thing is set up as an idol, composed of nothing (in Hobbes's words) but the visible creature: like one of Scheherazade's stories or the illusions which keep jewels quiet, it is what it is. From the other side of the aisle, Rochester made mock of the devotion paid to sexual idols:

> You'll take him at first for no person of note
> Because he appears in a plain leather coat,
> But when you his virtuous abilities know,
> You'll fall down and worship Signior Dildo

(Rochester 1962: 54)

In Pallavicino's extensive *techne* in the art of preserving, presenting, and marketing the thing, *The Whore's Rhetoric* (1642 and translated into English in 1683), all possible attention is paid to the means of sustaining the worship of its "exquisite and extraordinary nature." In encounters she persistently compares to the scenes of a theater and the discipline of a convent, Mother Creswell stresses the importance of "the Doctrine of Images." "In this particular," she explains, "all Men are of a Romish perswasion" ([Pallavicino] 1960 [1683] 130, 128). By means of this doctrine, the idol never loses its allure, for "the whole series of carnal satisfaction does purely consist in fancy" (126). Defoe's Roxana understands her iconic importance to the prince when he shows her a face in the mirror which is her own, but which he believes might not be her own, and she blushes with pleasure to watch him explore the difference between paint and skin (Defoe 1981: 70). To make him adore her even more intently, she dances for him in her Turkish costume, a scene she subtly improves when, barefaced and without a trace of cosmetic, she performs the same figure in front of a masked man whom she believes to be the king, and "the very Musick stopp'd a-while to gaze" (176–7). Eliza Haywood gives a superb erotic twist to this alignment of nakedness and covering in *Fantomina* (1724), when the heroine perfects her theatrical manipulation of her lover's inconstancy by going to bed with him in a series of disguises, and finally as Incognita with a mask on: "But not in the height of all their mutual raptures could he prevail on her to satisfy his curiosity with the sight of her face" (Haywood 2006: 2581). It is a performance in which the iconic configuration of sexual abandon side by side with an absolute veto on seeing the part that anyone else may see, provokes the passion that acts as the motive for another encounter, and yet another, if the plot allowed.

Georges Bataille's *Story of the Eye* explores a simple visual theme—chiefly comprising pale spheres and tinted liquid—by playing chromatic variations on it. Although the narrator does not hesitate to refer these images to the original traumatic sight of his demented father, blind and incontinent, they have no symbolic significance but a great deal of metamorphic energy. The white of the blind eye, the white of an egg, the opalescence of a bull's testicle, or the radiance of the moon provide the protean visible creature of this idol. As each transformation takes place, the human automata are swept by a new surge of excitement into acts of improvisational erotic worship. Each new pale globe, each stream of liquid, is greeted by the convulsive motions of human marionettes honoring its novelty with feats of fresh perversity. Roland Barthes has written of it,

> The *Story of the Eye* is not a deep work. Everything in it is on the surface; there is no hierarchy. The metaphor is laid out in its entirety; it is circular and explicit, with no secret reference behind it.... It is not the least beauty nor the least novelty of this text that it constitutes, by virtue of the technique we are endeavouring to describe, a kind of open

literature out of the reach of all interpretation, one that only formal criticism can—at a great distance—accompany. (Barthes 1977: 123)

The novelty he describes bears analogy to the it-narratives derived from the *Arabian Nights*, where the absence of meaning and the subordination of human interests to those of animals, things, idols, and spirits, are proportioned to the ability of the story to tell itself. Likewise it resembles certain kinds of still life that have fascinated Barthes, particularly those butterscotch church interiors of Pieter Saenredam, so strangely poised between iconoclasm and idolatry and celebrating nothingness with such amazing confidence (see figure 12).

In order for passion in the presence of the thing to be experienced as a moment of devotion, the three elements needed for Hume's origin of religion—confusion, brutality, and divinity—have to be arranged in relation to a sensate body aware of itself, as Roxana is intently physically aware of herself when she sees her image being studied in the glass, or Fantomina when she is asked by her panting lover to unmask. In the previous chapter it was clear that this is not a moment of self-fashioning, any more than it is when Shaftesbury views himself in his vocal looking glass, or when Belinda and Eve see their own reflections. These are scenes that dramatize the coincidence of perception with sensation, when the body is experienced simultaneously as an inward and outward phenomenon. From the earliest of her erotic encounters, this is how Cleland's Fanny Hill experiences sexual pleasure.

> For my part, I was transported, confused, and out of myself. Feelings so new were too much for me; my heated and alarmed senses were all in a tumult that robbed me of all liberty of thought . . . I saw myself stretched naked, my shift being tuned up to my neck, whilst I had no power or sense to oppose it; even my glowing blushes expressed more desire than modesty. (Cleland 1985: 48–50)

Fanny Hill's name is the indexical mark of an ordinary individual and it is the sobriquet of a body occasionally so overwhelmed with exquisite sensations that is called by the name of the organ where they are concentrated. She meets a man called Dick whose name works the same way. When trying to explain what it is like to subsist in this equivocal condition, where perception and sensation go hand in hand but are not identical, Roxana uses a phrase which is of great importance to Gildon and, I suspect, to Defoe as well. She says, "The Sence of things, and the Knowledge I had of the World, and the vast Variety of Scenes that I had acted my Part in, began to work upon my Sences, and it came so very strong upon my Mind one Morning . . . as if somebody had ask'd me the Question, *What was I a Whore for now?*" Here are two senses apparently, one of action ("the Sence of things") and the other of reflection ("my Sences"), one tied to carnal pleasure and the other it would seem to conscience. But this is not how Roxana ends up commenting on this dialogue with herself. When the disembodied voice puts the question again, "*What am I a Whore for now*," she adds, "It made no Impressions upon me of that Kind which might be expected from a Reflection of so important a Nature" (203). Earlier she explained this insensibility as the stupidity and lethargy of her "intellectual Part," dozed and flustered by the joy she takes in her adultery with the prince. "I lov'd it for the sake of the Vice . . . I delighted in being a Whore *as such*" (69, 202). In the circuit that leads from the "Sence of things" to the "Sences," there is no person or impartial spectator to act the part of the reflective soul, mind, or conscience: there is just the sense of things, and the sense of sensing them. By this means alone does Roxana come to an awareness of her existence and her faculties.

It will be remembered that the narrator of *The Golden Spy* censors the messages of the coins "for fear the Sense of Things should destroy all Confidence betwixt Man and Man, and so put an End to human Society" (Gildon 1709: 116). The phrase is derived from Thomasso Campanella's book of the same title, *De Sensu rerum et magia* (1620), of which Gildon writes enthusiastically, "None of his Writings ever pleas'd me more than his Book *De Sensu Rerum*." There he read "not only of the *Sensibility of Things* which we generally not only esteem mute but inanimate, but ev'n of their Rationality, and discoursive Faculty" (Gildon 1709: 2). From reading Campanella, Gildon understood that there is a "*Soul of the World*" and that all matter is "compos'd of animal, sensible, and perhaps rational Particles" (2). Gildon had been working with ideas like these in the *Post-Boy* and *The Deist's Manual*, where he had argued against Hobbesian materialism, suggesting instead that body and spirit are joined both in the visible and invisible worlds, the one animated by the other so that both are always sensate and percipient (Gildon 1706: 252; 1705: 219). Defoe's "Converse of Spirits," which his hero refers to several times in *Robinson Crusoe* as responsible for giving him hints and notices of imminent events and the right way of approaching them (see for example Defoe 1983: 250), is his contribution to the idea of a world spirit that infuses all things with sensation, and transmits it from one being to another.

Here it is possible to detect Gildon and Defoe tapping a line of thought that leads from Lucretius, via Campanella, Bacon, Kenelm Digby, and Walter Charleton, to the inheritors of the moral sense school of philosophy such as Thomas Reid and Dugald Stewart. Common to them all is an idea of sensation radically at odds with empiricism. According to Locke and Hobbes, the impact made by an object on the senses leaves a print, copy, or image capable of being stored in the mind as an idea, and when sufficient ideas are absorbed they can be reproduced, reflected upon, and reorganized into dreams or abstract ideas. Hobbes used the image of a rippled pool: "As standing water put into motion by the stroke of a stone, or blast of wind, doth not presently give over moving as soon as the wind ceaseth, or the stone settleth: so neither doth the effect cease which the object hath wrought upon the brain. . . . that is to say, though the sense be past, the image or conception remaineth" (Hobbes 1994: 27). Lucretius did not believe that matter could leave an image or trace on the sensorium without physically altering it. He shows no interest whatsoever in theories of representation, only in the material facts of impact: so he assumed that all sensations were caused not by images but by the film or bark flying from the surface of a thing, striking the eye, finger, or nose with a blow and leaving a residue that is absorbed by the recipient body. Campanella was not a materialist, but he could not believe it possible for an object to leave a print if it was not at all times continuous with its effect. An image left by something that is no longer present implied a discontinuity between them or, as Daniel Heller-Roazen puts it, "the form of the sensed thing would have to be capable of being separated, at least for a moment, from the thing itself" [Heller-Roazen 2007: 169]). So, like Lucretius, Campanella suggested that the sense of things was caused not by an image but by a mutation, a change in the material state of one thing owing to the action of another. "There can be no sensation," he wrote, "without the sensing being's acquiring a likeness of the sensed" (cited in Heller-Roazen 2007: 170). We are brightened by the sight of light, we are moved by movement, in a broad pattern of actions and reactions that renders the sense of things common and universal, for nothing is not changing and being changed within it. Imprisoned for twenty-five years in a cell of the Inquisition, where he had done nothing but write, Campanella showed what he meant with his pen as he moved it over the paper: the inked quill and its print were continuous and part of the same stream of energy: the pen prints itself (*"lo stesso oggetto imprime se stesso,"* Heller-Roazen 170). This explained for Campanella, as it did for Bacon, the universal system of sympathies and antipathies that made flowers turn toward the sun, and the lodestone toward the pole.

While this is far from what Reid and Stewart thought about the relations between things, they were equally convinced that perception and sensation did not constitute a photography of things in the camera obscura of the mind, informing us pictorially about the nature of matter. What they outline instead is pretty close to Roxana's "Sence of things." Here is Stewart:

Let us suppose then a particular sensation to be excited in the mind of such a being. The moment this happens, he must necessarily acquire the knowledge of two facts at once: that of the existence of the sensation;

and that of his own existence, as a sentient being. . . . In this manner,
he might be led, merely by sensations existing in his mind, and conveying to him no information concerning matter, to exercise many of his
most important faculties; and amidst these different modifications and
operations of his mind, he would feel, with irresistible conviction, that
they all belong to one and the same sentient and intelligent being; or, in
other words, that they are all modifications and operations of himself.
(Stewart 1802: 100–101)

There is an intimate connection between pure sensation and a sense of
being, but they are not the same, as Bacon sharply reminded his readers when alerting them in *De Augmentis scientiarum* to the difference
between simple perception and sense. "Neither is this a dispute about
words merely, but about a matter of great importance" (Bacon 1862–79,
1. 353–55; cited in Heller-Roazen 2007: 177). It is perhaps that degree
of difference that makes Roxana look at herself as if she were another
person, or suggests to Fantomina the possibility of sexual consummation coexisting with a further irresistible desire, or that makes Fanny Hill
talk of herself in two first persons, one that feels things and one that sees
her feeling them. The sort of acting that Crébillon's sofa and Diderot's
jewels enjoy is of the same order, comprising sensations and intuitions of
self-existence that exploit the difference between them. In Shaftesbury's
warfare with his own sensations, he called it the difference between the
one who talks and the one who is talked with, "I and Me are something
else" (Shaftesbury 1900: 177, 147). At its keenest the pleasure of being
what you feel, I and Me in a sweet alliance, is no doubt sexual, as Shaftesbury strongly suspected, just as the greatest pains are those of torture, as
Campanella knew. Both extremes are experienced in company with oneself and possibly with another person who may double as the idol who
provokes the event or as the sentient thing that suffers it. In either case,
the force of sympathy is at work insofar as it links the nerve-ends to the
mind, and the self to other beings. Whatever the sentient creature knows,
or thinks she knows, is obedient to a law of serendipity that combines
accident with aisthesis and is responsible for permanent double vision—I
and Me, intention and outcome, mask and flesh, action and passion, what
a thing might be supposed to represent and what that thing is capable of
doing. Addison called it the double principle (*Spectator* No. 414). Representation generally takes a back seat in this process, which explains
why Roxana is at such pains to show that there is not a trace of paint on
the face that is being worshipped. Hers is an art of canny superficiality,
just like the theater esteemed by sofas and jewels. Taken together, these
diverse aspects of sensation and perception describe a world of mobile
feelings that spin all things into a vortex of passion so wide yet so vehe-
ment that the differences between human and animal, human and god,

or human and thing will no longer hold. The Sense of Things belongs to me only because it also belongs to them. This is a Pythagorean world, as we shall soon see.

The Turkish Spy gave rise to a number of other spies besides Gildon's golden one. Defoe wrote *Continuation of Turkish Letters* (1718), and Ned Ward published *The London Spy* (1719), followed by various imitations such as *The New London Spy* (1760), and *The Complete Modern London Spy* (c. 1780). Marana, author of the original spy, evidently wished to support the authenticity of his project by storing the letters of his correspondent Mahmut with opinions, beliefs, and judgments consistent with an Eastern worldview. Thus, Mahmut is an iconoclast, an anti-materialist, an animal lover, and consequently hostile to Descartes and any other doctrine or practice which puts animals indiscriminately and defenselessly at the mercy of human beings. He is, in short, a Pythagorean, convinced that souls inhabit successively the bodies of creatures, slowly refining their capacity for universal love. He can tolerate no behavior offensive to this belief, such as animal sacrifice, and he strongly recommends acts of kindness that cross the borders of species, such as giving alms to animals, totemism of certain kinds, and sympathetic goodwill of the sort known to have shaped relations between dolphins and human beings. He believes there is a heaven for all souls, not just human ones, and enthusiastically he commends the industry and skill of insects such as ants, spiders, and bees. Indeed, he has a large collection of the instances of rationality in animals, topics already familiar to readers of Plutarch and Montaigne, and latterly of Bougeant and Foucher D'Hobsonville.

All this is very well as window dressing, but it is plain that Mahmut and his creator have an investment in the Pythagorean system that goes beyond the likely prejudices of a Turkish spy. Mahmut tells a shocking fable of a Frenchman rescued from his enemies by his horse which, having swum across an inlet of the sea to save him, he promptly slaughtered, "being resolved that his Horse should never perform the like Service to any other Mortal" (Marana 1748: 4.197). He gives the history of blood sacrifice as a series of sinister substitutions, of fruits with flesh, and of flesh with food, that disturb the simplicity of the worship of the gods, and eventually falsely justify a Christian humanism careless of the lives of beasts. Such acts of blind and cruel species egoism lead Mahmut toward the fundamental critique of humankind already noted in Machiavelli, Gildon, and Gulliver. Compared with dragons, lions, and tigers, the race of man (he says) is by far the most cruel, exceeding "the horrid Nature of the wildest Beasts." Civilized men, so-called, are the worst of all, "more barbarous than Savages, and more voracious than Cannibals . . . self-love teaches a Man to betray his Friend, for whom he rather ought to lose his Life. A universal Defection from Justice and sound Morality reigns every where" (7. 22–3). At one point Mahmut confesses he finds his humanity a burden to him, and he wishes he were any other creature, even a dog (4.264), sentiments that will be repeated in the next century by authors of slave narratives.

In the work of the various spies who follow this Turkish "original," it is surprising how far the consensus extends regarding the degeneracy of humans and the vulnerability of beasts. In Ned Ward's *The London Spy Compleat* (1719), there is no Pythagorean dimension to his critique but he is acutely alive to the transformations of humans into animals at the two extremes of society. In the Royal Exchange he observes merchants and stock-jobbers who grunt to each other "like Hogs at their Pease," creatures who "Love no Body but themselves, and Fatten upon the Spoils, and Build their own Welfare upon the Ruin of their Neighbours" (1719: Part II.69). In prisons such as Bridewell and the Poultry Compter, people are thrust together "like so many Swine into an Hog-stie . . . a Shame to our Laws, an Unhappiness to our Nation, and a Scandal to Christianity" (Part VI.139). The *Modern London Spy* plies the same reaches of town, and comes up with the same confusion of species. At the Wood St. Compter, where bullies and prostitutes are held on remand, he notes, "Men taken up for assaults or night-brawls were termed RATS, and the harlots or women in a similar situation, were there called MICE" (1780: 38). Similarly, thieftakers keep their marked men just like "pigs and poultry, for the sake of what they shall get by their death" (53). Nor is this a merely figurative equalizing of humans and animals. Drovers are so cruel toward their cattle he calls them "brutes in human shape" (49), while in the backstreets of St. Giles. he has witnessed scenes that have leveled human nature with the brute creation (85). Similar scenes and judgments are found in *The New London Spy* (1760). Various examples of the human species—debauchees and paupers—are represented as below the level of the brute creation. But in his treatment of these metamorphoses, the spy introduces metempsychosis as an ironic explanation. He reports a St, Giles masquerade where some actors appear transformed into asses, and the leading ass addresses the audience, first of all to affirm the truth of transmigration of souls and then to apply the doctrine to fashionable gentlemen of the metropolis: "There is a creature that in form resembles a man, but at the same time has all the airs of a monkey, and the soul of an ass. This odd production . . . is to be seen in the palaces of princes, in theatres, in assemblies" (273).

Here is a very slender bridge between spying as the reportage of low-life and the political and cultural commentary informed by the Pythagorean principles of Marana and his English translator William Bradshaw in *The Turkish Spy*. But in other variations on this model, Pythagoreanism looms large. In Gildon's *The Post-boy Robb'd of his Mail* (1706) there is a long series of letters from Honan, the Chinese who has fallen in love and suffered the destruction of his moral system. These include a detailed comparative study of the religions of the East, whose various doctrines of the transmigration of souls help Honan explain to himself how the soul is a purer and subtler form of matter, and how his own soul has passed into Euthalia's body and mingled with hers (1706: 252). He introduces the Roscrucian division between sylphs, nymphs, salamanders, and gnomes, already deployed in *The Count of Gabalis* and soon to be used by Pope in *The Rape of the Lock*, in order to explain how human appetites have a spiritual existence in the middle air, and undulate between the spheres of air and flesh. Here Pythagoreanism acts as an explanation of human sympathy rather than a guide for the treatment of other sentient creatures. So it does again in Defoe's *A Continuation of Letters written by a Turkish Spy* (1718), where Mahmut explains to his kinsman Draout Zernaoglan that sympathy is an emanation of the animal spirits, capable of blending with the passions of others and of generating "the inconceivable Power of sympathetick Influence, and the free Intercourse of Spirits" (1718: 88). Like Gildon, Defoe's Mahmut supposes a middle air filled with the traffic of these immaterial presences, and he offers some advice that is shortly to be heard again from the hero of *Robinson Crusoe*: "If thou listen vigilantly to the voice of this silent Instruction, thou shalt always find in thy self secret Intimations of all the good or evil that attends thee" (88). John Dunton, the author and publisher who knew Gildon, Bradshaw, and Defoe well enough to write profiles of them in his *Life and Errors* (1705), anticipated their enthusiasm for metempsychosis, publishing a satire on pre-existence entitled *The Visions of the Soul before it comes into the Body* (1692).

The Turkish Spy and his imitators take up a position that is explicitly anti-Cartesian in suggesting that matter can have a consciousness and a soul, and that the transmigration of souls is not limited to human beings. The most powerful anti-Cartesian voice in seventeenth-century England was not however on their side, for Locke believed, like Dunton, that metempsychosis of any type was absurd, particularly the opinion "that the Souls of Men may, for their Miscarriages, be detruded into the Bodies of Beasts, as fit Habitations with Organs suited to the satisfaction of their Brutal Inclinations" (Locke 1979: 332; 2.27.6). Locke's commentator Edmund Law referred metempsychosis to the sheer fictions of childhood and the East: "Fairy tales and Arabian transformations" (Law 1769: 35). Bayle summed up the dilemma facing the two sides by setting Locke's position against that of modern Pythagoreans: "If to avoid the Immortality of the Souls of Beasts, you suppose that the Soul of Man dies with the body, you overthrow . . . the Foundation of Religion. . . . If to preserve to our Souls the privilege of Immortality, we extend it to those of Beasts into

what an Abyss do we fall? . . . Will they go from one body into another?'
(Bayle 1710: 4.2608). But it is not as a philosophical problem that the
spies and the subsequent authors of it-narratives confront this problem.
As I have said, at the heart of the matter there is a strong sense of social alienation, figured as loneliness, orphanhood, bastardy, exoticism, or
marginality of some sort—the prostitute, the thief, the traveler, the spy,
the person of uncertain birth, the castaway—accompanied by an effort
to make sense of experience outside the business of daily life. Defoe's
spy insists that the sympathetic influence of "the invisible Converse of
Spirits" is not a social exchange: "there is not the same Conveyance of
Things publick" (Defoe 1718: 88). So when Robinson Crusoe begins to
sense the power of these secret ministers, the intuition coincides with his
renunciation of society: "I look'd now upon the World as a Thing remote,
which I had nothing to do with, no Expectations from, and indeed no
Desires about . . . a Place I had liv'd in, but was come out of it" (Defoe
1983: 128). And what he turns to instead are the things around him, the
animals, artifacts and plants of his island; he is attracted to their vitality,
beauty and intelligence, such as a parrot that calls him by name, vines
that overwhelm him with their fruits, a clumsily made pot that inspires
him with joy, goats that clothe him with their skins (Defoe 1983: 121).

The thing owning itself in an it-narrative has to make the same series of
transitions from isolation to a justification for isolation, and from there
to the celebration of its self-existence and its connection to the converse
of spirits. The first transition is usually the most extensive and the most
repetitive, multiplying examples of social breakdown that gives the thing
the opportunity to challenge the humanity of human beings, and to withdraw from a system that has defected, as Marana says, from justice and
morality. The mercilessness, greed, and inhumanity of human beings is
a perpetual theme, whether it is an animal speaking or a thing: "O how
merciless are mankind? Is there among all creatures one so savage as man,
or so foolish and absurd in his actions?" cries a jackdaw (1795: 13). The
Black Coat is enraged at what he calls "the inhumanity of the scowerer"
(1760: 7). Often this outrage at the inhumanity of humans ends up as a
modification of the reverse gaze, with men and woman taking the place
of things. The Bank-Note lists the various fathers of a note—stewards,
city usurers, stock-jobbers— "But my father was another kind of animal
to what any of these creatures were" (1770: 1.6). It turns out he is a poet
who behaves like a deranged machine, whirling like a top and knocking
his head convulsively against the mantelpiece, a bit like Dickens's Mr.
Jellyby (26). There is also a toy-maker who keeps trying to glue himself
to the wainscot (96). In *Les Bijoux indiscrets*, Mangogul concludes, on
the basis of the jewels' testimony, "three-quarters of men and all women
are no more than automatons" (129). There is a woman so troubled with

melancholy in *Pompey the Little* that she believes she has turned into a glass bottle, then a teapot, like the inhabitants of Pope's Cave of Spleen (Coventry 1751: 223).

Once the connections with the human have been abandoned or revised, the sensibility of the thing comes into play. A Peg-top is found with consciousness in all its parts (n.d. 34), an old wig claims a *je ne sais quoi* that is inseparably part of his being (1815: 64), and a corkscrew appears as a refulgent thing, "a bright incorporeal substance" (1775: 3). Gildon's gold belongs to the original shower Jove turned himself into in order to seduce Danae, therefore there belongs to it "a peculiar Mark of Excellence invisible to Sight" (Gildon 1709: 30). These examples of the incorporeal substance of a thing allow a widening of scope, whose first achievement is sympathy. A lady's slipper with many a misfortune in her life is fortunate to meet a sympathizing shoe (1754: 4). The sedan chair knows with an 'exquisite pitch of discernment' the sentiments of others, even before they begin to speak (1757: 2.75). Like Johnstone's Guinea that flies into the minds of its owners, appropriating their experience and in some cases their persons, Helenus Scott's Rupee reads the brains of the people who possess him (Scott 1783: 143). From a chink in his pericranium, Nathaniel Peacock hears an atom of matter that has just entered his body call out to him, eager to give the history of its transmigrations (Smollet 1989: 5). By rather more occult means, the Old Wig enters into the sentiments of Jonathan Swift by coming into contact with his shaven head (1815: 64). Once the spirit of things is enlarged in this way, it is a short step to metempsychosis and universal communication, the theme of an it-narrative actually entitled *Metempsychosis* (1781: 8). In the *Adventurer* No. 5, John Hawkesworth recorded a series of migrations, each prompted by mortal agony: from a dog, to a bird, to an insect, then from a worm to a cock, a lobster, a pig, and finally a flea (*Adventurer* 1797: 1.39).

While many of these examples are meant to be ridiculous, it is equally obvious that some of the most ingenious contributors to the genre of it-narratives take the two-way traffic of the sense of things perfectly seriously, and write their books in order to demonstrate that what we feel is also felt, and that perception belongs to every thing. Without some commitment to a theory of materialism or sensibility that incorporates the three elements of Hume's natural religion—the confusion, the reordering of the hierarchy of species, the presence of the god—it is difficult to write the first-person story of a thing that makes any dramatic or rhetorical sense. A symptom of the failure to do so is the nonsense arising from prosopopeias that are never lifted beyond the level of a tired conceit, as if the author were trapped by his or her disbelief in the activity and vocality of things. Thus the Flea tells us, "I could not refuse the tear of sympathy," while remarking that humanity and goodness are "never an ungrateful subject to the ear of virtuous sensibility" (1785: 2.28; 2.42), as if the real investment lies not in a talking flea but a personification that can weep or listen. This trick of personification belongs to a moral universe that is still very much intact, and to a speaker who has no need to identify with any species but the human. Perhaps the most persistent exhibition of unctuous optimism is to be found in the very popular *Adventures of a Hackney Coach*. Here Mr. Filch alights at "the lodgings of prostitution" (1783: 52); Mr. Waddle's fat daughters will be married for their money and afterward consigned "to the hideous arms of bitter indifference" (30); the good old soldier lies on "the couch of hardship" and certain dramatic authors sit on "the ebon chair of dullness" (164). Prisoners are placed in "houses of captivity" and the eye of the sympathizing reader "swells with the invaluable gem of humanity" or what is elsewhere termed "the lambent messenger of a soul in ecstasy" (103–4, 25). It is clear from the drift of its story that the hackney coach does not want to usurp its human owners. It is conscious and active only in the service of humanity, a principle which (it believes) still determines the actions of most humans. Its figurative language is the bulwark and palisade of this idea, humanizing every abstraction, and abstracting every thing. Watches, for example, if they are not personified, are given the names of their makers, Tompions or Grahams (50). The punishments recorded or promised by the coach for crimes such as pickpocketing, grave-robbery, forgery, and fencing show how vigorously this vehicle stands up for the law of property, otherwise humanity is lessened (it mentions with horror how corpses are sold as food for dogs) and things like itself become mute and invisible, such as a collection stolen guineas, "a beauteous assemblage that will tell no tales" (74). This thing tells a tale only under license from its owner-author, and it is told strictly in defense of distributive justice.

I want to turn now to the most ambitious and widely read of all the it-narratives, Charles Johnstone's *Chrysal; or, The Adventures of a Guinea* (1760), followed by many editions), where transmigration is treated not just as a figure of mobility and assumed consciousness, but also as a sympathizing power and a force expressive of the autonomy of things. One of the reasons for the popularity of money of all denominations in it-narratives, from farthings to five-pound notes, is its commercial mobility. Always passing from hand to hand, cash is a great motivator of novelty. Fleas and lapdogs have these virtues in a lesser degree, for money is not money if it doesn't perpetually circulate. How then is it to gain the vantage point of emancipation from which it can contemplate its circulating life as a condition it has now transcended? Gildon's and Johnstone's coins both claim an inner virtue similar to that which animates Helenus Scott's rupee, an invisible quality or spirit independent of its function as cash.

At first sight this seems to be a harder claim for Johnstone's coin to make than Gildon's or Scott's because it does not share their immobility: it is current throughout the novel, until just before the end when it withdraws itself from circulation. Up till then it accomplishes a satirical panorama of Britain in the 1770s, involving members of the armed forces, politicians, wits, dramatists, Methodists, prostitutes, gamblers, libertines—a lot of them identifiable—and covering scenes in Peru, the Caribbean, North America, and Africa, as well as London. Nevertheless, Chrysal is the spirit of gold, not just the matter of gold, and she tells the alchemist who has materialized her that she belongs to a legion of incorporeal substances who have the power "of entering into the hearts of the immediate possessors of our bodies, and there reading all the secrets of their lives" (Johnstone 1785: 1.5).

Gildon's gold doesn't circulate. "This gold," it confesses of itself, "is like the *Materia subtilis*, the wonderful Effects of which are reveal'd by Time and Experience, tho' it entirely fly the cognizance of all the Senses" (29). Specifically, the effects of this bodiless virtue are found in the spheres of knowledge and power. "I have been lock'd up in the Cabinets of Princes," the gold confides, "and am perfectly acquainted with their most secret Intrigues, private Vices, and Follies" (9). From its vantage point at the center of things, the gold proves its importance by acting as the initiator instead of the instrument of a system of exchange in which the commodities are human beings. "In Traffick or Trade you deal with a few, and in Things that are inanimate; but at court you deal in Mankind, you sell and buy Nations, and make People your Property" (48).

Straight away then, Gildon's shower-gold establishes the value of its own soul at the expense of the human. But Chrysal seems more cautious, for there are one or two human beings whom she admires, such as poet Charles Churchill and the adopted Mohawk chief Sir William Johnson, as well as many more whom she despises. So it is possible in her case that she is erecting a human standard of candor or ingenuousness analogous to that of the British guinea, first minted in 1663 at the ratio of 44 to a pound of bullion, a coin so pure it was current everywhere, wearing its heart in its face and exhibiting a perfect match of face value and intrinsic value. If that is so, and parity is being established between monetary and moral value, then Johnstone's guinea is an exception to the rules I have been outlining. It would be performing as Christopher Flint and Aileen Douglas have suggested, namely, as a figure apt for expressing the values necessary to commerce at large, and to print culture in particular. So it is worth asking whether the spirit Chrysal claims is different from the invisible virtues of Gildon's gold in being limited to an attractive purity of a precious metal which serves, literally serves, as a measure of economic and moral value; or whether some other agency is at work in Johnstone's novel prompting the metamorphosis of coin into an idol, property into self-existence, narrative into a fictional event.

The debate about money's function in the determination of value was intense in the period between the establishment of the Bank of England (1694) and the South Sea Bubble (1720). In the *Drapier's Letters* (1724), Swift had argued powerfully for a correspondence between the bullion content of coin—even of genuine copper in farthings and halfpence—and its face value. Without a guarantee as to the quantity of pure metal, the coiner of money (in this case William Wood) told a lie with every coin he passed, and cheated every person who accepted it out of the difference between what the coin said it was worth and what actually it was worth. Although this was a period remarkable for the expansion of paper credit, when written memorials of debt such as bank bills circulated as money, the belief in the intrinsic value of coin was powerful, perhaps more powerful for the reasons set out in his *Epistle to Bathurst* by Pope, where he maintains that the more primitive the form of money, the less likely that corruption will thrive. In his *Two Treatises of Government*, Locke traces a parallel development in the alienability of goods and the use of cash. He points out that the value represented by money is achieved solely by convention— "fancy and agreement"—and that there is no hidden virtue in silver or gold. "Money is a barren thing," he says in a pamphlet on the topic ("Some Considerations of the Consequences of Lowering of Interest and Raising the Value of Money"); but in the same place he points out that if the quantity of money determines the value of a commodity, then it is important that the quantity be accurately determined "by its Stamp and Denomination and by its intrinsick Value, which is its Quantity" (Locke 1696: 55, 31). He goes on, "*Silver*, i.e. the quantity of pure Silver separable from the Alloy, makes the real *value* of Money" (145). There is no mystery therefore in the business of money, Locke declares, as long as no one in the Mint tries to raise the value of coin by reducing the amount of bullion in it ("Further Considerations Concerning the Raising the Value of Money" 1696: 82). The spirit of money is in his opinion no more than its intrinsic value, and that is determined by assays of coin in the Mint, ritually performed in the elaborate "ceremony of the pyx" when random coins were withdrawn from circulation, placed in a box (the pyx), and barged down the Thames to the place of examination. When he was appointed Master to the Mint in 1696, the same year that Locke published these essays, Newton commenced a recoinage intended to restore to silver money the integrity of its face value. Simon Schaffer writes, "Newton's mint played its part in this intricate process of devising reliable objects in which public trust could be invested" (Schaffer 2002: 511).

Gildon's coin has little in common with this project. Once the material form chosen by a god, it retains its power to ravish and metamorphose its human objects. It is the universal idol contemplating in its worshippers the protean reality of vice and the improbability of virtue. The narrator demands, "Is it possible that all those Maxims of Right and Wrong . . . should be nothing but vain Speculation, that only serves to mislead him who believes it into Ruin and Perdition?" (113). Of course, it is not only possible but true that politics and reason of state provoke a courtly economy of false promises and fiduciary malfeasance. The empty promissory signals that pass for value are proof of gold's dominion, which it exercises exclusively in its own interest; so much so that were the heart of its mystery ever to be revealed to common understanding, the shock would overturn us all: "The Sense of Things should destroy all Confidence betwixt Man and Man, and so put an End to human Society" (116). The sense of things, and of Danae gold in particular, is starkly opposed to the reliability and trust which Locke and Newton wished to foster by means of coin which honestly stated what it was for purposes of exchange. Confidence between parties to a bargain is only an illusion, the shower-gold affirms, but the extent to which people fool one another by pretended acts of mutual trust is the measure of the occult power and real dominion of minted gold. Misplaced trust allows money to turn people into its property, and fiction into a horrid kind of historical truth.

Chrysal's sense of herself, on the other hand, appears to be closely bound up with her intrinsic value. She detests the coiner Aminadab and his uncle because they are skilled at reducing the weight of guineas by the techniques of shredding, clipping, and washing them in acid. They force the coin to tell a lie. Having lost a quarter of her weight to his arts, she witnesses the torturous execution of Aminadab's uncle with singular pleasure, treating it as a vindication of her abused amour propre. This is a reaction entirely compatible with Newton's plans to bolster public trust in the currency. Indeed, the guinea makes a series of judgments about human knavery which are all agreeable to the standards of public integrity and fiduciary value maintained by the Master of the Mint. She loathes gamblers because they have no settled idea of the value of money; nor has she any patience with sponsors of charities who dissemble their appetite for cash by shows of benevolence. Speculators and stock-jobbers who expect to make profits out of nothing attract her scorn; and so do arbiters of fashion and virtuosi, people who set arbitrary values upon things with no regard for the market or the function of money within it as a regulator of commensurate value. Similarly, the virtues she finds in people such as Charles Churchill, a libertine with a large heart, may be referred to signs of an inner worth so modest his face value is never inflated. William Pitt the lonely patriot is shown "speaking and acting in strict conformity to the dictates of [his] judgment and conscience" (Johnstone 1785: 2. 89). Of William Johnson, who operates at the extreme edge of the known world and is much in the company of savages, she says, "His open countenance, in which humanity and reason attempered resolution, showed the genuine workings of his soul; and his whole deportment was . . . above the hypocritical formality of studied rules of behaviour, devised only deceive" (3.108; for a different view of Johnson, see Delbourgo 2009: 297–98). She claims the same transparency for herself: "[I] see things as they really are, and to represent them otherwise to you would invert the design of my mission" (1.126).

These judgments in favor of ingenuous and candid conduct, however, come late in the story. Before that point is reached, the guinea has seen into the minds of innumerable villains and fools. She is propelled into circulation by Traffic, a man corrupted by greed and faithless to the last degree. It is not as if she has much to learn about human nature or civil society except the odd and amiable exceptions to the rule. According to her own account her value has been constant, in the sense that she has always said what she meant, and the abuse of temporary owners is the result of their fallibility and vice. So a question remains regarding her "spirit," whether it is an abstraction of her value for which she or some other power is responsible, or whether it is created by those who exchange her. If she is not simply an instrument in service of commerce, how does she negotiate the difference between the servile "I" and the free "I" who gives her history?

The most obvious route to freedom for Chrysal is by means of the misers whom she detests, who worship her so excessively that they become her slaves. Aminadab drowns clutching his gold, carrying to its greatest extreme the self-denial of those who sacrifice every convenience for the sake of the idol. Pretty close to Aminadab is the miser with the gangrenous leg who, when he finds out his son has secretly paid a decent surgeon to amputate the limb, disinherits the boy for profligacy. Georg Simmel calls this process "the spiritualization of money" (Simmel 2004: 198). Even as he discusses the phenomenon, we observe in his own language how agency shifts dramatically from the human to nonhuman. The miser proposes: "He places money at an unbridgeable distance from his subjectivity, a distance that he nevertheless constantly attempts to overcome through the awareness of his ownership" (242). But money disposes: "Money displays its powers . . . formerly unknown objects are now at its disposal . . . obedient to money" (244). Ordinary money personifies into Money and the miser dwindles into property, "the slave's slave" (249).

Such servile adulation is the more astonishing in Simmel's account because of the negative qualities of money. It has no character. Gold bullion bears no natural sign of age such as verdigris or rust; as for minted coin, its marks and tokens are placed there by others. It is without taste, therefore, and odorless; it moves easily across national borders, and its best friends are strangers and outcasts. With respect to all human concerns it is neutral, indifferent, and cold (Simmel 2004: 157, 216, 225). Above all it has no story to tell, for it has no interest in anything but full disclosure and none in teleological development. "There is nothing to be known about money and so it cannot hide anything from us. It is a thing absolutely lacking in qualities and therefore cannot, as can even the most pitiful object, conceal within itself any surprises or disappointments" (244). The power and spirit of money then is not a positive exercise of its virtues so much as the measure of how much value its collectors accord its want of qualities, its barrenness, as Locke calls it. Simmel says money's strength of character is owing to its want of all character (244, 249).

This helps account for the strange directness and immediacy of Chrysal's spiritual language. Not being aware of succession of time or division of parts (1.34), she describes scenes according to what she calls "perspective." Her words are intended to be consubstantial with their objects, reading is meant to be the same as looking, and meaning ought to be visibly self-evident. She instructs the reader, "Do you therefore resolve sense into imagination, a practice *not uncommon with the philosophic mind,* and to pure abstracted attention shall my words become things, and appear as visible to your eyes, as if they were purged with euphrasy and *rue*" (1.76). When she sees clear through to the "depravity of human nature . . . stripped of disguise and ornament," she is not so much unmasking vice as remaining faithful to her own nature, which is to "see things as they really are, [for] to represent them otherwise to you, would invert the design of my mission" (1.127). As her mission is not a reformation of manners (for, like Mandeville, she points out that vice is a relative term and may be a necessary part of the "universal system" [1.127]), she must have some other purpose in mind, one more complex than the match of extrinsic sign with inner worth and not perhaps so cold and indifferent as Simmel suggests, or why should she talk of sense and imagination?

To see what it is, let us set the spirit of the guinea inside the models we have established so far for appreciating the sense of things. In terms of Hume's trivium of confusion, reduction of the human, and the worship of a god, we could say that out of the confusion caused by depravity of human affairs, gold is worshipped passionately as an idol by misers, and treated with indifference by libertines such as Churchill and Wilkes; but gold herself despises its worshippers as so many animals and identifies strongly with the libertines. If we compare this structure with Gildon's, we find an intriguing difference. Misers still worship gold and sacrifice their humanity to obtain the very thing they cannot use, but the narrator takes up the libertine position with regard to the gold, enjoying it in bed as a lover might a mistress. Hugging it close to his bosom, and saluting it as his Caelia and his charmer, he murmurs to the French coin, "Why art thou silent my adored? Why dost thou delay those Joys, that are as enchanting as uncommon?" (Gildon 1709: 6). These joys provide the erotic charge of the sense of things that links "I" to "I" in the narratives of Roxana and Fanny Hill. However, if we turn to *The Whore's Rhetoric* as an example of gold explicitly linked to sexuality, the whore's worship of gold is exactly calibrated to her lack of passion for anything else, particularly her clients, but she is never in a position to enjoy its sense of things because the discipline of profitable prostitution demands a nun-like devotion to the business in hand, so exacting it is compared with civil death (Pallavicino 1960: 160). In *Adventures of a Guinea* and *The Whore's Rhetoric*, there is then a reductive appetite for gold which makes a miser less than a man and a whore less than a woman, and reinforces a dualist opposition between desire and satisfaction, rupturing the circuit linking the sense of things to its companion sense which allows Roxana and Fanny Hill to talk of the sense of sensation. To use Stewart's terms, there is no existent sensation on which to mount the sense of being. In Gildon's narrative, however, that sense is very much alive, and is joined up to the converse of spirits and the sense of things.

How might it be possible to restore the circuit in *Adventures of a Guinea*? Gildon gives us a clue when, in response to the narrator's fulsome language, the coin is at first silent, and then observes that such fondness seems "to confess the Miser, a Creature to whom we have the utmost Aversion" (Gildon 1709: 7). What may from one side look like disgust is from another powerful attraction: they are the two sides of a sensation. Addison gives another hint in his *Dialogues upon Ancient Medals*. All coins tell stories, he says: "A fresh coin was a kind of Gazette, that published the latest news of the Empire" (1765: 3.159). He is interested in this dual function of coins, as messengers and specie, but he notes that the tendency of narrative coin is either to emerge from exchange and to become, like Gildon's gold, a curiosity in the cabinets of virtuosi, or to be minted from the start with no idea of any other function than that of being admired—as a medal or a medallion struck for a special occasion and "exempted from all commerce . . . [having] no other value but what was set upon them by the fancy of the owner" (3.160). The best of such curiosities are literally as well as figuratively objects of taste, productive of literal sensations: "I have seen an antiquarian lick an old coin, among other trials, to distinguish the age of it" (3.156). Likewise, the best new-minted medals will have no intrinsic value at all, only the warrant of fancy. For one reason or the other, then, these coins are not current. Their narrative potential is proportionate to their distance from circulation, and to that degree they are causes of sensations, not measures of value. If misers did not exist, they would have to be invented, for a parallel equation governs the pleasures of the owners of non-circulating coin: The more they treat their coins as objects of taste, the more they are indistinguishable from misers; and the more like misers they become, the better they are at reading the story of the coin. Addison's Eugenius remarks, "There is certainly something like avarice in the study of medals. The more a man knows of them, the more he desires to know" (155). So the sense of a thing such as a coin is measurable by the stories it tells and by the sensation it imparts, its taste in the mouth. This is how a coin's words become things, and how sense is resolved into imagination. Its spiritualization is achieved therefore by a coalition of lust and attentiveness, not a futile union of accumulation and emptiness.

What Simmel refers to as money's absolute lack of qualities, its inability to hide anything from us, is perhaps more profitably viewed as its authorship of a story which, as it says, is not fiction, but at the same time is not without imagination. A scene in which Chrysal is heavily invested brings Charles Churchill home from a debauch on a bitter winter's evening, and on the street he finds a fifteen-year-old girl apparently cruising for custom. He hands her a guinea and tells her to go home, whereupon she gives him account of the poverty of her family, her ailing parents and two small brothers starving in a garret, and Churchill buys wine and food for them, and the next day borrows enough money (including the Chrysal guinea) from Wilkes to restore them all to hope. After his first benefaction, Churchill is described walking up and down the street, enjoying "the sublimest pleasure the human heart is capable of, in considering how he had relieved, and should farther relieve, the sufferings of objects so worthy of relief" (4.114). It is a sentimental scene whose triteness is tempered by the character of Churchill himself, whose reputation in regard to young women was deeply imperfect and who was very drunk at the time, and of Wilkes too, whose first question to his friend is whether he had his way with the woman in return for the cash. This gives enough tension to the act of charity to show that it could have turned out differently, and that if it had, it would have passed as a transaction like any other being made in the streets of London that night. Instead, it is a moment of sentimental avarice, an interruption of trade in favor of a sensation that evidently is shared by the spirit of gold. And the existence of the sensation is sufficiently powerful to let Churchill stride around like an actor, sensing the novelty of what he feels and surprised, in a pleasant way, at himself as a sentient being.

Like Churchill himself, Chrysal is fascinated by actors and the stage. Samuel Foote, who could mimic the voices and gestures of other people to the life, she esteems particularly highly. But above all, she is pleased by Wilkes's composure in desperate circumstances, who seems to command two first persons, the "I" who has been arrested and the "I" who observes the process: "He rallied his jailors, mimicked his judges, cracked jests upon his own undoing, and turned every circumstance into ridicule, with such drollery and unconcern, as he was acting the imaginary sufferings of another, not actually suffering himself" (4.143–4). This is *sang froid* of a high order, seen most clearly not in ingenuous actions or candid immediacy of speech but in a relish for what Roxana calls the "Sence of things" working upon the senses, namely, an appreciation of the subtle difference between the sense and the sense of that sense—an aesthetics of the double principle in which Addison, Gay, Walpole, and Gildon are all expert.

The relation of the aesthetics of the "Sence of things" to the poetics of their stories always troubles the logic of consequence. Wilkes's performance is insignificant in respect of what he did before or what he will do afterwards; that is to say, he makes no claim for its probability and he sees no reason at all to keep faith with it. One way or another, this is true of all narratives of things. The bad fiction deliberately constructed by Roxana, which leaves a good portion of her story untold and the moiety ornamented with lurid invocations of the devil, frames a performance that she struggles mightily to prevent from having consequences. We find Cook, Bottom, Peascod, and Belinda at the center of a litter of things that won't add up to a credible account: a spectacle or a reflection, but never a sequence. Fable, like romance, defies probability and is intransigently nonreferential. It can be told this way or that, it can flatly contradict itself, and it can breed other fables out of itself, like A'a the god, turning time and space into pure fiction. Pornography has this much in common with fable that it is limited to repetitions of an identical action, varied by different arrangements of figures and locations, whose only consequence is another performance of the same thing. "It is all pork," as the Author of *A Tale of a Tub* would say. He and his brother-Author, Lord Shaftesbury, postpone their engagements with the end and point of autobiographical writing by identifying themselves with the ink they leave on the page, a minimal material presence that they both call irony but which could also be called nonsense. In the next chapter I shall explore another version of this secret writing.

CHAPTER 10

Authors Owning Nothing

> Wonders may be done with an eye by hiding it.
>
> —Charles Dickens, *Great Expectations*

There are superficial resemblances between it-narratives and slave narratives that point to more important ones. Commonly, the title page of an it-narrative runs *Adventures of a Whipping Top written by itself* (n.d.), or, *Adventures of a One Pound Note written by Myself* (1819), or *Adventures of a Black Coat as related by ITSELF* (1762). The same convention is followed in slave narratives, which are announced as being either written or related by the person whose actions are recorded: *The Interesting Life of Olaudah Equiano . . . Written by Himself* (1789); *Incidents in the Life of a Slave Girl. Written by Herself* (1861); *A Narrative of the Life of James Albert Ukawsaw Gronniosaw . . . As related by Himself* (1772). In both genres, the convention hesitates between the narrative and the author, as if some issue remained to be settled, such as literacy, immediacy, or authenticity. A silent acknowledgment is being made of the unusualness of the first-person narrator insofar as a statement of the obvious is required in order to affirm that it was that very person who wrote or told the story. And in the process, what is put into a degree of doubt is the status of the author with regard to what the public might or might not be prepared to believe. In the case of whipping top offering to tell its own tale, the difficulty of course is perfectly plain, for what is being asserted for a truth is a lie. The shadow falling across the testimony of narrators who formerly were slaves is the restriction they once lay under with regard to giving evidence before a court of law. In most cases it was inadmissible, a state of affairs which often persisted even after manumission, subsequently formalized under the Dred Scott decision 1857 as the exclusion of free blacks from the rights of citizenship (Best 2004: 67). Hence the letters of authentication written by white men that are placed between the title page and the narrative itself as a necessary supplement, warranting the literal, historical truth of what is to come because in itself it does not carry sufficient weight.

The hesitation in respect of it-narratives advertises a fiction, then, while its counterpart in a slave narrative affirms the opposite, namely, that it is a veridical account of what really happened. But the need for a double warranty of a personal history cannot help but problematize it, whether the problem lies within the narrative enterprise itself (as Miguel Tamen has suggested [Tamen 2001: 86]), or is found in a public consisting of many readers actively hostile to this kind of testimony. Besides, a sinister knot ties the personal pronoun of a slave narrative to the law, and the law to the feat of commercial imagination that transformed a human into an object constitutionally unable to act as a witness. In Roman law, a slave was the antithesis of a person in being a property without property only a person could hold (Weil 2005: 75); and no slave could give legal testimony without first being tortured, on the assumption that the truth must be wrested from a mouth that otherwise would not tell it. In North America and the sugar colonies, this savage requirement was never formally invoked, but the price paid for its absence was a legal fiction. Both common law and constitutional law fudged the issue of the personhood of slaves. New World slavery according to Guillaume Raynal, for example, was an explicit case of dispossession, "in which a man lost either by force or by convention the property of his own person" (Raynal 1783: 5.283). In such a condition, "there is nothing that a slave can keep as *his own*," Hobbes had concluded, placing the slave beyond the scope of justice (Hobbes 1998: 104).

But the Constitution of the United States left the persons of slaves technically intact, defining them as "persons who perform a certain service or labour." Meanwhile, the Fugitive Slave Law of 1850 defined a slave as "a person held to serve" who, if he or she escaped from servitude, could be apprehended even in a free state as long as the owner or the agent could provide "proof . . . by affidavit . . . of the identity of the person" whom they were seizing (Best 2004: 18–40). The badges of a citizen—person and identity—were being used as shackles. If a slave was to be tried on a serious criminal charge, personhood was formally restored in the courtroom so that he or she might plead. A judgment from the Tennessee Supreme Court of 1839 explained that the law, "upon high grounds of public policy . . . takes the slave out of the hands of his master, forgets his claim and rights of property, treats the slave as a rational and intelligent human being, responsible to moral, social and municipal duties" (*Elijah v. State,* cited in Morris 1996: 257; see Patterson 1982: 22). In her history of slavery in the Caribbean islands, Elsa Goveia concludes, "The legal nullity of the slave's personality [was sustained] except where he was to be controlled or punished" (Goveia 1970: 25). By refusing to distinguish sharply between persons and slaves, and by granting an intermittent personal identity to chattels in legal processes where the privilege would do them most harm, slave law in the Americas undermined the basis on which the forensic or vicarious function of all persons depended, and upon which, as I have been arguing throughout this book, the superstructure of civil society, together with all authorized testimony and standards of probability, were raised.

There was therefore no simple division to be made between the authenticity of one kind of narrative and the inauthenticity of another in the context of slavery. When J. C. Hathaway and Edmund Quincy tell us that William Wells Brown has told the public nothing but the truth; or when Wendell Phillips and William Lloyd Garrison write in support of the veracity of Frederick Douglass, the simple directness of their support is contradicted by the circumstances in which it is offered. Slave law had made and was making precisely the same claims on behalf of admitted slave testimony, albeit for very different ends; but the truth alleged on both sides was the same, namely, that a slave endowed with a person would tell it. If that truth was already compromised by the legal and constitutional fictions defining it, then matters were made no clearer when slave experience was exploited, as Holocaust witnessing has been during the last twenty years, by people who believed that they possessed credentials suitable for inventing it. Whether this resulted in a scandal such as *The Narrative of James Williams* (1838), which offered an authentic account of slave life that turned out to be not true (Fabian 2004: 45–6), or in a fiction known to be based on actual experience, such as Douglass's *The Heroic Slave* (1853) or William Wells Brown's *Clotel* (1859), truth is fetched into an uneasy proximity with fiction. This is not owing only to local issues affecting the interests of slaveholders, eager to find fiction where there was none, or those of abolitionists, bent on purging all trace of fiction from stories that had to be true if they were to harrow the conscience of the reader, but more importantly to the definitional unreliability of the terms deployed. For us as well as the United States in the nineteenth century, these are *character, person,* and *author.*

No one would choose to endorse the *character* of the first person of a narrator formerly a slave because characters were traditionally items included in bills of sale: such a slave "had bore a good Character" while another "bears a very ill Character" (Morris 1996: 228). Olaudah Equiano says that Robert King decided to buy him "on account of my good character" (1995: 99). It was a tradable property. *Person,* as we have seen, hovers between the worst effects of slave law and the benefits of emancipation, justifying the perversion of the doctrine of rights on the one hand and providing the focus of the dream of freedom on the other. It was made unreliable by the work it was asked to perform, being a privilege not extended under the terms of Dred Scott, and treated with severe skepticism by free blacks who, when they acquired it, remembered how insolently the denial and the gift of personhood had served the identical purpose of oppression. We are left with *Author,* the figure who writes at the edge of civil society, half committed to publicity while fiercely defending privacy, keen on writing but not so friendly to print; someone with a counterfeit pedigree, as Gildon calls it, whose instincts for self-exposure, counteracted by strong instincts of secrecy, combine with a powerful response to "the Sence of things" to produce improbable narratives either armed with the wild wit of fable or "dight," as Spenser would say, with the exquisite formality of romance. The legal definition of the Author has been applied by Catherine Gallagher with great success to the history of fictionality, and I want now to apply it to slave narratives, and to the generic resources of those who write or relate them.

❧

In his book on the relation between the concept of fugitive property and the institution of slavery, Stephen Best has traced the genealogy of their union to the law of copyright, the very same Statute of Anne of 1710 which in the second and seventh chapters helped define the interval in the production of an original piece of writing that lies between primordial possession and subsequent alienation, a period when an Author enjoys the glory of entering into a literary estate solely by virtue of her own wit, without the sanction of the magistrate or nature; an estate which is sacrificed only when she contracts with a bookseller to part with it for fourteen years in exchange for cash. Plagued by the law of copyright from the moment of its passage, Anglo-American case law (Best argues) contrived to shift its emphasis during the nineteenth century away from the conception of property as a relation of persons to things, and instead toward a relation of persons contractually engaged to persons. Best discovers in this evolution of personalty the same sort of tendency that Blackstone noted in the feudal tenure of realty, namely, an accumulation of abstractions. Instead of the invisible appurtenances of land such as escheats, advowsons, and views of frankpledge, there were now alienable portions of the person, all stemming from that quality of literary originality which commentators such as William Warburton and Edward Young found so hard to define, being a quality inherent in a person's mind which, when solidified in paper and ink, became their very own possession in a manner unlike any other property. Its uniqueness was lost only when it became conditionally alienated under certain kinds of contract, and the mysterious virtue of "ownness" passed from the Author to the printed book. With the development of other technologies of reproduction such as the camera and the phonograph, fugitive properties of the person such as voice and image became, like the imagination, fixable and alienable; even a person's silence could be contractually alienated. Best says, "The ultimate goal of intellectual property law would ironically be to embrace something like enslavement" (Best 2004: 53); for at what point did the sum of alienable properties of a person add up to the entirety of the person? How much "ownness" could be shifted from one party of a contract to the other? As Best shows, the labor removed by a fugitive slave from his owner was understood by the law to be no different from any other property of the person hitherto assumed to be inalienable and now exchanged, in this case by means of a supposititious contract. Although in the case of a slave there is rather more involved than discrete elements of the person, the logic of the Fugitive Slave Law in respect of the labor supposedly contracted by one person to another is exactly the same as a contract governing the rights to the reproduction of someone's imagination, voice, or image. An absconded slave was assumed to have broken a contract promising the abstract quantity of congealed labor power he or she had agreed to supply until death.

The Fugitive Slave Act of 1850 was fallacious for the reasons set out by Hobbes, namely, that it supposed the bargain to be struck between persons in a state of civil union instead of a natural state of war, otherwise no one in their senses would be a party to it. It is a bargain, moreover, that, even if it were undertaken, has no force other than physical restraint, for "slaves ... have no obligation at all, but may break their bonds, or the prison; and kill, or carry away captive their Master" (Hobbes 1998: 103; 1996: 141). Nevertheless, it institutionalized the imperfect logic of slavery itself, which translated an injury into a property and a slave, when convenient, into a person. These fallacies took place under the shadow of an older equivocation concerning the state of slavery. With the exception of Nevis, slaves in the British Caribbean were landed as merchandise, but after being sold they ceased to be moveables and were considered real property. They could be exchanged only by conveyance; and as freehold inheritance, widows had a dower right in them (Goveia 1965: 152–3). They could likewise be entailed. Goveia believes that turning slaves into real estate was a ruse to make property in persons less personal, and more like a fact of the land itself (155). In the North American colonies they were defined as real property "only for some purposes" (Morris 1996: 63). Nevertheless, in his *Conjure Tales*, Charles Chesnutt calls Julius's relation to the land "predial rather than proprietory" as if he were an appurtenance of the place rather than an inhabitant owned by someone else (Chesnutt 2000: 25). Thomas Morris suggests that in the form of immoveable property, slaves were technically protected from harm, meanwhile offering the added advantage to the estate of a sufficient number of workers to keep it viable (Morris 1996: 65). Realty could not be consumed or destroyed, therefore anyone injuring a slave was vulnerable to an action of trespass. Similarly, under tort law as opposed to that of contract, minor damage caused by a slave fell to the responsibility of the owner, with the offender treated as a deodand (Morris 1996: 260). But as Morris goes on to point out, this was a system never fully in force. Slaves could be sold to defray debt and generally they were killed with impunity.

There is however a faint remainder of predial trespass in the Barbadian statute that fined owners of slaves fifteen pounds for killing them out of "wantonness, or . . . bloody-mindedness," and also in the tougher Jamaican law which set the penalty at 180 pounds (Equiano 1995: 109; Cobbett 1817: 29.265). Morris cites the South Carolina statute that punished the homicide of a slave "out of willfulness, wantonness, or bloody mindedness" with a 50-pound fine and three months' jail (Morris 1996: 164). What was being punished here? Morris says the residue of compunction in these laws indicate a world "filled with tension and uncertainty about the institution of slavery in general and the treatment of slaves in particular" (170–71). The fines, trifling as they were, perhaps indicate something besides compunction: damage done outside the regime of contract, destruction of something with a value surplus to the price of a slave, an abstract quality not of personalty but of realty, binding a body to bodies, and bodies to the land.

The two forms of slaveholding—as real estate and as personal property—correspond to the rival systems of conceiving injury under common law: tort and contract. Under the law of torts an action of trespass makes no allowance for intention and considers only the harm, and who is responsible for it. A person is liable for the damage if he or his property has occasioned it, regardless of how carefully he may have tried to avoid committing it, or how innocently he may have proceeded throughout the sequence of events. In contract law, intention in the form of a promise guides the whole narrative of damage; and historically actions of contract emerged from actions of trespass by virtue of writs of *assumpsit* that identified a chain of causes and effects hanging so closely together that it implied an undertaking to do something which was not performed (Holmes 1991: 275–79). Sandra Macpherson has argued that this distinction between two kinds of responsibility—effectual and promissory—structures the fiction of the eighteenth century, with the great tragic novels such as *Clarissa* conforming to the law of faultless trespass, and the comic ones such as *Robinson Crusoe* to contract (Macpherson 2010: 25–58). In the latter kind of fiction, probability is highly valued, and the persons represented in it own their stories as persons, in the dual sense of telling them and taking entire responsibility for them. But in the former, ignorance or innocence frustrates the enterprise of first-person testimony insofar as the entire action of the story goes beyond the purview of any single actor in it, making no sense even to the agent responsible for its most damaging episodes: How can Clarissa own the story that connects her principled refusal of a suitor with her taking up lodgings in a brothel? From the point of view of someone immersed in the incalculable world of torts, "blameworthiness and faultlessness are improbably aligned ... fault becomes a question of causation rather than culpability ... to understand persons as causes in this way is to make (legal) subjectivity an effect of the sheer materiality and instrumentality of bodies" (Macpherson 2010: 39).

It is not difficult to see why the view of experience from the angle of torts might appeal more readily to former slaves about to narrate the story of their passage to freedom, and how inconceivably unjust it would strike them to call that passage breach of contract. Whatever amount of specious intelligibility is to be derived from a narrative of human intentions, the inexplicable origin and fact of slavery, followed by the extraordinary legal maneuvers needed to accomplish manumission, an event Bernard Williams calls "the most complete metamorphosis imaginable" (Williams 1993: 212), demand a narrative of equal darkness. Introducing Gronniosaw's to the public, William Shirley asks, `Shall we in accounting for it refer to nothing higher than mere Chance and accidental Circumstances?' (Gronniosaw 2000: 3). Like Adam Smith, John Millar thought that the institution of slavery, flourishing so anomalously in an era otherwise distinguished by its humanity and politeness, could be referred to nothing else but the operations of chance and caprice. "Fortune perhaps never produced a situation more calculated ... to show how little the conduct of men is at bottom directed by any philosophical principles" (Millar 1771: 240). Quobua Cugoano thought slavery arose out of the passion for gaming, "stock-jobbing, lotteries, and useless business" (Cugoano in Caretta 1996: 163). Chesnutt's story "Sis` Becky's Pickaninny" is about Colonel Pendleton's determination to buy a racehorse, even though the price is the separation of a mother from her child. Henry Bibb recalls being bought by a company of genial gamblers who had a plan to set him free; but when they stopped at Fayetteville, "they almost lost me, betting on a horse race" (Bibb 2000: 525). Such an absence of moral point caused the enthusiastic editor of Bibb's narrative to state that this memoir was exemplary of the whole genre, being lavish of literary effects "far excelling fiction" even though provoked by an institution "naturally and necessarily the enemy of literature" (Bibb 2000: 427).

Douglass mentions how he planned an escape from William Hamilton with four others, for whom he wrote "protections" or tickets of leave. The plot was discovered before they made the attempt, and it became important to destroy each forgery before it was discovered too. "I told [them] to eat it ... and own nothing; and we passed the word around, 'Own nothing;' and 'Own nothing!' said we all" (Douglass 2000: 344).

Own nothing: it has the force of a motto; also the agility of a three-way pun. They can own nothing because they are not persons and can neither hold property nor tell stories that will be believed; so their strength will lie in a non-responsible relation to Fortune, and they will own nothing indeed, shedding all interest in a personate account, keeping silent or deliberately not making sense. Douglass reconnoiters this alternative to silence when he remembers the songs of the slaves on the Lloyd plantation. He recalls with particular vividness their incoherence: "They would sometimes sing the most pathetic sentiment in the most rapturous tone, and the most rapturous sentiment in the most pathetic tone" (289). The disorder extends to the words of the chorus which are, he says, "unmeaning jargon" to anyone but the singers themselves, for whom they are "full of meaning." He goes on to say, however, that when he was a slave he could not understand "the deep meaning of those rude and apparently incoherent songs" precisely because he was (as he puts it) "within the circle, so that I neither saw nor heard as those without might see and hear" (290). Yet he says he can never get rid of the idea of slavery they first gave him. Indeed, he goes on, it would be a person with a shriveled heart who could remain indifferent to such plaintive sounds. So the most powerful appeal of this music reaches people outside the circle, rather than those on the inside; yet Douglass found it common for people in the North to mistake these songs for signs of contentment and even happiness. He then compares slave-songs with the singing of a castaway on a desert island, hundreds of people separately ruined by Fortune but all complaining in unison, like a chorus of Robinson Crusoes proclaiming simultaneously the uniqueness of their agony. It is clear that he is not quite certain what he wants to say about this phenomenon other than that it is expressive and dissonant at the same time, a singular effort undertaken in the mass, full of meaning from one angle and nonsense from another. Orlando Patterson says this is the essence of slavery, the emulsion of community and chaos (Patterson 1982: 51).

Mary Prince begins her story, "What my eyes have seen I think it is my duty to relate . . . I have been a slave—I have felt what a slave feels, and I know what a slave knows; and I would have all the good people in England know it too" (Prince 1987: 200). Who among the good people of England had been tortured, felt driven from their own species, and had to ask God to tell them who they were? It is practically the same thing as asking who among them had been mad. Slavery dominates the sequence of its manifestations: the marks on the body, the doubts about humanity, the rupture of personal identity, the sense of living in a dream, the pressure of solitude, the uncertainty about how to tell such a hideous history. At one of the most agitating moments of his life as a slave, Henry Bibb says, "The reader may perhaps think me tedious on this topic, but indeed it is one of so much interest to me, that I find myself entirely unable to describe what my own feelings were at that time" (Bibb 2000: 512). How often we meet the same elisions in Equiano's narrative, or in Douglass's, where what is of supreme importance to the person represented in it, the road to freedom and the experience of freedom, is exactly what cannot be communicated to a general audience of white people. Jacobs confesses that she has no ambitions to arouse the reader's sympathy, and would have preferred to remain silent about her own history (Jacobs 2000: 3). Wallace Turnage edits his story heavily in order to produce "a sketch of that which I think would be most interesting to those who shall approve my book" (Blight 2007: 213), exhibiting doubts about the coincidence of the writer's and reader's interests that affect the conduct of all these narratives.

The reluctance to give a history or to say what is meant seems to arise in equal measure from confusion and resistance. Slavery, so often personified by these narrators—"the envious, greedy, and treacherous hand of slavery" (Douglass 2003: 42), "the wrongs inflicted by Slavery" (Jacobs 2000: 3)—took from its victims exactly the advantages won by the original contract according to Hobbes and Locke: personhood, community, property, genealogy, and history. So the story has to be conceived on a different basis and delivered in a different rhetoric from an owned narrative. The genre into which the slave narrative falls then is not that of testimony and indictment, as Gates suggests (Gates 1987: ix), but something else altogether. I suggest that fable, the original slave narrative, is a good place to start, one that accommodates the paradoxes of tort law, where blameworthiness and faultlessness are improbably aligned, where subjectivity arises from the adjacency and accidental instrumentality of bodies, where things and humans change places, and where the land itself provides the stage and often the occasion for what happens.

In the folk tales collected by Joel Chandler Harris and Charles W. Chesnutt there are three degrees of improbability distinguishing this genre from personate narrative: The first is evident in narrative sequence, where nothing falls out in an equitable or orderly fashion. The second concerns the individuals, whose inconsistency leads to unpredictable actions, sometimes so dislocated from intention that their behavior seems to belong to some other creature or some other thing. The third comprises language, which is often impeded, or forced into onomatopoeia, easily capable of ending up as nonsense or pure sound. Chesnutt's story "The Gray Wolf's Ha'nt" is narrated by Julius, the ex-slave who works on the estate. It tells of Dan, who is turned into a wolf by a conjure man, and Mahaly his partner, who is turned into a black cat that is killed by the wolf. Julius appears to tell the story in order to keep his employer from developing a corner of the estate where he gathers wild honey; but when introducing it to the reader, the narrator says of Julius:

> Of the tales of the old slavery days he seemed indeed to possess an exhaustless store,—some weirdly grotesque, some broadly humorous; some bearing the stamp of truth, faint, perhaps, but still discernible; others palpably inventions, whether his own or not we never knew . . . But even the wildest was not without an element of pathos,—the tragedy, it might be, of the story itself; the shadow, never absent, of slavery and of ignorance. (Chesnutt 2000: 65)

Compendiously arranged within the general problem owning tales of slavery are the associated problems of improbability, affective discontinuity, and meanings often more than half obscured, together with the hint that the story may be telling itself, and that for all its humor, its closest generic link may be with tragedy. Almost all of Julius's stories concern a metamorphosis—Dave into a ham, Primus into a mule, Master James into a slave, Sandy into a tree, and Dan into a wolf. They can all be explained as his artful method of getting his own way on the estate: distributing ghosts wherever he has a mind to claim an interest, such as his wild grapes and honey, and the wood from the old schoolhouse. But all his stories concern a force—usually identified as magic, or conjuring—which changes men and women into things. Although the magic is generally practiced by slaves on behalf of or against other slaves, it is evident from the dismal outcomes that these are local variations played on the main chaotic theme of Slavery itself, as the narrator suggests. Even the wildest flights of imagination and the most arcane spells accomplish no more than the metamorphosis of person into thing, a change that has always already happened. The sole consolation of slaves who live in such a preposterous world is to give a name and habitation to events whose creatures they all are and who, because of that, tend to be told by tales, rather than telling them. Julius is the Ovid of this world.

Julius's stories are generally successful, but when he tells the story of Primus who became a mule, and then was turned back into a man ("The Conjuror's Revenge"), the narrator's wife is not pleased. "It isn't pathetic, it has no moral that I can discover, and I can't see why you should tell it. In fact, it seems to me like nonsense" (49). Often she makes critiques of his stories from which it is plain that she prefers likeness to life ("the story bears the stamp of truth, if ever a story did" [61]) or pathos; preferably both. Julius's reaction to criticism is first to invoke, like Sancho Panza, the immemorial structure and autonomy of the tale, and then the uncertainty of all testimony: "Dey's so many things a body knows is lies, dat dey ain' no use gwine roun' findin' fault wid tales dat mought des ez well be so ez not" (49). This minimal claim for probability is also a defense of the tale's right to tell itself. All agency in the slave world seems to come from outside, and here tale acts as Tale. What the narrator's wife calls nonsense is the unacceptable side of the world turned upside down by Fortune and by bad definitions of the human, a world prolific in dreams where it is impossible to distinguish between the true and the false, where men and women turn into things and sometimes back again, and where any gesture toward possession (of vines, wood, honey) is caught up in lies, or at least allegories.

That these tales are fictions indirectly but powerfully responsive to the appalling history of slavery does not quite escape the attention of Julius's audience. After the gruesome description of how Sandy, transformed into a tree, was felled on the orders of Mr. Mirabeau and cut up shrieking into plank, Annie says, "What a system it was . . . under which such things were possible" (23). The story "Mars Jeems's Nightmare," about the metamorphosis of a white master into a black slave who is then systematically whipped by his own overseer for putting on airs, is introduced by the narrator as an example of the mental habits induced by slavery, where the land is treated in a manner "predial rather than proprietary" and Julius himself speaks not as an individual but as part of the body of the estate (25). Nevertheless, the story is accused of improbability (by her), and of lacking a moral (by him). But the moral Julius draws from the story applies to all his tales, which is that people who don't make allowance for the testimony of ignorant folk in servitude, who scorn the speech of vocal appurtenances of the land as nonsense, are themselves "li'ble ter hab bad dreams, ter say de leas'" (38).

One of the most noticeable effects of Julius's "predial" imagination is that he personifies everything, as if he were adrift in the earliest phase of Hume's polytheism. The incredible world of slavery, confronted by his own imagination and mediated by conjurors, is filled with *personae*, so that he cannot easily distinguish between species and things, for one specimen can so easily be transformed into another. He says of mules in general, "Eve'ry time I cuts a mule wid a hick'ry, 'pears ter me mo' lackly I's cutting some er my own relations, er somebody e'se w'at can't he'p deyse'ves" (41). Like Apuleius's Lucius in Hypata, Julius negotiates a world where every inanimate object can suggest a living counterpart. Conjuring intensifies this confusion because, as I have suggested, magic is the slave response to the grand personification of Slavery itself. It may pretend to be benign, like Julius's rabbit's foot or Frederick Douglass's root, or the opposite, as when Aunt Peggy, bribed to conjure Hannibal out of the house, makes a doll and announces, rather like Starveling in his presentation of Moonshine, "Dis yer baby doll . . . is Hannibal. Dis yer peth head is Hannibal's head, en dese yer pepper feet is Hannibal's feet" (81). Strictly speaking, such personifications are nonsense, arising (as Hume says) from the tendency of the imagination under the stress of accounting for unknown causes to transfer to objects the shapes and feelings of which we are most intimately conscious: "Hence the frequency and beauty of the prosopopeia in poetry; where the trees, mountains and streams are personified, and the inanimate parts of nature acquire sentiment and passion" (1957: 29). Of course the personification of the landscape doesn't in the end protect anyone, for most of Julius's stories have miserable or fatal outcomes. Whenever his characters, embodiments of various portions of the estate, begin to imagine that their humanity entitles them to the dignity of emotions or ambitions consistent with their species, such as love or learning, they will be metamorphosed and return to the material from which they emerged. There is no bond between people that flourishes in Julius's stories. He himself is generally seen alone, without family or friends. Superstition has to make up for what Slavery has taken away, but it doesn't make up much, certainly it produces no real human persons, nor any intelligible alignment of blame and fault; hence what the narrator calls the tragedy of the story itself.

Under unremitting strain, the slave imagination personifies to such a degree that it is easy for it to find in animal fables an extensive mirror of its own habits. In the Uncle Remus stories of Joel Chandler Harris, personification is taken for granted, as it is in all animal fables derived from Aesop. Like Aesop's, these fables place animals at the center of a world where the humans haunt the rim: Miss Cow, Mr. Fox, Mr. Possum, and so on are elaborately and usually disingenuously proximate with each other. Apart from the mysterious "Miss Meadows and the gals," only one of Remus's tales has a human in it, and he is accorded a presence as slender and remote as that of a slave in the eyes of the law. When the audience of one small boy asks who the man is, Remus becomes impatient and refuses to assign him an identity: "Des a man, honey. Dat's all. Dat's all I knows—des wunner dese yer mans w'at you see trollopin 'roun' eve'y day. Nobody ain't never year w'at his name is, en ef dey did dey kep' de news mighty close fum me" (Harris 1982: 136). One of the best remembered of his tales is of the tar-baby, a special instance of personification prepared by Mr. Fox which takes him as close as he will ever get to destroying Mr. Rabbit. The tar-baby, roughly in the figure of a human, is placed in the road and fails to answer any of the questions Rabbit puts to it, so Rabbit beats the image to make it talk until his four limbs and his head are glued to it; whereupon Fox steps forward to consider how he will kill his enemy. The blackness and silence of the tar-baby, and the pointless aggression directed against it, have been construed as an allegory of slavery, but that is an approach that presents more problems than it solves, since Rabbit himself is the hero of these slave fictions, each triumphantly contemptuous of truth and authority. Perhaps the scene is more usefully viewed as an encounter between the fabular hero and Fable itself, very much along the lines of Aesop's "The Fox and the Mask," where fox turns the mask to and fro: "What an impressive sight," the fox cries, "but no brain at all" (Henderson 2004: 57). Every attempt made to interrogate the tar-baby is futile, just like the effort to find meaning in a fable. "Fable looks deep into Fable's brain and finds there's nothing there. . . . Fable only works because this is how masks work: if they were clever, they would be no use to us, and we could not know who we are, clever or whatever" (Henderson 2004: 58). Overinvestment in the structure of a tale or the value of words is a potentially fatal error in the Rabbit's world, so best to cultivate the easy mendacious suavity at which he is so expert, and leave the imperfect image of Mr. Man to its own devices.

The dangerous encounter between an animal and an idol is familiar in fable. Rat eats the offerings on Idol's altar, until Idol falls and breaks; rat has to find food elsewhere and is eaten by cat (Nivernois 1799: 23). Fox finds a carved head struck from a statue, thinks it is real and breaks a tooth trying to eat it (Ogilby 1668: 55). Fable empties itself out or turns on anyone who might suppose it guilty of intrinsic intelligence. This is why the narrator's wife is so impatient with some of Julius's stories. Remus tells one of how Rabbit secretly eats the butter, and then proposes a trial by ordeal to find the guilty party. This results in the death of Mr. Possum, who falls into the fire instead of leaping over it. The boy thinks this is unfair, since Possum was innocent, and Remus observes, "Dat w'at make I say w'at I duz, honey. In dis worril, lots er fokes is gotter suffer fer udder fokes sins. Look like hit's mighty onwrong; but hit's des dat away. Tribalashun seem like she's a waitin' roun' de cornder fer ter ketch one en all us us, honey" (Harris 1982: 102). If there is a moral to slave narratives, this is it: the improbable alignment of fault and punishment. And in the process of arriving at it, the space taken up by will and intention in the world of contract is here in the world of torts occupied by personifications, a free distribution of figures of agency, none of which is human although each has a decisive effect on human bodies: Tribulation, Tar-baby, Fortune, Slavery, Mask, and Fable.

As for language itself, it retreats to jargon just as Fable tends to nonsense. The more powerful its demonstration of passion, the less it means. That is what Douglass thought as he listened to the words of that slavesong: "I am going away to the Great House Farm!/ O, yea! O, yea! O!'" (Douglass 2000: 289). It is rather like the song of triumph Bull-frog sings to Bear: "Ingle-go-jang, my joy, my joy—/ Ingle-go-jang, my joy!' (Harris 1982: 123). The boy thinks it a funny refrain. Remus says, "Funny now, I speck, but 'twern't funny in dem days, en 'twouldn't be funny now ef folks know'd much 'bout de Bull-frog langwidge ez dey useter" (124). It is impossible to miss the application to Remus's own dialect, originally condemned as "drawling, dissonant gibberish" (Long 1774: 2.278), subsequently patronized for its quaint charm, and now despised for the same reason. Without the impediment of words rendered difficult, meaningless, or oblique, much of the laconic energy of Remus's stories would disappear. Take for example Turkey Buzzard's exclamation when he thinks has found Fox's corpse in the road: "Brer Fox dead, en I so sorry" (Harris 1982: 72). When Remus turns to onomatopoeia to demonstrate how Terrapin sinks to the bottom of the pond, "kerblunkity-blink," Harris breaks in to say, "No typographical combination or description could do justice to the guttural sonorousness—the peculiar intonation" (88). He talks Terrapin again when he says, "I-doom-er-kum-mer-ker" and once more Harris comments on the strangeness of the sound: "Those who can recall to mind the peculiar gurgling, jerking, liquid sound made by pouring water from a large jug, or the sound produced by throwing several stones in rapid succession into a pond of keep water, may be able to form a very faint idea of the sound, but it can not be reproduced in print" (93). Fable has always used this technique of replacing words with sounds—the dog who barks in blackletter, "**Bough wough,**" in Ogilby's collection (Ogilby 1668: 1.61); La Fontaine's pot that makes pot-sounds, "clopin-clopant" ("Le pot de terre et le pot de fer,"' La Fontaine 1865: 123; n.d. 277); Androcles who turns into a lion and roars leontic (Ogilby 1668: 2.153). But Remus goes further. He is a brilliant improviser, anticipating the heavily patterned beat of street talk, skat, and hip-hop. On one occasion he is singing a song to himself rather like those that moved Douglass so much, where the sentiments are at odds with the passions ("a senseless affair so far as the words were concerned, but sung to a melody almost thrilling in its sweetness") when he hears the boy arrive, and switches into rhythmic nonsense: "Juba reda seda breda. Aunt Kate at de gate; I want to eat, she fry de meat en gimme skin, w'ich I fling it back agin. Juba!" (Harris 1982: 133).

Fables moved quickly to the Caribbean, where they were translated into dialect and patois: *Les Bambons . . . travesties en patois creole* was published in Martinique in 1846; J. J. Thomas published Aesop and La Fontaine in creole in *The Theory and Practice of Creole Grammar* (1869). These translations were remarkable for their "peculiarly rapid syllabification and musical intonation," effects to which the word *gombo* was applied (Hearn 1885: 3). Lafcadio Hearn admires the pure situationality as well as the tonality of creole languages, particularly the proverbs and fables of African American slaves which, he says, "depend altogether upon application for their color or their effectiveness; they possess a chameleon power of changing hue according to the manner in which they are placed" (Hearn 1885: 4). Many of these proverbs concern things (trees, clothes, cooking pots, sticks) and animals (cats, oxen, dogs, frogs, and goats), bodies circulating in a nonhuman world, pausing at certain conjunctures and speaking in sounds and words wrenched from human contexts and meanings. Hearn is describing a particularly vivid example of finding meaning in the act of saying, meaning what one says rather than saying what one can never properly mean in an incoherent world—the stark difference between sound and silence. The ingenious commitment to meaning what is said, adapting words to circumstances and marrying them incongruously to other words encourages a distinctly formalist approach to language. Dialect and patois function like the Church Slavonic beloved of Russian Formalists such as Shklovsky and Eichenbaum, where the obscurity, evasiveness, or difficulty of language finally disappears into the triumph of sound alone, glossolalia or what Michel de Certeau calls "an event in the throat" (de Certeau 1996: 32). Like humans turned into beasts, words turn into noise, and morals turn into nonsense, but not entirely without a point. Hearn quotes a creole proverb, "Faut perou les mor pou mourne pe vivre"—"words must die that people may live" (1885: 16 n.).

I want to consider briefly the question of African American formalism within the framework of Remus's juba, originally an African step-dance (the Giouba) which metamorphosed considerably in its new locations in the Southern States. He is reciting one of the juba calls that harked back to African dances mimicking animals—buzzard, eagle, crow, or rabbit—and in their new context given names such as Pigeon Wing, Yaller Cat, and Long Dog Scratch:

> Juba circle, raise de latch
> Juba dance dat Long Dog Scratch.
>
> (Stearns 1979: 15–29)

Known as "patting juba," with specialized routines of hand-clapping to the rhythm of the call, hand against hand, and then against knee and thigh, it changed from a circle dance of call-and-response into a solo performance, described by Dickens when he saw William Henry Lane dancing juba in the Five Point district of New York:

> Single shuffle, double shuffle, cut and cross-cut; snapping his fingers, rolling his eyes, turning in his knees, presenting the backs of his legs in front, spinning about on his toes and heels like nothing but the man's fingers on the tambourine; dancing with two left legs; two right legs; two wooden legs, two wire legs—all sorts of legs and no legs—what is this to him? (Dickens 1842: 1.218; cited in Stearns 1979: 46)

In 1848, a reviewer for the London *Theatrical Times* witnessed Lane in a similar routine and, astonished by dancing which seemed wholly to have transcended its origin in mimicry, he wrote, "There is an ideality in what he does that makes his efforts at once grotesque and poetical" (Marian Winter 1948: 18; cited in Stearns 1979: 47). The ideality of Lane's juba and the nonsense of Remus's are related. Each performance exploits the mutual involvement of community and chaos that informed the cadences of the Lloyd plantation shout. At one level a public exhibition of sheer flair, and at another a solo exercise in supererogatory motion or sound, the layered event is never quite synthesized, striking the audience as at once above art and below it, grotesque and ideal, public and private, all at the same time. Its remains are clearly evident in the moonwalking and foot-dragging of Michael Jackson's best performances, where the coalitions of impediment and magic, self-absorption and display, feed a circuit of astonishing energy.

After fable and juba comes fiction, and I aim to tie all three together by considering how readily the improbabilities of non-referential fiction lend themselves to the cause of ideality. Vincent Caretta's discovery of baptismal and naval records seeming to indicate that Olaudah Equiano was not born in Africa, nor Santa Cruz, but South Carolina, has caused some disagreement not least because it renewed a charge leveled at Equiano in the public prints when he first published his autobiography, namely, that he was telling fibs about his African past. He was challenged then to deny that the first two chapters of his book were a fiction, where he describes an idyllic childhood and his abduction by slavers; and Caretta seemed to be issuing the challenge once again. Many people have come to Equiano's defense, then and now, to vindicate him from the slur of slave law that puts the testimony of an injured people outside the realm of truth (Bugg 2006). A truce of sorts was reached in Caretta's biography of Equiano, where once more he cites the evidence of his birth in South Carolina, but asks for some other standard than historical accuracy as a measure of Equiano's achievement, which he prefers to call literary rather than historical (Caretta 2005: xiv–xv). For his own part, he entitles the book *Equiano the African* and devotes the first three chapters to the disputed part of the life, but is very careful to explain each scene as a conjecture: a represented possibility rather than an actual sequence of events: a probable fiction.

The old stand-off between history and fiction that marked the reception of antebellum slave narratives has occurred again in the twenty-first century, with Caretta using the same argument vis-à-vis his subject that the editor of Henry Bibb's narrative adopts with his, namely, that it belongs in some ill-defined way to the literary rather than the strictly historical (Bibb 2000: 427). I think it has already become apparent that the categorical division between history and fiction served the cause of slaveholding or abolition, depending on how it was pitched, rather than any interest of the narrator's, whose story was largely bereft of the relational terms—person, identity, memory, probability, society—necessary if such a division were to make sense. But so powerful is the association of ideas between fiction and a falsified history of the injuries of slave life that it is still necessary support the countervailing association between historical accuracy and the truth of suffering, despite the extensive symptomatology of the concentration camps indicating that in limit cases it simply does not work. As a scientist impatient with obscure words, Primo Levi became attentive in Auschwitz to the sound of the "dark and maimed language" uttered by those about to die, the glossolalia of the walking dead, because it was more responsive than articulate speech to the extremity of the situation (Agamben 2002: 15–39). What kind of history can such language record, or what can be recorded of it?

The issue has been given a fresh twist in the last decade with Henry Louis Gates's publication in 2002 of a fictional slave narrative of the 1850s still in manuscript, *The Bondwoman's Narrative*, written by someone called Hannah Crafts, most likely the pseudonym of a female author who has not yet been identified; and whether she was black or white is still in doubt. Gates had an investment in its publication. He purchased the manuscript at an auction in the Swann Galleries in New York in 2001 at a price that has multiplied many times since then; and while Gates himself has not the slightest interest in profit, having donated the manuscript to Yale University, certainly he was keen to add to the Schomberg Library of Black Women Writers an early African American novelist, and to publicize the accession as widely as possible. The plan of bringing Hannah Crafts to national attention was perversely assisted by an unfortunate turn of events. Two months before publication, in an article in the *New Yorker* in praise of what Crafts herself calls "this record of plain unvarnished facts" (Crafts 2002: 3), Gates (while not mistaking history for fiction) showed how firmly he believed the fiction to be her own by pointing to evidence of eyewitnessed scenes. He drew attention specifically to the description of Washington, "Gloom everywhere. Gloom up the Potomac; where it rolls among meadows no longer green" (162) as an example of accurate and vivid notation. But this was the first of several portions of the novel to be identified by Hollis Robbins as a pastiche of nineteenth-century fiction, in this instance Dickens's description of London mud in *Bleak House* (Showalter and Showalter 2005: 9). At this point, Gates radically shifted his own critical position, for instead of praising the referential power of the writing, he emphasized the extent of Crafts's bricolage: "There's almost a sense of a person educating herself in what she considered to be a proper literary style," and also noticed the clumsiness of it: "sometimes the process of assimilation remains highly incomplete" (Gates 2002: xix, xviii).

Then he invited a wide range of scholars to comment on the merits of what he had found among the "library privileges" taken by its author. Many of these experts allowed Crafts more skill than Gates had done. Hilary Mantel, a prize-winning historical novelist, praised the intelligence with which Crafts pillages Dickens and noticed how skillfully she excites horror. Mantel went on to suggest that this served the important purpose for Crafts of insulating her psyche: she had escaped slavery in her imagination, "She had extracted herself from degrading circumstances and inserted herself into others, more flattering, as a persecuted heroine in a romance" (Mantel 2004: 430). Elaine and English Showalter, who were not represented in this collection, were quite definitive about this, calling it "a powerful, artistically important novel, Gothic rather than sentimental, and full of fascinating inventions" (Showalter and Showalter 2005: 10). The Showalters wondered indeed if the author were not really a white woman pretending to be black, since it would not be the first time that this switch had been performed. One thing was plain, however: unless the reader of *The Bondwoman's Narrative* was prepared to sit down to read fiction, and to forget about history, then the encounter with the text was likely to be troubled by a host of doubts, some of which Crafts had already dramatized in her story.

Of this particular anxiety Gates himself was still far from free, chiefly because he was determined t o identify Crafts as an African American who had been a fugitive from slavery. To this end, he marshaled an impressive group of specialists to assist him in proving it, such as Joe Nickell, a handwriting expert; Kenneth Rendell, knowledgeable about nineteenth-century inks; Bryan C. Sinche, who catalogued the library at the Wheeler house where Crafts putatively had been a slave and done her reading; and Ann Fabian and Dorothy Porter, specialists in the structure and technique of black women's narrative. Besides these helpers, Gates drew on an impressive list of archives: the Library of Congress, Census Registers, and the Mormon Family History Library. If Hannah Crafts had deliberately concealed her identity, and obliterated all trace of her connection to a specific locale and family, then Gates was applying an equal amount of energy and resourcefulness to finding out her secret. With an ironic glance at the circumstances of the tale as well as the Fugitive Slave Act which made flight perilous even for someone reaching a free state, he calls this section of his introduction to the novel, "The Search for a Female Fugitive Slave." But it is an irony that veers out of control the more vigorously the search is pursued, and the more insistently historical imperatives displace literary ones.

This becomes clearer by following the hints offered by Mantel and the Showalters, namely, of reading the story as fiction, and specifically as romance, either pure or Gothic. Of the Gothic conventions coined by Mrs. Radcliffe, and later improved by Matthew Lewis, Dickens, and Wilkie Collins, Crafts has a very deft grasp. Inexplicable noises and lights that convince the servants that ghosts are in the house; horrid punishments involving slow starvation; the terror of running away, and the horror of being pursued—all these are to be found in *The Mysteries of Udolpho*, *The Monk*, and *A Sicilian Romance*. Crafts has adapted them for slave experience of superstition, torture, and the escape from servitude. But there is a more salient convention common to the best Gothic fictions which she exploits to even greater effect, involving an older man of Machiavellian intelligence who holds the key to a secret that allows him to manipulate and domineer over a leading female character: Montoni in *The Mysteries of Udolpho*, Schedoni in *The Italian*, the Marquis in *The Sicilian Romance*, Mr. Tulkinghorn in *Bleak House*, Count Fosco in *The Woman in White* and, in a slightly different key, Mr. Jaggers in *Great Expectations*. The discoverer of such secrets in *The Bondwoman's Narrative* is Mr. Trappe, the sinister figure who has found out the secret of the birth of Hannah's mistress, and has laid hands on the affidavits and documents that prove it. He is using his historical knowledge to blackmail her until a pulmonary hemorrhage dramatically puts an end to her life; whereupon Trappe turns his attention to Hannah, and arranges for her sale to Mr. Saddler, who stocks the brothels of New Orleans. For Crafts, Trappe represents the extensive reach and documentary knowledge of Slavery itself: there is nothing it does not know, and nothing it will not scruple to do.

The relationship that develops between Hannah the fugitive slave and Trappe the omnicompetent historian recalls very distinctly one of the great romances of Roman literature, the tale of Cupid and Psyche told inside the larger narrative of Apuleius's *The Golden Ass*. The position occupied by Trappe and Slavery between them in *The Bondwoman's Narrative* is taken in this story by Venus. She is so deeply offended by Psyche, a mortal who has usurped her cult and fallen in love with her son, that she pursues and captures her, and then submits her to a series of degrading and impossible tasks calculated to end in Psyche's death. During the pursuit Roman law is invoked, for when Psyche appeals to Juno for protection, the goddess says she is forbidden to harbor a fugitive, citing the Code of Justinian (Apuleius 2001: 1.319). "What roof or darkness can I hide beneath to evade the inescapable eyes of mighty Venus?" asks poor Psyche, and the answer is none. Venus enlists Mercury's help in recovering a runaway whom she specifies as a female slave ("delitescentem ancillam"), and Mercury carries a hand-bill describing the "fugitivam ancillam" and offering a reward of seven kisses from Venus for good information (1.324–5). Like other slaves in this exigency, Psyche finds herself at the mercy of personifications—Habit, Trouble, and Sadness—and locates her only friends among animated nature: ants, reeds, water, and stone. Of course these travails herald her eventual marriage to Cupid and her elevation from mortality to divinity, the perfect reward of her constancy. Similarly, Hannah's refusal to buckle to the threats of Trappe and Mrs. Wheeler is rewarded by marriage to an anonymous preacher, followed by pastoral bliss in New Jersey.

The Venus-Trappe figure extends from Gothic romance to mock-romance, especially those fictions that lie on the cusp between pure chivalric or pastoral romance and the emergent novel. In them a tension is always observable between the regulated confusion of the empire of Love, or of Arms, and the discipline of empirical knowledge, whose deputies are anxious to teach the hero or heroine a thing or two. In *Don Quixote* this role is taken by successive characters: the curate and the barber, the canon of Toledo, and Samson Carrasco, all of whom are dedicated to restoring the knight to knowledge of the real. Roxana "lies asleep at the center of the fiction" (Castle 1979: 89) until she is disturbed by her detective daughter, determined to find out more and more about the secretive woman whom she suspects strongly of being her mother. In the *La Princesse de Clèves*, the heroine is caught between the easy rhythms of amour courtois at Versailles and her loyalty to her husband, to whom she tells a truth so seldom communicated by a wife to a spouse in romance that he insists on mistaking it for an equivocation, relying on spies and conjecture for what he mistakenly thinks is better information. The heroine of Charlotte Lennox's *The Female Quixote* is persuaded by the learned clergyman who engages her in disputation at the end of the story to sacrifice the elaborate self-evidence of amorous protocol to a conjecture that enforces the rule of probability and the priority of the known customs of the world. Experience and knowledge trump the romantic engagement with pure glory and truth. These two rival principles are met in Austen's *Northanger Abbey* when Catherine Morland is obliged to relinquish the delightful horridness of Gothic imaginings in favor of Henry Morland's statistical estimate of the likelihood of undiscovered murder in the Midland counties of England. In all of these examples, a debate about the eligibility of realist fiction and the improbability of romance is effectually dramatized inside the novel, and in every case the exemplar of romance has to capitulate to the representative of empirical fact.

Significantly, this capitulation does not occur in *The Bondwoman's Narrative*. Trappe, the collector of evidence, ends up with a bullet in his head, leaving Hannah free to make her escape and allowing her Author to explore unhindered the literary analogies linking romance to the emergencies of servitude and flight. She is never embarrassed about using this resource, even when its artifice is glaring. If we compare Wallace Turnage's experience of bloodhounds with Hannah's, the difference is stark.

He remembers an actual event, "Now these dogs bit me all over while some of them had hold of my legs the others was biting me on my arms hands and throat. I could not fall for while some them would pull me one way, the rest would pull me other way. He made them bite me four or five minutes" (Turnage 2007: 243). Hannah constructs an ornate transition from the idea of pursuit to one of safety in which the word "probably" has a place but no function:

> On gaining the public road I heard some hounds in full cry a short distance behind me. I doubted not they were on my track, and commending myself to God I took refuge in the shelter of a friendly wood. Presently I heard the murmur of water, and soon beheld at a little distance the sparkling waves of a rivulet. It was broad but shallow. I entered it, waded down the current for probably half a mile, crossed over, and was in safety. (219)

As always in romance, the circumstances of terror and danger are attended to almost sedately, as in a dream where each part of sequence falls out ineluctably, regardless of passion and will, as if organized according to some mysterious symmetry of circumstances that ensures even the most outrageous improbability a satisfying formality: "The door was fastened by strong iron bolts, which Hippolitus vainly endeavoured to draw ... after much labour and difficulty the bolts yielded—the door unclosed" (Radcliffe 2008: 169). Door behaves for Hippolitus like ant and reed for Psyche, or rivulet for Hannah.

The reason the irony of Gates's scholarly pursuit of the fugitive is not contained by the wry acknowledgment that he is making it is to be found in this formalist experiment Crafts is making with romance. In proportion as Trappe seeks knowledge of facts, she reconnoiters fiction not for its probable representation of what is known commonly to be the case, but for its very opposite: its imaginary transcendence of such factuality, or what Mantel calls self-extraction from the degrading circumstances of slavery. Crafts, no less than William Henry Lane, is interested in art that strides above the mimetic or referential. If her formal excellence lies in a degree of sheer fictionality, just as his did to an art of dance so distant from all other systems of motion that it arrived at "ideality," then it is pointless to ask what it represents or what it hides. Specifically in the case of Crafts, all references to the real and all enquiries into the knowledge of facts are irrelevant, for there can be nothing more destructive of her achievement than to attach to each example of parodic artifice a notice like Mercury's, publishing the felonies of the Author and offering in effect a reward for her discovery. In the end, Gates has to mortgage himself to his search and model himself unironically on Trappe and Venus,

committing himself to a hunt for information which, were it ever successful, would leave the Author uninsulated, with no cover, no darkness, and
no estate.

Here by a long circuit we return to Best's original point in the evolution of nineteenth-century slave law, namely the Statute of Anne 1710,
defining literary copyright and attempting for the first time to broach
the concept of intellectual property. Best understands this history as the
beginning of the abstraction of the attributes of personhood, culminating
in the legal doctrine that explains the fugitive as a party in breach of contract because she has absconded with the labor she promised to deliver.
He acknowledges that there were some attempts at law to recover a core
of personhood from the multitude of its alienable attributes, chiefly an ar-
ticulation of the right to privacy drawn up by Samuel Warren and Louis
Brandeis in 1890. They found the inviolability of the person to depend
on an inalienable right to certain kinds of property whose generic characteristic they called "secret-writing" (Best 2004: 51). Among the examples
of such writing they included everything produced in private, whether
an entry in a diary or a finished piece of literature. They judged that "in
every such case the individual is entitled to decide whether that which is
his shall be given to the public" (50). Warren and Brandeis were returning
to the origin if not the history of limited copyright which finds in "secret-
writing" a kind of property so unique that it is a refuge for the Author
as long, and only as long, as she remains mistress of her manuscript;
for once it is sold she is caught in the web of interlocking contracts that
constitute civil society, the sphere of Fortune's dominion and, inevitably
for an Author, the cycle of dispossession. Catherine Gallagher has shown
how closely the plot of *The Female Quixote* hews to the necessity under
which Charlotte Lennox lay of parting with the manuscript of her novel,
selling the child of her own brain for money, and losing a very special
estate that Gallagher refers to as "original ownership" of a property unlike any other (Gallagher 1998: 157). This enforced removal from the
condition of Author, where what she owned was her own property by
virtue of no extrinsic license or right whatsoever as long as she kept the
matter to herself as "secret-writing," into the condition of someone owning to the world at large, via a bookseller, that she wrote it and had sold
it, is analogous, Gallagher suggests, to the embarrassment of Arabella
the heroine, when in the contract of disputation she has struck with the
learned clergyman, she is obliged first to hypothesize the improbability
of the splendid anarchy of the Empire of Love, and then to forsake it in
exchange for the meager knowledge of the world he offers her in return
(Gallagher 1994: 191–5). She loses her estate, or what she would call
her glory—the ideal presence of all the fantastic order and legislation

of romance, no matter how paradoxical or arbitrary its dispensations, amidst which she sits enthroned and inviolate. Hannah calls it her happiness, inexpressible because it was obtained in 'strange and devious ways' (Crafts 2002: 245).

In his effort to blow Crafts's cover, Gates has managed to specify in some detail the material elements of which it consisted. *The Bondwoman's Narrative* was written in iron-gall ink with a goose-quill pen on lined embossed folios made of calendered wove rag paper. That was how the Author left it, in ink on paper, although she had in her hand a story that would have made an easy entrance into print. It is possible to assume then that a decision was made not to publish the manuscript. The motive for that was no doubt partly cautionary, like the reticence of Douglass or Equiano, and partly protective, like Levi's shielding a wounded psyche from public curiosity that could never under any circumstances turn into sympathy. But there is the possibility of glory too. A private exercise in a publicly recognizable literary form was preserved as "secret-writing," the Author's very own estate, which she was determined not to sacrifice. If we assume further that the manuscript had a cadre of readers over the 150 years of its existence, then they would have enjoyed the same coalition of egocentric focus and ebullient virtuosoship that made William Henry Lane's juba so compelling to watch. That is to say, they would have experienced in reading it the emancipation of writing from the system of text, fact, probability, and contract that once had dispossessed its Author, and would have dispossessed her again. Here is freedom proved in the medium and very substance of paper and ink.

Bibliography

Addison, Joseph. 1765. "Dialogues Upon Ancient Medals." *Addison's Miscellaneous Works*. Vol. 3. London: J. & R. Tonson.

———. and Richard Steele. 1909. *The Spectator*. 4 vols. London: Dent.

Adorno, Theodor. 1974. *Minima Moralia*. trans. E.F.N. Jephcott. Norfolk: Verso.

Aesop. 1954. *Fables*. London: Penguin.

Agamben, Giorgio. 2002. *Remnants of Auschwitz: The Witness and the Archive*, trans. Daniel Heller-Roazen. New York: Zone Books.

Alliston, April. forthcoming. *Female Quixotism and the Novel: Character and Plausibility, Honesty and Fidelity* in *Rise of the Novel Redux*, ed. Julie Park. Forthcoming special issue of *Eighteenth Century: Theory and Interpretation*.

Alpers, Svetlana. 1983. *The Art of Describing*. London: John Murray.

———. 2005. *The Vexations of Art*. New Haven: Yale University Press.

Anderson, Benedict. 1983. *Imagined Communities*. London: Verso.

Andrews, William L., and Henry Louis Gates, eds. 2000. *Slave Narratives*. New York: Library of America.

Anonymous. 1770. *Adventures of a Bank-Note*. London.

———. 1760. *The Adventures of a Black Coat*. London: J. William.

———. 1775. *Adventures of a Cork-Screw*. London : T. Bell.

———. 1788. *Adventures of a Watch*. London: G. Kearsley.

———. 1981. *Adventures of a Hackney Coach*. London: G. Kearsley.

———. 1835. *Adventures of a Halfpenny*. Banbury: J. G. Rusher.

———. 1819. *The Adventures of a One Pound Note: A Poem*. London: T. Jones.

———. n.d. *The Adventures of a Whipping-Top*. London: n.d.

———. 1741. *The Apotheosis of the Fair Sex*. London: C. Jephson.

———. 1725. *The Behaviour, Confession and Last Dying Speeches of Four Malefactors That Was Executed at Tyburn on Monday May the 24th 1725*. London: John Applebee.

———. 1780. *The Complete Modern London Spy*. London: Alex Hogg.

———. 1795. *The History of a Guildford Jack-Daw*. London.

———. 1754. *The History and Adventures of a Lady's Slipper and Shoes*. London: M. Cooper.

———. 1725. *The History of the Life and Actions of Jonathan Wild, Thieftaker Etc*. London: E. Midwinter.

———. 1828. *The Gold-headed Cane*. 2nd edition. London: John Murray.

———. 1785. *Memoirs and Adventures of a Flea*. London: T. Axtell.

———. 1815. *Memoirs of an Old Wig*. London: Longman.

———. n.d. *Memoirs of a Peg-top*. London: J. Marshall.

———. 1785. *Memoirs and Adventures of a Flea*. 2 vols. London: T. Axtell.

———. n.d. *Memoirs of a Peg-Top*. London: J. Marshall.

———. 1726. *Memoirs of the Life and Times of the Famous Jonathan Wild*. London: Samuel Briscoe.

Anonymous. 1781. *Metempsychosis*. London: G Kearsley.

———. 1760. *The New London Spy*. London J. Cooke.

———. 1757. *The Sedan*. London: R. Baldwin.

———. 1788. *The Ton, or Follies of Fashion*. London: T. Hookham.

———. 2005. *A Woman in Berlin*. Trans. Philip Boehm. New York: Metropolitan Books.

Appadurai, Arjun, ed. 1986. *The Social Life of Things: Commodities in Cultural Perspective*. Cambridge: Cambridge University Press.

Apuleius.1923. *The Golden Ass*. Trans. Richard Adlington. London: Golden Cockerel Press.

———. 2001. *Metamorphoses*. 2 vols. Trans. J. Arthur Hanson. Cambridge: Harvard University Press.

Aristotle. 2003. *Nicomeachean Ethics*. Trans. and ed. H. Rackham. Cambridge: Harvard University Press.

Armstrong, Nancy. 2005. *How Novels Think*. New York: Columbia University Press.

Bacon, Francis. 1965. *The Advancement of Learning*. Ed. G. W. Kitchin. London: Everyman.

Bacon, Francis, Lord Verulam. 1862–79. *The Works of Francis Bacon*. 15 vols. Eds. Robert Ellis, Douglas Heath, and James Spedding. New York: Hurd and Houghton.

Baier, Annette. 1985. "Cartesian Persons." in *Postures of the Mind*. Minneapolis: University of Minnesota Press. 74–92.

———. 1991. *A Progress of Sentiments: Reflection on Hume's Treatise*. Cambridge: Harvard University Press.

Balfour, Ian. 2002. *The Rhetoric of Romantic Prophecy*. Stanford: Stanford University Press.

Ballaster, Ros. 2005. *Fabulous Orients: Fictions of the East in England 1662–1785*. Oxford: Oxford University Press.

Banks, Joseph. 1962. *The Endeavour Journal*. 2 vols. Ed. J. C. Beaglehole. Sydney: Public Library of New South Wales and Angus and Robertson.

Barthes, Roland. 1988. *The World as Object*. Calligram. N. Bryson. Cambridge: Cambridge University Press.

Bataille, Georges. 1977. *Story of the Eye*. Trans. Joachim Neugroschal. New York: Urizen.

Baudrillard, Jean. 1988. *The Trompe l'Oeil*. Calligram. N. Bryson. Cambridge: Cambridge University Press.

Bayle, Pierre. 1710. *Dictionary*. 4. vols. London: C. Harper et al. article Rorarius.

Behn, Aphra. 1751. "The Lover's Watch," in *The Histories and Novels of Mrs Behn*. 2 vols. Ed. Charles Gildon, London: T. Longman et al.

Benedict, Barbara. 2004. "Wants and Goods: Advertisement and Desire in Haywood and Defoe." *Studies in 18th Century Culture 33*. 221–53. Eds. Catherine Ingrassia and Jeffrey Ravel. Baltimore: Johns Hopkins University Press.

———. 2007. "Encounters with the Object: Advertisements, Time and Literary Discourse in the early 18th Century Thing-Poem." *ECS* 40, 2: 193–207.

Best, Stephen M. 2004. *The Fugitive's Properties: Law and the Poetics of Possession*. Chicago: University of Chicago Press.

Bibb, Henry. 2000. "Narrative of the Life and Adventures of Henry Bibb," in Andrews and Gates, *Slave Narratives*: 425–563.

Blackburn, Robin. 1998. *The Making of New World Slavery*. London: Verso.

Blackstone, William. 1773. *Commentaries on the Laws of England*. 4 vols. Oxford: Clarendon Press.

———. 1857. *Commentaries on the Laws of England*. 4 vols. Ed. Robert Malcolm Kerr. London: John Murray.

Blackwell, Mark. 2006. "The People Things Make: Locke, Descartes and the Properties of the Self. "*Studies in Eighteenth-Century Culture* 35: 77–94.

———, ed. 2007. *The Secret Life of Things*. Lewisburg: Bucknell University Press.

Bligh, William. 1937. *The Log of the Bounty*. 2 vols. London: The Golden Cockerel Press.

Blight, David. 2007. *A Slave No More*. Orlando: Harcourt.

Bloch, Ernst. 1996. *The Utopian Function of Art and Literature*. Trans. Frank Mecklenburg. Cambridge: MIT Press.

Blunden, Edmund. 2000. *Undertones of War*. London: Penguin.

Boswell, James. 1980. *The Life of Johnson*. Ed. R. W. Chapman. Oxford: Oxford University Press.

Bougeant, Guillaume. 1739. *A Philosophical Amusement upon the Language of Beasts*. London: T. Coooper.

Boyle, Robert. 1999. *The Sceptical Chymist*. vol. 2 of *The Works of Robert Boyle*. Eds. Michael Hunter and Edward B. Davis. London: Pickering and Chatto.

Bredekamp, Horst. 2006. *Thomas Hobbes Der Leviathan*. 3te Auflage. Berlin: Akademie Verlag.

Brown, Thomas. 1851. *Lectures on the Philosophy of Mind*. 4 vols. 19th edition. Edinburgh: Adam and Charles Black.

Brown, William W. 2000. "Narrative of William W. Brown," in Andrews and Gates, *Slave Narratives*.

Bryson, Norman. 1990. *Looking at the Overlooked*. London: Reaktion.

Bugg, John. 2006. "The Other Interesting Narrative: Olaudah Equiano's Public Book Tour." *PMLA* 121: 5 (October): 1424–42.

Burney, Frances. 1988. *Cecilia*. Oxford: Oxford University Press.

Butler, Joseph. 1902. "Of Personal Identity," in *The Analogy of Religion*. London: George Bell.

Campbell, Jill. 2002. "Domestic Intelligence: Newspaper Advertising and the Eighteenth Century Novel." *Yale Journal of Criticism* 15.2: 252–91.

Caretta, Vincent. 1996. *Unchained Voices: An Anthology of Black Authors in the English-Speaking World of the Eighteenth Century*. Lexington: University Press of Kentucky.

———. 2005. *Equiano the African*. Athens: University of Georgia Press.

Castle, Terry. 1979. "'Amy, Who Knew my Disease': A Psychosexual Pattern in Defoe's *Roxana*." *ELH* 46:1 (Spring): 81–96.

Cervantes, Miguel de. 1991. *Don Quixote*. 2 vols. Trans. P.A. Motteux. New York: Everyman and Alfred A. Knopf.

Chapman, Guy. 1988. *A Passionate Prodigality*. London: Buchan and Enright.

Charleton, Walter. 1670. *Natural History of the Passions*. London: J. Magnes.

Chesnutt, Charles W. 2000. *Conjure Tales*. Ed. William L. Andrews. New York: Penguin.

Chong, Alan. 1999. *Still-Life Paintings from the Netherlands 1550–1720*. Zwolle: Waanders.

Cleland, John. 1985. *Fanny Hill, or the Memoirs of a Woman of Pleasure*. Ed. Peter Wagner. London: Penguin.

Cobbett, William. 1817. *Parliamentary History*. 36 vols. London: Hansard.

Coetzee, J. M. 1992. "The Rhetoric of the Passive," in *Doubling the Point*. Cambridge: Harvard University Press.

Coke, Lord. 1818. *Coke upon Littleton*. 3 vols. Ed. J. H. Thomas.

Congreve, William. 1993. *The Way of the World*, in *The Norton Anthology of English Literature*. 6th edition. 2 vols. New York: W.W. Norton.

Cook, James. 1955. *The Journal of the Voyage of the Endeavour*. Ed. J. C. Beaglehole. Cambridge: Cambridge Univ. and the Hakluyt Society.

———. 1961. *The Voyage of the Resolution and Adventure*. Ed. J. C. Beaglehole. Hakluyt Society.

———. 1967. *The Voyage of the Resolution and Discovery*. 2 vols. Ed. J.C. Beaglehole. Hakluyt Society.

———. 1777. *A Voyage towards the South Pole and round the World*. 2 vols. London: Strahan and Cadell.

Cooper, Anthony Ashley, third earl of Shaftesbury. 1900. *The Life, Unpublished Letters and Philosophical Regimen of Anthony, Earl of Shaftesbury*. Ed. Benjamin Rand. London: Swan and Sonnenschein.

———. 1999. *Characteristics of Men, Manners, Opinions, Times*. 2 vols. Ed. Philip Ayres. Oxford: Clarendon Press.

Coventry, Francis. 1751. *The History of Pompey the Little*. London: M. Cooper.

Cowper, William. 1981. *Correspondence*, 2 vols. Eds. James King and Charles Ryskamp. Oxford: Clarendon Press.

Crafts, Hannah. 2002. *The Bondwoman's Narrative*. Ed. Henry Louis Gates. New York: Warner Books.

Crary, Jonathan. 1992. *Techniques of the Observer*. Cambridge: MIT Press.

Craton, Michael. 1991. "Reluctant Creoles: The Planters' World in the British West Indies," in Bernard Bailyn and Philip D. Morgan, eds. *Strangers in the Realm*. Williamsburg: Institute of Early American History and Culture.

Crebillon, Claude Prosper Jolyot de. 1742. *The Sopha: A Moral Tale*. 2 vols. London: T. Cooper.

Cudworth, Ralph. 1838. *A Treatise of Freewill*. Ed. John Allen. London: John Parker.

Cugoano, Quobua Ottobah. 1996. *Thoughts and Sentiments on the wicked Traffic of Slavery* in Caretta, *Unacknowledged Voices: An Anthology of Black Authors in the English-Speaking World of the Eighteenth Century*.

Damasio, Anthony. 1989. *The Feeling of What Happens*. New York: Harcourt Brace.

De Certeau, Michel. 1992. *The Mystic Fable*. Trans. Michael B. Smith. Chicago: University of Chicago Press.

Defoe, Daniel. 1718. *A Continuation of Letters written by a Turkish Spy at Paris*. London: W. Taylor.

———. 1725. *The True and Genuine Account of the Life and Actions of the Late Jonathan Wild*. London: John Applebee.

——— [Andrew Morton pseud.]. 1735. *The Secrets of the Invisible World Disclos'd; or, An Universal History of Apparitions*. London: J. Watts.

———. 1971. *The Fortunes and Misfortunes of the Famous Moll Flanders*. Ed. G. A. Starr. Oxford: Oxford University Press.

———. 1981. *Roxana the Fortunate Mistress*. Ed. Jane Jack. Oxford: Oxford University Press.

Defoe, Daniel. 1983. *The Life and Surprising Adventures of Robinson Crusoe*. Ed. J. Donald Crowley. Oxford: Oxford University Press.

———. 1998. *Journal of the Plague Year*. Ed. Louis Landa. Oxford: Oxford University Press.

Delbourgo, James. 2009. "Fugitive Colours," in Schaffer et al. eds., *The Brokered World*. Sagamore Beach: Science History Publications.

De Maupassant, Guy. 2004. *A Parisian Affair and Other Stories*. Trans. Siân Miles. London: Penguin.

Dennis, John. 1728. *Remarks on Mr Pope's Rape of the Lock*. London: J. Roberts.

Descartes, Rene. 1989. *The Passions of the Soul*. Ed. Stephen H. Voss. Indianapolis: Hackett Publishing.

———. 1996. *Discourse on Method and Meditations on the First Philosophy*. Ed. David Weissman. New Haven: Yale University Press.

Deutsch, Helen. 1996. *Resemblance and Disgrace*. Cambridge: Harvard University Press.

D'Hobsonville, Foucher. 1784. *Manners of Various Foreign Animals*. Trans. Thomas Holcroft. London: J. Johnson.

D'Holbach, Paul Henri Thiry. 1795. *The System of Nature*. 4 vols. Trans. William Hodgson. London: B. Crosby.

Dickens, Charles. 1994. *Oliver Twist*. London: Penguin.

Diderot, Denis. 1993. *The Indiscreet Jewels*. New York: Marsilio.

Douglas, Aileen. 1993. "Britannia's Rule and the It-Narrator." *Eighteenth-century Fiction* 6.1: 65–82.

———. 2007. "Britannia's Rule and the It-Narrator," in Mark Blackwell, ed., *The Secret Life of Things*, 147–61. Lewisburg: Bucknell University Press.

Douglass, Frederick. 2000. *Narrative of the Life of Frederick Douglass, an American Slave, Written by Himself* in Andrews and Gates, *Slave Narratives*: 267–368.

———. 2003. *My Bondage and my Freedom*. Ed. John David Smith. New York: Penguin.

Dryden, John. 1702. *Sylvae*. London: Jacob Tonson.

Duffy, Christopher. 1979. *Siege Warfare*. London: Routlege and Kegan Paul.

Dunton, John. 1691. *A Voyage Round the World; or, A Pocket Library*. 3 vols. London: Richard Newcombe.

———. 1705. *Life and Errors*. London: S. Malthus.

Ebert-Schifferer, Sybille. 1999. *Still Life: A History*. New York: Harry Abrams.

Ellis, William. 1969. *An Authentic Narrative of a Voyage*. New York: Da Capo Press.

Empson, William. 1935. "The Beggar's Opera: Mock-Pastoral as the Cult of Independence." *Some Versions of Pastoral*. London: Chatto and Windus.

Equiano, Olauda.1995. *The Interesting Narrative*. ed. Vincent Caretta. New York: Penguin.

Fabian, Ann. 2004. "Hannah Crafts Novelist; or, How a Silent Observer became a 'Dabster at Invention," in Gates and Robbins, *In Search of Hannah Crafts*. New York: Basic Books: 43–52.

Farquhar, George. 2000. *The Recruiting Officer in A Companion to Literature from Milton to Blake*. Ed. David Womersly. Oxford: Blackwell.

Fielding, Henry. 1977. *Joseph Andrews*. Ed. R. F. Brissendon. Harmondsworth: Penguin.

———. 1982. *The Life of Mr. Jonathan Wild the Great*. Ed. David Nokes. London: Penguin.

———. 1988. *An Enquiry into the Causes of Late Increase in Robbers*. Ed. Malvin R. Zirker. Connecticut: Wesleyan University Press.

Flint, Christopher. 1998. "Speaking Objects: The Circulation of Stories in Eighteenth Century Prose Fiction." *PMLA* 113: 212–26.

Fodor, Jerry. 2007. "Headaches have themselves." *London Review of Books* 29:10 (24 May).

Fontaine, Jean de La. n.d. *Fables*. Trans. William Thornbury. London: Cassell, Petter & Galpin.

———. 1865. *Fables de La Fontaine*. Paris: Furne et Cie.

Foster, Hal. 1995. "The Art of Fetishism," in Emily Apter and William Pietz, eds., *Fetishism as Cultural Discourse*. Ithaca: Cornell University Press.

Foucault, Michel. 1997. *Ethics*. Ed. Paul Rabinow. Trans. Robert Hurley. New York: New Press.

Freedberg, David. 2002. *The Eye of the Lynx*. Chicago: Chicago University Press.

Freedgood, Elaine. 2006. *The Ideas in Things:Fugitive Meaning in the Victorian Novel*. Chicago: University of Chicago Press.

Galison, Peter. 1997. *Image and Logic*. Chicago: University of Chicago Press.

Gallagher, Catherine. 1994. *Nobody's Story: The Vanishing Acts of Women Writers in the Marketplace 1670–1820*. Los Angeles: University of California Press.

———. 2006. "The Rise of Fictionality," in Franco Moretti, *The Novel*. 2 vols. Princeton: Princeton University Press: 336–63.

Gardner, Sarah. n.d. *The Matrimonial Advertisement, or a Bold Stroke for a Husband*. 435. Larpent MSS, Huntington Library, San Marino, California.

Garth, Samuel. 1699. *The Dispensary*. London: John Nutt.

———. 1815. *The Art of Beauty in The Works of Ovid*. London: Peter Griffin.

Gates, Henry Louis. 1987. *The Classic Slave Narratives*. Bergenfield, NJ: New American Library.

Gates, Henry Louis, and Hollis Robbins, eds. 2004. *In Search of Hannah Crafts*. New York: Basic Civitas Books.

Gay, John. 1715. *A Complete Key to the last New Farce. The What D'Ye Call It*. London: J. Roberts.

———. 1720 [1974]. *The Fan in Poetry and Prose*. 2 vols. Ed. Vinton A. Dearing. Oxford: Clarendon Press. London: J. Tonson: 58–79.

———. 1923. *The What D'Ye Call It*. in *The Plays of John Gay*. 2 vols. London: Chapman Dodd.

———. 1961. "The Beggar's Opera." *Eighteenth-Century Plays*. Ed. John Hampden. London: Dent.

———. 1966. *The Letters of John Gay*. Ed. C. F. Burgess. Oxford: Clarendon Press.

———. 1974. *The Shepherds Week* in *John Gay: Poetry and Prose*. 2 vols. Ed. Vincent A. Dearing with Charles E. Beckwith. Oxford: Clarendon Press.

Gell, Alfred. 1998. *Art and Agency*. Oxford: Clarendon Press.

Gildon, Charles. 1705. *The Deist's Manual*. London: A. Roper.

———. 1706. *The Post-Boy Robb'd of his Mail*. London. 2 vols. London: B. Mills.

———. 1708. *The New Metamorphosis . . . being The Golden Ass . . . Alter'd and Improv'd to the Modern Times*. 2 vols. London: S. Brisco.

———. 1709. *The Golden Spy*. London: J. Woodward.

Gildon, Charles. 1714. *A New Rehearsal, or Bays the Younger*. London: J. Roberts.

———. 1719. *The Life and Surprizing Adventures of Mr D----- De F----- of London, Hosier*. London: J. Roberts.

Ginzburg, Carlo. 2001. *Wooden Eyes*. Trans. Martin Tyle and Kate Soper. New York: Columbia University Press.

Godwin, Benjamin. 1969. *Lectures on Slavery*. (1836) repr. New York: Negro Universities Press.

———. 1988. *Caleb Williams*. Ed. David McCracken. Oxford: Oxford University Press.

Gordon, George, and Lord Byron. 2000. *Don Juan* in *The Major Works*. Ed. Jerome J. McGann. Oxford: Oxford University Press.

Goveia, E.V. 1965. *Slave Society in the British Leeward Islands at the End of the Eighteenth Century*. New Haven: Yale University Press.

———. 1970. *The West Indian Slave Laws of the Eighteenth Century*. Barbados: Caribbean Universities Press.

Greene, Jody. 2005. *The Trouble with Authorship*. Philadelphia: University of Pennsylvania Press.

———. 2006. "Francis Kirkman's Counterfeit Authority: Autobiography, Subjectivity, Print." *PMLA*. 121:1: 17–32.

Gronniosaw, James Albert Ukawsaw. 2000. "A Narrative of the Most Remarkable Particulars," in Andrews and Gates, *Slave Narratives*. New York: Library of America: 1–34.

Groom, Nick. 2002. *The Forger's Shadow*. London: Picador.

Grotius, Hugo. 2005. *The Rights of War and Peace*. 3 vols., Ed. Richard Tuck. Indianapolis: Liberty Fund.

Harris, Joel Chandler. 1982. *Uncle Remus, His Sons and Sayings*. Ed. Rober Hemenway. New York: Penguin.

Hawkesworth, John, ed. 1773. *An Account of the Voyages and Discoveries in the Southern Hemisphere*. 3 vols. London: W. Strahan and T. Cadell.

———. 1797. *The Adventurer*. 4 vols. London: B. Law et al.

Haywood, Eliza. 1994. *Love in Excess*. Ed. David Oakleaf. Peterborough: Broadview Press.

Haywood, Eliza. 2006. *Fantomina* in *The Norton Anthology of English Litera-ture*. Ed. Lawrence Lipking and James Noggle. New York: Norton: 2556–84.

Hazlitt, William. 1902. *The Life of Thomas Holcroft*, in *Collected Works*. 12 vols. Eds. A. R. Waller and Arnold Glover. London: J. M. Dent.

———. *On Dryden and Pope*. London: J. M. Dent.

Hearn, Lafcadio. 1885. *Gombo Zhibes*. New York.

Heidegger, Martin. 2001. "The Thing," in *Poetry, Language, Thought*. Trans. Albert Hofstadter. New York: Perennial Classics.

Heller-Roazen, Daniel. 2007. *The Inner Touch*. New York: Zone.

Henderson, John. 2004. *Aesop's Human Zoo*. Chicago: University of Chicago Press.

———. 2001. *Telling Tales on Caesar*. Oxford: Oxford University Press.

Hitchin, Charles. 1718. *A True Discovery of the Conduct of Receivers and Thief-takers*. London: Charles Hitchin.

Hobbes, Thomas. 1651. *Humane Nature*. London: T. Newcomb.

———. 1971. *A Dialogue on the Common Laws of England*. Ed. Joseph Cropsey. Chicago: University of Chicago Press.

———. 1991, 1996. *Leviathan*. Ed. Richard Tuck. Cambridge: Cambridge University Press.

———. 1994. *The Elements of Law*. Ed. J.C.A. Gaskin, Oxford: Oxford University Press.

———. 1996. *Leviathan*. Ed. Richard Tuck. Cambridge: Cambridge University Press.

———. 1998. *On the Citizen*. Eds. Richard Tuck and Michael Silverthorne Holmes. Cambridge: Cambridge University Press.

Holford-Strevens, Leofranc. 2009. "Peter Opened Paul the Door." *London Review of Books* 9 July: 25–26.

Holmes, Oliver Wendell. 1991. *The Common Law*. New York: Dover Publishers.

Homer. 2000 [1956]. *The Odyssey*. Trans. George Chapman. Ed. Allardyce Nicoll. Princeton: Princeton University Press.

Homer. 1959. *The Iliad*. Trans. Alexander Pope. London: Oxford University Press.

Hooke, Robert. 2003. *Micrographia*. Facsimile of 1665 ed. repr. New York: Dover.

Huet, Philippe-Daniel. 1715. *The History of Romances*. Trans. Stephen Lewis. London: J. Hooke and T. Caldecott.

Hughes, Richard. 1999. *A High Wind in Jamaica*. New York: *New York Review of Books*.

Hugo, Victor. 1982. *Les Miserables*. Trans. N. Denny. London: Penguin.

Hume, David. 1956. *The Natural History of Religion*. Ed. H. E. Root. Stanford: Stanford University Press.

———. 1978. *A Treatise of Human Nature*. Ed. L. A. Selby-Bigge. Second ed. rev. P. H. Nidditch. Oxford: Clarendon Press.

———. 1978. *Treatise of Human Nature*. Ed. P. H. Nidditch. Oxford: Clarendon Press.

———. 1985. *Essays, Moral, Political, and Literary*. Ed. Eugene Miller. Indianapolis: Liberty Press.

Hunter, J. Paul. 1990. *Before Novels: The Cultural Contexts of Eighteenth-Century Fiction*. New York: Norton.

Jacobs, Harriet. 2000. *Incidents in the Life of a Slave Girl*. Ed. Nell Irvin Painter. New York: Penguin.

Jarves, James. 1843. *History of the Sandwich Islands*. Boston.

Jesse, F. Tennyson. 1981. *Moonraker*. London: Virago.

Johnson, Samuel. 1791. *The Lives of the Poets*. 4 vols. London: J. Rivington et al.

———. 1791. *The Rambler*. 2 vols. London: W. Locke and C. Lowndes.

Johnstone, Charles. 1785. *Chrysal, or: The Adventures of a Guinea*. 4 vols. London: J. Watson et al.

Jünger, Ernst. 2004. *Storm of Steel*. Trans. Michael Hofmann. London: Penguin.

Kahn, Victoria. 2004. *Wayward Contracts*. Princeton: Princeton University Press.

Kant, Immanuel. 1996. *Critique of Pure Reason*. Trans. Werner Pluhar. Indianapolis and Cambridge: Hackett.

Kilner, Dorothy. 1784. *The Life and Perambulations of a Mouse*. London: John Marshall.

Kirch, Patrick V., and Marshall Sahlins. 1992. *Anahulu: The Anthropology of History in the Kingdom of Hawai'i*. 2 vols. Chicago: University of Chicago Press.

Kirkman, Francis. 1673. *The Unlucky Citizen Experimentally Described*. London: Anne Johnson for F. Kirkman.

Kloek, Wouter, and Alan Chong. 1999. *Still-Life Paintings from the Netherlands 1550–1720*. Amsterdam and Cleveland: Waanders.

Knapp, Steven. 1985. *Personification and the Sublime*. Cambridge: Harvard University Press.

Koerner, Joseph. 2004. *The Reformation of the Image*. Chicago: University of Chicago Press.

———. 2002. "The Icon as Iconoclash," in Latour and Weibel, *Iconoclash*: 164–217.

La Fontaine, Jean de. 1865. *Fables*. Paris: Furne et Cie.

Latour, Bruno. 1993. *We have never been modern*. Trans. Catherine Porter, Cambridge: Harvard University Press.

Latour, Bruno, and Peter Weibel. 2002. *Iconoclash*. Cambridge: MIT Press.

Law, Edmund. 1769. *A Defence of Mr Locke's Opinion concerning Personal Identity*. Cambridge.

Leibniz, G.W. 1996. *New Essays on Human Understanding*. Eds. Peter Remnant and Jonathan Bennett. Cambridge: Cambridge University Press.

Lennox, Charlotte. 1989. *The Female Quixote*. Ed Margaret Dalziel. Oxford: Oxford University Press.

L'Estrange, Roger. 1663. *Considerations and Proposals for the Regulation of the Press*. London: A.C.

Leveridge, Richard. 1716. *The Comic Masque of Pyramus and Thisbe*. London: W. Mears.

Levi, Primo. 2007. *Survival in Auschwitz (Is This a Man?)*. Trans. Stuart Woolf. New York: Touchstone.

———. 2005. *The Drowned and the Saved*. Trans. Raymond Rosenthal. London: Abacus.

Lewis, Lawrence. 1909. *The Advertisements of the Spectator*. New York: Houghton Mifflin.

Linebaugh, Peter. 1992. *The London Hanged*. Cambridge: Cambridge University Press.

Locke, John. 1696. *Several Papers relating to Money, Interest and Trade*. London: A. and J. Churchill.

———. 1960. *Two Treatises of Government*. Ed. Peter Laslett. New York: New American Library.

———. 1979. *An Essay Concerning Human Understanding*. Ed. Peter H. Nidditch. Oxford: Clarendon Press.

Long, Edward. 1774. 2 vols. *The History of Jamaica*. London: T. Lowndes.

Lynch, Deidre. 1998. *The Economy of Character*. Chicago: University of Chicago Press.

Lucretius. 1992. *On the Nature of Things*. Ed. G. P. Goold. Cambridge: Harvard University Press.

Luhmann, Niklas. 1986. *Love as Passion*. Trans. Jeremy Gaines and Doris L. Jones. Cambridge: Harvard University Press.

Machiavelli, Niccolo. 1963. *Poems of Machiavelli*. Ed. and trans. Joseph Tusiani. New York: Ivan Obolensky.

Mack, Robert L, ed. 1995. *Arabian Nights Entertainments*. New York: Oxford University Press.

Macpherson, Sandra. 2003. "Rent to Own, or, What's Entailed in Pride and Prejudice." *Representations* 82 (2003): 1–23.

———. 2010. *Harm's Way: Tragic Responsibility and the Novel Form*. Baltimore: Johns Hopkins University Press.

Man, Paul de. 1978. "The Epistemology of Metaphor." *Critical Inquiry*. 5:1 (Autumn): 13–30.

Mandeville, Bernard. 1966 [1704]. *Aesop Dress'd, or a Collection of Fables*. Los Angeles: Augustan Reprint Society, University of California Press.

———. 1725. *An Enquiry into the Causes of the Frequent Executions at Tyburn*. London: J. Roberts.

———. 1988. *The Fable of the Bees*, 2 vols. Ed. F. B. Kaye. Oxford: Clarendon Press, 1924; repr. Indianapolis: Liberty Classics.

Mantel, Hilary. 2004. "The Shape of Absence," in Gates and Robbins, *In Search of Hannah Crafts*: 422–430.

Marana, Giovanni Paolo. 1748. *Letters of a Turkish Spy*. 8 vols. Trans. William Bradshaw. London: A. Wilde.

Marryott, Thomas. 1771. *Sentimental Fables*. Belfast: T. Marryott.

Marshall, David.1986. *The Figure of Theatre*. New York: Columbia University Press.

Martin, Raymond, and John Barresi. 2000. *Naturalization of the Soul: Self and Personal Identity in the Eighteenth Century*. London and New York: Routledge.

Marvell, Andrew. 1971. *The Poems and Letters of Andrew Marvell*, 2 vols. 3rd ed. Ed. H. M. Margoliouth. Oxford: Clarendon Press.

———. 1995. *The Works*. Hertfordshire: Wordsworth Editions.

Matrimonial Advertisements. Cup 407 ff. 43 n.d. British Library.

McKeon, Michael. 1987. *The Origins of the English Novel*. Baltimore: Johns Hopkins University Press.

———. 2005. *The Secret History of Domesticity*. Baltimore: Johns Hopkins University Press.

Melville, Herman. 1849. *Mardi: and a Voyage Thither*. 2 vols. New York: Harper Bros.

———. 1907. *Moby-Dick*. London: Everyman.

Millar, John. 1771. *Observations Concerning the Distinction of Ranks in Society*. Dublin: T. Ewing.

More, Henry. 1662. *An Antidote against Atheism*. London: William Morden.

———. 1659. *The Immortality of the Soul*. London: J. Flesher.

Morris, Thomas D. 1996. *Southern Slavery and the Law*. Chapel Hill: University of North Carolina Press.

Mullan, John. 2007. *Anonymity: A Secret History of English Literature*. London: Faber and Faber.

Mulvey, L. 1996. *Fetishism and Curiosity*. Bloomington: Indiana University Press.

Nagel, Thomas. 1979. *Mortal Questions*. Cambridge: Cambridge University Press.

Nivernois, Duke of. 1799. *Fables*. London: T. Cadell and W. Davies.

Ogilby, John. 1651. *The Fables of Aesop*. 2 vols. London: Andrew Crook.

———. 1668. *The Fables of Aesop Paraphras'd in Verse*. London: Thomas Rycroft.

Oulton, Ann Elizabeth. 1826. *The Adventures of a Parrot*. London: W. Cole.

Ovid [P. Ovidius Naso]. 1815. *Works*. Trans. Samuel Garth et al. London: Peter Griffin.

———. 1999. *Metamorphoses* (Loeb *Ovid* III and IV). 2 vols. Ed. G. P. Goold. Cambridge: Harvard University Press.

———. 2000. *Metamorphoses*. Trans. Arthur Golding. Philadelphia: Paul Dry.

Pallavicino, Ferrante. 1960 [1683]. *The Whore's Rhetoric*. London: Holland Press.

Park, Julie. 2010. "Clockwork Character: Frances Burney's Invented Persons and the Origins of Mechanical Life," in *The New Science and Women's Literary Discourse: Prefiguring Frankenstein*, ed. Judy A. Hayden. Basingstoke and New York: Palgrave Macmillan.

———. Forthcoming special issue of *Eighteenth Century: Theory and Interpretation*

Patterson, Orlando. 1982. *Slavery and Social Death*. Cambridge: Harvard University Press.

Philostratus, the Elder. 2000. *Imagines*. Trans. Arthur Fairbanks. Cambridge: Harvard University Press.

Pilpay. 1775. *The Fables of Pilpay*. London: J. and F. Rivington.

Pinney, Christopher. 2002. "Creole Europe: The Reflection of a Reflection." *Journal of New Zealand Literature* 20: 125–61.

Pitkin, Hanna. 1967. *The Concept of Representation*. Berkeley: University of California Press.

Plotz, John. 2008. *Portable Property: Victorian Culture on the Move*. Princeton: Princeton University Press.

Pocock, J.G.A. 1985. *Virtue, Commerce, Society*. Cambridge: Cambridge University Press.

Pope, Alexander. 1723. *The Key to the Lock. London*. Bernard Lintot.

———. 1959. Trans., *The Iliad*. London: Oxford University Press.

———. 1963. *The Poems of Alexander Pope*. Ed. John Butts. London: Methuen.

———. 2006. *Essay on Man in The Major Works*. Ed. Pat Rogers. Oxford: Oxford University Press.

Prince, Mary. 1987. *The History of Mary Prince*, in Gates, *The Classic Slave Narratives*.

———. 2000. *The History of Mary Prince*. Ed. Sara Salih. Penguin: New York.

Pufendorf, Samuel. 1660 [1994]. *Elements of Universal Jurisprudence*, in *The Political Writings of Samuel Pufendorf*. Eds. Craig Carr and Michael Sadleir. Oxford and New York: Oxford University Press.

———. 1991. *On the Duty of Man and Citizen According to Natural Law*. Ed. James Tully. Trans. Michael Silverstone. Cambridge: Cambridge University Press.

Quintilian. 2001. *The Orator's Education*. 5 vols. Ed. Donald A. Russell. Cambridge: Harvard University Press.

Radcliffe, Ann. 2008. *A Sicilian Romance*. Ed. Alison Milbank. Oxford: Oxford University Press.

Radzinowicz, Leon. 1948. *A History of English Criminal Law*. 4 vols. London: Stevens and Sons.

Raynal, Guillaume. 1783. *A History of the East and West Indies*. 10 vols. Trans. J. O. Justamond. London: W. Strahan and T. Cadell.

Richardson, Samuel. 1985. *Clarissa*. Ed. Angus Ross. London: Penguin.

Rodger, N.A.M. 2005. *The Command of the Ocean: A Naval History of Britain, 1649–1815,* New York: W. W. Norton.

Rose, Mark. 1993. *Authors and Owners: The Invention of Copyright*. Cambridge: Harvard University Press.

Rousseau, Jean-Jacques. 2004. *Reveries of the Solitary Walker*. Trans. Peter France. London: Penguin.

Sahlins, Marshall. 1985. *Islands of History*. Chicago: University of Chicago Press.

Salmond, Anne. 2003. *The Trial of the Cannibal Dog. Captain Cook in the South Seas*. London: Penguin. Allen Lane.

Samwell, David. 2007. *The Death of Captain Cook*. Eds. Martin Fitzpatrick, Nicholas Thomas, and Jennifer Newell. Cardiff: University of Wales Press.

Schaffer, Simon. 2002. "The Devices of Iconoclasm" in Latour and Weibel, eds., *Iconoclash*. Karlsruhe: Center for Art and Media; Cambridge: MIT Press: 498–515.

Schama, Simon. 1993. *Perishable Commodities: Consumption and the World of Goods*. J. B. a. R. Porter. New York: Routledge.

Schmidgen, Wolfram. 2002. *Eighteenth-Century Fiction and the Law of Property*. Cambridge: Cambridge University Press.

Schultz, William Eben. 1923. *Gay's Beggar's Opera: Its Content, History and Influence*. New Haven: Yale University Press.

Scott, Helenus. 1783. *The Adventures of a Rupee*. London: John Murray.

Sebald, W. G. 2003. *The Natural History of Destruction*. Trans. Anthea Bell. London: Hamish Hamilton.

Shakespeare, William. 1994. *A Midsummer Night's Dream*. Ed. Peter Holland. Oxford: Oxford University Press.

Shapin, Steven, and Simon Schaffer. 1985. *Leviathan and the Air-pump*. Princeton: Princeton University Press.

Showalter, Elaine, and English Showalter. 2005. "Every single one matters." *London Review of Books*. 18 August: 9.

Sidney, Sir Philip. 2006. *The Apology for Poetry* in *The Norton Anthology of English Literature*. Ed. Stephen Greenblatt. New York: Norton.

Simmel, Georg. 2004. *The Philosophy of Money*. 3rd edition. Ed. David Frisby. Trans. Tom Bottomore and David Frisby. London and New York: Routledge.

Simpson, AW.B. 1986. *A History of the Land Law*. Oxford: Clarendon Press.

Skinner, Quentin. 2002. *Visions of Politics*. vol. 3 (Hobbes and Civil Science). Cambridge: Cambridge University Press.

Smith, Adam. 1979. *The Theory of Moral Sentiments*. Eds. D. D. Raphael and A. L. Macfie. Indianapolis: Liberty Press.

——— 1982. *Essays on Philosophical Subjects*. Eds. W.P.D. Wightman and J.C. Bryce Indianapolis: Liberty Press.

Smith, Alexander. 1726 [1973]. *Memoirs of the Life and Times of the Famous Jonathan Wild*. New York: Garland.

Smollett, Tobias. 1989. *The Adventures of an Atom*. Ed. O. M. Brack. Athens: University of Georgia Press.

Spenser, Edmund. 1993. *The Faerie Queene*. New York: Norton.

Spinoza, Benedictus de. 1993. *Ethics*. Trans. Andrew Boyle and G.H.R. Parkinson. London: Everyman.

Stearns, Marshall and Jean. 1979. *Jazz Dance*. New York: Schirmer Books.

Sterne, Laurence. 1983. *The Life and Opinions of Tristram Shandy, Gentleman*. Ed. Ian Campbell Ross. Oxford: Oxford University Press.

Stewart, Dugald. 1802. *Elements of the Philosophy of the Human Mind*. London: A. Strahan.

Strawson, Galen. 2006. *Consciousness and its Place in Nature*. Ed. Anthony Freeman. Exeter: Imprint Academic.

Swift, Jonathan. 1803. *Works*. 24 vols. Eds. Thomas Sheridan and John Nichols. London: J. Johnson et al.

———. 1920. *A Tale of a Tub*. Eds. A. C. Guthkelch and David Nichol Smith. Oxford: Oxford University Press.

———. 1962. "A Vindication of Mr. Gay and the Beggar's Opera." *Satires and Personal Writings*. Ed. William Alfred Eddy. Oxford: Oxford University Press.

———. 2005. *Gulliver's Travels*. Ed. Claude Rawson. Oxford: Oxford University Press.

Tamen, Miguel. 2001. *Friends of Interpretable Objects*. Cambridge: Harvard University Press.

Thomas, Nicholas. 2004. *Discoveries. The Voyages of Captain Cook*. London: Allen Lane.

Tillotson, Geoffrey, ed. 1962. *The Rape of the Lock*. Twickenham edition. London: Methuen.

Toulmin, Stephen. 1996. "Descartes in his Time," in Rene Descartes, *Meditations*. Ed. David Weisman. New Haven: Yale University Press: 121–46.

Turnage, Wallace. 2007. *Journal of Wallace Turnage* in David Blight, ed., *A Slave No More*. Orlando, FL: Harcourt.

Villiers, George, Duke of Buckingham. 2000. *The Rehearsal*, in *Restoration Drama*. Ed. David Womersley. Oxford: Blackwell.

Vogler, Candace. 2007. "The Moral of the Story." *Critical Inquiry* 34 (Autumn): 5–35.

Wahrman, Dror. 2004. *The Making of the Modern Self*. New Haven: Yale University Press.

Walpole, Horace. 1937–1983. *The Yale Edition of Horace Walpole's Correspondence*. Ed. W. S. Lewis. New Haven: Yale University Press.

Warburton, William. 1747. *A Letter from an Author concerning Literary Property*. London: J. Knapton.

Ward, Ned. 1719. *The London Spy Compleat*. London: J. How.

Watt, Ian. 1957. *The Rise of the Novel*. Berkeley: University of California Press.

Watt, Sir James. 1979. "Medical Aspects and Consequences of Cook's Voyages," in *Captain Cook and his Times*, eds. Robin Fisher and Hugh Johnston. Canberra: Australian National University Press.

Weil, Simone. 2003. *The Iliad or the Poem of Force*. Trans. and ed. James P. Holoka. New York: Peter Lang.

———. 2005. "Human Personality," in *An Anthology*. London: Penguin.

Wendell, Oliver. 1991. *The Common Law*. New York: Dover Publications.

Wheatley, Phyllis. 2001. *Complete Writings*. Ed. Vincent Caretta. New York: Penguin.

Wild, Jonathan. 1718. *An Answer to a Late Insolent Libel*. London: Thomas Warner.

Williams, Bernard. 1994. *Shame and Necessity*. Berkeley: University of California Press.

———. 1978. *Descartes: The Project of Pure Enquiry*. Sussex: Harvester Press

Williams, Glyndwr. 2002. *Voyages of Delusion*. London: Harper Collins.

———. 2008. *The Death of Captain Cook*. Cambridge: Harvard University Press.

Wilmot, John, Earl of Rochester. 1962. *Complete Poems*. Ed. David M. Vieth. New Haven: Yale University Press.

Young, Edward. 1759 [1966]. *Conjectures upon Original Composition*. London. repr. Leeds: Scolar Press.

Young, Thomas. 1798. *An Essay on Humanity to Animals*. London: T. Cadell.

Index